10-20-2013

2009

CREATIVITY & MADNESS

PYSCHOLOGICAL STUDIES OF
ART AND ARTISTS
Volume 2

CREATIVITY & MADNESS

PYSCHOLOGICAL STUDIES OF
ART AND ARTISTS
Volume 2

Edited by
Barry Panter, MD, PhD

AIMED PRESS

CREATIVITY & MADNESS—Psychological Studies of Art and Artists.
Volume 2
Copyright 2009 by Barry M. Panter, MD., PhD. editor
All rights reserved.
Printed in Manipal, India.

Every effort has been made to locate the copyright holders of the illustrations and quotes reproduced in this book. Omissions brought to our attention will be corrected in the subsequent printings.

Published by AIMED PRESS
AMERICAN INSTITUTE OF MEDICAL EDUCATION
3255 Cahuenga Blvd. #111, Los Angeles, CA 90068
(800) 348-8441 (323) 874 5500 FAX (323) 874 5502

Cover art by Mary Lou Panter

Includes bibliographical references, index and glossary
ISBN 0-9712560—5—5
1. Artists–Biography. 2. Artists–Psychology. 3. Creative ability.
4. Psychology–Biographical methods. I. Panter, Barry.
N40.C743 1994 709.22
QB194-1319

ACKNOWLEDGMENTS

We would like to thank the authors who made contributions to this book: Mary Baures, PhD, George Campbell, MA, Scott Carder, MD, PhD Arthur Colman, MD, Catherine Evans, PhD, Todd D. Evans, MA, Robert Feder, MD, Gail Carr Feldman, PhD, Lance Fogan, MD MPH, David C. Frauman, PhD Benjamin Garber, MD, Louis A. Gamino, PhD, Dana L. Hadley-Carder, RN, MA, Janet Helton Hasegawa, PhD, Lewis Mehl-Madrona, MD, PhD, Richard A. Paskowitz, MD, Carol Salus, PhD, Fabian Ulitsky, MEd, Lisa M. Wayman MSN, RN-BC, AHN-BC, and Johan Wouterloot, MD. Their chapters were given originally as presentations at CREATIVITY & MADNESS-Psychological Studies of Art and Artists, conferences sponsored by the American Institute of Medical Education. It was in the fine work that the authors did as presenters, and the warm reception their works received, that this volume is conceived.

Thanks also to Jacques Winter, MD, Marlene Paley, PhD, Donna and Jack Salem who made valuable contributions to the introduction.

We are grateful for the invaluable help of Ken Rubin, of Garden Wall Graphics for much of the formatting, editing, contacting the printer and many other necessary aspects of creating this book. Ken's contact information is: 800-508-9028 and kenmozo@earthlink.net.

Thanks also to Denise Forlizzi and Sue Cain, our wonderful office staff who unfailingly handle the needs of the office and help in so many ways.

We also thank all the presenters and attendees at our conferences over the past 27 years. They have greatly enriched and broadened our lives, and it was their support and interest that encouraged us to bring this work to fruition.

We are gratified that Creativity & Madness—
Psychological Studies of Art and Artists Volume 1
is in its third printing.

It was first published in 1995, reprinted in
1999 and 2008

AIMED Press
A Division of
The American Institute of Medical Eduction
and
The Creativity & Madness Conferences
3255 Cahuenga Blvd. West #111
Los Angeles, CA 90068

800 348 8441   323 874-5500
Fax 323 874 5502
www.aimed.com
Email   aimed@earthlink.net

August 2009

Contents

Preface

The material artists use for their art comes from the primitive levels of their inner lives. As we mature and are "civilized"' we suppress these forces. But the artist stays in touch with, and struggles to understand, them. And to remain so in touch with that primitive self is to be on the fine line between sanity and madness.

The passions and inner conflicts of the creative artist often are revealed in studies of the artists' lives and works. They are the passions and conflicts with which we all struggle. Our studies illustrate what we all know to be true, pain and turmoil do not always result in disability and disease, but can lead to that triumph of the human spirit we call creativity.

Creativity, uniquely human, has allowed mankind to reach its highest levels of achievement. We can approach the understanding of creativity in many ways: psychological, neurological, sociological, biochemical, genetic, environmental, political. This book emphasizes the psychological aspect, and gains understanding of the artist's personality. What forces parental, societal, internal mold an individual's psyche to allow use of creativity as a reaction to the world?

A major thread throughout this book is that creativity, a factor in the lives of many artists, is the highest level of reaction to injury. The artist is wrestling with inner demons that torment many of us: depression, as in Anne Sexton; lack of self-cohesion and aggression as in Jackson Pollock; feelings of unworthiness and the inability to tolerate success as in Vincent van Gogh; fear of and rebellion against authority as in Dmitri Shostakovich. Instead of being paralyzed or beaten by their psychological problems, artists wrestle with the problems and use the conflicts and torments as elements of the creative process. In this way, the artist discovers a transcendent path through the great universal emotional issues that confront all of us. Dr. Feldman's article on resilience emphasizes this. Dr. Feder's article on Gustav Mahler shows how his grief was an essential component, a stimulus, for his great music. Dr. Catherine and Todd Evans' article on John Lennon and Paul McCartney also illustrates the stimulating power of loss. Others were not so fortunate. We can see in the tragedies and suicides of Mark Rothko, Vincent Van Gogh, Anne Sexton, and others, the failed attempts to resolve the emotional wounds of early life.

Artists are driven to create by their psychological issues. Yet paradoxically, the artist does not need to be consciously aware of these issues or conflicts. Indeed, many artists shun anything, and especially psychotherapy or psychoanalysis, that would bring these issues into awareness, fearing that such knowledge would cause their creativity to dry up. In Creativity & Madness—Psychological Studies of Art and Artists Volume 1 Dr. and Mrs. Warick describe in their article on Edvard Munch, how his somewhat successful psychiatric treatment led to a change in the nature of his paintings. Many art critics think his later works are not as powerful as the early ones. Dr. Jones, in his article on Leonardo and Magritte, again in Volume 1, states the opposite; that neurosis or psychological conflicts are obstacles to creativity rather than the fuel for the artist.

The psychological approach to creativity is only one of many approaches to understanding art and artists. For us, it is the most interesting way of studying our greatest abilities. However, we realize that no matter how comprehensive our psychological studies are, they constitute only one of many avenues into the secrets of creativity. Even if all the known avenues were traveled, the innermost secrets would still remain. We can know parts of the truth about creativity; we are will never know all of it.

The book is intended for both the intelligent layperson interested in psychology, art and the creative process, as well as the mental health professional. We appreciate that, although many of the chapters deal with sophisticated psychological theories, the authors have followed our request to avoid psychoanalytic and psychological jargon.

Introduction

What is creativity?

Creativity is the ability to bring something new into existence, by seeing things in a new way. Those who have this in the greatest degree are considered geniuses, and greatly honored and rewarded, but frequently considered strange, disturbing, and even mad. Picasso liked to live in a house of chaos— paintings, object, clothes strewn in disarray, in which his eye would behold unusual combinations. One of his most famous works is the handlebar of a bicycle above the metal seat of the bicycle making the form of a bull's head. He saw it that way in his house. Einstein was riding the trolley to work one day when his attention was caught by a clock tower he passed every day. He wondered what would happen to his perception and understanding of time if he were traveling at the speed of light. His musings turned into the theory of relativity, and changed the world we live in. Freud wondered about the bizarre behavior of patients few other physicians wanted to treat. His early musings led to the opening of the unconscious and he too changed the world we live in.

From where does creativity come?

Perhaps Plato knew as much as anyone can know, when he wrote that creativity is a divine madness...a gift from the gods. There are many examples of inspirations that seem to come from the gods. The chemist Kekule was trying to discover the chemical structure of the benzene ring. One night during his sleep he dreamed of snakes chasing their own tails. When he awoke, he realized he had discovered in his dream exactly what he had been looking for. George Handel was asked how he composed the magnificent Hallelujah Chorus. He replied he really hadn't composed it, he heard it. Sleeping, he dreamed of huge doors opening. As they opened he heard music. The wider they opened, the louder the music became. When he awoke, he wrote down the music he had heard. So creativity is not limited to conscious effort. Freud would say that creativity takes place in the unconscious.

Who is creative?

On the one hand there are those precious few, Mozart, Michelangelo, da Vinci, Shakespeare, Einstein, whose creativity is so great that the gifts they give the world are unfathomable. But there is also the creativity of everyday life. The simple task of making a meal is an act of creativity. No two people do it the same way. It combines elements into something new. It brings pleasure. The same can be said for giving a party or writing a letter. In this sense we all are creative.

Who fosters creativity?

Pasteur wrote, *Chance favors the prepared mind*. Artists must learn their craft. Usually early in life the artist learns the technique necessary for his or her medium. Virginia Woolf came from a long line of writers. She observed her father and her mother in the act of writing and discussing the process. Rossini's parents were musicians. The child's natural idealization of the parent turns into the wish to be like the parent, to learn what the parent knows, and to become the artist the parent was perceived to be. Mozart's father was a skilled and accomplished musician and composer. Van Gogh's mother was only marginally talented but in her son's eyes she was an artist. That was enough for him to idealize the act of painting. The Bach and Strauss families are examples of how observation enhances the development of inherent gifts. It is no accident that families of musicians produce musicians, such as the Bach and Strauss families. Parents are models for idealization and emulation.

Being exposed to the techniques of art was once considered a necessary part of an education. Children were expected to learn a musical instrument or to paint or to mold clay. Unfortunately, these skills increasingly are seen as unnecessary for making a living, and they are being dropped from curricula. However, Grandma Moses is an example that the craft of art may be learned at any age.

XVI

But craft is not enough. The prepared mind includes a willingness to experience and express without inhibition. The favorable soil frequently is the accepting, approving, non-critical atmosphere created by a parent or benefactor. In the early stages of creation there should be no editing. Unusual questions should be encouraged; unusual responses should be admired. Everything should be allowed to flow to find its expression on paper, or canvas, or stone. Editing comes later. To edit early, to feel disapproval or criticism too early, stifles the creative process. Parents can provide the encouraging, approving, educating environment for their children that fosters the joy of creativity, as well as helping them learn healthy techniques for coping with life's adversities.

"Genius is laid down at birth, probably as athletic ability which finds specially favorable soil for its evolution in families where there is also a good inheritance of intellect, and a favorable background for identification."

Phyllis Greenacre

The fostering, encouraging person need not be a parent. Michelangelo's parent punished him for wanting to be an artist, but he found another fostering benefactor, Lorenzo de Medici of Florence. There are certain people and times in history who have provided the fertile soil for creativity. Among these was Lorenzo de Medici, in the second half of the 15th century. He loved the arts and wanted Florence to be a world leader. He supported and encouraged artists. Among his rewards, and the world's rewards, are Botticelli, Michelangelo, Fra Angelico, and Leonardo da Vinci. Other enlightened governments include Paris in the late 1800's and Vienna at the turn of the century. Their leaders encouraged the arts, and their cities and the arts flowered.

The artist must tolerate and enjoy being alone. He or she needs the time to allow thoughts and feelings to roll around in the head, to ruminate, to come together in new combinations. Einstein said he got his best ideas while shaving. Beethoven, Brahms and Strauss loved to walk in the Vienna woods. How many of us have had wonderful, creative ideas while on vacation, when our minds are not occupied with the usual tasks and routine of life?

"Certain springs are tapped only when we are alone."

Anne Morrow Lindbergh

"Genius, whether locked up in a cell or roaming at large is always solitary."

George Sand

"The artist must be courageous, with the strength and boldness to stand behind the new ideas, new combinations, new techniques that emerge. Many new ideas are greeted at first with scorn or ridicule. Sometimes the worth of a creation is appreciated at first only by the artist. Sometimes recognition comes long after the artist's death."

"Greatness breaks laws."

Louise Nevelson

Every work of art is an act of faith, or we wouldn't bother to do it. It is a message in a bottle, a shout in the dark. It is saying, *I am here, and I believe you are somewhere, and that you will answer, if necessary, across time.*

Jeanette Winterson

Are creative artists mad?

Artists see the world differently, and for this they pay a price. Dr. Kay Jamison and Dr. Nancy Andreason have found in their studies that a high percentage of artists have manic-depressive and depressive disorders. Many artists have disturbances in the regulation of their moods, with a higher than normal degree of alcoholism, drug addiction, depression, and mood swings than is found in the general population. Is this a natural association with creativity? Is it caused by the way they perceive the world, or the way the world receives them?

Or is creativity a response to trauma? Artists may have a greater sensitivity to emotional trauma than others. They must be able to experience and endure their primitive emotional storms, with the capacity and technical ability to express their torment in their art form. Artists, like Orpheus, must descend into their particular Hades, and return to tell about it. If they turn back to look at Eurydice, she will be lost. Only by turning toward life can artists emerge with their treasure. For many artists, art is their salvation.

Must the artist suffer?

Not all artists suffer. Marc Chagall and Felix Mendelssohn are among many artists who seemingly did not suffer from neurotic problems and who did not live lives of misery; but many artists attribute their works to their misfortunes, which they see as the fuel for their creativity. We think that emotional suffering, and the struggle against it, is found in most great artists. Creativity is humanity's most heroic struggle against adversity. The artists studied in this book are examples of this.

Why do we enjoy art?

Great art puts us in touch, often on a subliminal level, with unconscious parts of ourselves. Great artists put something that is universal, that touches each of us, into their works. The sorrow expressed in the music of Mahler is an example of how great art expresses what each of us, on some level, has felt. Our emotional response to music has both neuroanatomic and biochemical correlates. The intense and sometimes immediate pleasure or sadness experienced in the presence of many varieties of music (i.e. *What A Wonderful World* by Louis Armstrong or the final adagio movement of Mahler's *Ninth Symphony*) involves brain regions implicated in arousal and reward; in particular, the frontal cortex and ventral striatum. A small structure, the nucleus accumbens (in the ventral striatum) is known to be active in the pleasure derived from gambling and many forms of drug use and addiction. These pleasurable responses are mediated by a specific neurotransmitter dopamine present in the nucleus accumbens. Sophisticated neuroimaging techniques (functional MRI) performed in people listening to music demonstrated activation of these brain regions.

Great art can function as a catharsis, helping us relieve the tension of some of our own repressed elements. As it resonates with the deepest levels of our emotional lives, often the repressed unconscious feelings and thoughts, we are expanded. Great art encourages us to see more, to feel more, to understand ourselves more. This expansion of the self may explain why two hours in a great museum, or an evening at a concert or play, is often followed by a sense of comforting, of gladdening, of feeling uplifted, of euphoria. We are expanded. We are more than we were before the experience. We are more alive when we experience great art.

"Even in the most sophisticated person, it is the primitive eye that watches the film."

Jack Nicholson

What can we learn from these creative artists?

Creativity is a constructive outlet for painful feelings and confused states of being. Creativity is a healing force in an individual, and in a society in turmoil. Teaching our children, and learning ourselves, how to paint or play an instrument or sculpt is not just idle use of time. It is an important, even a necessary element if we are to deal with the inevitable problems in our lives, if we are to be a civilized society, and, possibly, if we are to survive as a society.

Dreams occur during REM (rapid eye movement) sleep. Researchers are able to observe and wake someone when he or she enters REM sleep. It is possible to deprive someone of his or her dreams. After 4-10 nights without dreams psychotic elements begin to enter our thought processes. The poets have known this for centuries. *Simply stated, without our dreams, we go mad.*

Barry Fauntum MD

Dearest Jacqueline,

My Beloved Wife,

My Inspiration, My Friend,

Principessa,

This book is for you.

Barry

Benjamin Garber, MD, Is A Child Psychiatrist and Child Psych analyst with an active practice of Children and adults In Chicago Illinois. For The past 15 years he has been the Director Of The Barr-Harris Children's Grief Center of The Chicago Institute For Psychoanalysis. As A result he has written extensively on the impact of parent loss on children. Other writings include a book "Follow-Up Study Of Hospitalized Adolescents." He Is currently the guest editor of The 2008 Annual Of Psychoanalysis which Is devoted to the therapeutic work with children. Dr. Garber enjoys teaching, reading, running, playing tennis, basketball, rock music, gardening and traveling. He is happily married For 45 years to Wylie who is an ice skating teacher. They have three children and eight grandchildren. His primary office is at The Chicago Institute For Psychoanalysis At 122 S. Michigan. Chicago Illinois, 60603.

*"Before the problem of the arts,
psychoanalysis, alas, must lay down its arms."*

Sigmund Freud

PSYCHOPATHOLOGY, LOSS, MOURNING AND CREATIVITY

BY BENJAMIN GARBER, MD

CREATIVITY AND PSYCHOPATHOLOGY

Folklore and mythology assert that madness and genius are somehow interrelated. The possible link was suggested very early, expressed in pre-Grecian times in myths about the close relationship between the creators, gods and madness. Aristotle thought that great artists, philosophers, writers and politicians were vulnerable to melancholy. However, systematic studies about the association started only in the nineteenth century when a romantic myth was created about the relationship between genius and madness (Goodwin and Jamison 1990).

Lombroso, in his *The Man of Genius* (1891), suggested that genius was a "degenerative psychosis." He also proposed that genius and mental illness might run in families; however, most of his material was anecdotal. Galton,, in his classic study *Hereditary Genius* (1892), observed a familial association between mental disorder and creativity. While there have been numerous gifted persons or selected groups of gifted individuals with mental disorders, many studies showed no association between the two (Lucas and Stringer 1972).

Most of the studies in this area have been based on biographical and autobiographical writings (Juda 1949: Post 1994). These studies assessed psychopathology at a distance via lay reports or through material produced by the participants themselves. Waddell (1998) has systematically reviewed the literature on the relationship between creativity and mental illness. She evaluated twenty-nine studies about the possible link: In fifteen studies, there was no link; in nine, a relation was found; and in five, the findings were unclear. She concluded that scientific evidence of the positive relationship between mental illness and creativity is limited but it cannot be discounted. In scientific research, the relationship between creativity and psychopathology is largely unresolved. Many creative individuals with mental disorder have been described. Most seem to have bipolar disorder and some form of depression. Despite an overwhelming interest in this topic, the association between creativity and mental disorder is almost impossible to study epidemiologically. In part, the problem has to do with the inherent difficulty in defining creativity and mental disorder.

There is no universal standardized definition of creativity. It is difficult to separate creativity from other special capacities. Creativity may be intertwined with intelligence, talent and recognition, and somewhere near these, there is genius. Oremland (1997) separates talent from creativity. Whereas talent implies special abilities, skills, and making fine distinctions, creativity stands for originality and the production of something new. He considered that creativity has something in common with play.

Mental disorder is equally difficult to define, although psychiatrists have struggled with this for many years. Most authors will now make use of the American Association's Diagnostic and Statistical Manuals (DSM) to come up with a coherent diagnosis. Mental disorder is defined as a behavioral or psychological syndrome which is clinically significant and which is associated with distress, disability and suffering with the risk of losing freedom. In spite of the various definitions, assessing diagnosis is extremely difficult especially in atypical or mild conditions.

In addition to the inherent difficulties in the definitions of creativity and mental disorder, linking the two entities poses further complications. While there is much speculation about a possible link, it is exceptional that the two may coexist in the same person. Consequently, it is difficult to assemble large samples of subjects, and so by necessity, the clinical data is mostly anecdotal. While there are numerous empirical studies of the possible linkage, most have methodological difficulties and variations in definitions. According to Lauronen (2004), who reviewed most of these studies, there is a fragile association between creativity and mental disorder but the link is not obvious for all groups of mental disorder and for all forms of creativity. Evidence exists for some form of association between creativity and mental disorder, however the direction of any causal link is obscure. In spite of such questions, uncertainties and draw-backs, psychiatrists have indulged in a lengthy ongoing search of the connection between the two. To understand the origins of creativity has remained an all-consuming passion for mental health professionals. In part, it has to do with an overriding wish to find the key to unlock the mysteries of the creative mind.

Creativity And Mood Disorders

While the association between creativity, schizophrenia and other forms of psychopathology is vague and unclear, the association between creativity and affective disorders seems more prominent. Mood disorders include deviances in emotional states ranging from depression, which is more common, to mood elevations. There is some evidence for the predominance of mood swings in writers, especially during or after a creative crisis (Andreasen 1987).

Many famous composers, writers, artists and poets such as Robert Schumann, Anne Sexton, Virginia Woolf and others, have suffered from severe mood disorders (Goodwin and Jamison 1990). A remarkably high number of writers have committed suicide in-cluding Ernest Hemingway, Sylvia Plath, John Berrymore, Anne Sexton, and Virginia Woolf.

Andreason (1987) investigated 30 successful writers from the prestigious University of Iowa Writers Workshop and compared them with 30 matched controls. She found an extraordinarily high rate of affective illness among writers (80%) when compared with controls (30%). Post (1996) found similar results in that 82 out of 100 writers had some kind of affective psychopathology, and that almost one half

3

had been through major depressive episodes. Ludwig (1994), who concentrated on the psychopathology of creative women, found that 54% of writers suffered from depression compared to 14% of controls. They also had more suicide attempts and mania (19% of subjects vs. 3% of controls). Andreasen (1987) also found that relatives of people with literary gifts have an excess of mood disorders.

Richards et al. (1988) investigated creativity in 33 manic depressive and cyclothymic patients in conjunction with their 11 healthy relatives and 33 controls who were healthy or who had unrelated psychiatric diagnoses. In this study, more creativity was found among the manic depressive and cyclothymic persons and their normal relatives compared to controls. Higher creativity was also found among the normal, index relatives and cyclothymic patients than in manic-depressives. This suggests that people who show milder expressions of potential liability to bipolar disorder may be more creative than those with more severe mental disorder or persons with no tendency to bipolar disorder at all. When comparisons were made between creativity and mood disorders versus creativity and schizophrenia, the association was much more striking. While some creative people can develop schizophrenia, in most cases schizophrenia is associated with lower ability.

Many prominent artists have written accounts of their moods that describe bouts of depression followed by periods of elation. It has been reported that Robert Schumann composed his first symphony in a four-day manic frenzy soon after his marriage to Clara Wieck. Examples such as this are consistent with a diagnosis of bipolar disorder. From descriptions of the illness, it is evident that manic and hypomanic phases may enhance cognitive states. The various symptoms that are a part of the syndrome are; flight of ideas, lowering of inhibitions, heightened creativity, sensitivity and productivity. The potential of such attributes to bolster the creative drive are self-evident. Furthermore, mania is characterized by improvements in memory and cognition that may also enhance creativity. Clinical studies have demonstrated that individuals in a manic state tend to rhyme and use alliteration more and can find more synonyms and word associations than those without bipolar disorders. The enhanced cognitive state of mania may thus contribute to a fluency of ideas that is essential to innovation and by extension creativity. One may assume that in areas of writing, the above listed attributes of the hypomanic may enhance that skill. However, one could probably make an equally valid case for painting, sculpting or musical composition.

Another way of looking at creativity in the manic depressive individual is that the cycles of depression and mania facilitate the development of artistic insight by allowing the sufferer to experience extreme emotional lows and highs that in and of themselves may allow them to get in touch with affective states that to some extent exist in all of us. They may experience things more deeply and more intensely; love more and be more loved, laugh more and cry more often, and appreciate the changing moods of nature more intensely than the rest of us. Unfortunately, only a small percentage of such creative individuals are capable of setting down, organizing and then transmitting to us these feelings and emotions in a manner that touches the very core and being of who we are. The bulk of individuals with affective disorder may become so paralyzed with sadness and anxiety as to become nonfunctional and unable to set an emotional distance from the psychopathology in order to transmit their impressions and feelings to others folklore.

In conclusion, it would seem reasonable to assume that there is some form of positive association between creativity and mental disorder and that creative people have more psychopathology, especially affective disorder. However, we should not forget that the stressed link between bipolar disorder and creativity, or for that matter, any emotional disorder and creativity, is only theoretical. A causal connection has never been proven. Furthermore, the biological mechanisms for such a link remain totally speculative. An obvious argument against such a link is that most people with bipolar disorder are not creative or artistic, and it has not been established that most artists and creative individuals are affected by bipolar disorder.

Consequently, if such a relationship does exist, it is influenced by many factors that we do not yet understand. Yet, our need to idealize and to romanticize the artist and his or her productions is so consuming and our search for the holy grail of understanding creativity is so pervasive that we automatically attribute unusual and peculiar qualities to individuals who seem to be so inclined. In fact, the notion of a stable and well adjusted artist (of which there are many) or creative individual escapes us as there is the automatic focusing on what is strange and peculiar, bizarre and eccentric, in their productions and their very being.

Loss, Mourning And Creativity

Since all forms of affective disorder are more common in individuals who have been traumatized and experienced significant losses in childhood, we may extend our speculations to a connection between childhood loss, mourning, vulnerability to affective disorder and creativity. Mental health professionals and psychoanalysts in particular have always been fascinated by the twin mysteries of creativity and genius, and their relationship to psychopathology. Starting with Freud's *Jensen's Gradiva* (1907) and the use of applied psychoanalysis, psychoanalysts have pursued the understanding of creative genius with a passionate fervor. The list of world famous artists such as writers, composers, and painters, who have lost a parent, sibling or other important caretaker in childhood is quite lengthy. Dr. George Pollock compiled a list of 3800 such individuals. What has been described repeatedly in the individual case histories of these famous individuals is that the mourning process and its ultimate resolution were pivotal stimuli for the artist's creativity. It has been suggested that there may be a fundamental connection between the mourning process and the creative process. To bolster that assertion, there have been numerous studies in the psychoanalytic literature of artists who have experienced significant losses early in life and these losses intertwined in some manner with their creative productivity. The psychoanalytic examination of authors' lives or works involving the thorny methodological problems of "analysis in absentia" is sometimes facilitated by picking a subject with a relatively simple and straightforward lifeline, whose psychological preoccupations occur with regularity in thinly disguised form. When an author presents statements about himself or herself that seem to coincide with feelings and events in the fictional creations, there is some justification for such an analysis. Although I do not believe we can analyze someone from his or her literary works alone, much can be learned about the creator. Where loss issues are concerned, the aspects of mourning dealt with in authors' productions can give us valuable information about how they experienced and dealt with the significant losses in their lives.

A classic example of such an association occurred in Freud. By his own account, after his daughter's death, he plunged himself into his work to escape the pain of the loss. He said that the loss of a child is so severe a blow to one's narcissism that mourning will only come later. It is legitimate to postulate a causal link between death, or the threat of death, and the creative activity; it is as if his psychic activity was intensified in order to ward of disorganization.

Virginia Woolf, whose history is available from her writings and letters, was described by Dalsimer (2001) as a classic example of an artist using the creative process to come to terms with her mother's death. Woolf had her first breakdown shortly after her mother's death. She said that until she was forty-four and wrote the novel *To the Lighthouse*, she had been obsessed with and haunted by her mother. With the completion of the book, Woolf wrote: "I ceased to be obsessed by my mother and I no longer hear her voice: I do not see her." Virginia was haunted by her mother's ghostly presence and she tried to give her tangibility through her writing.

Sylvia Plath, one of the most gifted poets of our time, committed suicide after an abbreviated life of prodigious creativity in poetry and her novel The *Bell Jar*. Due to her creative genius and self-revelatory writings, she has become a prime subject of psychologically oriented researchers (Garber 1995). The break-up of her marriage to

7

the writer Ted Hughes echoed the loss of her father at age eight. She had a hostile dependent relationship with an unempathic mother that lent linearity to events that ultimately culminated in suicide. Her writings demonstrated her rage against an empty unresponsive mother.

Plath was preoccupied with death. She wrote and spoke of dying as a young girl. This points to a lifelong depression. For her, the creative urge and the need for literary success were intertwined with her need to overcome her depression. Her poetry gave her the chance to check and ameliorate her strong aggressive and destructive urges by constructive activity. Her poetry afforded her the opportunity to establish order and control over her desires and the emotional storms that tore her apart. Why there came a point in her life where the adaptations did not work awaits further exploration.

Edvard Munch, a world-renowned painter, gave birth to an art style that would later be known as Expressionism. Munch was affected by the many losses he experienced in his life, and his grief became a major motif in his art (Warick and Warick 1995). The most painful events in his life were the premature death of his mother when he was five years old and the death of his older sister when he was thirteen. These blows were compounded by the loss of his father who became emotionally unavailable when he suffered from a psychotic agitated depression. The family experienced much poverty after all of these losses. In attempting to work through his grief, Munch visually recreated his mother, father and sister many times. He waged a life long struggle to recover his lost love object, using a series of defenses often seen in pathological grief. In a normal grief process, these would have been effective in diminishing the pain of the loss. However, in this instance, it was not effective. There is little doubt that Munch's creativity saved him from total psychological disintegration and eased to some extent the pain of his many losses.

Hamilton (1969) examined the poetry of John Keats to determine if there is a meaningful connection between the early and repeated losses of essential people in his life, his failure to mourn adequately, and his creative output. Keats resorted to poetry in an attempt to complete the mourning process and to make restitution for the lost object, most importantly his mother. He did this by externalizing his dreams in the form of poems. Because of the intense ambivalence and hypercathexis of the introject, this method was only partially successful. Keats had to repeat this process over and over again. These attempts to heal the same wound led to one of the richest and most profuse efforts in literature. Keats, as many artists, was like Sisyphus, attempting repeatedly to accomplish his impossible task. Pollock described this as "perseverative creativity." Other artists who struggled in this way include Kathe Kollwitz and Vincent Van Gogh.

Clowell (2004), in her study of loss and mourning, shows how the elegy itself becomes a consoling substitute for the lost one. The very act of writing moves the poet from bereaved despair to resolution. This resolution converges with the elegist's assessment and affirmation of his surviving powers, one of the most important of which is the use of language. The successful completion of mourning signals that the lost one has transcended death by achieving aesthetic immortality in a timeless literary artifact (Sacks (1985).

According to Pollock (1978), in talented individuals, the death of a sibling can stimulate creativity. The creative product can show evidence of the sibling's loss event, the type of mourning process utilized, and at times it becomes a restitutional or reparational product to replace the lost object. Loss itself however does not account for the creative potential.

As a major contributor to the understanding of children's reactions to parent loss, Wolfenstein (1973) wrote about how the death of a mother influenced the work of A.E. Housman, an eminent British poet, and the painter Rene Magritte. In the works of both artists, there was evidence of the derivatives of the persisting image of the lost parent as both dead and alive. In both artists, there was evidence of a splitting of the ego as the child both acknowledges and denies the reality of the parent's death. In the images of the poet and

9

the painter, both of these opposites are fused. The lost parent is both dead and alive, absent but enduring, far and near. This exemplifies the artist's ability to dissolve the inner barriers of the mind and to combine the devices of primary and secondary process. What is otherwise a contradiction, assumes for the artist the aspect of rich ambiguity.

All of the above mentioned creations depend on memory of the lost object. Perhaps the experience of early loss makes memory itself a matter of urgent concern. It is memory that maintains our living connection with the dead: it is the most palpable way to preserve what is otherwise irrevocably lost.

According to McDermott (2001), Emily Dickinson, one of America's foremost poets, was capable of capturing extreme emotional states in her work. By dating her poems, one can see the chronological patterns of her affective illness. She may have suffered from a recurrent affective disorder with the obvious emotional and cognitive fluctuations that are a part of its course. She, as so many others, experienced multiple losses during her lifetime. Such speculation addresses the mystery of her poetic drive, which resulted in much creativity over a short period of time. While these patterns of her productive creativity seem evident, they do not explain the phenomenon of her rich imagination.

What then are the critical factors that distinguish losses and changes that give rise to emotional difficulties and those that can result in creative outcomes? In order to attempt to answer that question, we need to examine some of the salient factors that contribute to creativity in childhood as a response to trauma and loss. It is extremely difficult, if not impossible, to differentiate potentially talented children from the less gifted ones. Due to developmental shifts, whatever appears precocious at one point may appear commonplace at a different period in a child's development. Some children show prodigious development early and that pattern continues as the child gets older, while others may not demonstrate talent until later childhood or even adolescence. Child prodigies may be subdivided into three somewhat distinct yet overlapping groups.

First, there are those in whom precocious development appears as a spontaneous, rapid unfolding of inner pressure for growth in some way inherent in the child himself. It is similar to an inherited drive that is akin to something biological. Then there are those children whose astounding performance is mainly the result of demands exerted by significant adults. The parents who push the child use him as an extension of themselves in an attempt to realize some personal frustrated ambition. Then there are those children whose remarkable performance is the result of overcoming a psychic conflict, more specifically a significant loss.

The following clinical material illustrates all three of these possibilities manifesting in one patient:

Case Study

This is the clinical material of a talented adolescent girl who used the loss of her father as a stimulus for her creative potential.

Loren was an attractive fourteen-year-old adolescent girl referred by her mother because of an unusual concern. She worried that Loren was working too hard and spending too much time on her schoolwork. She wished that her daughter would be more rounded in her interests and not be such a "bookworm." She was a good student until the death of her father from a melanoma eight months earlier. Soon after his death, she went into a pattern of staying up late to do schoolwork and write. She became an exceptional student and rose to the top of her class. After his death, she became overly conscientious. She neglected her friends and social life. She also quit the volleyball team and spent all of her free time studying, reading and writing. While she had always enjoyed writing short stories and poems, doing so became an obsession. She began to stay up until all hours on school nights and on weekends she spent most of her time at the library or combing through bookstores.

Loren had had a very close relationship with her father who was an English professor at a local college. They went for walks, read together and discussed books. He encouraged her to write, for which

11

she had an aptitude and an interest. Her father fought a valiant battle against the cancer, which went into remission, but then spread suddenly. He deteriorated and died within a six-month period. Initially, Loren was crushed by his death. She cried and was inconsolable; however, after the first few weeks, she became even tempered as she retreated to the privacy of her room and her books. She seldom talked about her father but he was always on her mind as she had his photographs, made a memory book and used some of his belongings. Her eleven-year-old sister dealt with the loss by becoming very involved in her social life and spent much time away from home.

Her mother was forty-four years old and she went back to work as a teacher. To her credit, she became uneasy about her daughter's overly studious behavior and felt that it might be a problem. Most parents would probably consider such a preoccupation by their child a blessing and even brag about it to relatives and friends. While the teachers were excited and supportive of Loren's academics and writing skills, the mother remained uneasy.

At first Loren was puzzled as to why her mother brought her to me. She enjoyed reading and writing and had become an exceptional student. So why was that a problem? Initially Loren was suspicious and uneasy about seeing me, but when I reassured her that this was only an evaluation, she relaxed and became more open.

In the beginning, she was eager to talk about her poetry. However, when I asked for a sample she hesitated. When I pointed out that perhaps the poetry and her stories were a connection between her and her father, she agreed to let me see it the next time. She seemed rather well modulated emotionally when telling me how much she missed her father and that she thought about him all the time. After our first meeting, I suggested a few more sessions and then periodic follow-up. She agreed but her mother remained skeptical about my not recommending therapy.

The next time she brought me two poems, one about fall and the other about the stars in heaven. When I noted the sadness in the poems, she became visibly anxious and her eyes welled up with tears.

She told me that at night before going to bed, she thinks about her father, cries and then reads her stories and poems aloud which makes her feel better. Her mother noted hearing her daughter's voice late at night.

I pointed out to the mother that adolescents usually deal with the loss of a parent in private as there is a wish not to emote openly, and in that way not to appear different from one's peers. Loren had two close friends with similar interests but she would not talk to them about her father. It was too upsetting. I reassured her mother that all these interests, especially the writing, were Loren's way of mourning. Her mother was pleased that I agreed to follow up with her daughter.

I saw Loren again four months later when the mother told me that her behavior had not changed. In our meeting, she seemed the same and once again expressed unease in talking about her writing. I wondered if she was afraid that talking about it would in some way remove her interest in writing. She agreed. She knew that her mother tried to distract her from writing and she was angry because she was interfering in her relationship with her father.

I saw her again six months later and in this meeting she was silent most of the time. I pointed this out and she became anxious. I witnessed an intense internal struggle after which she told me with great difficulty that at night she read to her father whom she felt was watching her. I said that he must be proud of her writing and academic success. She started to sob and haltingly admitted that she loved to write because it made him happy and proud. She said, "I have to do it now because I don't know much longer he will be close by to witness and enjoy my writing." She was afraid to tell her mother about this interaction because she would think of her as crazy. She was equally afraid to tell me because I would think that she was "loony" and lock her up. She heard that creative people are often seen as crazy. She knew that she was not crazy but she worried that others would think she was.

I reassured her that I did not think that she was crazy and I understood how important her writing was to her in dealing with the

13

loss of her father. She then proceeded to elaborate how her father was bitter about his parents discouraging him from being a writer when he was in high school. So he decided to do the next best thing and teach language appreciation to others. He never forgave his parents for telling him that he would be a ne'er-do-well if he proceeded in that direction. Before his death, he told her to continue writing because she was good at it and not let anyone discourage her from this career path.

I didn't saw Loren again but received a call from her mother at the time of the anniversary of her husband's death. It seemed that Loren was much better. She was more social and going to the prom with her boyfriend. She was the editor of the school paper and had won state and national contests with her poetry. She mentioned that Loren said that she wanted to send me one of her poems but had never gotten around to it.

Discussion

Children who have been subject to traumatic situations such as exposure to multiple environments, parental divorce or the loss of a parent by death are more likely to grow up quickly to become hyper mature and develop a reactive precocity. This is in part a matter of necessity of survival as well as something that has been encouraged by the surviving parent and other significant adults. Consequently, if such a child has a particular skill or talent whether it is for writing, drawing, painting, music or sports, these talents and abilities are used in the service of mastering the trauma. The child may use this particular talent to master such a psychic trauma as the death of a parent. It is equally plausible that the significant adults would be supportive of and encouraging the child in the further elaboration and use of these talents (Garber 1981). While in this case, the mother was uneasy about her daughter's excessive studying and use of writing skills, she did not interfere actively but tried to understand the meaning of the behavior and to determine if it was pathological.

In some children, isolation and a loneliness that is not over-whelming may heighten ones sensitivity to one's environment. It may also heighten the capacity for an awareness of the relationships and connections between the various stimuli, which may lead then to a higher level of empathy for a wider range of phenomena. During these periods there may be a diminution of repression and material newly released from the unconscious, and items recently recruited from the environment may be conjoined by the ego into an idiosyncratic organization which may then be presented to the external world as something creative and new. Once this creative work is shared with others, especially those individuals important to the child for approval, appreciation, support and encouragement, it will perpetuate the existence of the work and perhaps stimulate further productions. There may then come about a fundamental connection between the mourning process of the child and the child's ability to be creative.

According to Pollock (1978), the universal transformational process that results from successful mourning has a positive outcome when completed and can then be viewed as a "liberation" process, which frees one from the past that no longer exists. In a sense, the positive outcome of the mourning and liberation process is creativity; creativity to live happily with one's self and with others, to creatively participate in various sublimatory pursuits, and in the gifted, to have freed energy to have inspirational ideas and to participate in their elaboration. Consequently, the creative genius is not the result of the mourning process but the creative product may be strongly influenced by this process and may show evidence of its presence in theme, content and style.

What are the critical factors that distinguish losses and changes that give rise to emotional difficulties and those that can result in creative outcomes? This question demands further study and the critical analysis of the clinical data of creative individuals.

In talented children, the death of a parent can stimulate creativity. The creative product can show evidence of the parental death and its accompanying sense of loss. The type of mourning utilized at times becomes a restitutional or reparational product to replace the lost object. But it is important to underline that loss itself does not account for the creative potential. In children, due to the immaturity of the psychic apparatus, it is sometimes easier to tease out the loss elements that seem so intertwined with the child's creativity. Creativity in children may be the result of a unique conjunction between conflictual material and external elements recruited by means of an increased perceptual sensitivity (Baum 1978).

For example, an inventiveness of original productions, to engage in figure ground reversal, and the fusion of specific with abstract situations are abilities which are elements of creativity. These are ego executive functions that may be rooted in adaptive and defensive reactions to conflict. Another hallmark of creativity is the ability to depict abstractions and an affect unto a specific form. Creative children may derive much pleasure and enjoyment from cognitive contradictions and exceptions as well as from cognitive manipulations, inversions, reversals and shifts. This type of cognitive experimentation and play may indeed be another element in the creative process.

In children, drawings and stories may be viewed as transitional objects. Greenacre (1969) speaks of the use of the transitional object as a companion with which to meet the unknown. The illusory sense of connectedness between the child and his transitional object is analogous to the illusory connection between the creative symbol of the Paleolithic artist and the real object that the symbol denotes.

This essay does not claim to explain creative genius but it does focus on some of the factors that awaken the creative impulse in the artist and how that affects his or her choice of subject matter. The reworking of childhood trauma, especially loss, is but one factor in the creative work. It will influence the content, subject matter, and tone but it will not determine the creative process itself.

Why do most children recreate their play in a repetitive and monotonous way whereas a few geniuses can introduce enough variety into their recreations so that audiences are taken by them and accept them time after time? What in these few individuals allows them to rise above their childhood ordeals and to free themselves enough to be creative? That is something we are unable to answer at this time but maybe someday a genius will come up with the answer to this complicated puzzle (Terr 1985, 1987). Psychoanalysis has made major contributions to the understanding of artistic contents by demonstrating that forms and themes are often manifested enactments of various traumas, mastery and compromise formations. Yet, when it comes to understanding the origins and genesis of creativity, psychoanalysis has yet to contribute greatly. However, there are some promising beginnings that may give us some general clues about the essence of the creative process.

Winnicott's (1953) explorations of the "part me and part not me" aspect of the personality may be an element of what constitutes the creative process. In this metaphoric "transitional space", he locates play, the dream and creativity. Kris's emphasis on intrapsychic fluidity may be another element of the creative process. The traditional psychoanalytic emphasis on mastery and resolution of conflict, especially loss and mourning, may be all motivational elements in creativity.

With these starting points in mind, it may be up to another generation of psychoanalysts to unravel the mystery of the creative mind. However, it may be that some things should be left alone and remain mysterious because, after all, the magical mystery of it all is one of the main attractions of creativity.

REFERENCES

Andreasen, N.C. (1987) "Creativity and mental illness: Prevalence rates in writers and their first-degree relatives". *American Journal of Psychiatry*, vol. 44. pp. 1288-1292.

Baum, E., (1978) "Creative responses to early trauma". In the *Annual of Psychoanalysis*. Edited by the Chicago Institute for Psychoanalysis. Pp.257-273. International Universities Press. New York.

Clewell, T., (2004) "Mourning Beyond Melancholia". *Journal American Psychoanalytic Association*. Vol.52. pp. 43-69.

Dalsimer, K., (2001) "Virginia Woolf: On becoming a writer". *The Psychoanalytic Study of the Child*. Pp. 324-357. New Haven, Yale University Press. DSM-IV., (2000) Diagnostic and Statistical Manual. American Psychiatric Association. Washington D.C.

Freud, S., (1907) Delusions and Dreams in Jensen's *Gradiva*. Std. Edition vol. IX pp. 3-87. Hogarth Press. London.

Freud, S., (1921) *Dostoevsky and parricide*. Standard Edition vol.21; pp. 177-198. Hogarth Press. London.

Garber, B., (1981) "Mourning in children: Toward a theoretical synthesis". *Annual of Psychoanalysis*. Edited by the Chicago Institute for Psychoanalysis. Pp.921. International Universities Press. New York.

Garber, B., (1995) "Comment on Sylvia Plath" by Robertson, *In Creativity and Madness*. Edited by Panter, B., pp.202-205. Aimed Press. Los-Angeles.

Goodwill, F.K., & Jamison, K.R., (1990) *Manic-Depressive Illness*. Pp. 153-162. Oxford. Oxford University Press.

Galton, F., (1892) *Hereditary Genius*. London: Macmillan and Company.

Greenacre, P., (1957) "The childhood of the artist". *The Psychoanalytic Study of the Child*. Vol. XIII. Pp. 47-73. International Universities Press. New York.

Hamilton, J.W., (1969).Object loss: Dreaming and creativity: *The poetry of John Keats*. The Psychoanalytic Study of the Child. Pp.488-532. International Universities Press. New York.

Juda, a., (1949) "The relationship between high mental capacity and psychic abnormalities". *American Journal of Psychiatry*. Vol. 106. pp. 296-307.

Lauronen, E., et al., (2004) "Links between creativity and mental disorder". Psychiatry. Vol. 67. Pp.81-98. Guilford Publications.

Lombroso, C., (1891) *The Man of Genius*. London. Walter Scott.

Lucas, C., & Stringer, P., (1972) "Interaction in university selection, mental health and academic performance". *British Journal of Psychiatry*. Vol.120.pp. 189-195.

Ludwig, A.M. (1994) "Mental illness and creative activity in female writers". *American Journal of Psychiatry*. Vol. 151. pp. 1650-1656.

McDermott, J., (2001) "Emily Dickinson; A study of periodicity in her work". *The American Journal of Psychiatry*. Vol. 158. pp. 686-690.

Oremland, J.D., (1997) *The Origins and Psychodynamics of Creativity*. International Universities Press. New York.

Pollock, G.H., (1978) "Siblings, childhood sibling loss and creativity". *The Annual of Psychoanalysis*. Edited by the Chicago Institute for Psychoanalysis.

Vol. 8. pp. 443-483. International universities Press. New York.

Pollock, G.H., (1988) Personal Communication.

Post, F., (1994) "Creativity and psychopathology. A study of 291 world famous men". *British Journal of Psychiatry*. Vol. 195. pp. 22-34.

Post, F., (1996) "Verbal creativity, depression and alcoholism: an investigation of one hundred American and British writers". *British Journal of Psychiatry*. Vol.168.

Richards, R., et. al., (1988) "Creativity in manic-depressives, cyclothymes, their normal relatives, and control subjects". *Journal of Abnormal Psychology*. vol.98. pp. 281-328.

Sacks, P., (1985) *The English Elegy: Studies in the Genre from Spenser to Yeats*. Baltimore Johns Hopkins Press.

Terr, L., (1985) "Remembered images and trauma". *The Psychoanalytic Study of the Child*. Vol.40. pp. 493-533. New Haven. Yale University Press.

Terr, L., (1987) "Childhood trauma and the creative product: A look at the early lives and later works of Poe, Wharton, Magritte, Hitchcock, and Bergman". *Psychoanalytic Study of the Child*. Vol.12. pp. 531-545.

Waddell, C. (1998) "Creativity and mental illness: Is there a Link?" *Canadian Journal of Psychiatry*. Vol.43. pp. 166-173.

Warick, L., and Warick, L., (1995) "Edvard Munch: A study of loss, grief and creativity". Panter, et, al., *Creativity and Madness*. Aimed Press. Los-Angeles.

Winnicott, D.W., (1953) "Transitional objects and transitional phenomena". *International Journal of Psychoanalysis*. Vol. 30. Pp.79-87.

Wolfenstein, M., (1973) "The Image of the Lost Parent". *The Psychoanalytic Study of the Child*. Vol. 28. Pp.433-455. Yale University Press. New Haven.

Before Mary Baures, PsyD, became a psychologist, she was a writer. She earned a master's degree in creative writing at Boston University where she worked with Anne Sexton the year before her death.

Dr. Baures first shares what it was like to watch her mentor suffering from emotional problems, and then she uses her clinical training to explore what was happening with Anne Sexton as she slid toward suicide.

Mary Baures is the author of Undaunted Spirits: Portraits of Recovery from Trauma (Charles Press, 1994) and co-producer of Strong at the Broken Places: Turning Trauma into Recovery (Cambridge Documentary Films, 1998).

In addition to her master's in creative writing, she has a doctorate in clinical psychology from Antioch New England, a Certificate of Advanced Graduate Study in Human Development from Harvard University and a Master's in psychopharmacology. Dr. Baures also has a Master's in counseling from Boston University

She has a private practice in Massachusetts where she paints and gives shows of her oils and watercolors.

Her web page is www.marybaures.com.

"Art should serve as the axe for the frozen sea within us."

Kafka

Anne Sexton "One Writes Because One Has To"

Anne Sexton — Battling One's Demons with Poetry or Using Poetry to Battle One's Demons

I came to Boston in 1973 to study with Anne Sexton in the master's program in creative writing at Boston University. I was fascinated by her honesty, her wise profound observations, and the way she mocked her fears with humor.

One day stands out vividly. Anne and I had just crossed Commonwealth Avenue, and headed for the Dugout, a bar where we met after class. A young woman stepped in front of our path. She had mailed Anne some poems and wanted a reaction.

"Oh, yes," Anne said, making her voice gentle. "There are some good lines in them, but I teach a graduate class. I don't think you are ready for that."

"Should I be a writer?" the woman asked.

"One does not choose to write," Anne answered. "One writes because one has to. It is not an easy life. Look at me. I am staying in a mental hospital. I only come out to teach my class."

Speechless, the woman stood there staring at the backs of cars, their little red lights saying, "Let me out of this lane." Anne wished her good luck with her writing.

It was a sunny fall day and our eyes adjusted to the darkness of the bar. Two other members of the workshop waited for us at the dimly lit table. The nurse from the hospital had gone to the car, and, since she wasn't watching, Anne borrowed a dollar for a beer since the hospital made her give up her money. Her hand fumbled over five packs of Benson and Hedges in her purse to an opened pack. She stuck the soft white stick in her mouth and leaned toward an orange flame.

"That was a marvelous poem you had today," she raved, her blue-green eyes looking brightly across the table at the woman who had written it. After we finished talking about the poem, Anne said, "It's a horrible place." Everyone knew she referred to the hospital.

"At least you will get some gripping poems out of it," another classmate said.

"No," Anne replied her voice a bit loud. "I do not want to be known as the mad suicide poet, the live Sylvia Plath."

Anne was an attractive Pulitzer Prize winning poet who seemed to squeeze every bit of enjoyment from life. It was sometimes hard to see how fragile she was.

She taught us about images and metaphors. They were more powerful when you found connections between unlike things—a fist and a fetus, eyelids and riding boots, a tongue and fish, flies and small black shoes, a girl curled like a snail. She showed us how to "image-monger" by spewing out a torrent of metaphors in a process called "storming the image." We would "unrepress" by creating an unconscious for an object, like a can of Coke. Our associations became rapid as we talked over each other to get our ideas out. We became raunchy and laughed wildly.

I couldn't understand how such a fun-loving person like Anne could obsess about dying. And if she really wanted to die, why did she have so many failed attempts? Were they expressions of ambivalence? Did part of her want to die, while another part was terrified of dying? Clearly another part wanted to live.

In our group, which had become a kind of family for Anne, she rarely discussed her suicidal impulses. She said she loved being with us because we were not used up or dirty with life. What I knew about her suicidal impulses came from her work. In *Live or Die*, she decided to live like the Dalmatian puppies she was unable to drown in the pails of water waiting for them. Like the Saul Bellow quote at the beginning of her book, she decided to "...live or die but not poison everything."

Another time she had admitted herself to a hospital, and she looked around at the brains rotting and the hearts going flat and decided to flee on her donkey, "...flee this sad hotel, ride out on some hairy beast, gallop backwards pressing your buttocks to his withers, sit to his clumsy gait somehow. Ride out any old way you please!"

She attempted suicide in 1970 when she was psychotic. Colors and sounds were either far away or very loud. She became convinced that her best friend, Maxine Kumin, was dead. Anne drove to a mutual friend's house and described her confusion. When the mutual friend called Maxine, Anne was convinced that Maxine's voice was a tape recording. Her friend came home with Anne, and when Anne's husband left to drive the friend home, Anne overdosed.

Her doctors found that teaching was life-giving for her, so they allowed her to leave the hospital with a nurse just to teach her class. Soon *The Death Notebooks* came out and Sexton was released from the hospital. She began a series of readings around the country in her "performance mode." "I could perform just before I die, but it's a performance of the poems. I know the lines—it's a practiced emotion."

Her dramatic public personae contributed to her popularity and the sales of her books. She missed our class twice for hospitalizations after suicide attempts, but we were told that she was away with a busy reading schedule. A few students found her a bit unstable to be an effective mentor, but only on one occasion did I see her inappropriately angry. A male classmate attempted criticism of a poem by counting the number of references to music. I saw that something was "off" with Anne some days, but most days she was charismatic. Her laugh was deep and gusty, she was sometimes silly and the class was fun.

Although she could not hide her instability from us, she hid the worst part of her illness from her students. She'd been suicidal so many times before, and I thought she'd get through this crisis too. When she killed herself in October of 1974, I was dazed and shocked.

Now Anne Sexton's handwriting in my copy of *Live or Die*: "Live, dear friend, and write on and on…" seems to stretch out impossibly over the years. Back in 1973 when she gave me the book, it did not seem possible that I would have gone on to become a psychologist with some specialization in suicide evaluations. Anne would have laughed at the posthumous absurdity.

Now, with my training, I can see more clearly how Anne was careening toward her death and taking with her the bright distractions and warm touches that enabled her to endure so far.

Many of her losses were from her illness. Her diagnosis changed over time but she seemed bipolar with some dissociative features. As Kay Jamison says in *Touched with Fire*, thinking by people with bipolar can range from unusually clear, fast, and creative to retardation so profound there's no meaningful mental activity. In her section on Sexton, Jamison says Anne had a rapid cycling quality to her illness.

Sexton's ability to dip into primitive, irrational sources while being in reality helped her live on close terms with life's dark forces that she wrote about. Her compass needle was easily set ajar. Gaiety, fiery thoughts and feelings, and grand visions soon swung into grim and stormy moods.

The first time I saw Anne, she was high on love. In August of 1973, just before the fall term, Anne read at the Bread Loaf Writer's Conference. The room was dark as she stood in spotlights reading with dramatic gestures—the clench of a hand to her throat, raising her hands to the heavens, pregnant pauses. Passion in her voice was palpable as she read her love poems.

> My nerves are turned on.
> I hear them like musical instruments.
> Where there was silence, the drums,
> the strings are incurably playing.
> You did this. Pure genius at work.
> Darling, the composer has stepped into fire.

At the conference, Anne was with Phil Legler from Northern Michigan University. Legler had previously arranged her readings and fees at various colleges. As the sparks between them grew hotter, he wrote, "You live at such a screaming intensity, it's almost too painfully beautiful to bear. You've got both a lifetime fan of your work and a mad mad mad lover to cope with." Soon he checked himself into a psychiatric hospital because he was torn between his love for Anne and for his marriage and family.

She wrote to him that poets were always writing each other love letters but it was hard for the wives and husbands to understand. She explained that her husband was good-looking, stern, hated poetry, her abundance, and didn't desire her as a woman. "I went a bit haywire over getting some love."

Sexton began to consider divorcing Kayo, although she depended on him for a stable home. He shouldered many responsibilities she was not up to and made her work possible. As she wrote about in *Man and Wife*: "A soldier is forced to stay with a soldier because they share the same dirt, the same blows....Even their song is not a sure thing. It is not a language....It is a kind of breathing." Her life really began to unravel when she went through with the divorce, after twenty-four years of marriage.

Although her therapist advised her to go slowly with Legler, she soon flooded him with long erotic letters to leave his marriage and marry her. He was also desperate for her company, but feared he and Sexton had resonant weaknesses and might destroy each other.

As the complicated alliance with Legler unraveled, Sexton's psychiatrist, Dr. Constance Chase, went on vacation. Anne started having fugue states where the walls and floors seemed to shift. Her fear mounted to panic. When Legler finally decided to remain in his marriage, Sexton overdosed and spent a month in a hospital.

"Men," she told us were "...fraidy cats." She joined a dating service, and, terrified of being alone, hired live-in companions. Family rituals had contained some of her sickness but Kayo was gone and her daughters were away at school.

25

Going off Thorazine was another reason for Anne's decline. Dr. Chase was against it since Sexton said that it kept her sane and made her too tranquil. (Thorazine is not the best medication for bipolar illness. A better medication would have been lithium, but by the time she tried it in 1972, alcohol undermined the medication's effects.) After going off her medication, her periods of sickness were longer and the chaos was deeper.

One wonders if she would have stayed married to Kayo had she stayed on her medication. Although her illness was frustrating to him, he helped her through her breakdowns, starting at the beginning of them, when she was twenty-eight.

Anne's first breakdown came when she was unable to tolerate the stress of motherhood and she overdosed on barbiturates. "I was trying to lead a conventional life...but one can't build little white picket fences to keep nightmares out." Her mother-in-law, Billie, did a great deal of the parenting when her children were toddlers. Conflicts developed because Billie had a lot of authority over the children and Anne resented it.

When Sexton recovered some stability, she felt guilty for leaving her children. She wrote to Joy: "In naming you I named all the things you are except the ditch where I left you once...while I sailed off into madness." Her daughters were four and six when Anne emerged as a poet. She shared with them her passion for music, writing and acting. One game she played was upsetting to Linda because Anne played like a baby and insisted on them mothering her. Perhaps Anne didn't understand the effects of her instability and years of sickness and couldn't see her daughters' problem with it.

Anne started writing poetry at her psychologist's suggestions. Poetry, she said, led her by the hand out of madness. After the fragmentation of a psychosis, she knitted together the pieces of her life—faded pictures in scrapbooks, toys from childhood, the broken ends of things.

Most poems went through endless revisions—one 300 times and another over four years—until she found just the right juxtaposition of images, just the right voice. Giving artistic form to her madness gave her a sense of control over it, and she was able to explore it without being overwhelmed.

> I have gone out, a possessed witch,
> haunting the black air, braver at night;
> dreaming evil, I have done my hitch
> over the plain houses, light by light;
> lovely thing, twelve-fingered out of mind.
> A woman like that is not a woman, quite.
> I have been her kind.

Anne's psychologist, Dr. Martin Orne, told her that she couldn't kill herself because her poems might be helpful to others going through similar things who couldn't express themselves as well. "That gave me a purpose," Anne said, "A little cause, something to do with my life, no matter how rotten I was."

She gave shape to the chaos that threatened to drown her and ordered her experiences so the world was sensible and real again. In poetry, she revealed things she needed to conceal from herself. After seeing it in her work, she integrated it into her therapy. "I alternate between hiding behind my own hands protecting myself anyway I can and this other this seeing, ouching other."

During therapy, a persona called Elizabeth (her paternal grandmother's name) emerged by scrawling in childlike letters across a notebook. In this dissociative form, she remembered an incestuous relationship with her father. Later, Anne questioned this memory, but her symptoms—the way she sexualized significant relationships—fit the picture of sexual abuse. Dr. Orne disengaged from acknowledging the Elizabeth persona as distinct from Anne because he did not want to encourage her dissociative states.

In her first interview with Dr. Orne, who was a clinical psychologist as well as a medical doctor, she said her best talent was making men feel sexually powerful and that she should become a prostitute. At the beginning, Orne said Anne pushed reality away and "...you had to see deeply into her to know there was someone there." He began to see that she brought powerful resources to her healing: imagination and a facility with words, deep pleasures in living that gave her motivation to work hard. He helped her re-channel her energy and see herself as a capable person.

When dealing with her psychosis, as words crowded and pressed for headroom, Anne worked in strict form. When she arrived at the meaning, there was a change in her psyche. The form of the poem, she said, worked as a kind of super-ego for her. She said that it was a miracle she came out of it whole.

She began "Kind Sir: These Woods" with a quote from Thoreau: "For a man needs only to be turned around once with his eyes shut in this world to be lost...Not til we are lost...do we begin to find ourselves." In the poem, she compares her illness to a game she played as a child in Maine at her grandfather's cottage. In the game, she turned around with her eyes shut and the world was rearranged. A bell buoy's cry of doom told her that her nursemaid was gone and she was dead. In her illness, "...the woods were white and my night mind saw such strange happenings, untold and unreal. And opening my eyes, I am afraid of course to look—this inward look that society scorns—Still, I search in these woods and find nothing worse than myself, caught between the grapes and the thorns."

Her first teacher, John Holmes at The Boston Center for Adult Education, told her that her poetry was such a narrow diary that she wasn't giving anything to the readers that teaches them, but she developed a huge following among others with emotional problems.

She saw her suicide attempt as a rebirth that separated her from her former life. Before she wrote poetry, Anne felt frozen or like a doll: shellacked, grinning and planted in an all-American kitchen. After madness cracked the surface of her life, a buried self emerged. Writing enabled her to develop a new self and she found positive meanings in her illness. She emerged from her grief with her head held high, holding a finished book in her hand. When she wrote, she said she knew she was doing the thing she was born to do. Suicide, she said, was the opposite of the poem.

Sexton enrolled in Robert Lowell's class at Boston University along with Sylvia Plath and George Starbuck. When Lowell won the National Book Award, his acceptance speech distinguished between two types of poetry: "cooked" formal, expert and remote and "raw." The raw kind—written by Lowell, Sexton, Plath, Allen Ginsburg and Adrienne Rich—started a new movement in the culture. Some referred to the new style as "confessional." Sexton and Plath both tapped the constraints of conforming to feminine stereotypes at the beginning of the woman's movement. Both used mental illness as a generating motor for transcendent truth and beauty. Both used writing as escape from themselves.

Lowell told Sexton: "You stick to the truth and the simple expression of very difficult feelings." He must have resonated with her poems in her first book *To Bedlam and Part Way Back*. Lowell was manic-depressive himself and had frequent hospitalizations. He wrote about seeing too much and feeling it with "one layer of skin missing." He called mania "a magical orange grove in a nightmare."

Anne Sexton became an American success story. She won the Pulitzer Prize and taught in a prestigious graduate writing program, yet she had little formal education.

On one level, Anne mastered her madness and found a purpose in her illness that she integrated into a new life-course attuned with the best in herself. She converted psychological pain into truth and beauty and taught her terrors to sing.

In a severe trauma such as a psychosis, the lifeline has been broken and the survivor must establish her life on a new basis. Images are a powerful way to compose a new truth and metaphors tap preverbal violations.

On another level, she blamed herself for her illness. As in literature where heroes are rewarded and villains are punished, she felt she suffered because of some essential badness. She pursued love and lust and finally God, but nothing took her hunger or her feelings of badness away.

As she careened toward her death, she distorted her experiences more and more. Her distortions and her anguish stressed all of her relationships, including those with her doctors. During a discussion over her divorce settlement, Anne revealed a financial status that did not warrant the reduced fee that Dr. Chase gave her. Anne insisted that Dr. Chase had lost professional objectivity and had confused her own needs with those of her patient. Anne was bitter. When Dr. Chase ended the therapy, Sexton said, "This is no termination of any sort but an amputation, and I feel pretty damned desperate." Although Sexton did see a psychiatric social worker for a while, in the nine months of her remaining life, poetry became her principal therapy.

Anne depended a great deal on her doctors. When an earlier relationship with Dr. Orne dissolved, Anne felt that she lost part of herself. "For him to leave is to leave myself….I need someone, aside from pain, to rock me out, away alone." Her doctors helped her keep the voices away and became sustaining others, like her mother and Nana before, and her Muse and God afterwards.

After the termination of Dr. Chase, Anne became more and more suicidal and typed out her thoughts: "Can I save myself? I can try….I can keep right on trying. Granny, you electric Smith Corona heart, you buzz back at me and I pray you do not break."

During this time, she was unable to visit the dentist or go shopping alone. Earlier, she thought she could make her demons go away if there was enough love to put them down. Depending on her friends may have been how Anne stayed out of the hospital, but when they refused to care for her like a child, she felt abandoned. Similar to how her moods shifted from euphoria to depression, she viewed people as all good or all bad. When an unrealistic request was refused, she felt rejected.

As the others she depended on for psychic integration deserted her, she spiraled inward and became bitter, weary, frightened and alone.

The more chaotic her inner states, the less careful her craft. Although her poetry still had brilliant lines, its structure didn't seem to contain her chaotic emotions. Her critics said she reduced a once graceful style to its barest, crude essentials and showed little progression in her themes.

> Mrs. Sexton went out looking for the gods.
> She began looking in the sky
> expecting a large white angel with a blue crotch.
> Ms. Dog, how much time you got left?
> Ms. Dog when you gonna feel that cold nose?
> You better get straight with the Maker.
> Cuz it's a coming, it's a coming.

These lines are from *The Death Notebooks*. Herbert Kenny of *The Boston Globe* called the book a "deeply spiritual manifesto." Ben Howard of *Poetry* said she reduced her religious quest to a kind of verbal cartoon and evoked a sense of succession and repetition of events following one another in predictable and usually empty patterns. Another critic said, "...musically her instrument became the kazoo... yet her writing dazzled."

Earlier, her writing led to a process of discovery, surprise and synthesis. As many of her relationships went sour, she turned to God with a stubborn fanaticism and clung to her obsession of meeting Him and feeling His healing embrace. She visited an elderly priest who said he could not give the last rites but that God was her typewriter. Maxine Kumin believes that this down-to-earth wisdom may have kept Anne alive another year and enabled her to write her next book.

From January 10 to January 30 in 1973, she wrote *The Awful Rowing Toward God*. With five to seven poems pouring out a day, she called it a frenzy of despair and hope. Her goal was to rescue herself from chaos, but she was unable to progress beyond her one theme. Previously, one topic merged into another until she found themes she never considered before.

31

Earlier in *Transformations*, published in 1971, she modernized *Grimm Fairy Tales* and the center of gravity in her work shifted. She fused both public and personal themes and exhibited a gift for knocking social and moral conventions. Each poem-story was built around some dark psychic core, turned on a magical transformation.

The more she became isolated and cut off, she searched for some magical transformation in her psyche. After all, previously she had been transformed from a housewife into a poet. More and more, she inhabited a private self-contained world.

> To be without God is to be a snake
> who wants to swallow an elephant.
> The curtain falls.
> The audience rushes out.
> It was a bad performance.
> That's because I'm the only actor
> and there are few humans whose lives
> will make an interesting play.

This poem may have been in response to critics who said Anne was narcissistic. The more she lost perspective, how others viewed her took on an exaggerated importance, and the harder it was for her to regulate her self-esteem.

On March 7, she was scheduled to give a reading to promote *The Death Notebooks* at Sanders Theatre at Harvard. When she saw a mimeographed flyer (including a typo in the book title) to announce the reading, she shifted into high gear. She sent copies of the book to local radio stations and dared them to read poems such as "The Fury of Cocks" to announce the event. She hired an advertising agency to produce a poster and had it inserted into newspapers as a flyer.

When she arrived at the reading, wearing a long black and white skirt split to the knee, the hall was filled to the rafters. Some people sat in window frames, others on the fire escape. Her opening words sounded slurred, but then her voice gathered confidence and deepened. She joked that she was reading from her "posthumous work." She bantered with the audience, made cracks about *The New Yorker*, read about her madness in "Music Swims Back to Me" and ended with "The Touch." The audience gave her a standing ovation.

The reading had been an overwhelming success and she received many positive reviews, but she focused on the negative. A *Boston Globe* critic accused her of commercialism and said she was filled with "middle-brow anguish." When she was healthier, she would have been able to see that most of the reviews were positive, but she was unable to laugh off the criticism. She read it aloud in class and said: "See, even when you're at the top, people still throw spitballs at you."

In June of 1974, I went to Anne's house in Weston to go over my thesis—a collection of poems and short stories. When I drove into her driveway on Black Oak Road, she and her dogs came out to greet me. (These were the Dalmatians she refused to drown when she decided to live and stop poisoning everything.) One of them had a lame paw. She said in a poem: "Come forth with a dog who is spotted and smiling and holds up his paw for the awful stars."

She had just finished a short story and handed it to me for feedback. In it, a man who had just died waited at the gates of heaven to be judged for all the lives he ever lived. An amazing series of flashbacks, reeled through his mind. In earlier years, Anne wrote about death but grounded it in other themes: her parents, love, loss, lust, and motherhood. Now death was her only topic.

After I'd been there an hour, her voice became slurred by tranquilizers. Pills, she said, were time bombs she used to kill herself in small amounts.

She mentioned that she wanted to give a summer workshop, so I offered to put up some posters. A week later, she called to ask what I'd done because she'd received a huge response. I said, "Lots of people want to work with you because you are a wonderful teacher and writer."

"Me?" she asked, "The confessional poet?"

As Anne careened toward her death, her poetic voice, which was authentic and original because it was so personal, began to feel shameful. When she was healthier, she could shrug off the complaints that she wrote confessional poetry.

The legal system had given the concept of confession a new twist. Some of her poems were about extramarital affairs, and during her divorce process, Anne felt unclothed in court. The only cure of such confessions, as she wrote in a poem, was to "…sit in a cold bath for six days, a bath full of leeches, drawing out your blood into which confessors heated the devil."

Anne felt that something essential in her was missing, like her characters in an early poem, "The Lost Ingredient", when they sat in tubs in Atlantic City, patting towels over their shivered skin and praying for impossible loves or new skin or another child.

When Anne divorced, she believed freedom was the lost ingredient, but just like the promise of lust, love and God, nothing made her whole. She wrote to her daughter Joyce that the divorce had been a mistake. "A little love is better than no love at all." Friends could not pick up the pieces the way Kayo did. Her neediness strained her relationship with both of her daughters, and Maxine Kumin was angry with her for her rude behavior toward two professors when they read at Douglass College. Anne felt alone and poetry made little difference.

She attempted suicide in the spring of 1974 and complained to Maxine that the attempt aborted. She vowed to tell no one of her plan the next time.

On October 4, 1974, she read the proofs of *The Awful Rowing Toward God* and had a visit with Maxine who felt Anne was doing better because she'd been gay and silly. "I could perform just before I die," she had said years earlier.

When Anne came home, she fixed a drink of vodka and wrapped herself in her mother's old fur coat. Then she went to the garage and sat in her red Cougar. With her mother's coat embracing her, she breathed in the carbon monoxide poison in the exhaust fumes. Her final act was the dramatic end of *The Awful Rowing Toward God*.

After John Holmes complained that her writing was too narrow, she wrote a poem to him: "To John Who Begs Me Not to Enquire Further." In it she tells him that the commonplaces of the asylum where "…the cracked mirror of my selfish death out stared me were her education. And if you turn away because there is no lesson here I will hold my awkward bowl with all its cracked stars shining like a complicated lie."

Now I imagine Anne up there, somewhere, still holding out her awkward bowl. We do not want to turn away from the lessons among her cracked stars.

As Denise Levertov said at one of Anne's memorial services, "We who are alive must make clear, as she could not, the distinction between creativity and self destruction."

One reason Anne killed herself is that she vividly imagined death as a healing place where she would get rid of the rat inside her, "the gnawing pestilent rat," where "God would take it with His two hands and embrace it." Finding God and death became fused into a place where she would find her lost self. She had looked for this healing place between herself and others, but because of her illness, was unable to find it.

As A. Alvarez said in his study of suicide: "Each suicide is a closed world with its own irresistible logic." As Anne said in *The Awful Rowing Toward God*, "God was there like an island I had not rowed to." As in the fairy tales she wrote, after a transformation, she'd enter another kingdom where she would be whole.

When Anne lost perspective, her illness made it hard for her to correct herself. She became alienated from friends who could have helped her. Robert Mazzocco wrote in *The New York Review of Books* that what killed Anne was not unhappiness, but something deeper—the horror of being unable to see or feel clearly, to be always only part way back from bedlam. "It's the sense of the fragmentary that barriers us, because things don't connect, so we don't add up, we become useless to ourselves and to others."

From the time of Anne's breakdown at twenty-eight until her death at forty-five, poetry kept her alive. On one level, writing transformed Anne, but on another level, as Robert Lowell said, "...it became a monologue in which her brave heart drowned."

Anne's inner sense of badness—of the rat inside —may have been a factor in her suicide. She may have been seeking a merger with God that in her fantasy would make her whole and good.

In life she never realized how beautiful she was, how she enriched the lives of others, how much she inspired others, and what a brilliant and wonderful contribution she made to the world. She wished, in death, to achieve that sense of wholeness and goodness that she was unable to achieve in life.

George Campbell. MA, holds a Masters in Clinical Mental Health Counseling from Lesley University. He has an undergraduate degree in biology from Earlham College and is a graduate of the Art Institute of Boston's photography program. Over the past decade he has participated in numerous trainings and workshops related to the interface of mind and body, with particular attention to energy healing and intuitive phenomena. He agrees with Gerald Steckler that truly ethical behavior is contextually felt and not a product of reasoned thinking-- a concept that can be expanded to include all genuine matters of the heart. This is particularly so if behavior arises organically from the non-reactive depths of our shared humanity.

George credits his own desire to authentically explore the deeper nature of things to his father. George grew up in a remote Quaker community in the mountains of Costa Rica and from an early age was imbued with idea that creativity and art were essential to one's development as a whole person. The isolation contributed to George learning, in a hands-on manner, from his father, just as his father had learned in a hands-on manner while a student at Black Mountain College.* George is a past presenter at the Conference on Creativity & Madness in Santa Fe and founder of an experientially oriented Artists & Writers Group in Cambridge, Massachusetts.

*During the 1930's and 1940's Black Mountain College was a radical experiment in education whose roster read like a who's who of the art world of the time.

An Artist/Psychotherapist Reflects
on the Parallels between the
Artistic & Psychotherapeutic Processes

By George Campbell, MA

I'm writing to share my reflections on the artistic process, the psychotherapeutic healing process, and their common interface with spirituality. I will begin with my own journey. As long as I can remember, I have wanted to better understand the deeper nature of things. Although I have a longstanding interest in art, I initially thought of science as the medium best suited for a life of exploration. I have not now, rejected science, but have found a need to also embrace mystery, not-knowing, and subjective truth as part of my essential toolkit. These latter factors best serve me in terms of allowing meaning and purpose to become manifest in my life. My push to pursue science professionally, stopped with a BA in Biology. Adversity had skewed my participation in life, and a background force within me insistently sought realignment towards a vision of wholeness, beauty, and meaning. In college I spent four years attending to the mind and the intellect. Throughout this time I had largely ignored the body part of the mind-body continuum, but a quiet stirring within my very core now demanded attention. There was no logic, words, or clear thought process; just that, something in me needed to create.

It was in photography school that I finally began to understand that my body was an integral part of the creative process. I was introduced to the idea of using my body as an instrument of attunement. For example, if I was photographing a plant I might move my body in parallel harmony so as to feel a gesture that I sensed the plant was making. In this way I would develop a more intimate relationship with my subject, and it could begin to tell me how to photograph it.

39

Some time after photography school, I came to understand that my images were more powerful when I intuitively surrendered to a felt sense in my body. Through my body I would open myself, defocus my vision, and allow the image to be felt as an overall Gestalt. When all the elements came together in a way that "felt" right I would record the image.

I have come to think of my fine art photography of nature as capturing patterns of wholeness and meaning. With certain images I have felt a quickening within me, a release, and a realignment with a larger oneness. Others have described a sense of wellbeing, calmness, and release when viewing these photographs. I'm in accord with the idea that healing often involves a reminder of wholeness. That the creative process involves the body makes sense given how we also use the body to give meaning to events in our lives through emotional responses. Although the particularity of the individual response in the moment may be important to authentic artistic expression, a universality is often captured that transcends the artist as an individual. Perhaps artists, surrendering more fully to who they are in the act of creation, awaken something authentic in the viewer or listener. There is a Sanskrit word (and yogic greeting) "Namastè" that somehow seems relevant to the bond that can be formed as one person creates art and another participates by experiencing it. Under the best of circumstances, this is what ideally happens in psychotherapy as well. According to the website, WikiHealth ("Namaste," 2006, para. # 3), Ram Dass is quoted as defining Namastè thus:

> I honor the place in you
> in which the entire universe dwells.
> I honor the place in you
> which is of love, of truth, of light, and of peace.
> I honor the place in you where,
> if you are in that place in you,
> and I am in that place in me,
> there is only one of us.

In 1995 I went through a spontaneous Kundalini (Spiritual) Awakening that turned my world upside down, inside out, and seemed to spin me around 180 degrees. A sequential process began unfolding from within my body as if I were a player piano. Someone else had written the score, and I could do little more than alter the speed of unfolding by attending to the breath. It began with markedly heightened sensitivity on the part of all of my senses. Everything was brightly illuminated by a pervasive and wonderfully soft sense of transparent light. It was as if the heavens had opened up and every pore in me drank in the experience. The natural environment became so exquisitely beautiful that tears welled up in my eyes and gratitude filled me to the inner core of my being.

My heart, now more open than it had ever been before, had feelings of all-encompassing love and deep compassion. Night after night in lucid dreaming I reviewed my life and replayed events for which I had not been able to forgive myself. As I held myself within the compassionate vastness of the eternal, I came to forgive myself and let go of persistent self-judgments. I no longer felt so powerless and aggravated by the evening news. Instead of an emotional reactiveness to atrocities, I felt a poignant sadness stab through to the very center of my heart. In response, I lightly touched my hand to the center of my chest and felt a resolve to better heal myself as my most available solution, holding the difficult knowledge of evil as a whole part of who I am. I no longer thought so dichotomously in terms of "us" and "them;" it was now "we." This didn't mean that terrible things were now OK, but I came to better understand the web of life to which I am inextricably bound. The older vision of controlling or "fixing" life was becoming obsolete.

A twenty-fifth reunion with dear friends in the Fall of 1994 had set the stage for my Awakening. In the reunion, I was reminded how much I cared for them based on the two years we had worked together, doing community development work in Mexico. Post reunion, it came to me that part of love is being better known, and I set out to rectify the ways I had previously hidden my authentic self. In a six page epistle I revealed, to the best of my ability, who I was and how I felt back then. Out of this process came a strong desire to live courageously from a place of authenticity and truth. The Awakening seemed to arise out of this commitment and a friend's authentic response to me and my epistle. It felt very right to my heart and brought me greater awareness, joy, and purpose. However, there were periods of intense vulnerability and pain that nearly knocked me off my path, highlighting the challenges I would face if I was to consistently surrender to the dictates of an open heart.

The Kundalini process, the psychic healing process and the creative process seem to share a lot in common. In the Kundalini awakening I found myself engaging in a child's sense of freshness, wonderment, aliveness, and vitality. I also felt a spontaneous welling up of love, goodwill, and a wonderfully receptive and nurturing feminine energy. Despite becoming aware of the tremendous potential that is available to each of us as we awaken, I was simultaneously aware that not everything was in place and integrated. Few of us can successfully pull off the Greek goddess Athena's trick of springing full-grown from the forehead of Zeus, and I was no exception. There was a long developmental process ahead of me, albeit with a fresh start.

The Kundalini process could be dismissed by some clinicians as hypomania or psychotic process-- something requiring a mood stabilizer or antipsychotic medication to eradicate. The confusion is understandable. In a way there is a bit of an ungluing that happens, and those who don't maintain a solid grounding and a good connection to others can become psychotic in the classical sense. Nevertheless, even classical psychotic expression, although viewed by some as mere dreck, may contain seeds of healing. Unintegrated material, as unreal as it may seem, can sometimes be the manure that fertilizes new growth when the client feels safer, more grounded, and ready. Just because someone has psychosis, it does not mean that this person is altogether unaware. For example, clients may be very attuned to my feelings and relational stance towards them, so I try my best to maintain a calm, non-judgmental presence of respect and compassion. When a client is psychotic, I can find it challenging to stay very present and self-aware. In the interest of being non-judgmental, I try to remember that the opposite extreme has limitations as well. When we get very stuck in stale patterns, an ungluing may allow for change that can make the experience of life more precious and vital. There is risk involved in the sense that we may seem to descend a bit into "insanity" in order to ultimately become more sane. It is useful to remember that crisis is also opportunity.

The creative process benefits from initially holding things loosely in all their potential so that they aren't tightly bound or lock-step ordered. Similarly my Kundalini process involved a freeing-up of things that had become tied into emotional knots or ossified into a well ordered, but constricted, worldview. The state of being unglued or unaligned is the potential on which the creative process draws. Although the goal is to ultimately have concrete artistic output, it is equally important to devote sufficient time and space for a seasoning process to optimally coalesce that which begins as pure potential. Artistic expression can be nudged, through slight initial variations, onto paths that play out quite differently just as very slight changes in value affect greatly the final product in mathematically-based fractal drawing.

Although I might have in mind a general idea of what I want to photograph, I try to start with embracing possibility. As I do my fine art photography, I've found that my reasoning mind is a fairly blunt instrument compared to my body when it comes to making initial visual choices. I begin with a body-based tuning-in that involves feeling my way through successive approximations. I continue until there is a sense of completion or that it is close enough. The tuning-in is present at all stages from taking the picture to developing the print, but each alternate choice has a progressively more subtle impact.

There is the story of Frank Lloyd Wright who was commissioned to build a house in the environs of a stream. He took many measurements, made mental notes, and spent a lot of time mulling over how to accomplish this challenging task. However, he had no architectural drawings to show for this effort. His client, who had

43

become impatient, called him out of the blue and asked if he could stop by to see the drawings that very day. In a flurry of activity Wright produced the drawings for one of his seminal works, "Falling Water," in a matter of a few hours. This could be viewed as a classic example of procrastination or alternately as an example of an artist who didn't want to prematurely foreclose the open-ended creative process. The creative process owes much of its vitality to the bottom-up processes known as emergence; but we don't have a packaged product until we reach for hierarchical top-down processes to achieve something that persists through time and is predictably ordered.

The dance between taking-charge and letting-go has always been a complicated one for me. A real letting-go had proven fairly elusive in my life, and my need to control had often gotten me stuck. Well before I did a good job of letting-go in my life, I discovered it in the open-endedness of the creative process. Perhaps the spiritual awakening was fundamentally a creative process. This seems particularly true considering that both processes benefit from a kind of open-endedness that balances an optimal letting-go with an optimal taking charge at just the right time. I see another similarity. The painter brings overt intention and skill to the process of painting but there is also a way that the hand seems to unconsciously know how to make the painting more whole and vital. It might be said that there is a spontaneous, integrative, and expressive coming together of loosely-held elements not unlike the healing I experienced for myself. Like the hand seemingly guided in how to paint, my mind-body knew how to heal itself, given a genuineness of intention and the proper conditions such as safety, love, and trust.

Diagnostic formulations and theoretical explanations are expected from those of us who practice psychotherapy. As important as it is to be guided by a theoretical framework, I think of the session as particularly benefiting from those factors that nurture creativity rather than those that provide clear-cut explanations. Perhaps it is wise to pause and reflect on the Jewish tradition of leaving God unnamed, or to consider the Native American concept of the

"Great Mystery." The reality, of course, is that the person in psychotherapy has to work effectively within certain constraints and limitations, just as the artist needs to realistically work within the constraints of the medium. Nevertheless, there is no need to close down possibility prematurely. I think of the heart and not the mind as the center of healing. The fully opened heart, though bound by the truth, need not be shackled by "what-is." It is most unfortunate that the "love" of clients by psychotherapists has become so widely associated with boundary violations. Genuine mutually mirroring love can be especially helpful in keeping possibility open. Love is, after all, the language of the heart and should not be confused with a narcissistic gratification of needs.

I see artistic expression and psychological/spiritual healing as being involved with transmitting underlying patterns of meaning. The ancient Greeks imbued Gods and Goddesses with particular sets of characteristics. Jungian theory notes the universality of the energy that these Gods and Goddesses carry by naming archetypes for them. These Gods and Goddesses weren't constructed out of thin air as idle fantasies, but represent widely observed patterns that guide everyday humans in the ways they manage life and relationships. Perhaps healing, in part, involves tuning-in to or aligning-with new patterns to guide us. However, these patterns are not continuously variable, but seem to come in discrete groupings. Larry Dossey (1982), for one, notes that healing appears to take place in discrete jumps. This is reminiscent of the way Quantum Theory describes electrons in an atom as only being capable of occupying particular energy states to the exclusion of intermediate states. However, changing to a more energized state is only possible when a threshold value of energy input is attained or exceeded.

Archetypes, and other patterns that guide our behavior and perception, may best be thought of as patterns we intuitively attune-to rather than ones that we learn through formal instruction. With respect to patterns, I've noticed for myself a process of tuning-in or resonating that somewhat parallels that of a radio. A good quality

45

radio has the ability to select, out of a vast jumbled soup of electro-magnetic radiation, an exceedingly weak signal with great specificity and clarity. My own tuning-in is mostly an unconscious process, but I'm occasionally aware of my mind-body titrating successive approximations until it seems that I have gotten it right. Sometimes I only have a felt-sense. At other times I'll perceive just a faint outline as if seen through an obscuring fog or mist. If I'm really attuned I might see an image with clarity. Regardless of the degree of clarity with which the image is perceived, it invariably references a "whole" and not just one segment. The image in a developing black and white print gradually emerges in a similar fashion. The emergence is some-what discontinuous, but it generally appears to arise out of the out-line of the image as a whole. This always referencing of the whole is also reminiscent of the way a hologram functions. Even when a holo-gram is cut into successively smaller pieces, each piece retains the ability to recreate the entire image, albeit with less distinctness as each piece becomes smaller.

Some patterns may be perceived and understood in terms of images. Other patterns are powerfully tuned-in, but in ways that are a bit mysterious. Even when images are involved, the images them-selves may be best thought of as ways that underlying patterns are brought to light rather than the images being the patterns per se. William Blake (c.1800), in Auguires of Innocence, seemed especially aware of patterns:

> To see a World in a Grain of Sand
> And a Heaven in a Wild Flower
> Hold Infinity in the palm of your hand
> And Eternity in an hour.

I believe that Blake envisioned the universe as replete with pat-terns and that each small unit was inherently capable of referencing a much larger whole. In everyday terms we can sometimes implicitly intuit quite a bit about someone based on ever-so-subtle changes in facial expression, expressive qualities of the voice, or how the body

46

presents itself. If we tap into an essence that is true enough, and free enough of our own biases, we may be able to sense a much bigger picture regarding the circumstances surrounding a particular person, and how he or she has been engaging life. I suspect that nearly everything leaves traces in the space-time continuum whether or not we can perceive it.

We all do relationship according to underlying patterns that follow a syntax specific to those with whom we have sustained intimate contact; in particular patterns associated with our families of origin. How we learn the language of intimate relationship is a bit mysterious, but Lewis, et al. (2000) propose a relational pattern-recognition mechanism called "limbic attractors" or "limbic attunement." The limbic system is the part of the brain associated with emotion, and how we feel about things has a lot to do with what we pay attention to and how we assign meaning to our individual experience. Early in childhood, we tune in to emotional patterns of relationship and form durable inner templates of how relationship is done in our family. Although not hardwired, the patterns can be amazingly persistent. Even years after leaving home, who amongst us has not had the experience of emotionally responding to someone unrelated, as if they were in fact our parent? If relational patterns in the family of origin were faulty, there are times when limbic attunement can draw someone into an abusive relationship like a moth to a flame. Stolorow (2005, p. 101), in his discussion on intersubjectivity, seems to also touch on this topic using very different language. In brief he discusses how the attunement or malattunement is felt within the intersubjective context in a way that can't be separated from that context in which the experience takes place.

At its best, artistic expression involves taking something we are attuned-to and bringing it out into the world in a manner that can be shared. It can be very personal in nature, but when it arises from an authentic place in the artist, it can transcend the vision or experience of one person and have great meaning for others as well. Patterns that reference the eternal or universal, may be woven into the very fabric of the artistic expression regardless of the artist's explicit intentions. I suspect that the patterns of meaning are imbedded and retrieved in a manner reminiscent of holograms. The wave patterns captured in the hologram don't have meaning until they are viewed under "tuned" light. But, under those conditions, a three dimensional image can be recreated seemingly out of thin air. As with the hologram, there may be a tuning-in process that allows us to resonate to the imbedded meaning in art or, alternately, we may tune-in and form intuitive images (sometimes called psychic images) as we resonate to the accessible archetypal, relational, and identity-associated patterns in those around us.

I'll give an example of what I understand as tuning-in to imbedded meaning in a work of art. Several months after my Kundalini Awakening began I met a presenter, Ericha Scott, at the summer of 1995 Conference on Creativity and Madness in Santa Fe, New Mexico. She shared with me a group of four guided self-portraits that she had done. I was very drawn to one of the guided self-portraits with antlers and an unusual look associated with the eyes. A month later, following a guided meditation in a workshop, I went to the restroom. There in the restroom mirror I saw that same look in the eyes, now overlaying my own features. I quickly intuited that it had something to do with a healing archetype. Two years later, in 1997, I wrote this piece about what that look in the eyes represented to me.

The Eyes of the Healer

The eyes of the healer look strange and yet I know them. I see them for the first time peering out at me as I look in the mirror. I have not been consciously aware of them before but my soul acknowledges them with comfortable familiarity. I am awakened to the divinity within me and feel truly blessed by this moment.

As I gaze in the mirror I contemplate the quality of the psychic vision I am seeing. The words are hard to find but gradually I begin to discern certain features in the healer eyes. There is that prescient immanence about the eyes, the quality of having seen and known everything for all time and a sense that time seems irrelevant. There is a softness, a deep compassion and love but no pity. There is an unadorned starkness and a pervasive immutable quality where things are seen as they are without judgment.

These are not the eyes of innocence but bear witness to both the good and the evil alike. Adapted as they are to seeing in the dark they maintain a full pupillary dilation. As a sturdy ship against the tempest, they embody truth held unchanging in the face of an exquisitely intimate knowledge of pain and suffering. Even as I experience the full weight of adversity, the healer maintains me unyielding in the truth as I pass through the veil of illusion that has held me fettered in pain. Once I see, know and fully embrace things as they are, holding that truth consistent with who I authentically am and where I have been, then I can relinquish the need to hold onto symptoms and illness as a thwarted expression of truth.

-George Campbell

Ever since I was first introduced to the "eyes of the healer" I have periodically seen this look associated with my features when looking in the mirror. It is sometimes stronger and sometimes almost imperceptible, or it commingles with other features. It is a fairly reliable indicator of how present I am to the Whole aspects of Truth. It is an archetypal energy that can stand me in good stead when listening as witness to someone's story of trauma. I once saw an image of exquisite beauty overlaid on a friend as she told her story of being raped. This healer archetype held me present, and my heart guided me, as I instinctively became her mirror, restoring a piece of what had been robbed from her by a truly ugly act.

My conscious mind had stepped aside, as something greater than me came through me and guided my response in a manner that artists sometimes speak of when producing their art. In both cases, we are a prepared channel through which a creative force flows and enters the world. We cannot take full credit, for we are but the privileged midwives who have assisted in the birth of something, which is both of us and not of us, simultaneously. Therapists, like artists, benefit from being skilled with the medium; i.e. having the proper tools, setting, and intention. However, healing (or art) often comes through us as an act of grace. Finally, both artists and psychotherapists, in the act of being very fully who they authentically are, can be unwitting messengers for serendipitous healing that wasn't consciously intended.

The healer archetype helps keep me in a place where I can give myself over to a larger purpose and, like Viktor Frankl (1963), find ways to give meaning to suffering. Offering something up to the altar of the eternal can be an essential part of bringing meaning to traumatic experience, suffering, and pain. Cruelty and acts that deliberately harm often fall outside of our ordinary ability to make sense of the world. For that which cannot be articulated in words, or is beyond our ordinary capacity to understand, expansively referencing the vastness of the eternal can bring a felt-meaning in the heart.

I have often wondered why many artists have led particularly difficult lives. I see their gifts and their curses as inextricably intertwined. Often artists tap the pulse of "what is" to a greater degree than the average person, going beyond an awareness of their own particular circumstances to an uncanny awareness of ageless truths or even the zeitgeist. Being allied in some measure with that which is authentic and true can be deeply meaningful, and at times ecstatically joyful and satisfying; but the process that an artist goes through in producing authentic art can also involve much angst and torment. Perhaps some of the angst and torment arises

50

from staying in a certain authentic space of attunement to life that is not so clouded by society's rules, prescribed viewing lenses, and amnestic machinations.

In the interest of a higher good, life may sometimes demand to be experienced without anesthesia or the full benefit of defensive mechanisms. Goya's depictions of the atrocities associated with the Napoleonic Wars carry a very stark truth that simply cannot be made palatable by depicting warfare as heroic. Whether he is a witting or an unwitting messenger, there seems to be a compulsion through which a truth inexorably emerges, a truth that cannot simply be replaced by the expediency of political formulations or the detached abstractions of the human mind.

Recently I had a wonderful exchange with my friend Pat Hill about the creative process. She is a self-taught artist as well as a professional writer who finds doing art to be essential to her own journey of healing and integration. I mentioned to her that the artist seems to have the capacity to remind us all of wholeness but that being in touch with wholeness can also be associated with pain and angst. I further suggested that maybe there is a sense of immediacy and urgency associated with artistic expression that provides a powerful incentive to do art. Here is her response to me:

> True. For me, it feels like something must "come up."
> It is like the birth process--you get a rumbling, then morning sickness, then there's pain and some frustration. The process takes over your life, and more acutely your body, and then it must be expunged into the world! a piece of you--a part of you, yes, but more so, a creation that comes through you for the sole reason to exist in the physical world/form. My best work comes when I allow myself to be the vessel, not the captain. (Pat Hill personal communication, 2006)

In a strict sense art may not be seen as essential for survival in terms of our mere physical persistence. Yet it may be experienced as essential, particularly for the life of the soul, by allowing us to feel more complete, integrated, and connected. That the life-affirming energy of the Greek deity Eros is often counterbalanced by the death force of Thanatos in our struggle to live meaningfully and purpose-fully, stands as a tribute to the complexity of what it is to be human. I believe that Thanatos represents more than a simple nihilistic force to be eliminated as an abject defect in human nature.

If life isn't experienced as having meaning, perhaps contrasting it with death is the impetus that helps reorder life so as to regain meaning. The point isn't necessarily to kill oneself, rather the sense that one is aligned with a self that is emotionally dying or emotionally unviable means that one may feel in that moment that he/she is a member of the "living dead", physically alive but emotionally walled off without access to life. Since we all have a powerful intrinsic force in us that seeks to align with living meaningfully, ironically one may face death in order to live. For trauma survivors who feel the pull of suicide and self-destructive behavior, artistic expression may create movement towards reconnecting with a body that otherwise feels numb or dissociated. From beneath the surface of consciousness, an endogenous psychic healing force may be persistently seeking to break ground through the artwork.

I'm struck by the way meaning, identity and truth are intertwined. Embracing truth with sincerity is important because of the way that the experience of self is tied in to autobiographical memory. Realistically we can't always be truthful or follow truth all of the time. Nevertheless a pattern of consistently doing one's best to stay with the truth despite pain or fear can promote the development of a cohesive and integrated sense of self. By contrast, an optimally inte-grated self-identity can suffer if we are overly identified with certain distortions of the survival instinct. For example, we might get caught up in creating a version of relational reality that seems to always give ourselves the edge, or we might identify our sense of self too closely with a carefully crafted face we present to the world. In some cases an inner emptiness or void may be created as progressively greater portions of true autobiographical memory are relegated to the disallowed-self or, in Carl Jung's terms, relegated to "the shadow."

Distortions of the survival instinct are almost unavoidable with exposure to trauma. Those who have experienced trauma often find that a stable and cohesive sense of self-identity can be especially elusive. Dissociation is one obvious way that autobiographical memory and identity are disrupted. Additionally, trauma and abuse can spawn narcissistic spectrum issues that impact identity and autobiography in major ways. Even without obvious dissociation, relational history can be somewhat absent, not just with respect to past traumatic events, but on an ongoing basis with contemporary relationships. As seductive as it may be to mostly remember positive events and things that positively reference one's self-image, moving forward developmentally requires adjustments based on more inclusive self-memories.

Pain and suffering can be very hard to bear for client, therapist, and artist alike. Our natural inclination when confronted by intense psychic or physical pain is how to get rid of it, and soon. Sometimes a quick reflexive response in the moment is best. For example, we may need to quickly separate ourselves from something that is very hot lest there be damage to the flesh. At other times an impulse to alleviate pain can get us off track, off our path, and even lead to more pain. Although we all might like to do the best we can, in the face of pain many of us can succumb to one or more of the following strategies to alleviate or manage pain: these include avoidance, denial, suicidal and self-harm behavior, addictions, numbing/dissociation, or even psychosis. These strategies unfortunately limit growth, as do the outwardly directed strategies of blame, projecting, inflicting pain on others, or forcing others to be our empathic mirrors. In addition to spiritual practice, acupuncture or medical intervention, healthier strategies might involve such things as going into the pain and addressing, from a place of honesty and truth, any messages that the pain might have for us.

In my own journey of healing I have found it useful to sometimes make friends with pain and not only view it as an archenemy to be defeated. Pain need not relegate us to victimhood or cause us to cynically lose faith in God. Discomfort or pain can be viewed as letting us know that something is amiss. There are some caveats to consider: things don't generally play out well if we actively seek out pain, if we have a relationship with pain that attracts pain to ourselves, if we induce pain in others, or if our identity becomes too intimately defined by pain. If we can circumnavigate the depersonalizing defense mechanisms such as dissociation and psychosis, pain has the capability of potentiating a focused awareness that can move us towards new understanding and new growth. That focused awareness may also greatly enhance the sense of presence and poignancy in artistic output. This is the impression I get when I view paintings done by Frieda Kahlo. In terms of the bigger picture, our movement towards God, spirit, or universal oneness may be associated with a desire to maintain integrity in the face of pain.

Simply avoiding pain without paying homage to Truth circumvents pain's message and purpose... and can lead to addictions. I think of Truth, not as involving strict adherence to an inviolate set of facts or stridently speaking whatever comes to mind, but as something subjective that arises from a heart-centered place of genuineness and authenticity. By contrast, the too-diligent pursuit of power, control, and perfectionism can be antithetical to Truth. I believe that Truth is that which avoids expediency and addictive processes by maintaining a willingness to be subject to the inconvenience of "what is."

Sticking to factual literalness is not what I mean by being subject to Truth, and imagination that lacks the intention to deceive should not be confused with lies. For example, there is a legitimate place for dreaming and expansively imagining new possibility as is sometimes the case with an artist or even an exuberant two-year-old staking out attention and space. Nevertheless, the artist is ideally responsive to the artistic process as well as acting on it and the two-year-old ideally begins forming a viable identity as others respond authentically in a give-and-take manner. In writing this chapter, I've noticed myself having periods of expansiveness and getting "puffed up." The voice of the "expert" eventually showed up, and then the editor in me strived to make the writing more "perfect," only to find the magic beneath the words beginning to slip away into the never-never land of "carefully-crafted." Striving for perfection works well as a direction, but can be very problematic when I try to make it an actual destination. Yet, without the expansiveness and perfectionistic pull, I could never have written this chapter. I've needed all whole parts of myself to do this work; but, as a final editor, my heart has thankfully transcended my conscious self.

For me, Truth is not about "creating" meaning through selecting the right words, which is the currency of politics and advertising, but is about the use of words to best convey meaning that is authentically understood and authentically experienced in a spirit of open inquiry. The latter is art and psychotherapy at its best, and is intimately intertwined with the ability to heal. The openness that is conducive to optimal functioning of the artistic process seems to parallel the conduciveness arising from a therapist's stance of deep respect within the psychotherapy session. Perhaps this deep respect is best conceptualized as the ability to see clients anew in each moment as if, once again, seeing them for the very first time. The truth, when squarely faced in psychotherapy, can be very freeing and cathartic but ever so painful. Likewise, some of the angst and torment that an artist can experience while producing art may be associated with adhering to the truth to the best of his or her ability. The reward in each case seems to be an enhanced sense of sustainable wholeness, integrity, and resilience to life.

REFERENCES

Blake, W. (c. 1800). *Auguires of Innocence.*

Bolen, J. S. (1984). *Goddesses in everywoman: A new psychology of women.* San Francisco: Harper & Row.

Bolen, J. S. (1989). *Gods in everyman: A new psychology of men's lives and loves.* San Francisco: Harper & Row.

Dossey, L. (1982). *Space time and medicine*. Boston: Shambhala Press.

Frankl, V.E. (1963) *Man's search for meaning*. Boston: Beacon Press.

Grof, S. and Grof. C. (Eds.). (1989). *Spiritual emergency: When personal transformation becomes a crisis*. New York: Tarcher/Putnam.

Henshaw, J. (2006). Carl Jung and the Kundalini. *Knowledge of Reality Magazine*. http://www.sol.com.au/kor/12_02.htm

Lewis, T., Amini, F., Lannon, R. (2000). *A general theory of love*. NY: Vintage.

Stolorow, R.D. (2005). *The contextuality of emotional experience*. Psychoanalytic Psychology,22(1), 101-106.

WikiHealth contributors (2006). Namaste. *WikiHealth*. Retrieved August 4, 2006 from http://www.wikihealth.com/Namaste.

Arthur Colman, MD, was born in New York City and educated at Harvard College and Harvard Medical completing his psychiatric residency at University of California Medical Center. Drafted into the Vietnam War, he worked at Walter Reed Army Institute of Research and was discharged as a Major. Afterward he spent several years in Jerusalem working at Bet Etonim, a large multilingual state mental hospital, and at the University Mental Health Clinic at Hebrew University.

In 1971 he coauthored the book Pregnancy: the Psychological Experience a best seller examining the psychological changes in women and men during the pregnancy and post partum period. From 1970 thru 1977 he worked as a Career Investigator in psychiatry at U.C.S.F. and the Department of Architecture at U.C. Berkeley where along with a small team of architects and planners he helped design and develop "birth centers" at San Francisco General Hospital and Mt. Zion Hospital in San Francisco, the first in the U.S. He also wrote the influential book, Earth Father Sky Father, which elaborated the archetypal, historical and impending role of men in the parenting process.

His interest in the psychology of composers and musical composition began as part of an interest in choral singing; —Studying with Brian Baker and Robert Geary, he sings tenor with the S. F. Choral Society and Marin Symphony Orchestra and the Festival Chorus (directed by Donald Runnicles) in Teton Village, Wyoming. Together with his life partner Pilar Montero he has published psychological commentary on major choral composers including Monteverdi, Mozart, Handel, Bach, Brahms, Beethoven, Brahms, Faure, Bernstein, and Vaughn Williams. He has recently published a chapter on Benjamin Britten entitled Music and the Psychology of Pacifism Benjamin Britten's War Requiem' for Terror, Violence and the <None>Impulse to Destroy, Edited by John Beebe.

Dmitri Shostakovich

PTSD Casualty or Russian Holy Fool

Arthur Colman, MD

Introduction

Dmitri Shostakovich (1906–1975) is universally acknowledged as one of the great classical composers of the twentieth century and Russia's greatest composer of the Soviet era. His music is extraordinary. His Fifth Symphony and Eighth Quartet are well known, but increasingly, aided by the celebrations of the centennial of his birth in 2006, most of his major works are in the repertoire of symphony orchestras, string quartets, lieder singers, and opera.

His life as a composer and a man was also extraordinary and the subject of considerable controversy.[1] Except for occasional trips to the United States and Europe, Shostakovich lived most of his adult life in Soviet Russia under the rule of Josef Stalin. Because Shostakovich was so famous in a country that valued classical music, and because, like Hitler, Stalin was interested in the arts as a manipulative tool for his regime, Shostakovich's relationship with Stalin was direct and almost intimate. This relationship and its consequences had a major effect on his musical compositions. Shostakovich is probably unique among all great composers in the extent to which his work was directly influenced by a political regime and its leader.

For the last ten years, Pilar Montero and I have been studying the lives of great composers from the perspectives of collective and individual psychology.[2] These perspectives have their roots in our experience as organizational consultants, as Jungian analysts, and as members of choruses singing classical works.

Through our work as group consultants and group theorists, we are interested in the effect on music composition of what we have called *collective consciousness*, a construct analogous to individual

59

consciousness but applied to larger systems, such as groups, organizations, and even nations.[3] It has proved a useful model with which to understand the largest social, emotional, and intellectual milieu in which the composer is imbedded and from which he creates. Our studies suggests that many great composers, from Bach and Mozart to Beethoven to Richard Strauss, are peculiarly sensitive to their polity, which may also offer a key to the mystery of their creativity. In Shostakovich's case, the national consciousness embodied by the dictator Stalin was a primary influence on every aspect of the music Shostakovich composed.

Related to this approach is our desire to integrate this collective model with a psychological and developmental approach to musicians' lives, in particular the factors that transform prodigies into great composers.[4] Obviously, personal experiences profoundly shape the creative process of all composers, and important life cycle and family influences and crises are rightfully emphasized in biographical studies. The death of two of Dvorak's children preceding the composition of his wrenching *Stabat Mater*, and the death of Brahms's mother before he composed parts of his *German Requiem*, are famous examples of the latter. Most twentieth century European composers such as Shostakovich (and Britten and Richard Strauss as well) were also, and sometimes primarily, dealing with the horrific reality of their times. Shostakovich displays all the familiar childhood hallmarks of prodigy and had his share of personal family tragedy; yet, in his case at least, we must underline the dominating influence of political events as both the central trauma and dark inspiration in his music.

From our perspective as members of the healing profession, the study of composers and their music has been a wonderful way to enrich our knowledge of the relationship of creativity and the healing process, including the fascinating task of untangling the mysteries of creativity and madness. In the case of Shostakovich, political trauma—including its personal, pathological, and collective effects—and creative transcendence in his art are inextricably bound together.

60

It is important to consider all these factors if we are to better understand his musical development and his oeuvre.

The Nature Of Music And Collective Consciousness

The musical composer is defined by a unique sensitivity to the vibrations of the world, human and nonhuman, animate and inanimate. Only rare individuals are capable of mastering music as both an abstract, mathematical language and a language of human emotions and sensibilities. The impossibility of separating personal and collective in the creative act is part and parcel of the nature of music itself. The developing artist draws inspiration from many sources, including his or her own life experiences. But one of the measures of artistic development is the ability to plumb the collective psyche and speak from it in a way that moves the entire society beyond itself.

In this regard, it is interesting that of all the arts, music is the least *species specific*; as recent articles in *Science* suggest, there is no adequate way to distinguish human music from auditory productions of other species, such as complex birdcalls.[5] If you have followed a lion through its nightly rounds and listened to its auditory territorial displays—its roars—not to mention its erotic and awe-inspiring mating symphonies, you will understand what the article is logically showing. Created sound, the music of all species, including our own, is by its very nature collective, serving the ritual ceremonies of life: love and mating, territoriality and aggression, loss and death.

This biological and cultural imperative that empowers the composer's collective voice is at the heart of his creativity. It is my belief that the greatest composers become ciphers, codified representatives for the broadest range and depth of a vast vibrational consciousness, which surrounds them, the collective speaking through the composer even as the composer speaks to the collective. As musical mediums, great composers may become muses to their nations to their political leaders, and eventually to the world.

It is perhaps counterintuitive to think of music as the stuff of prophecy and interpretation. Music is abstract and mathematical, but it is this very abstractness that links it to the larger collective context in every non literal and nonlinear way possible—its forms, structures, notation, and instruments all distilling the spirit and culture of the age. Musicians must master a complex array of intuitions, skills, and competencies to begin their work as composers. But as they develop, they also learn to use the refining fire of auditory visions as an "other world" to interpret the hidden, the mysterious, and the problematic to their audience. The great musicologist philosopher Theodor Adorno described this idea beautifully: "Music gazes at its listener with empty eyes, and the more deeply one immerses oneself in it, the more incomprehensible its ultimate purpose becomes until one learns that the answer, if such is possible, does not lie in contemplation but in interpretation."[6] From this perspective, Shostakovich composed and spoke from, and for, the most disturbed collective consciousness we can imagine: one dominated by war and murder, by agonizing fear, betrayal, revenge, and despair—emotions that are never far from our musical heritage. His interpretation of this world was from both its center and its edge, from a place of great loyalty and of great deceit, from his deepest self as well as his most pitiful traumatized ego.

The Development Of A Composer

I find it extraordinary that every great composer we have studied began his or her life as a musical prodigy (although the converse is not true—few musical prodigies become great composers). The talents of child musical prodigies certainly feel otherworldly, even to those who are musically competent or gifted. To have known a musical prodigy close up, or to have studied the unfathomable early achievements of a Mozart, Beethoven, or Bernstein, is to cross a boundary from ordinary to extraordinary. True to form, Shostakovich was a prodigy, although a late bloomer as prodigies go. He was introduced to the piano at nine and all but mastered it in six months. He was soon able to play the most difficult piano music by heart, and to compose complex music in all genres. Some of the qualities that Shostakovich shared with other prodigies were an intense pleasure in musical scores and notation, an infallible memory of all things musical, and an eye-hand coordination genius in their chosen instruments. Shostakovich had it all. Stories about his feats are legion.

A brief apocryphal example of the pre-teen musician, one among many: A piece of chamber music was to be played at the Shostakovich household in St. Petersburg. It was four-part music for string quartet —and the violist had not shown up. Shostakovich had heard the piece only once before. Without any score, he proceeded to play the viola part, a difficult inner part, on the piano with the other three string parts and made almost no mistakes. Those of you who know music will appreciate that this is a real feat, far beyond the fake claims of spiritual masters and certainly beyond the influences of nurture, support, lessons, or even immense talent.[7]

For musical prodigies, the familiar nature/nurture polarity is dominated by nature. Many children are introduced to music early and enjoy the privilege of having great teachers. They may become proficient musicians, although that rarely extends to composing. But almost all great composers have had musical parents or close relatives, whether or not the composers benefited directly from having them as parents or teachers—but of course they often did. The musical childhood of Dmitri Shostakovich is no exception. Shostakovich's father was a gifted tenor, musician, and scientist. His mother studied at the St. Petersburg Conservatory (as did Dmitri) but gave that up to raise her family. Shostakovich's sister was a professional musician. Prodigies need and benefit from support and, above all, recognition by family and community, but their gifts are not learnable in the usual sense; in the world of prodigies and therefore composers, genetics rules. Overzealous parents, be forewarned!

After recognition, the next step in the musical destiny of the prodigy's life is musical education. Young Shostakovich's talents were dramatic. They were particularly prized in his cultured professional Russian family in musical St. Petersburg, although after 1917, being

63

cultured and professional in revolutionary Russia was a political liability. Great prodigies can be nurtured in many musical styles, but they all seem to almost physically require the kind of vibrational complexity that only the classical music of the world, Western and non-Western, provides. But even with such innate skills, there is a grand edifice to be learned. Ten years of immersion and studying music theory and practice counts as a minimum even for the musical genius of a Shostakovich. He studied with the great teachers of his city and at the renowned St. Petersburg Conservatory even when there were personal and financial reasons to dissuade him. His father died when Dmitri was in his early teens, and he earned money as an improvising pianist for silent films—Brahms did the same in bawdy houses—to help support his family. Shostakovich was also present at the riots in St. Petersburg during the Russian Revolution in 1917. These were strong influences on the young man and his music, but through this turmoil he never deviated from acquiring the skills he needed to become a composer.

By this stage in Shostakovich's development, many other prodigies would have fallen by the wayside; their special talent might have disappeared or become integrated into other more practical (and lucrative) endeavors. Some would simply not be psychologically up to the enormous work required of great (not just competent) musicians. But Shostakovich was not only brilliantly talented but a juggernaut of energy. Despite the loss of his father and the drama of political revolution, he was by all accounts a psychologically healthy young man firmly and inspirationally connected to a composing career.

In 1932, at the age of twenty-four, he finished his second opera, the first in what he and colleagues projected to be his own four-opera "Ring cycle" à la Wagner. Titled *Lady Macbeth of the Mtsensk District*, it was produced in Moscow and St. Petersburg (a major triumph in itself for a twenty-four-year-old), and eagerly awaited by the musical community already familiar with his exciting compositions.

(A procedural aside: Writing about musicians and music does not easily allow examples, as is the case with painters or poets. So, as

64

the reader continues with this chapter, I suggest watching and listening to the excerpted portions of this opera.[8] It was the fulcrum of Shostakovich's transformation from young hero to a far more difficult life phase and will provide a necessary taste of Shostakovich's presumptuous virtuosity and brilliance pre-trauma before his dramatic fall.)

The libretto was inspired by but not based on Shakespeare's and Verdi's Macbeth. Katerina, our tragic heroine, is a bored, passionate beauty now married to a less-than-exciting, nay, flaccid businessman's son. This classic situation soon leads to adultery, murder, exile, and death.

In the last refrain from an aria, Katerina describes her loveless, indolent life in a way that presages the subsequent tragedy. It contains lyricism and strains of folk songs so familiar in the Russian tradition and a constant aspect of all of Shostakovich's music.

In it we see and hear the seduction/rape of Katerina by Sergei, a laborer in her husband's factory. We are dealing with brilliant musical storytelling of overtly sexual and violent material. It expresses passion, rape, lust, and even the humor of a few postcoital seconds.

Leading up to this moment in the opera, Katerina has poisoned her father-in-law, a failed seducer himself, who savagely whipped her lover Sergei when he was caught escaping from her window. Katerina and Sergei are now living as a couple, but the husband/bereaved son is coming home. The scene begins with Sergei hiding as the husband enters. This is the Italian Shostakovich: fanfare, contrapuntal duet, extravagant, exuberant, passionate—dramatic stuff.

This is young Shostakovich's brilliant and lusty opera. Those of you who have seen the opera performed know how dramatic and soul-stirring this piece can be. In the musically knowledgeable Moscow and St. Petersburg of 1932, its genius was more than evident. It was a huge success. In the first two years, there were ninety-four productions in Moscow alone! Almost immediately, it was being sung everywhere in the Soviet Union that had an opera house, as well as in the international opera world, including the United States, Argentina, England, Sweden, and Czechoslovakia. And then, suddenly, it was not heard at all. There was total silence from Katerina, Sergei, and the rest. No more stirring arias from the stage or brilliant music from the orchestra pit. There were, in fact, no more productions. The opera was not produced again in the Soviet Union for twenty-three years! And there were to be no more operas composed by Shostakovich. Not one!

What happened? Stalin happened, and a *danse macabre* between two very different geniuses happened. Two years after *Lady Macbeth* burst into the world's musical consciousness, Stalin and his retinue went to the Moscow opera house to see what all the fuss was about. The next morning there was a review of it in Pravda, probably the most infamous and influential review in musical history. It was understood by the cognoscenti to have been dictated by Stalin himself.[9] Here is an excerpt from the review: "The listener is flabbergasted from the first moments of the opera by an intentionally ungainly flow of sounds, snatches of melody, embryos of musical phrases drown, escape, and drown once more in crashing gnashing and screeching." And, at the end, an ominous phrase; "This is playing at abstruse things that could end very badly."[10]

The objective facts of Stalin's regime are well-known: the gulags; an estimated 35 million people dead, most of them as a result of exile from within Russia itself, systematic terror and murder directed against many dissidents, including the prominent intelligentsia. From the moment of Stalin's musical critique of the opera, Shostakovich became a special object of sadistic control, the mouse in a cat-and-mouse game that lasted until Stalin's death and beyond.

Stalin's words had immediate disastrous effects on Shostakovich's music and reputation. All productions of *Lady Macbeth* were immediately canceled. Previously positive critics now "saw the light" and spoke out against his opera and its musical heresies. And much to their disgrace, most international opera houses, fearing political pressure and the loss of visiting Soviet artists, followed suit. In addition, the premiere of Shostakovich's Fourth Symphony, an eagerly awaited event, suddenly found no orchestra or concert house willing to play it. A quarter of a century passed before *Lady Macbeth* was played again and the Fourth Symphony finally premiered.

Political censorship has been all too common in the artistic world. Oppressive governments and dictators are usually attuned to the potential incendiary effect of art and music on a repressed populace and also on the humanitarian sensibilities of onlookers.

I felt this keenly as I listened to a recent performance of Shostakovich's *Lady Macbeth* in San Francisco. After all, it is not just the members of imprisoned nations that suffer from censorship. It is all of us who are denied access to the great art and its effects on us. After the performance, I found myself crying uncontrollably. Of course, this outburst was catalyzed by the powerful music and the dramatic story, but there is something more. *Lady Macbeth's* theme was the death of hope, the death of the free, wild, and politically dangerous. Women and men such as Katerina could never be allowed to exist in Stalin's repressive world.

To me, the opera was Shostakovich's preternatural prophecy of the death of a portion of his musical future. I believe my tears were for all that was lost, including Shostakovich's unborn operas, which no one would ever hear. Surely, Shostakovich became a great composer despite Stalin, but he was a far different composer than he might have been. That evening helped me to grasp what Shostakovich himself suggests: that opera could have been Shostakovich's preeminent medium. Like Verdi in *Lady Macbeth*, young Shostakovich showed that he already had that rare and magical gift— rare even among great composers—of creating passionate and dramatic music that is both personal and political.

One of Verdi's main operatic inspirations was his call for the liberation of Italy, which he and his music actually helped bring about. (The famous chorus from his opera *Nabucco*, "Va pensiero," became a unified Italy's national anthem.) But the Austrian monarchy that ruled and divided Italy's people was not the government of the Soviet Union. Verdi had to put up with annoying and sometimes disruptive censorship, which is why so many of his operas were reframed in older historical contexts. However, Stalin's pragmatic terror was far more destructive and obviously too much for Shostakovich to combat. Under these life-threatening conditions, he was simply unable to write another opera, a lifelong post-traumatic inhibition. In his later years, Shostakovich struggled with this inhibition and began adding more and more lyrics, mostly poems, to his symphonic works. For example, he used "Baba Yar," Yevtushenko's controversial poem, as text and leitmotifs for his music. Still, much was lost to the Russian people of the time, and ultimately to all of us.

*　　*　　*

Almost immediately after Stalin's review, Shostakovich developed acute psychological symptoms that we now would diagnose as post-traumatic stress disorder (PTSD).[11] His symptoms were classic: fear, anxiety, sleeplessness, nightmares when he did sleep—and these and many other responses to the terrorizing juggernaut behind Stalin's words were to last his entire life. A description of Shostakovich by a friend captures something of the effect: "...stiffening in front of a microphone like a rabbit caught in a snake's gaze—nervous, twitchy, crankiness, worn-out, weak."[12]

Symptoms of acute and chronic trauma were always with him, as were their stimuli, and their effects on his music and his psyche multiplied. Stalin understood that Shostakovich was psychologically malleable and therefore a political gold mine for his regime. He kept Shostakovich continually within his gun sights. Shostakovich fully expected to be dragged with his family out of their apartment every night for the next decades—the fate of many of his artistic colleagues. But Stalin needed a live scapegoat, so these threats were potential, more potent because they never needed to be actualized. His bureaucratic torture machine did the work for him; the official musical

68

community and the critics became his loyal and willing lieutenants in this scapegoating. Shostakovich's music was played, applauded, and then blasphemed and banned; and then played again to cheering countrymen. He was shamed by critics and shunned by soloists and orchestras; then his music was played and honored again. For him, as with every composer, each new composition carried with it the question of how good it was, what it was saying that was new and creative; but additionally in his case, each new composition also held the question of his actual survival and the survival of his family.

A candid description by Shostakovich in a letter to his good friend Isaak Glickman, written in 1974, just before Shostakovich's death, gives us an intimate and candid portrait of the inappropriate anxiety and self-doubt infusing his personality and social relationships. He was to hold a seat at a concert of *his own music* for Glickman, who went out for a smoke. Evgeny Mravinsky, a renowned symphonic conductor, appeared and sat in the saved seat. "I ought to have said, 'This is Isaak Davidovich's seat' but I didn't say anything," wrote Shostakovich. "I didn't have the courage, and was afraid of offending Mravinsky. So I sat there, quietly angry with myself."[13] In 2006, the famous Russian cellist and of late, orchestra conductor, Mstislav Rostropovich described his mentor in a telling reminiscence: "He was the most important man in my life after my father. Sometimes when I'm conducting, I see his face coming to me. Sometimes it's not really a happy face—I conduct maybe a bit too slowly, so I conduct faster, and the face disappears."[14]

Shostakovich was never physically abused or imprisoned, and as his fame spread, he received many financial and status rewards from the Soviet system. But beyond all the rewards and punishment that music brought him was his need to compose and his need for his works to be performed. Despite personal and political trauma of a kind that most of us cannot begin to imagine, he could not stop the music in his head and could not stop creating from those sounds—he composed right up until the day he died.

The real trauma that Stalin imposed on Shostakovich was to his creative soul. There was a monster loose in that sacred world, paired forever with his own monster of increasing self-doubts about his political compromise and cowardice. Musical composition was Shostakovich's lifeblood, and now he, like so many of his countrymen, had to dance to Stalin's nightmare tune as much as his own.

Shostakovich's adaptation to this nightmare is a subject of great debate in the academic and critical musical world today. Books, memoirs, biographies, symposia, journals, blogs and web sites regularly debate how much or how little Shostakovich capitulated to the Soviet system—and there is much evidence for both. The standard biography, written by Laurel Fay, suggests that he was an opportunist who succumbed and then benefited.[15] Musical critics and musicologists, including some who came from the Soviet Union to the West, made their reputations from this point of view. So it was a political and professional bombshell when Solomon Volkov, a music critic and younger friend of Shostakovich, arrived in the United States and published a book called *Testimony*, purporting to be a memoir by Shostakovich himself, that gave a glimpse of the relationship between his inner life, his politics and his music.[16]

This was a different Shostakovich than the public man that Fay and others portrayed: a Dostoyevskian underground man, an artist who, despite appearances, despite phobic symptoms and depression and despair, never really capitulated to the regime. Using Shostakovich's commentary, Volkov and then others reinterpreted his compositions as coded messages to his Russian people reflecting his and their inner desolation. Most personally and concretely (and the best documented example of this coding) was Shostakovich's use of a specific musical theme derived from his initials whenever he particularly wanted to emphasize material as reflecting his personal views, most notably in his gripping Eighth Quartet. Many of his symphonic works are seemingly about the victory over the Germans in 1945, but they have hidden and powerful allusions to the simultaneous oppression of the Russian people by Stalin's regime. Throughout his music, Shostakovich used overtly supra patriotic themes and lyrics but undercut them with sly musical references and quotations reflecting a dissident position.

And perhaps because music is abstract and non-literal, he could mostly keep what he was up to veiled in double entendre. He was like a spy communicating in cipher from an enemy land. His compositions had implicit alternative messages: an unusual harmony, a musical quotation, a transformation of inner structure, all pointing in other directions than the overt. The bleak world of a repressed people and culture became his muse inspiring music, parsed with coded, oblique paraphrased messages, to the desolate collective, parables to cognoscenti and peasant alike, and also perhaps for us, the future generations to which every composer gazes.

After Stalin died, there was a brief thaw in political oppression. During that time, Shostakovich expressed his anti-Soviet views more openly in his compositions. He began composing more programmatic music—that is, music that directly expresses an unambiguous point of view within the composition, either through the words it sets or the story the music itself tells. (A classic example of the latter is Richard Strauss's early symphonic composition *Ein Heldenleben*, in which Strauss illustrates the stages of a hero's life in simple and graphic musical terms clear to anyone listening.) In later symphonies, Shostakovich used both music and libretto to make a political point, and although he was still humiliated, there were fewer repercussions. His own fame and the withering political will of leaders who came after Stalin made his personal danger less immediate. For example, he used songs with revolutionary and rebellious themes to represent his hope for a better political order. In his song cycle From *Jewish Folk Poetry*, he used Jewish themes—he was not Jewish—as a metaphor for those who suffered but continued to live with joy in their lives.

Most famously, he asked the young poet Yevtuchenko if he could use "Babi Yar" as the libretto in his Thirteenth Symphony. This poem implicated all anti-Semitic Russia in the massacre of the Jews by the Germans in World War II, and then identified Russians and Jews together as part of victimized humanity. Even in the now

71

more liberal post-Stalinist soviet regime, this composition was deemed unacceptable. The musical bureaucracy required change in the poetry and its setting if the symphony was to be played. Shostakovich (but not Yevtuchenko) refused to alter his work and the orchestra members accepted the risk of playing the uncensored version. Even then, no baritone could be found to sing Yevtushenko's most seditious words. But Shostakovich persevered, and when the symphony was finally played, it was with the original text and music intact. The audience was jubilant, but there were no reviews and it was not mentioned in the newspapers.

Volkov was the first to connect Shostakovich's paradoxical role in Soviet Russia with the *Yurodivy*, or "holy fool," the Russian variation of the archetype of prophet or shaman or court fool. In Russian folktales, the *Yurodivy* has the gift to see and hear what others cannot, but he tells the world about his insights in an intentionally paradoxical way, in code. He plays the fool while he exposes evil and injustice. Opera buffs will know of the holy fool from the character of the same name in Mussorgsky's *Boris Godunov*, and spiritual buffs will know of the Russian holy fool in the anonymous mid nineteenth-century Russian mystical classic *The Way of the Pilgrim*.[17] In Volkov's view, now supported by letters and documents that became available after the Soviet Union collapsed, Shostakovich used his music to transcend the trauma by becoming a creative light to his enslaved nation.

My own tendency to agree with Volkov is informed by a visit to Moscow in August, 1991. A year before, Pilar Montero and I were asked by the State Department, through a senator enamored with Jungian analysis, to consult to an august group of artists, politicians, academics, and business people from Russia and the United States. The occasion for the conference was a growing awareness on both sides of the coming collapse of the Soviet Union. A year later, a second conference with the same group took place in Moscow on the day of the collapse. Overnight, people who, the day before, were identified members of the Communist party refused to acknowledge that

72

identity. Translators from Lithuania refused to translate Russian, saying that they no longer understood the language of their oppressors. We saw people living in apartments that looked impoverished from the outside, but inside them we found "subversive" libraries full of spiritual tracts, "immoderate" novels, decadent art objects, and other signs of "moral collapse." It was indeed a country of duplicity, doublespeak. The psychopathology inspired deception and deviousness to survive amidst the constriction, pain, and despair engendered by a malignant dictatorship. In my mind, Shostakovich mirrored this adaptation by speaking to his people on their own terms as a PTSD victim and interpretive artist.

Ultimately, we will judge him by his music. I want to end this chapter by briefly commenting on one Shostakovich's greatest pieces, his Eighth Quartet, composed in 1960 in Dresden. Its official legend was "In memory of war and fascism," but there is little question that this "In memory" was also directed to himself and to the plight of Soviet artists and other oppressed people in his land.

Shostakovich marked this piece as autobiographical with an anagram of his initials coded in musical notation—"D, E, C, B"—as its major theme. In typically self-denigrating and coded language, Shostakovich explained the nature of the quartet to a friend: "I wrote this ideological flawed quartet which is of no use to anybody. I started thinking that if some day I die, nobody is likely to write a work in memory of me, so I had better write one myself. The title page could carry the dedication 'to the memory of the composer of this quartet'."[18]

Throughout the quartet, he uses musical "quotes" as thematic landmarks of his life: a Jewish folk melody, a theme of victimization from his opera *Lady Macbeth*, the well-known revolutionary folk song "Tormented by Grievous Bondage," and most of all the prison theme with the famous "knocking at the door" fragment. All are communications that would have been familiar to his knowledgeable listeners much as themes from *Star Wars* would be familiar to today's movie audiences.

The work is an emotional unburdening of a tormented soul, an unrelenting portrait of the struggle of a man in despair. It begins in a slow largo with a mournful cello playing the four-note anagram of Shostakovich's signature. The theme is taken up by the other instruments and woven into a haunting fugue. The second movement begins without break. Shostakovich marks it *"attaca"* (attack). The sullen fabric of the first is smashed with a repetitive, frenzied, and violent refrain in which the "Jewish" theme is introduced with shrieking violins. The third movement is a weirdly ironic waltz, a danse macabre, gradually slowing to the ghostly monologue of a single violin. The sustained note in the violin that begins the fourth movement is dramatically broken by three dissonant chords marked *"sforzando"* (straining) in the three lower-voiced instruments. These chords, the famous knocking-at-the-door theme, redolent of the fearful KGB sound of doom in apartment houses throughout Russia, repeats intermittently, each time disrupting the bits of other themes—beautiful, sad, and sweet—that struggle unsuccessfully for a foothold against the unrelenting hammer blows. The end of the fourth movement returns us to the personal anagram; and the fifth, the final movement, leads us to mournful ruminations on this theme and other painful voices. At the very end, there is one brief moment of a bombastic ending (as in the finale of his Fifth Symphony), but again it is not to be. Instead, the Eighth Quartet ends in a slow diminuendo to an almost funereal meditation on the mournful anagram, and then ... nothing.

There are many moments of great sadness and great beauty here, and the listener feels the passion and creative genius of the composer in almost every note. But it is above all a work expressing the rage and despair of a reflective man in chronic physical and emotional bondage. There is nowhere for the listener, the performers, or the composer to rest; no silence, no respite between movements, no way out of the pain and anxiety expressed in the music. Shostakovich has composed a musical portrait of his life in Soviet Russia, and he has also forced us to live in his psyche as he struggles with and adapts to a world dominated by terror. The twenty minutes that it takes to play

74

the Eighth Quartet depict a lifetime of suffering to which we as listeners are witness.

Lurking just below the surface of this quartet is the template for a musical language of subterfuge. Shostakovich could not take the way of Verdi, creating operas and anthems based on historical stories that were thinly veiled metaphors for his country's plight. Shostakovich had tried that in his opera *Lady Macbeth* with horrendous results. Instead, he refashioned his palette and struggled to create music that simultaneously suggested rousing patriotism and abject disloyalty. His compositions openly celebrate Soviet victories, and yet there is always an implicit subtext of an opposite story or sentiment. He could commemorate the victory of courage over terror in the defeat of Germany at the siege of Leningrad or the triumphs of the revolution over the repressive czars, but the piece would also be a parable of the horror of life under Stalin and the struggle to survive a brutal dictatorship. Shostakovich's music rouses the emotions of the audience and merges them with his. We are forced through his openness to confront the prisons not only of our own personal lives, but also of our polity and our citizenship. His fame gave him increasing license to goad his nation toward a vision of freedom that it would actually grasp a generation after his death.

Shostakovich did not believe in God, and he was cynical about the potential of improvements in human nature. He expressed little hope of transcendence through religion or humanism. But he always retained an acutely reflective appreciation of his fate and strove to represent its ramifications in his art. The creative spirit never left him, and as he matured, he used it increasingly to show the plight of man caught in the psychological and material web of the malevolent dictatorship—a chronicle of suffering, his people's suffering, human suffering without relief. Shostakovich himself could not play the Eighth Quartet without breaking into tears. Most string quartet musicians playing this work or an involved audience intent on listening feel the sadness, the pain and the suffering.

75

His music, far more than his words or the words of critics and musicologists, helps us to understand the life and times of this complex, tortured genius.

REFERENCES

[1] J. R. Oestreich, Shostakovich: New Questions, New Clues (New York: New York Times, 2004).

[2] A. D. Colman, *Music and the Psychology of Pacifism: Benjamin Britten's War Requiem in Terror Violence, and the Impulse to Destroy* (Beebe J. Canada, Diamon Verlag, 2003)

[3] P. Montero and A. D. Colman, "Collective Consciousness and the Psychology of Human Interconnectedness, *Group* 24, nos. 2/3 (2000).

[4] C. Kenneson, *Musical Prodigies: Perilous Journeys, Remarkable Lives* (Portland, Oregon: Amadeus, 1998).

[5] Science references

[6] Adorno reference

[7] Story reference

[8] *Lady Macbeth of Mtsensk: A Film by Peter Weir*, video (1992 tv2000/zdf/kf).

[9] D. D. Shostakovich, *Letters to a Friend* (New York: Cornell University Press, 2001), 214.

[10] S. Volkov, *Testimony: The Memoirs of Dmitri Shostakovich* (New York: Limelight Editions, 2000), ppxxix

[11] DSm PTSD reference

[12] Volkov, *Testimony*, xvi.

[13] Shostakovich, *Letters to a Friend*, 214.

[14] M. Rostropovich, *International Herald Tribune*, 2006

[15] L. Fay, *Shostakovich: A Life* (New York: Oxford University Press, 2000).

[16] Volkov, *Testimony*.

[17] Anonymous, *The Way of the Pilgrim* (New York, Ballantine, 1974).

[18] Glickman, 91.

Lewis, T., Amini, F., Lannon, R. (2000). *A general theory of love*. NY: Vintage.

Stolorow, R.D. (2005). *The contextuality of emotional experience*. Psychoanalytic Psychology, 22(1), 101-106.

WikiHealth contributors (2006). Namaste. WikiHealth. Retrieved August 4, 2006 from http://www.wikihealth.com/Namaste.

Catherine Evans, PhD

Catherine received her PhD in 1990 from Brigham Young University, and specialized in neuropsychology at the University of Minnesota Medical School. She has been in practice as a neuropsychologist in Des Moines, Iowa, with the Iowa Health System for 16 years. Subjects of her published research articles include rare brain diseases, the chemical brain pathway for anorexia, and attachment disorders.

Catherine is also credentialed, through USA Track and Field, to coach endurance running at the college level.

Todd D. Evans, MA

Todd received his MA from Western Illinois University in 1983, specializing in Electronic Media. He is a professor of Journalism and Mass Communication at Drake University, in Des Moines, Iowa. He teaches within the electronic media department, specializing in new media technologies, applications and broadcast production. Todd also teaches popular music and culture classes in the classroom and on the web.

Todd is an active member of the Popular Culture Association and the Broadcast Education Association, and holds coaching certification through USA Track and Field.

And in the end,
the love you take,
is equal to the love you make.

—John Lennon and Paul McCartney

CHAOS TO CREATIVITY: DISRUPTED PARENTAL RELATIONSHIPS AND THE MUSIC OF JOHN LENNON AND PAUL MCCARTNEY

BY CATHERINE EVANS, PHD
AND TODD D. EVANS, MA

John Lennon and Paul McCartney, the primary writers for the extensive library of Beatles music, reveal much of their inner struggles with attachment issues through their lyrics and music. John Lennon spent his youth living primarily with an aunt and uncle, though turning frequently to his absentee mother for guidance. His mother died tragically while Lennon was in his teens, and his father remained absent until long after he had become a pop music icon. Paul McCartney was raised in a stable family environment but also lost his mother at an early age. The creative output of Lennon and McCartney offers a means to explore how their disrupted parental relationships impacted their collaborative song writing efforts.

Attachment Theory

Parent child relationships can be characterized by the attachment relationships they develop. Attachment theory was a development in personality theory initially proposed by John Bowlby in 1969. Starting from the psychoanalytic perspective, Bowlby integrated psychobiology, evolutionary theory, and Piaget's approach to development to suggest human behavior is framed by the early interactions of the mother and infant.

79

Infants demonstrate a consistent interest in maintaining close physical proximity to the primary caregiver, using this individual as an anchor or base from which they can explore the world, returning to the base for security. When conflict or threat arises in the infant's world, security and reassurance is sought from the caregiver. The intensity of the infant's response is related to the degree of threat; hence, stronger responses are seen in increasingly threatening situations.

Common behavior patterns among infants suggest different types of attachment. These variations in attachment patterns are related, in part, to the experiences the infant has over time with the attachment figure. An internal representation of the attachment figure seems to develop and the infant tries to predict the reactions of the attachment figure based on previous experiences. These patterns established during infancy with the primary caregiver are typically exhibited similarly across the life span. Disruption or loss of the primary caregiver during critical phases of the establishment of attachment patterns influences the nature of attachment in future relationships.

Three classifications of attachment have been suggested: *secure, avoidant*, and *resistant ambivalent/anxious*. Secure infants are typically sensitive, responsive and warm in caregiver infant interactions. Caregivers who demonstrated an aversion to physical contact with their infants during stress, and frequently rejected or ignored the attempts to attach were found to develop avoidant attachment patterns. Inconsistency and unpredictability in interactions occurred in infants with resistant/ambivalent attachment relationships. While caregivers of these infants were not actively rejecting or avoiding physical contact, their interactions were inept and disorganized. Attempts by the caregiver to soothe the infant were seen as awkward and uncoordinated.

As individuals move toward adolescence and adulthood, attachment systems are activated during conflict that threatens the stability of relationships. An adult with *resistant ambivalent* or *anxious* attachment style attempts to maintain a relationship at all cost.

The relationship validates the adult's self-concept, driving the individual to maintain the status quo of a relationship, even if all interpersonal needs are not being met. These individuals are more sensitive to anger and demonstrate less control over emotions and behavior. Compared to others, they report more intense negative emotions, less confidence in controlling emotions and are generally more fearful in relationships. They tend to demand excessive attention to combat their excessive fears.

Individuals with avoidant attachment styles exhibit behavior that minimizes concerns and negative emotions. They tend to withdraw and express emotions "coolly" and in a detached manner. They exhibit core issues of trust and dependability.

The Childhood of John Winston Lennon

Julia Stanley and Alfred "Freddy" Lennon impulsively married in 1938. Employed as a ship's waiter, he departed soon after the marriage, leaving his pregnant wife to fend for herself. John Winston Lennon was born on October 9, 1940, during a fierce WWII bombing raid on Liverpool. All four of Julia's sisters helped care for John, but from the time he could speak, he expressed a preference for his aunt Mimi. Mimi and her husband George took primary physical custody of John when he was two years old. Julia had become involved in a new relationship but continued to make daily visits to see John after his move.

John's behavior and expression of affect demonstrated a pattern of core issues including fear of abandonment and rejection. Resistant ambivalent attachment patterns, sometimes referred to as anxious attachment patterns in relationships, seemed to develop both privately and publicly. The inconsistency and unpredictability of John's relationship with his mother seemed to cause him to develop ambivalent attachment behavior patterns in his relationships.

John's childhood was marked by general rebelliousness and hooliganism. He was the leader of a small group of troublemakers at the Quarry Bank Grammar School. School records indicate that he spent a great deal of time in the headmaster's office and endured corporal punishment during some of these visits. He rarely displayed remorse for his actions and demonstrated little fear of reprisal for his bad behavior.

When John was twelve, his uncle George died of a hemorrhage. He and John had forged a close relationship in the decade that they lived together. George had taken on the role of father and had given John his first harmonica. Loss of structure in John's family life seemed to intensify with George's passing. By age thirteen, his discipline problems escalated with school records indicating John had been caught gambling, cutting classes, and smoking.

John frequently visited his mother Julia on days when he skipped school. She had subsequently remarried and seemed to enjoy her son's personality. He was developing a talent for writing verse and drawing cartoons. Julia taught John how to play the banjo and guitar. It was Mimi who purchased his first guitar, but she was not particularly comfortable with John's musical aspirations. He had formed his first band, "The Quarry Men" by age fifteen. Julia allowed them to rehearse at her home while keeping the band a secret from Mimi. John failed all of his Ordinary level examinations and dropped out of the Quarry Bank School during his final term.

John and Mimi had numerous heated arguments during this period of his life. She not only disapproved of his band, but also criticized his clothing, choice of friends and lifestyle in general. He had taken to retreating to his mother's house for extended periods after such arguments. After one, John headed for Julia's house to find that she had just left to visit him at Mimi's. Julia arrived at Mimi's only to discover that John had just left for her home. She stepped through a hedge on her trip back to her own home and was struck and killed by a motor vehicle. The car was driven by an intoxicated off-duty police officer.

After Julia's death, John began drinking heavily. He became increasingly angry and rebellious. Although his expressions of affect were not outwardly sad, his grief over the loss of his mother served as a muse for his music.

The inspiration for the song "She Said, She Said", recorded and released on the Beatles Revolver album in 1966, is often credited to an encounter Lennon had with actor Peter Fonda. However, the song can also be interpreted as reflecting the primary conflicts and contrast of his relationships with Mimi and Julia. The lyrics continue to shift between the voices of two women, each revealing a different attitude about the narrator. The words seem to reflect comments, either real or imagined, that Mimi and Julia made to John during this tumultuous period of teen years. The lyrics define one of the females to be dead. The narrator explains that when he was a boy, everything was right, but now he knows what it is like to be sad. The other female is in conflict with the narrator, and it makes him crazy that they can't seem to understand each other. He feels so diminished that she makes him feel as though he'd "never been born."

During an interview in the 1970's, John admitted that he frequently wrote of personal experiences and feelings, as he felt contrived characters were too "phony." While not the only reference to his family in lyrics, the song, "She said, She said" clearly reflects the type of family conflict John felt during his youth.

The Childhood of James Paul McCartney

James Paul McCartney, known simply as Paul, was born to Jim and Mary McCartney on June 18, 1942. Their second son, Michael, was born two years after Paul. The family lived in a working class neighborhood in Liverpool, and the boys were raised in a relatively typical home environment. Paul was more reserved than Michael, but was talented and popular. As young boys, their personality differences were pronounced; Michael was disinterested in academics and more argumentative than Paul was. Paul was quiet and intelligent, earning good grades in school. An award Paul received from a local art show recognized a developing interest and skill in painting.

Michael was more prone to trouble than his older brother was, and the use of corporal punishment demonstrated the difference between the boys. While Michael would scream in pain, Paul would silently endure his punishment. He has admitted that after such episodes, he would make tiny rips in his parents' bedroom curtains to retaliate for his punishment. Despite their youthful differences, brother Michael, made his appearance in McCartney's lyrics in the song, "Let 'em in."

Mary McCartney was employed as a public and private nurse. In spite of her medical training, or perhaps because of it, she did not discuss a persistent pain in her side with the physicians or other nurses where she worked. In her late forties, having dismissed the pain and growing lump in her breast, Mary finally saw a specialist. In spite of a mastectomy, her breast cancer was too advanced for successful treatment. On October 31, 1956, she passed away. Paul was fourteen years old when she died.

Mary's death had a profound impact on Paul, and he used music as his primary coping strategy. He took his guitar with him everywhere, reportedly even to the bathroom. He wrote his first complete song, both music and lyrics, after his mother's death. The song, "I Lost My Little Girl", described the experience of having loved and lost a girl. Paul once remarked that the song was not consciously written about the loss of his mother, but that he understood that "any psychiatrist would say that it was."

With the illness and death of Mary, Paul lost the access to his nurturing mother during the formative adolescent development years. While she did not actively reject Paul, or refuse to facilitate attachment, she was unable to meet his attachment needs during a time of excessive stress. His denial of negative affect and his tendency to minimize distress are consistent with avoidant attachment patterns.

The Songs of Lennon - McCartney

John Lennon and Paul McCartney wrote the bulk of the library of Beatles catalog. They agreed to share songwriting credit on all of their compositions, regardless of the genuine amount of contributions either had to any song. Despite the appearance of equality in effort, it is apparent that each had major influence on different compositions. Many Lennon-McCartney compositions reflect either avoidant or ambivalent resistant anxious attachment patterns.

In "Tell Me Why", we see several attempts to desperately maintain a relationship as in the anxious attachment style. John sings lyrics suggesting he is devastated that his love is trying to end the relationship. Looking to understand what has gone wrong and promising to do anything to reconcile, he asks her, after offering repeatedly to apologize, why she lied to him. While he was wronged in the relationship, he begs to reconcile. In this example, John's interpersonal needs were not met, yet maintaining the relationship at all cost is emphasized.

Fear of abandonment and rejection are apparent in "If I Fell." While the relationship has not yet begun, the lyrics John sings seem to seek assurances that the relationship will not end. He is hesitant to start a romance without a promise that his new love will not hurt him.

In contrast, Paul sings lyrics that point to avoidant attachment styles. His words tend to express interpersonal withdrawal and express emotions in a detached manner. In "Things We Said Today", he sings about ending a relationship with a girl. She attempts to change his mind by telling him how much he will miss her, and that it will be too late to reconcile when he realizes his mistake.

Downplaying the negative aspects of a situation is demonstrated in the song, "I'll follow the Sun." Paul's lyrics suggest a desire to avoid negative consequences in the future. He sings that ending the relationship now will mean he will lose a friend, but because things are good right now, he should end it before anything bad happens. The notion that he expects the other shoe to drop drives him to end a good relationship while it is still good.

Perhaps the most powerful direct example of John's issues relating to his mother is reflected in the song "Julia." He sings to his mother as a means of connecting with the memory of her. Within the lines of the song, John sings that "Ocean Child" (a rough translation of "Yoko" in Japanese) is calling him. He sings the song so that Julia will know that he has fallen in love.

"Julia," recorded in 1968, is a turning point for both Lennon and McCartney. This is the first time either composer dares to reflect on his loss directly by name. McCartney makes a similar direct reference to his mother and her spiritual presence in his life in "Let It Be". His words reveal that the internalized representation of his "mother Mary" helps him to manage his affect in times of conflict.

The only example of Lennon or McCartney providing a named reference within the specific content of displacement is the McCartney-influenced "Hey Jude." Paul was influenced by the emotional pain he believed John Lennon's son Julian was experiencing during Lennon's divorce from his first wife Cynthia. In the song, McCartney encourages Jude (Julian's nickname) to avoid keeping the pain within him.

Accepting the Past

One hundred and seventy-three songs were written and commercially recorded by Lennon and McCartney. A simple broad interpretation of the lyrics suggests thirty-eight (Table 1) have themes that seem to have been influenced or referenced by their disrupted relationships. While many of the lyrics express negative emotions, "In My Life" seems to best represent Lennon and McCartney coming to terms with the deaths of their mothers. The song clearly lists positive and negative aspects of growth and change, but resolves on a note of acceptance to remember and love those from the past.

Table 1

Please Please Me	1963
Misery	1963
There's A Place	1963
Not a Second Time	1963
You Can't Do That	1964
I Call You Name	1964
I'm A Loser	1964

If I Fell	1964
Tell Me Why	1964
I'll Cry Instead	1964
Things We Said Today	1964
I'll Be Back	1964
Baby's In Black	1964
I'll Follow The Sun	1964
HELP	1965
You've Got To Hide Your Love Away	1965
I Need You	1965
Yesterday	1965
You Won't See Me	1965
Nowhere Man	1965
Girl	1965
In My Life	1965
We Can Work It Out	1965
Here, There and Everywhere	1966
She Said She Said	1966
Tomorrow Never Knows	1966
She's Leaving Home	1967
A Day In The Life	1967
All You Need Is Love	1967
Hello Goodbye	1967
Hey Jude	1968
I Will	1968
Julia	1968
Carry That Weight	1969
Oh Darling	1969
The End	1969
Let It Be	1970
The Long and Winding Road	1970

Robert Feder, MD is a psychiatrist with an active private practice in Manchester, New Hampshire. His professional activities have included Medical Directorships of inpatient, partial hospitalization, and outpatient psychiatric services. He also served for many years as the Medical Director of Behavioral Health Network, on the State of New Hampshire Board of Medicine, and in governance roles with the American Psychiatric Association. Dr. Feder has been an avid music listener ever since his mother Helen introduced him to the Nutcracker Suite at the age of 2. Mahler is a relatively recent fascination for Dr. Feder; he had found Mahler's music largely incomprehensible for many years until learning more about the composer. Dr. Feder enjoys playing the clarinet, didgeridoo, psaltery, and electronic instruments. In addition to being an avid concertgoer, he also spends a lot of time at the theater and art museums. His photographs have been exhibited at the American Psychiatric Association, the Beaver Brook Association, the Hollis Library, and the Nashua Area Arts Association. Dr. Feder is also an avid runner, skier, and boogie-boarder. He has been happily married for 35 years to Marsha, a high-school special education teacher. He has two wonderful children – Daniel, a revolutionary journalist, and Elana, an urban anthropologist-educator. He is hoping they will make him a joyful grandfather some day. He can be reached at 753 Chestnut St., Manchester, NH 03049, or feder@charter.net.

DEATH AND GUSTAV MAHLER

BY ROBERT FEDER, MD

My heart is quiet and awaits its hour!
Everywhere the dear earth blossoms in
spring and becomes green anew!
The blue horizon shines everywhere
and eternally Eternally...eternally...

Gustav Mahler (Das Lied von der Erde)

Figure 1 — *Gustav Mahler*

The composer Gustav Mahler (Fig. 1) was focused on death and mourning in most of his musical works. His life-long preoccupation with death, the forms this took in his life and music, and Mahler's ultimate resolution of this subject are a source of knowledge and inspiration for all of us struggling to come to terms with this issue.

Mahler, who lived from 1860 to 1911, is now seen as one of the major figures in the history of music, a bridge between the Romantic and Modern eras. He might easily have fallen into obscurity as a result of the active suppression of his work by anti-Semitic elements in the European musical community and later by the Nazis. During the first half of the twentieth century, Bruno Walter, a protégé of Mahler's, almost single-handedly kept the music alive by actively conducting Mahler's works throughout the world. In the second half of the twentieth century, Leonard Bernstein was largely responsible for a Mahler renaissance and the current enthusiasm for this composer's work.

In examining what Mahler was trying to express in his musical compositions, we are more fortunate than with most composers in that we have a wealth of sources to draw on. Natalie Bauer-Lechner was a conservatory classmate of Mahler and, from 1890 to 1901, his closest personal friend. Mahler discussed his musical, emotional, and philosophical ideas with her openly and regularly. Bauer-Lechner recorded these in great detail in her diary that was later published. She ended her close relationship with Mahler in 1902 after he married Alma Schindler. Alma also published a detailed diary of her intimate and intellectual conversations with Mahler. Through these two diaries, as well as numerous surviving letters of Mahler, we are afforded a unique window into the themes and ideas contained in his music.

Mahler completed fourteen major works (nine symphonies, two symphonic songworks, and three song cycles). Ten of these fourteen works deal primarily with themes of death or the mourning process. Death was a life-long preoccupation of Mahler's, an aspect of existence that he struggled to describe, understand, and accept. This fascination with death was related to his belief that only if we understand death can we truly understand existence. His obsession with death was also strongly rooted in the actual events of his life.

Gustav Mahler was born in 1860 to Bernard and Marie Mahler, Bohemian Jews. Gustav showed a remarkable command of music at an early age. At the age of one, he could hum tunes; at three, he could play the accordion; at five, he was taking master piano lessons; at seven, he was teaching piano lessons; and at ten, had his first public recital.

Death became a pervasive element in Gustav's life even before he was born. His parents' first child had died an accidental death at one year of age, a year before Gustav's birth. When Gustav was five, two younger brothers, aged six and sixteen months, both died.

Shortly afterward, Gustav wrote his first musical composition, which he titled Polka With Introductory Funeral March. At age eleven, Gustav suffered the loss of another two younger brothers (aged six months and three years), both of whom succumbed to scarlet fever. At age thirteen, Gustav lost a one-year-old brother to congestive heart failure. At age fifteen, Gustav lost his closest sibling (his only sibling who had survived most of Gustav's life until then), a fourteen-year-old brother who died of pericarditis. Traditional Jewish rituals include a weeklong intensive mourning period after the death, and a one-year period during which mourning prayers are said on a daily basis and various joyful activities are avoided. Thus, between the ages of five and fifteen, Gustav Mahler was living in a house of mourning for almost six of those ten years. Ultimately, he would experience the deaths of ten of his thirteen siblings.

Mahler completed his formal musical Conservatory education and his first major composition at age twenty. Das Klagende Lied (The Song of Lament) is a long and beautiful cantata that is based on an old Germanic folktale involving a fratricide. One year after completing this work, he lost yet another brother, aged two, to diphtheria.

Mahler also obtained his first conducting post, with the Linz Bad Hall, when he was twenty. He would make his living as a conductor, as his complex and revolutionary musical compositions never became popular during his lifetime. His success as a conductor was truly remarkable. He rapidly gained a reputation of being able to bring forth previously unheard strength and beauty from every orchestra he conducted. He achieved this by his grueling rehearsal schedules and demand for perfection, driven by his underlying compulsive personality. He had a flamboyant, energetic style on the podium. Working his way up in the conducting world with successively more prestigious posts, by age thirty-seven Mahler had obtained the pinnacle of the musical world when he was named conductor and musical director of the Vienna Court Opera and the Vienna Philharmonic.

Mahler had his first love affair at age twenty-five. It ended unhappily when broken off by Johanna Richter. This experience led directly to the composition of Songs of a Wayfarer. In this work, each of the four songs represents a stage in the process of mourning a lost love. He identified these stages as grief, denial, anger, and resignation. He apparently had some doubt with this order and formulation, however, and was to return to the musical expression of the mourning process seventeen years later in his fifth symphony.

Mahler was twenty-eight when he composed his Symphony No. 1, which was destined to become his most well-known and popular work, a symphony that chronicles the life of a hero. The third movement, a bizarre funeral march based on the nursery rhyme "Frère Jacques", is an attempt to examine the childhood deaths that had pervaded his life. Shortly after completing Symphony No. 1, both of Mahler's parents died, as well as his twenty-six-year old sister Leopoldine with whom he was extremely close.

Mahler's first major composition that does not deal with death was Des Knaben Wunderhorn, written when he was thirty-two. This is a collection of German folk poetry that Mahler beautifully sets to music. Many of the musical themes in his symphonies were later based on the phrases that he created in these songs.

Symphony No. 2 (The Resurrection) was written at age thirty-four. This is an enormous work that called for an orchestra and chorus larger than that for almost any previously written symphony. It deals not with resurrection in the Christian sense, but rather the more archetypical notion of death as a return to God. The publication of this work was followed shortly afterward by the suicide of Mahler's twenty-two-year old brother.

Symphony No. 3, even longer and requiring an even larger orchestra and chorus than Symphony No. 2, was completed when Mahler was thirty-six. This was his second work that was free of death themes. It is a beautiful, lyrical examination of love and the natural world, the primary non-thanatological themes that perfuse Mahler's work.

Mahler completed Symphony No. 4 at age forty. This is another lyrical piece that presents a child's innocent view of life and heaven, with heaven represented in an ideal and positive fashion. It was after completing this opus that he married Alma Schindler. He then seemed to look back on his musical work, questioned what he had done, and began to examine death in a much more complex and realistic fashion, as opposed to the idealistic approach in his earlier works.

Symphony No. 5 is a return to looking at the mourning process in the academic style that Mahler had used in Songs of a Wayfarer. Mahler takes this to a much more sophisticated degree in Symphony No. 5 where he examines the process of mourning death rather than the loss of a love affair. In this five movement work, each of the movements represents a successive stage in the mourning process. Mahler identified these stages as Grief, Anger, Denial, Resignation, and Acceptance. There is a remarkable similarity between Mahler's conception of mourning in Symphony No. 5 and the results of research done almost seventy years later by Elizabeth Kubler-Ross on the dying process. The symphony ends in a rousing finale that Mahler uses to inspire in the listener an affirmation of the positive aspects of life, a stage that he felt the living individual needed to achieve in order to complete the mourning process and make it meaningful.

Symphony No. 6 is another musical depiction of the hero. Unlike the largely joyous depiction of Symphony No. 1, however, Symphony No. 6 is a heavy, agonizing work that depicts a hero's tragic downfall due to fate. In the same year that this work was completed, Mahler also finished Kindertotenlieder (Songs on the Death of Children). He felt driven to look back one more time on this subject that dominated his childhood. He felt he had not yet examined this sufficiently, or perhaps the births of his own two children in 1902 and 1904 compelled him to revisit this topic. Kindertotenlieder sets to music the poetry of Friedrich Ruckert, largely inspired by Ruckert's loss of his two children.

Mahler then turns to more joyous subject matter. In 1905, at the age of forty-five, he completed Symphony No. 7, a beautifully mysterious piece that depicts the romantic music of the night. This was followed one year later by Symphony No. 8, or The Symphony of a Thousand, that calls for the largest collection of musicians in the history of Western classical music. At its premiere, there were over one thousand orchestra and chorus members on the stage at one time. It is a powerful, complex work based on Goethe's Faust describing the glory of God in the archetypes of masculine creator and feminine provider of love and mercy.

Mahler was forty-seven in 1907 when three events occurred that shaped the remainder of his life. As a result of increasing pressure and unpopularity (due to his being a Jew, the complexity of his musical works, and his unrelenting demands as a conductor), he resigned as conductor of the Vienna Opera. He was also diagnosed with valvular heart disease, probably a remnant of childhood scarlet fever that had spared him but claimed so many of his brothers. Finally and most significantly, his beloved daughter Maria died at age four from scarlet fever and diphtheria. Mahler was never to recover from these events, and his remaining compositions took on a depth and seriousness regarding death that they had not previously possessed.

Das Lied von der Erde (The Song of the Earth), completed when Mahler was forty-nine, is a symphonic-like song cycle dealing with a full compendium of the emotions of life—joy, loneliness, beauty, and loss. The final long movement is a musical treatise on the nature of grief and death. In this piece, the depiction of death takes on a benign, soothing, infinite, otherworldly atmosphere of acceptance that was unique at that time in Western music.

Symphony No. 9 was finished less than a year before Mahler's death at age fifty, and is his last completed work. In the first movement, envisioning his own impending death, Mahler says goodbye to love. In the second movement, he bids farewell to the pleasures of the country life. The third movement is a farewell to the chaos and corruption of urban society. In the fourth and final movement, Mahler depicts death and says goodbye to life itself. This movement is a truly remarkable and unique musical experience in which the agony of death and the fight to hold on to life gradually give way to a transcendental, blissful, serene acceptance of one's fate, followed by nothingness.

Mahler's death was a gradual one that ended in triumph and beauty. He suffered for six months from subacute bacterial endocarditis (related to his valvular heart disease) before succumbing on May 18, 1911, at the age of fifty-one. The artist Gustav Klimt, a friend of Mahler's, described the "regal calm and unworldly beauty" of Mahler's expression in death. This can easily be seen in the death masks of Mahler made by Alma's step-father Carl Moll. In these molds made immediately after he died, Mahler's face clearly expresses the serene bliss of death that he had depicted in Das Lied von Der Erde and Symphony No. 9 (Figs. 2 and 3). He was buried beside his daughter Marie. At his prior instruction, his tombstone contains only his name and no epitaph. "Any who come to look for me," he said, "will know who I was, and the rest do not need to know."

The relationship of the events of Mahler's life to his music are summarized in Table 1.

Although not understood or appreciated by many in his life-time, Mahler's music is now recognized as some of the greatest ever written and lives on in his absence. His exploration of new sounds, harmonies, rhythms, and collections of performers heralded the profound changes in music that the twentieth century was about to bring. Equally profound was his examination of the themes of death and mourning. His ability to depict in music the feeling, meaning, and significance of death was as great as any who have attempted this in the arts, philosophy, or science.

REFERENCES

Bauer-Lechner, Natalie. *Recollections of Gustav Mahler*. Cambridge: Cambridge University Press, 1980

Collins, Dean. "Gustav Mahler's Summer of 1910," *Bulletin of the Meninger Clinic* 46(1982): 255-279

De La Grange, Henry-Louis. *Mahler, Volume 1*. New York: Doubleday, 1973

De La Grange, Henry-Louis. *Mahler, Volume 2*. Oxford: Oxford University Press, 1995

De La Grange, Henry-Louis. *Mahler, Volume 3*. Oxford: Oxford University Press, 1999

Feder, Stuart. "Gustav Mahler, Dying," *International Rev. of Psychoanalysis* 5(1978): 125-148

Floros, Constantin. *Gustav Mahler: The Symphonies*. Portland, OR: Amadeus Press, 1997

Franklin, Peter. *The Life of Mahler*. Cambrige: Cambridge University Press, 1997

Hindley, Geoffrey (Ed.). *The Larousse Encyclopedia of Music*. Seacaucus:Chartwell, 1977, 360-362. 362.

Greenberg, Robert. *Great Masters: Mahler – His Life and Music*. Chantilly, VA: The Teaching Company, 2001, 63.

Kaplan, Gilbert. *The Mahler Album*. New York: Abrams, 1995, 201

Kubler-Ross, Elisabeth. *On Death and Dying*. New York: MacMillan, 1969

Mahler, Alma. *Gustav Mahler : Memories and Letters*, third edition. Seattle: University of Washington Press, 1975

Mooney, William E. "*Gustav Mahler: A Note on Life and Death in Music*". Psychoanalytic Quarterly 37(1968): 80-102

Figures

Figure 1 – *Gustav Mahler at age 42*

Figure 2 – *Death Mask of Mahler, lateral view*

Figure 3 – *Death mask of Mahler, frontal view*

Table 1

Year	Age	Life Events — Event	Musical Compositions — Title	Major Themes
1859	-1	Death of brother Isidor, age 18 months		
1860	0	Birth of Gustav Mahler		
1865	5	Death of brother Karl, age 16 months Death of brother Rudolph, age 6 months	Polka With Introductory Funeral March	Mahler's first musical Composition
1871	11	Death of brother Friedrich, age 6 months, of scarlet fever Death of brother Arnold, age 3 years, of scarlet fever		
1873	13	Death of brother Alfred, age 1 year, of congestive heart failure		
1875	15	Death of brother Ernst, age 14, of pericarditis		
1880	20		Das Klagende Lied (The Song of Lament)	Mahler's first major work. A cantata based on an old folktale about a fratricide
1881	21	Death of brother Konrad, age 2 of diptheria		
1885	25	Unhappy love affair with Johanna Richter	Songs of a Wayfarer	The stages of mourning a lost love
1888	28		Symphony No. 1	A hero's life, including a funeral march based on Frère Jacques
1889	28	Death of father		
1889	29	Death of sister Leopoldine, age 26, of meningitis Death of mother		
1892	32		Des Knaben Wunderhorn (Songs)	German folk poetry set to music
1894	34		Symphony No. 2	Death seen as a return to God
1895	34	Death of brother Otto, age 22, of suicide		
1896	36		Symphony No. 3	Love and the natural world
1897	37	Becomes conductor of the Vienna Opera		
1990	40		Symphony No. 4	A child's view of life and heaven

Table 1, Continued

Year		Life Events	Musical Compositions	
	Age	Event	Title	Major Themes
1902	41	Marries Alma Schindler		
1902	42	Birth of daughter Maria	Symphony No. 5	The mourning process
1904	44	Birth of daughter Anna	Symphony No. 6	A hero's tragic downfall brought about by fate
			Kindertotenlieder	Songs on the death of children
1905	45		Symphony No. 7	Romantic music of the night
1906	46		Symphony No. 8	The glory of God the creator (masculine) and God the loving and merciful (feminine)
1907	47	Resigns as conductor of Vienna Opera Mahler diagnosed with valvular heart disease Death of daughter Maria, age 4, from scarlet fever and diphtheria		
1909	49		Das Lied von der Erde (The Song of the Earth)	Songs of loneliness, joy, beauty, loss, and the acceptance of death
1910	50		Symphony No. 9	Mahler's farewell to life and description of his own death
1911	50	Death of Mahler		

101

Gail Carr Feldman, PhD, is a clinical psychologist, an award-winning author and a popular public speaker. She is also an ontological life coach. Dr. Feldman has appeared on radio and television programs across the country, including Larry King Live. In addition to numerous talks in the United States, she has spoken on creativity and resilience psychology in Puerto Rico, Greece and Viet Nam. She served for twenty-two years as clinical assistant professor, Psychiatry Department, University of New Mexico School of Medicine. Dr. Feldman is the author of five books and numerous articles.

THE LIGHT OF CREATIVITY, THE PSYCHOLOGY OF RESILIENCE

GAIL CARR FELDMAN, PhD

CLINICAL PSYCHOLOGIST,

ALBUQUERQUE, NEW MEXICO, U.S.A.

FROM THE PAPER PRESENTED AT THE
AMERICAN INSTITUTE OF MEDICAL EDUCATION
CREATIVITY AND MADNESS CONFERENCE,
VIET NAM, MARCH 2007

In recent years, I've become aware of a connection between resilience, the ability to overcome difficult life events, and the power of creative self-expression. Two blind men inspired this realization—two men from different generations, different countries, and different cultures. In both cases, even though their eyes of physical sight had been blinded, both men lived their lives in an expanded realm of sensation, awareness, and confidence, and both made contributions to the world that most of us could never dream of.

Jacques Lusseyran was born in Paris in 1924, the only child of "marvelously wise and loving" parents—warm, protective, and attentive. When he was eight years old, he was blinded from an accident at school. As he struck his head on the sharp corner of a desk, the arm of the glasses he wore drove deep into the right eye. He lost consciousness and at the hospital, doctors removed the eye. The retina of the left eye was badly torn and sympathetic ophthalmia led to permanent and complete blindness.

He spoke of the feeling "adults call despair" in the days following his surgery. He was trying to look out at the things he knew were there and see them in the old way, and when he could not, it was anguish. And then one day, he had a revelation. Instead of looking out, he went to a place deeper within. "I was aware of a radiance emanating....I could feel light rising, spreading, resting on objects, giving them form, then leaving them....I felt indescribable relief and happiness so great it almost made me laugh. Confidence and gratitude came as if a prayer had been answered. I found light and joy at the same moment, and...from that time on light and joy have never been separated in my experience. I have had them or lost them together...every waking hour and even in my dreams, I lived in a stream of light.

"I saw the whole world in light, existing through it and because of it. Colors, all the colors of the rainbow also survived. For me, the child who loved to draw and paint, colors made a celebration so unexpected that I spent hours playing with them....Light threw its color on things and on people....The colors were only a game, while light was my whole reason for living....In a few months my personal world had turned into a painter's studio."

Lusseyran would discover that only one thing could cause him to become blind, to lose "sight" of color and light—that was FEAR. A brilliant student, he learned Braille, became head of his class, studied languages, literature, art, theater, and philosophy. On March 12, 1938, Germany invaded Austria. Thirteen-year-old Jacques listened to the news on his radio and decided he must perfect his German. Intuition told him he would play some role in the coming conflict. When France fell and the Gestapo entered the scene, Lusseyran formed his own resistance movement with fifty-two boys between the ages of seventeen and twenty-one. He was only fifteen. Within a year, there were more than six hundred young people calling themselves the "Volunteers of Liberty." They created, printed, and distributed a newspaper, with Lusseyran able to keep all data, including fifteen hundred telephone numbers, in his head to avoid incriminating evidence being found on paper.

While they were successful at disseminating information, "a country in disaster is swarming with traitors." Lusseyran judged the French Nazis to be even more treacherous and sadistic than the Germans. In July of 1943, he was arrested by the Gestapo, held in a cell and interrogated for 180 days before beginning his next nightmare journey—to Buchenwald. He survived there for eighteen months. Of the two thousand Frenchmen who entered the camp with him, only thirty survived to be liberated by General Patton. Three hundred and eighty thousand men from twelve different countries died in that camp. Several months into his imprisonment, Lusseyran lay dying in Les Invalides where there were more dead bodies than living ones. He had dysentery, pleurisy, and a fever of 104 degrees.

Lusseyran said that the illness saved him. During the time he was unconscious, he became aware of light "like a shimmering wave....I could see it beyond my eyes and my forehead and above my head. It touched me and filled me to overflowing. I let myself float upon it. I drew my strength from that...celestial stream." After that, he was known as "the blind Frenchman" and "the man who wouldn't die," and he became a friend and an inspiration to hundreds of men. Because he could speak French, Russian, German and Polish, they all came to him. In the end when there was so much despair and many thousands being killed by the SS, he would stand and recite poetry. "I learned that poetry is an act, an incantation, a kiss of peace, a medicine....We loved Victor Hugo... Baudelaire also worked on us....But the real winners, the tonics, those who worked upon us like wine, were the poets who sang. I found some in the Middle Ages. Then there were Villon, Ronsard, Verlaine Apollinaire, Aragon. They surmounted all obstacles. They spoke from another realm, or rather, it was their step, the rhythm of their gait, which had nothing in common with our cowering. They flew past and carried us on their wings." All of Lusseyran's recitations came from his memory, and "that poetry was completely lived by us..." It nourished the soul and "it was the soul which first had to be nourished." He had learned early that those who could not nourish their souls died very quickly.

After the liberation, once in the United States, Lusseyran became a husband, father, university professor and writer. He was a full professor at Western Reserve University, teaching on sabbatical at the University of Hawaii in 1971 when he and his wife were killed in an automobile accident. His credo, the two truths he believed in were:

"Joy does not come from outside, for whatever happens to us it is within. The second is that light does not come to us from without. Light is in us, even if we have no eyes."

*   *   *

On Christmas day of 1968, Michael Naranjo was with the Ninth Infantry in the Mekong Delta, Viet Nam. He was nineteen years old, a Native American Indian from Taos Pueblo. "We were in a rice field when the Viet Cong opened fire. Six guys were killed immediately. In the movies, they call them 'men,' but it's boys who fight wars— babies really. Several of us had run off to the right into the jungle where some of the gunfire was coming from. A medic had just been shot trying to get to two of the guys. I'd dropped to my belly two or three times. Every time we stood, someone was shot. I crawled as far as I could and took off my pack. I took out two grenades and threw one. When I looked up, only a few yards away I could see a Viet Cong soldier in a 'spider hole.' I fired, then let go of my rifle with my right hand to reach for another grenade. My sergeant yelled, but I couldn't hear what he was trying to say. He'd seen another VC throw a grenade. It rolled right into my right hand. I turned to my right to look as I began to throw it, and it went off."

I have written elsewhere about the details of Michael's evacuation and his stay in hospitals, first in Japan and then in the U.S. His grieving process and his fight to become a sculptor are extraordinary examples of psychological resiliency. The first thing he asked for in the hospital was a ball of clay. He began making small figures with his left hand, as his right hand was damaged. At the Veteran's Hospital for the Blind in Palo Alto, California, he was informed that his intention to become a sculptor again was "completely unrealistic." During his rehabilitation, he first refused to make wallets. When he was allowed to attend a woodworking class, he refused to make a bench. He found a small piece of smooth wood and began to carve a bear.

"I had always been a sculptor. My mother was a potter, and I grew up fashioning clay figures while she worked first at Santa Clara, then at Taos Pueblo where we moved when I was nine. My father was a Baptist minister and a skilled carpenter. He built the first Protestant church in any pueblo. I was raised with the expectation of attending college. Most of my nine brothers and sisters completed college and some are professionals, but I couldn't tolerate that structure. I attended Highlands University for a while and even the Institute of American Indian Art in Santa Fe, taking drawing, design, and sculpture. I'd end up back home though, where I could be outdoors."

Michael told me about his ongoing love for the Taos Mountains, the forest images that filled his eyes as a boy, the fishing trips that resulted in pockets filled with tiny, wriggling cutthroat trout. "A few years ago," he said, "I went for a hike in the mountains with a friend. It was a lovely day, and my friend could see, but I was the man who knew the way." Both Michael Naranjo and Jacques Lusseyran had the uncanny ability to move around in the world and know where objects were, and even estimate the distance between them and people, buildings, trees, as well as a far off mountain.

Michael Naranjo knew the way to his passion, his art, and he insisted on finding it. "Disability is destroyed by doing something you love, something you're excited about," says Michael. "Of course it's a challenge. Life is a challenge, a game. If you accept it, though, it's a gift and the inspiration and the dreams you have can come true.

"I had a dream—I often have colorful, vivid dreams—a dream that I could see and touch Michelangelo's sculptures. Not too long after that, I was invited to Rome to have an audience with the Pope. Following the Papal audience, I was taken to a chapel and allowed to examine the sculpture of Moses. I crawled all over him for about a half hour, and for days after I would have flashes of feeling the softness of that flesh. Two years later, I went back to Italy and was allowed to see the David. On top of scaffolding, I felt the beauty of the eyes, the tear ducts hiding in the corners, the pupils like hearts. I cried. My dream had come true. I felt the lips; so soft you could feel the

107

heart beating and pumping blood to them...the veins in his neck, the tension of the hands. It was amazing to feel the flesh and feelings of a man eighteen feet tall. Afterward, I had new life in my hands. I could see twice as much."

Being with Michael gives one the sense of being with a holy man, a man who reveres and accepts every aspect of life. Everywhere you look in his house in Santa Fe, his sculptures, with their gleaming bronze or alabaster surfaces, seem to be moving; an eagle being released to fly; a "Spirit Maiden" dancing gracefully with feathers in her hands; "Grey Fox" skillfully performing the Hoop Dance; a nude female figure, "Joy," extending both hands upward as though greeting the morning sun.

Michael's exhibitions, awards and honors are vast. His sculpture is found in many collections, including those of The Vatican in Rome and the White House in Washington D.C. "My blindness is a gift," he insists. "It has given me a new way of looking at life." Always, with these two blind men, there is the allusion to inner sight, to "seeing."

*　　*　　*

Psychologist Gina Higgins begins her book on resilient adults with the following words: "Clinical psychology and psychiatry typically study the dire, the deadly, and the derailing. We admire or envy—but rarely puzzle over—dazzling psychological success. Although a lot is known about the genesis of illness and dissolution, the origins of mental health are often ignored. Moreover, even less is known about the origins of healthy loving...." She goes on to define resilient adults as those "individuals who have surmounted even the most turbulent pasts in order to love well, work well, struggle well, and expect well in the present."

Dr. Higgins studied forty adult subjects clustered around age forty, who were referred to her for their resilience from clinicians in the Greater Boston area. In most all cases, the therapists noted that they had puzzled over the considerable mental health of their subjects, all of whom had histories of multiple and significant stressors in childhood. Half of the group, in addition to poverty, alcoholism, or mental illness in their family experience, also had a history of repeated physical and/or sexual abuse. Not only were these subjects deemed "psychologically mature and healthy," they were also chosen because they "love well." Each subject had established and sustained a satisfying intimate love relationship for an average of twelve to eighteen years.

Professors Karen Reivich and Andrew Shatte at the University of Pennsylvania define "resilience" as "the capacity to respond in healthy and productive ways when faced with adversity or trauma." They also relate resiliency to "self efficacy," or the sense that one is effective in the world and believes in one's own ability to solve problems. Resilient people live with vitality, curiosity, and engagement with the world. They are fully self-expressed, and take responsibility for all aspects of their lives.

In a landmark study begun in 1955 by developmental psychologists Emmy Werner and Ruth Smith, 698 high-risk children were studied from their prenatal year until their thirtieth birthdays. Two out of three of these vulnerable children suffered learning deficits and behavior problems by the time they were ten. By eighteen, arrests, pregnancies, and serious mental health problems were common. "But there was one child in every three who developed into a confident, accomplished, connected adult."

Psychologists, Reivich and Shatte are among those who have made it their life work to study resilience in children and adults. In the early research, these survivor/thrivers were referred to as "invulnerables." Reivich and Shatte found one primary distinguishing characteristic among people who had survived extraordinary stress—a positive cognitive style, a way of looking at the world and interpreting events that allowed them to maintain a sense of personal strength in spite of assaults on body, mind, and soul. The researchers discovered seven abilities in the resilient that reflect their cognitive style and lead to successful behaviors. These are: 1) emotion regulation, 2) impulse control, 3) empathy, 4) optimism, 5) causal analysis, 6) self-efficacy, and 7) reaching out.

The first two—emotion regulation and impulse control—are closely related. Those who stay calm under pressure will act calm under pressure. They are better able to think clearly, evaluate the situation, and see options. Because their thoughts are free of self-reference and the contamination of false beliefs, they cannot only problem-solve under pressure, but they can experience empathy for others involved in the adverse condition. "Resilient people are optimistic. They believe that things can change for the better. They have hope for the future and believe that they control the direction of their lives. Compared to pessimists, optimists are physically healthier, are less likely to suffer depression, do better in school, are more productive at work…"

Causal analysis refers to the ability to accurately identify the causes of problems. Researchers have found that resilient people have an "explanatory style" that reflects cognitive flexibility and they can identify the significant causes of the adversities they face. They are realists; they do not reflexively blame others, nor do they ruminate about their own mistakes. They channel their energy into looking at the factors they can control, even, as in the cases of Michael Naranjo and Jacques Lusseyran, when the only thing that can be controlled is one's emotional integrity.

Self-efficacy, or faith in our ability to succeed, implies confidence and leadership. Reaching out, engaging with others, asking for and giving help, or what we might currently call having a "secure attachment style", are all powerful aspects of resilience. When I imagine Jacques Lusseyran reciting poetry to men in rags who are barely still alive, I see the power of love and connection through creative self-expression to inspire the will to live. His resilience saved his life and strengthened all of those around him.

The good news is that resilience can be taught. Reveitch and Shatte have created programs ("Adaptive Learning Systems") that have proved successful in teaching what they call "real-time resilience." Self-calming methods of controlled breathing, progressive muscle relaxation, and positive imagery, in conjunction with quick-change cognitive strategies make it possible for coping skills to take the place of self-defeating unconscious patterns. Their program has been used in schools, with parenting groups, in marriage counseling, and in work settings from non-profit organizations to government departments to Fortune 500 companies.

A "real-time resilience" exercise works like this: 1) Identify the adversity, stressor, or the event that has occurred. 2) Look at your beliefs about the event. What do you tell yourself about it? What are the automatic thoughts that come up? Listen to that inner voice that is always making meaning of the world—and often the wrong meaning. 3) Look at the consequences, the impact on you of holding those beliefs. It is usually an emotional impact. 4) Begin to analyze and challenge those beliefs so that you can come to an acceptance of the experience.

I will give you a small personal example. (You will also want to start with the small issues before taking on the more significant stressors in your life.) I received a call from one of the offices of an insurance plan for which I am a provider. They asked for a copy of a W-9 form for my Federal ID number. I immediately became upset because I had gone through a lot of paperwork with this company when I had moved my office location six months earlier. My secretary had responded and then several months later I had responded, and I thought it had been taken care of, and now again, many months later, they asked for the same information.

First, I notice my upset: A simple act of getting a form and putting it in the fax machine is completely overshadowed by my anger. I tell myself I shouldn't have to be bothered in this way. I don't have time for this—my secretary retired last year. The office worker requesting the form is most likely new and lost the previous paperwork. Why can't they get their S--- together? I've been doing this work for thirty-five years; why do I need a number anyway...? You get the picture. The event is the request for a piece of paper.

My automatic thoughts about that event could go all the way into paranoia if I let them. The consequences are that my relatively peaceful but busy body has now become a tiny tornado of noisy swirling upset. I'm also losing precious time with this reactive ruminating. I quickly go to the challenge: What's really happening here is about reasons that have nothing to do with me—an office simply needs a W-9 form. Period. I get the paper and put it in the fax machine. I then smile at my tendency towards arrogance, and I forgive myself for wanting to be treated like a queen rather than like everyone else. I can then move into my day with greater ease and a healthier mind-set.

Dr. Suzanne Kobasa, a psychologist at the City University of New York, has studied thousands of executives and managers in order to differentiate those who are resilient to stress from those who are more vulnerable. She, like the other researchers, found that the critical factor for resilience is a particular thinking style. A positive thinking style is evident in three areas she calls "control, commitment and challenge": 1) Those who experience better health and low stress in jobs that are rich in stressors believe they can control and directly influence events that occur in their lives; 2) Resilient people score higher on measures of engagement or commitment to their work. For them, the job is a source of meaning in their lives; 3) Change is seen as challenge or an opportunity for growth.

In their book, *The Power of Resilience*, psychologists Robert Brooks and Sam Goldstein echo the importance of nurturing resilience. Not only can resilience training help the nearly forty million adult Americans who suffer from depressive and anxiety disorders, it also increases the resistance to stress and lowers chances of developing PTSD (post traumatic stress disorder) following a life crisis.

Those who write about resilience and the extraordinary individuals whose lives illustrate the phenomenon credit their unusual success to a powerful, supportive relationship, "an adult from whom they gathered strength." For Jacques Lusseyran, it was his parents who never faltered in their confidence in their son's ability to accomplish anything he chose to take on. For Michael Naranjo, it was his older brother Tito, "my best friend...my model for unconditional love." Over the twenty-eight years of his marriage, it is Laurie, Michael's wife, who is "the sustaining force behind everything."

For those whose misfortune was to have parents who were unavailable or even perpetrators of abuse, the task of learning compassion for oneself and others was achieved because of a special, caring relationship. In all the research on resilience, compassion and empathy are cited as driving the motivation to connect with others and to monitor the thoughts and behaviors that would interfere with "loving well."

Psychiatrist Frederic Flach listed twelve attributes of resilience:

1) strong self-esteem, 2) independence of thought, 3) a strong network of friends, 4) discipline/responsibility, 5) ability to recognize and develop one's gifts and talents, 6) open-mindedness, 7) willingness to dream, 8) a wide range of interests, 9) keen sense of humor, 10) insight into the feelings of others as well as one's own and the ability to communicate them, 11) high tolerance for distress, 12) commitment to life, including a philosophy for meaning and hope, even under the worst circumstances.

Micheal Naranjo did not overcome blindness and live happily ever after. He has continuously dealt with medical problems, some from his injuries from the explosion in Viet Nam, others unrelated. In 1994, he began to suddenly experience "horrendous pain" in his head, pain that would only abate somewhat if he were lying prone It took over a year until a physician at the University of California, San Francisco, diagnosed a very rare cyst on his spinal cord at T3-T4. Spinal fluid was leaking out into the soft tissue, diminishing the fluid that would normally "float the brain." After spinal surgery, he was pain-free for a few months, and then the headaches began. He has tried every treatment imaginable, but the pain continues. He can only work now about one-third time.

"Pain or no pain, we still travel and look at art," said Michael. He and Laurie were in Paris just prior to 9/11 on a walking tour of France. They were in the Louvre, Michael looking (feeling) Michelangelo's "The Slave." "It was so exciting....Art fills my life," he said. "When I do it, I'm extremely happy." He spoke of his disappointment in not being chosen, after a long bidding process, for a very large art installation. "Yes, it was disappointing," he said, "but it's just one thing that didn't happen. So many other things have, and many more things will. I always think I'm gonna win. If I try, if I work at it, I'll win. My job is to find a way around obstacles. There are no problems, just challenges. You find a purpose and go forth.... The whole world is an inspiration."

The Dalai Lama wrote in The Art of Living, "...a pessimistic attitude. I consider that to be the real seed of failure." And holocaust survivor, psychiatrist Viktor Frankl, wrote, "...everything can be taken away from a man but one thing...to choose one's attitude in any given set of circumstances."

And finally, Helen Keller said: "No pessimist ever discovered the secret of the stars, or sailed to an uncharted land, or opened a new doorway for the human spirit.

For those in the mental health field, the similarities between "positive psychology," or the psychology of resilience, and the methods of cognitive restructuring or cognitive-behavioral therapy as developed by Aaron Beck MD are immediately apparent. The other giant, if not the originator of this new field is Martin Seligman, whose work in depression and "learned helplessness" led him to realize the need for studying personal strengths and helping children and adults identify their strengths in order to learn optimism and handle negative conditions in life with responsible actions.

The study of resilience has expanded the audience for this work from the field of psychology and psychotherapy to apply the usefulness of these teachings to skills-development trainings in the workplace, for managers and CEO[1]s, and also to a thriving new field of "life coaching." Men, especially, tend to be more comfortable and open to the concept of being "coached" and taking action on the coaching, but both genders can be empowered when they are helped to find solutions to problems and personality patterns that allow them to move forward more quickly to accomplish their life goals.

It should be remembered that the understanding of resilience evolved from studying people who have overcome sometimes brutal life conditions to become highly effective, creative, and loving human beings. These people represent a small percentage of the population of traumatized individuals. The majority of us require supportive help to deal with the impact of negative experiences, gentle teaching about the naturalness and necessity of grief work, and ongoing permission to "work through" our feelings and be patient in moving toward self-acceptance and coming-to-terms with change and loss. Any attempt to by-pass grief and move quickly into positive thinking will not only most likely fail, but does not honor the pain inherent in loss, nor the courage necessary to re-establish a sense of self and create a new life.

(Two issues that should not be over-looked include: 1) the similarities to cognitive behavioral therapy and the new field of life coaching; and 2) the importance of dealing with the impact of trauma and helping people process grief; that positive psychology cannot nor should it be used to bypass the pain of loss.)

REFERENCES

Brooks, Robert & Goldstein, Sam. *The Power of Resilience*. New York: MaGraw-Hill, 2004.

Feldman, Gail. *From Crisis to Creativity*. Bookpartners, 1999. 2nd ed. Taking Advantage of Adversity. London: Time Warner, 2002.

Flach, Frederic. *Resilience*. New York: Fawcett Columbine, 1988.

Harris, Thoresen, Lopez, "Integrating Positive Psychology Into Counseling" *Journal of Counseling & Development*. Winter 2007: Vol 85.

Higgins, Gina O'Connell, *Resilient Adults*. San Francisco: Jossey-Bass, 1994.

Kamins, Michael, Producer. "Colores: Michael Naranjo- A New Vision." Albuquerque, NM: KUNM-TV, 1996.

Lusseyran, Jacques, *And There Was Light*. New York: Parabola Books, 1987.

Lusseyran, Jacques, *Against the Pollution of the I*. Idaho, Sandpoint: Morning Light Press, 2006.

Nelson, Mary C., *Michael Naranjo*. Minneapolis, MN: Dillon Press, 1957.

Nelson, Mary C., *Artists of the Spirit*. Sonoma, CA: Arcus Publishing Co., 1995.

Reivich, Karen & Shatte, Andrew. *The Resilience Factor*. New York: Broadway Books, 2002.

Seligman, Martin. *Authentic Happiness: Using the New Positive Psychology...* New York: Free Press, 2002.

Gail Siebert, Al. *The Resiliency Advantage*. San Francisco: Berrett-Koehler, 2005.

Lance Fogan, MD, MPH, is Clinical Professor of Neurology at the David Geffen School of Medicine at UCLA in Los Angeles, CA. He is a 1965 graduate of the State University of New York at Buffalo School of Medicine, his home town. Following neurology training at Case Western Reserve University Hospitals in Cleveland, OH, from 1968-1971, he joined Kaiser Permanente in Southern California. After a 26 year career practicing clinical neurology with that health plan, he retired in 1997.

Literature classes at his local junior college stimulated his interest in Shakespeare's medical knowledge. His paper, The Neurology in Shakespeare, *won the 1988 American Academy of Neurology History of Neurology Prize, and he continues to give presentations on that subject around the country. For the past eight years he has participated in a weekly private literature/writing class, to finally "get educated," and to read the great literature that, he believes, should be read. A written record of the lives of his five year-old and nine year-old grandsons, and how their experiences re-kindle his own childhood memories, has been the nexus of his current work-in-progress.*

WILLIAM SHAKESPEARE: RENAISSANCE PHYSICIAN

LANCE FOGAN, MD, MPH

The few facts known about William Shakespeare can be listed in one short paragraph. They include that he was born in Stratford-upon-Avon in April 1564, probably on the twenty-third. He died on the same date in 1616 in Stratford, a wealthy man in retirement. He owned New Place, the second largest home in town, and he was possessor of other local real estate. He married and had a family. None of his personal papers survive. He left a famous will, in which he bequeathed his wife their second-best bed. In Elizabethan England, that was the marriage bed; the best bed was reserved for guests. Six copies of his signature survive and three of these are in his will; several of them appear to be written by a different hand, possibly because it was common for scriveners of documents, such as wills, to sign the subject's name. No signatures are on literary/dramatical works. Any of his plays that survive – the quartos and folios – were transcribed by his colleagues. He was known to be an actor, to have lived in London, and he was a member of acting troupes, including the Kings' Men. No record exists to attest to his family visiting him in London. Did they attend any of his performances? During his productive years, did he return to visit Stratford, and when?

The fact that he was known to attend school in Stratford for only several years, with an emphasis on Greek, and on Latin, to enable reading scripture, leaves us to wonder how he gained his oceanic knowledge. How could any one person, genius or no, have acquired all of the sophisticated knowledge and insights that are so evident in Shakespeare's canon? The works display intimate knowledge of all levels of society from the royal court to legal, religious, military and diplomatic offices, down to the servant classes, common street people, and criminals. The bountiful biblical and mythological references denote profound background study and knowledge.

One-third of his thirty-seven plays take place outside of England. Foreign lands and languages are accurately described, yet there is no mention, no record, of Shakespeare ever leaving England. Herein lays the reason why an industry has arisen questioning the authorship of the thirty-seven plays, poems and one hundred and fifty-four sonnets attributed to William Shakespeare of Stratford. His parents, his wife, and his children seem to have been illiterate, yet Shakespeare had a vocabulary of about 20,000 words. Most modern authors use a vocabulary of around 7,500 words. He left no literary works and no library of books in his will; curiously, books were a successful man's most prized possessions at that time. This is most puzzling if Shakespeare were more than just the actor whose name was "borrowed" by any of a number of contemporary poets and scholars. Edward de Vere, the seventeenth Earl of Oxford, Sir Francis Bacon, Queen Elizabeth I, Christopher Marlowe and others are currently championed to be the "real" Shakespeare. The reason why an upper class personage might hide his or her true identity as the actual author was that playwrights and actors were considered to be on the same level as beggars and prostitutes.

This paper will focus on Shakespeare's medical knowledge, and more specifically, his apparent understanding of the nervous system. I believe that any intelligent observer of life in Elizabethan England would have witnessed signs and symptoms of many physical maladies. He would absorb much of what the trained physicians and barber-surgeons of the time knew and offered to their patients. Yet, his medical knowledge was far beyond the understanding of the average person, even in our day. Shakespeare's daughter, Susana, married John Hall, a leading physician in Stratford. Is he the source of Shakespeare's medical knowledge? But the marriage didn't occur until 1607, when most of his writings were behind him. Doctor Hall moved to Stratford in 1601. The accuracy, and Shakespeare's apparent understanding of many symptoms and signs of neurological disease, will amaze the reader. His writing calls out to the most astute clinicians of disease phenomena that could not be described any more accurately or succinctly, and, for lovers of creative drama and literature, expressed more beautifully. He conveys emotions of greater range and depth than any other author. English speakers, fortunately, can experience his prose and poetry in the original language.

> "Shakespeare might have been a neurologist...he was so good at it... His wonderful descriptions and delineations in this great field of our science show that he had thoroughly mastered the subject in all its branches."

This comment was recorded in medical transactions in Detroit over a century ago.[1]

Neurologists cannot solely claim Shakespeare as one of their own. The bibliography at the conclusion of this paper lists some of the medical research on Shakespeare's knowledge of rheumatology [2], chest diseases [3], obstetrics [4], syphilis [5], pediatrics [6], ear, nose, and throat diseases [7], gerontology [8], teeth [9], and even a tongue-in-cheek paper on radiography, wherein atoms are mentioned in *As You Like It*.[10] Psychiatrists document extraordinary depth and insights into their specialty based on his works.[11,12,13] Over 700 quotations containing references to medicine and psychiatry appear in the canon. [14]

Medical practitioners weren't always presented in his works in an honorable fashion, and much of Elizabethan writing referred to physicians quite critically. They were considered by many as pretenders, pedants and mercenary scoundrels who were impotent in the face of disease. Physicians and lay people alike believed in the humoral hypotheses of Hippocrates, Empedocles, and Galen in postulating the cause of disease. Restoring the "correct" balance of Galen's four humors, through purging, bleeding, blistering, sweating, etc., was the principle followed to restore health up until the nineteenth century. This emphasis on the humoral balancing stultified English medical education and practice, in contrast to the more scientifically sound advancements of the use of medications incorporated into the continental practice. That Shakespeare had access to the ancient Greeks Hippocrates and Galen, and to the Swiss practitioner Paracelsus, is

121

certified in his works. Falstaff announces, in *Part 2 Henry IV* (I,2,10): "I have read the cause of his effects in Galen." Aristotle is mentioned twice, Galen five times, and Paracelsus once.

Neuroanatomy

Still controversial for the Elizabethans was the "seat of the soul." The Encyclopedia Britannica defines the soul as an immaterial principle, or aspect, that with the body constitutes the human person.[15] Shakespeare appeared to believe the soul resided in the brain, but he acknowledges the controversy in sixteenth century England in *Bassanio's song upon referring to fancy (or love) in The Merchant of Venice* (III, 2, 63): "Tell me where is fancy bred / Or in the heart or in the head?" And in King John (V, 7, 2), Prince Henry describes: "...his pure brain, which some suppose the soul's frail Dwelling house."

Shakespeare recognized the brain's pre-eminent position in the nervous system; in *Antony and Cleopatra* (IV, 8, 21), he has Antony say: "...yet ha' we a brain that nourishes our nerves..." Pia mater is one of the three membranes covering the brain. In the Renaissance, it also referred to the brain itself. In *Twelfth Night* (I, 5, 108), the clown says: "Whose skull Jove cram with brains ... one of thy kin has a most weak pia mater." In *Troilus and Cressida* (II, 1, 66), Thersites exclaims: "I have bobbed his brain more than he has beat my bones ... and his pia mater is not worth the ninth part of a sparrow." A locus for the foundations of memory appears in *Love's Labor's Lost* (IV, 2 66): "These are begot in the ventricle of memory, nourished in the womb of pia mater..." Four hundred years later can we be that much more precise in "locating" memory?

How could Shakespeare have known of these anatomical structures? A nineteenth century English physician, Benjamin Richardson, wrote in 1888 that Helkiah Crooke published a vast work on anatomy in 1615. Crooke's publisher was W. Jaggard, the same printer employed by Shakespeare [sic]. Richardson speculates that Crooke's anatomical drawings, plates and letterpresses "...would for long seasons be the most remarkable press works of the time. To that office the indefatigable playwright would often be drawn by his own business, and there he would hardly fail to see unfolded before him the anatomy of man from a sure source…that would appeal to his ever absorbing mind."[16]

Shakespeare approaches the question of defective intelligence, or irrational and dumb decisions, in *Othello* when he has Lodovico declare about *Othello* (IV, 1, 260): "Are his wits safe: Is he not light of brain?"

The famed Renaissance Professor of Medicine at the University of Montpellier, Andreas Laurentius, noted in his writings that low foreheads often correlated with low intelligence.[17] Shakespeare employed this concept in *The Tempest* (IV, 1, 246) when Caliban says: "…We shall lose our time and all be turned to barnacles / or to apes with foreheads villainous low." Julia disparages her rival in love in *Two Gentlemen of Verona* (IV, 4, 191): "Ay, but her forehead's low, and mine's as high." And a love rival is disparaged by a messenger in *Antony and Cleopatra* (III, 3, 36): "…And her forehead as low as she would wish it."

Lear utilizes the test for the perception of sharpness in a fashion common to all physicians (IV, 7, 55): "I will not swear these are my hands. Let's see – I feel this pin prick. Would I were assured of my condition."

Sciatica And Leg Cramps

One of the several references to this affliction is offered by the "deformed and scurrilous Greek" Thersites in *Troilus and Cressida* (V, 1, 25), as he includes sciaticas as one of the "rotten diseases of the south," i.e., on the southern end of the body. Treatment of sciatica must have been frequently disappointing in Shakespeare's day, just as today, for Thersites expounds: "…sciaticas, lime-kilns i' the palm [or arthritic calcifications], incurable bone-ache…" Also, in *Timon of Athens* (IV, 1, 25): "…Thou cold sciatica, cripple our senators, that their limbs may halt as lamely as their manners…"

123

Leg cramps and leg spasms, common complaints brought to modern physicians, afflict Shakespeare's characters as well. Prospero, midst an angry flurry of expletives, adds, in *The Tempest* (IV, 1, 258): "...shorten up their sinews with aged cramps."

Headache

There are very few direct references to headache. A character mentions "hardening of the brows" in *Winter's Tale* (I, 2, 143), but the precise meaning of this phrase is not known. In King John (IV, 1, 41), Arthur says: "When your head did but ache, I knit my handkerchief about your brows..." In *Othello* (III, 3, 282):

Desdemona:	Why do you speak so faintly? Are you not well?
Othello:	I have a pain upon my forehead, here.
Desdemona:	Let me bind it hard, within this hour it will be well again.

In *Romeo and Juliet* (II, 5, 48), Nurse says: "Lord, how my head aches! What a head have I! It beats as it would fall in twenty pieces." A migraine, vascular-type, "sick" headache, would be the diagnosis.

Olfactory Function

Anosmia is implied by the Fool in *King Lear* (II, 4, 66). Head injuries and upper respiratory and sinus infections were the likely causes:

Fool:	"All that follow their noses are led by their eyes but blind men; and there's not a nose among twenty but can smell him that's stinking..."

The sense of smell and autonomic reflexes are effectively intertwined by Lafeu in *All's Well That Ends Well* (V, 3, 117): "Mine eyes smell onions: I shall weep anon."

Nasal Speech

Pharyngeal/palatal abnormalities and/or cranial nerve lesions that can cause nasal speech are referred to by Shylock in *The Merchant of Venice* (IV, 1, 49): "And others, when the bagpipe sings i' th' nose..." And in *Othello* (III, 1, 3), the Clown asks: "Why masters, ha' your instruments been in Naples, that they speak i' the nose thus?" Syphilitic gummas, which occur in tertiary syphilis, erode the palate and nasal septum; these are implied as Naples was notorious in Elizabethan England for its association with venereal disease.

Blindness/Double Vision

Schmidt's *SHAKESPEARE LEXICON* notes "squint" means to turn the eye to an oblique position, and that "pin and web" indicates a disorder of the eye consisting of a dusky film hindering the sight, a cataract.[18] In *King Lear* (III, 4, 109), Edgar's nonsensical word salad on the moor includes: "He gives the web and the pin, squints the eye..." Leontes, in *The Winter's Tale* (I, 2, 289), turns the same phrase: "...and all eyes blend with the pin and web but theirs."

Gloucester's eyes are plucked out from their sockets in *King Lear* by the hands of the Duke of Cornwall in an especially brutal scene. This episode, which Gloucester survives, is a turning point in his own self-awareness. From this point on, he can "see" with great insight into the realities that surround him. Prior to this, although his eyesight was sound, he was "blind" to reality – he was easily duped and betrayed without realizing it. Shakespeare often used this convention, this symbolic display of insight midst physical blindness, and emotional "blindness" when the literal sight was intact. The gelatinous vitreous humor was known to Shakespeare, as demonstrated by Cornwall's statement in the above scene (III, 7, 83): "...Out vile jelly. Where is thy luster now?"

Shakespeare obviously was acquainted with the several extraocular muscles and their apparent function, as demonstrated in the following two speeches. *Cymbeline* (I, 3, 18): Imogen: "I would

have broke mine eye strings, cracked them but to look upon him..."
In *A Midsummer Night's Dream* (IV, 1, 188), Hermia: "Me thinks I
see these things with parted eye, when everything seems double."

Dizziness/Vertigo

Shakespeare refers to giddiness to imply vertigo, and our
English colleagues are still partial to this expression. In *The Taming
of The Shrew* (V, 2, 20), the widow says: "He that is giddy thinks the
world turns round." In Romeo and Juliet (I, 2, 47), it is suggested that
when one becomes giddy from spinning around, then he should turn
in the reverse direction: Benvolio: "Turn giddy, and be holp by
backward turning." Troilus and Cressida (III, 2, 16) offers Troilus
saying: "I am giddy; expectation whorls me around." *Part II Henry
IV* (III, 1, 18) has the King stating: "Wilt thou upon the high and
giddy mast seal up the ship-boy's eyes, and rock his brains in cradle
of the rude imperious surge..."

Another sensation, possibly different from vertigo and more
suggestive of light-headedness and cerebral hypoperfusion, is offered
by the following application of the word "giddy" in *Part II Henry IV*
(IV, 4, 110) from the King: "...And now my sight fails, and my brain
is giddy."

Deafness

Caesar's unilateral deafness is noted in Julius Caesar (I, 2, 213)
when he says: "Come on my right hand, for this ear is deaf, and tell
me truly what thou thinkst of him." In *A Midsummer Night's Dream*
(III, 2, 177), the Bard offers a physiological observation on adaptation
in the nervous system for why the hearing sense is augmented when
vision is simultaneously compromised:

Hermia: Dark night, that from the eye his function take
           The ear more quick of apprehension makes.
           Wherein it doth impair the seeing sense,
           It pays the hearing double recompense.
           Thou art not by mine eye, Lysander, found;
           Mine ear, I thank it, brought me to thy sound.

Tremors

There is a paucity of people with apparent paralysis agitans (Parkinson's disease) or other tremulous conditions among Shakespeare's contingent of symptoms and diseases, but a description of tremor in the senium is in Troilus and Cressida (I, 3, 172):

Ulysses:	And then forsooth, the faint defects of age
	Must be the scene of mirth; to cough and spit,
	And with a palsy fumbling on his gorget
	[armor],
	Shake in and out the rivet...

Paralysis

An enticing clinical description that is highly suggestive of stroke is offered by the incorrigible Falstaff in *Part II Henry IV* (I, 2, 101):

And I hear…his highness is fallen into this same whoreson apoplexy…This apoplexy, as I take it, is a kind of lethargy…a kind of sleeping in the blood, a whoreson tingling…It hath it original from much grief, from study and perturbation of the brain…

Shakespeare is describing what we know in the early twenty-first century is interruption of cerebral blood flow, resulting in focal dysfunction, which is so often associated with physical and emotional distress. Apoplexy is a "sudden stop of sense and voluntary motion, from an affection of the brains", according to the 1902 edition of Schmidt's Shakespeare Lexicon and Quotation Dictionary.[18] Later, in this play (IV, 4, 110), this same king again suffers apoplexy:

King:	And now my sight fails, and my brain is giddy,
	O me! Come near me. Now I am much ill.
Warwick:	You do know these fits
	Are with his highness very ordinary.
	Stand from him, give him air, he'll straight be well.
	…Speak lower for the king recovers.
Gloucester:	This apoplexy will certain be his end.

The king recovers enough to converse with his son and others, and shortly thereafter, he dies. No further useful mention is made of symptoms, focal or otherwise. We can speculate that he suffered from stroke, and/or transient ischemic attacks (TIAs) and/or seizures.

York, an old man in Richard II, has a palsied arm, which implies "paralysis, cessation of animal function," according to Schmidt.[18] In II, 3, 103, York says: "...O' then how quickly should this arm of mine, now prisoner to the palsy, chastise thee..." In a passage from *Measure For Measure* (III, 1, 34), the Duke expounds upon the toils, stresses, and worthlessness of life, and refers to one of the features of old age – paralysis:

> Duke: ...for all thy blessed youth,
> Becomes as aged, and doth beg the alms
> Of palsied eld...

King Richard III – the deformed, hunchbacked, villainous murderer! This image is embellished by the Tudor chroniclers who clearly had an interest in maligning him in order to justify the usurpation of his crown by their hero Henry VII, grandfather of Shakespeare's own reigning Queen Elizabeth I. Writers of that time state, "It is... reported that the Duchess, his mother, had so much ado in her travail that she could not be delivered of him uncut, and that he came into this world with the feet forward...and not untoothed" – a breech birth with probable birth anomalies.[19] Holinshed's Chronicle As Used In Shakespeare's Plays, based on the source book of the Chronicle, states that Richard III was little of stature, ill-featured of limbs, crook-backed, his left shoulder much higher than his right.[20] In Richard III (I, 1, 19):

> Richard: Cheated of feature by dissembling Nature,
> Deform'd, unfinish'd, sent before my time
> Into this breathing world, scarce half made up.
> And that so lamely and unfashionable
> And that dogs bark at me, as I halt by them.

Richard's withered arm was described by Raphael Holinshed in *The Chronicles of England, Scotlande, and Irelande* in 1578.[20] Richard accused the mistress of his dead brother of having "wasted my body" by sorcery, and therewith he plucked up his dublet sleeve to his elbow, upon his left arm, where he showed a weerish withered arm and small. But, did Shakespeare describe these abnormalities from the street scenes of Elizabethan England? Brachial plexus, or cervical radiculopathic lesions, resulting in Erb's and Klumpke's palsies correlate with difficult deliveries; unequal-sized legs can result in a limp, possibly representative of a hemiparetic or spastic paraparetic gait which in turn could be secondary to a spinal cord lesion associated with a kyphoscoliosis. Richard says (III, 4, 68): "…Behold, mine arm is like a blasted sapling, withered up."

Sleep And Neurology

It is known that learning can continue even during sleep; the brain can register external stimuli. Shakespeare seems to be aware of suggestion under narcosis in *Part I Henry IV* (I, 3, 221) when Hotspur says: "…But I will find him when he lies asleep / And in his ear I'll hollo 'Mortimer'."

Descriptions of Falstaff's drunken, snoring sleep and whether Shakespeare was describing obstructive sleep apnea elicited a minor controversy in the New England Journal of Medicine in 1983.[21],[22] After imbibing much sack (sherry), as was his wont, and passing out, Falstaff was discovered snoring heavily in *Part I Henry IV* (II, 4, 503):

Peto:	Falstaff! Fast asleep behind the arras, And snorting like a horse.
Prince:	Hark how hard he fetches breath.

Insomnia is depicted countless times by the great dramatist; typical is the king lamenting his insomnia while his lowliest subjects can easily find that soft nurse of nature, sleep, in *Part II Henry IV* (III, 1, 4):

How many thousands of my poorest subjects
Are at this hour asleep! O sleep, O gentle sleep
Nature's soft nurse, how have I frighted thee,
That thou no more wilt weigh my eyelids down
And steep my senses in forgetfulness?

A superb description of insomnia is this excerpt from sonnet number twenty-seven:

Weary with toil, I hast me to my bed,
The dear repose for limbs with travel tired,
But then begins a journey in my head
To work my mind when body's work expired;
...Lo thus, by day my limbs, by night my mind,
For thee and for myself no quiet find.

Somnambulism (sleepwalking) and somniloquy (talking while asleep) are symptomatic disturbances of stage IV sleep. They can be symptoms of the dissociative form of hysteria. Among the best-known literary examples of these phenomena are the sleepwalking and sleep-talking of Lady Macbeth, as depicted in *Macbeth* (V, 1, 4). Charcot characterized the somnambulic stage of sleep as that in which "all the senses are intact...although the conscience is in abeyance...", i.e., the motor centers are awake but the higher centers are asleep.[23]

Gentlewoman:	I have seen her rise from her bed, throw her nightgown upon her, unlock her closet, take forth paper, fold it, write upon it, read it, afterwards seal it, and again return to bed; yet all this while in a most fast sleep.
Doctor:	A great perturbation in nature, to receive at once the benefit of sleep and do the effects of watching! In this slumbry agitation, besides her walking and other actual performances, what (at any time) have you heard her say? (Lady Macbeth then enters holding a candle).
Doctor:	You see her eyes are open.
Gentlewoman:	Ay, but their sense are shut.

Recent emotional turmoil and anxiety, the troubled subconscious mind, seem to be the bed from which these sleep disturbances arise. It is no wonder that Lady Macbeth walked and talked in her sleep after her involvement in multiple murders. However, so real are the characters Shakespeare created out of his imagination that modern scholars can argue about and dissect their motivations, personal attributes/faults, and the implications of their statements and actions four centuries later. One can consider that Lady Macbeth's sleepwalking is not due to a stage IV sleep parasomnia because sleepwalkers are generally silent. Lady Macbeth vocalizes while sleepwalking, and the observing gentlewoman and doctor overhear her guilt lamentations concerning the murders and blood-letting in which she was involved. Therefore, one should consider, in her parasomnia differential diagnosis, the REM (rapid eye movement) Sleep Behavior Disorder Syndrome, a recently described sleep disorder.[24] REM sleep is a fifth sleep stage, one which we all experience every ninety minutes during natural sleep. This is the stage of dreaming, and because normally there is inhibition of impulses down the spinal cord resulting in atonia or mild paralysis of our limbs, we do not physically act out our dreams, e.g., we don't run, or thrash, and yell out. This is a protective mechanism. The REM Sleep Behavior Disorder Syndrome is associated with violent striking out and/or kicking and vocalizing due to an abnormal loss of the muscle atonia.

Epilepsy

A saunter down a busy Tudor London thoroughfare would reveal citizens harboring countless maladies. If epilepsy is estimated to occur in almost one percent of the population today, there must have been at least that incidence available for Shakespeare to observe. Two of the plays include people described in the throes of a fit, three others refer to altered behavior and/or responsiveness, and a sixth makes reference to an ill-defined "epileptic" expression. In *Julius Caesar* (I, 2, 246):

131

Casca:	...for he swounded and fell down at it ... He fell down in the market place and foamed At the mouth and was speechless.
Brutus:	'Tis very like he hath the falling sickness. ...What did he say when he came unto himself?
Casca:	...and so he fell. When he came to himself Again, he said, if he had done or said anything Amiss, he desired their worships to think it Was his infirmity...

In *Julius Caesar*, Cassius describes Caesar during a febrile illness. Rigors of febrile chills, possibly accompanied by another of Caesar's convulsions, were described (I, 2,119):

> He had a fever when he was in Spain, and when the fit was on
> him, I did mark how he did shake. 'Tis true, this god did shake.
> His coward lips did from their color fly, and that same eye
> whose bend doth awe the world did lose his luster. I did hear
> him groan...

Othello presents an actual seizure on stage, preceded by extreme emotional upset and agitation, then mental confusion, followed by Iago advising Cassio, who is also witnessing the seizure, that the lethargy of the post-ictus must play its course. He also warns of the "savage madness" that is so often the agitated, confusional, feature of partial complex seizures (IV, 1, 41):

Othello:	It is not words that shakes me thus. – Pish! Noses, ears and lips? Is't possible? –Confess? -Handkerchief? –O devil! (Falls in trance).
Iago:	...My lord is fall'n into an epilepsy. This Is his second fit; he had one yesterday.
Cassio:	Rub him about the temples.
Iago:	No, forbear. The lethargy must have his quiet course. If not, he foams at mouth, and by and by Breaks out to savage madness. Look, he stirs. Do you withdraw yourself a little while. He will recover straight.

132

Later in *Othello*, Shakespeare depicts this epileptic Othello committing the strangulation murder of his beloved wife while in a rage. Today, defense lawyers would attempt to lessen the perpetrator's responsibility and guilt with a plea that the act occurred during a partial complex seizure when the patient lost all voluntary control. The victim, Desdemona, even supports this plea that he may be in the midst of a seizure by her uttering (V, 2, 40): "And yet I fear you; for you're fatal then / When your eyes roll so…"

In Macbeth, upon hearing discomforting news, Macbeth alludes to an alteration in his well-being (III, 4, 21): "Then comes my fit again. I had else been perfect / Whole as marble, founded as the rock…" Macbeth then experiences visual hallucinations, seeing the form of Banquo, just murdered on orders of Macbeth, and he reacts to his companions in a confused manner. His wife makes excuses, alluding to a fit (II, 4, 51):

Lennox:	What is't that moves your Highness?
Macbeth:	Which of you have done this?
Lords:	What, my good lord?
Ross:	Gentlemen, rise. His Highness is not well.
Lady:	Sit, worthy friends. My lord is often thus, And hath been from his youth. Pray you keep seat. The fit is momentary; upon a thought He will again be well…

Part 2 Henry IV related symptoms compatible with a vasovagal attack, or retino-cerebrovascular hypoperfusion, more than a seizure, but the observers refer to the event as a fit. Schmidt's Shakespeare Lexicon defines "fit" in several ways: a violent attack of disease, a paroxysm; an attack of mental disorder; any irregular and violent affection of the mind18 (IV, 4, 102):

King:	And wherefore should these good news make me sick?
	...I should rejoice now at this happy news, And now my sight fails, and my brain is giddy. O me! Come near me. Now I am much ill.
Warwick:	...You do know these fits Are with his highness very ordinary...

The romance comedy *The Tempest* includes Caliban, a savage and deformed slave. Shakespeare makes reference to fits, which could imply shaking chills, or possibly a seizure, in the following exchange of Stephano to Caliban (II, 2, 72):

Stephano:	He's in his fit now and does not talk after the wisest. He shall taste of my bottle: if he have never drunk wine afore, it will go near to remove his fit....Open your mouth. This will shake your shaking, I can tell you, and that soundly. [Gives Caliban a drink.]

The Earl of Kent, in *King Lear*, exclaims in anger (II, 2, 76): "A plague upon your epileptic visage!" This probably refers only to a face contorted in a grin, but Shakespeare demonstrates his descriptive talents.

Malingering And Hysteria

Feigning neurological symptoms to achieve a goal must have been at least as common in Tudor England as it is in many of our clinical practices. The hard-drinking, amoral, lecherous rogue Sir John Falstaff, who willingly would march his squad of soldiers to their deaths on the battlefield so that he could collect their pay, was certainly not above malingering. When the Lord Chief Justice sought him out suspecting that Falstaff had committed a robbery, Falstaff pretended that deafness prevented him from understanding what the Chief Justice had to say, in *Part 2 Henry IV* (I, 2, 63):

Falstaff:	Boy [to his page], tell him I am deaf.
Page:	You must speak louder; my master is deaf.
Chief Justice:	I am sure he is, to the hearing of anything good.
	Go, pluck him by the elbow; I must speak with him…

And what follows is Falstaff maintaining his pretense and wandering on with gossip as though he had heard none of the serious charges previously brought against him.

Another sham episode that is skillfully written by Shakespeare occurs in the first scene in *Part 2 Henry VI* (II, 1). The mayor and townsfolk of St. Albans carry Saunder Simpcox in a chair before the King and royal party. Simpcox claims to be crippled, but also to have been cured of lifelong blindness just one-half hour before by Saint Alban. The Duke of Gloucester questions Simpcox and his wife. When Gloucester queries Simpcox how long he had been blind, a woman volunteers to confirm that Simpcox had been born blind. Gloucester asks for her identity and upon being told that she was his wife, Gloucester shrewdly offers, "Hadst thou been his mother thou couldst have better told." The interview proceeds to the point where the skeptical Gloucester, to carry the sham to the point of resolution, examines Simpcox in a neurological manner in line 103:

| Gloucester: | A subtle knave. But yet it shall not serve. Let me see thine eyes. Wink now. Now open them. In my opinion yet thou seest not well. |
| Simpcox: | Yes, master, clear as day. I thank God and Saint Alban. |

Gloucester continues by asking Simpcox to name the colors of clothing articles that Gloucester has on, which Simpcox does in spectacular fashion:

| Gloucester: | Then, Saunder, sit there, the lying'st knave in Christendom. If thou hadst been born blind… [you wouldn't have known the names of colors]. |

> My lords, Saint Alban here hath done a miracle;
> and would ye not think his cunning to be great
> that could restore this cripple to his legs again.

Simpcox: O master that you could!

Gloucester: My masters of Saint Albans, have you not
beadles [constables] in your town, and things
called whips? [As Simpcox is set upon he leaps
from the invalid's chair and runs away.]

The Bard's psychological insights and skillful descriptions of the unbalanced and disturbed mind and personality were maximally displayed in countless of his characters and works. In *King Lear*, Edgar malingered insanity while living on the cruel heath in order to survive assassination. This occurred after an evil brother tricked him and he was forced to flee from his father's household. Shakespeare was able to recount Lear's true insane delusional periods and to contrast them with Edgar's feigned madness; so accurately displayed is the malingerer employing dramatic exaggeration of his mental symptoms. The richness of *Hamlet* is manifested by the enigmatic complex character of the protagonist. Shakespeare's genius is proclaimed by the fact that four centuries later, libraries of volumes are devoted to interpreting Hamlet's motives and behavior. Some believe the character represents a true feigned psychosis in a weak and indecisive soul; others argue that the character represents a combination of feigned and actual psychosis.

Lear felt that he was losing control of his reason because of passion, great turmoil of emotions, and in ancient times, as in Shakespeare's age, it was believed that the uterus was the source of the great hysterical passion, metaphorically termed "mother" or a "fit of the mother." Its action could ascend and control the brain, as in *King Lear* (II, 4, 54):

Lear: O, how this mother swells up toward my heart!
Hysterica passio, down, thou climbing sorrow;
Thy element's [i.e. proper place] below.

Dementia

The works of William Shakespeare are as fertile a field as any extant from which to harvest literal examples of people who have lost their fullest intellectual powers. Price noted that "...Nowhere do we find so many, and such remarkable, descriptions of senility as we find in the writings of Shakespeare."[25]

Shakespeare portrays both the physique and mentality of age: a broken voice, white hair and wrinkles, secreting orifices, weakness of limb and sense, various diseases, ugliness of face and crookedness of stature, talkativeness, lack of friends, and most skillfully of all, especially as illustrated in King Lear, its failing mental powers.

The sonnets (#63, 64, and 65) exquisitely describe when age steals beauty, love and life from us, so too our reason. In *Henry V* (IV, 3, 49), the King tells us: "Old men forget." In *Much Ado About Nothing* (III, 5, 33), it is Dogberry who says: "...When the age is in, the wit is out." Jacques' famous 'seven ages of man' speech in As You Like It (II, 7, 163):

> ...Last scene of all,
> ...Is second childishness and mere oblivion,
> Sans teeth, sans eye, sans taste, sans everything.

Renaissance writers considered old age to start at fifty.[17] Some, such as Henry Cuffe, believed old age began at thirty-five.[26] Cuffe cited classical authorities and applied astrology and Galen's humoral theories; astrologically the declining years were unfortunate and the body was then dominated by black bile, a cold, dry, melancholy humor. Draper has reviewed Shakespeare's depictions of old age.[27] He noted that this melancholy humor was the one found in conditions of bodily decrepitude and mental instability. This, Draper reports, then easily deteriorated into the childishness of dotage. Thus, the evolution of Lear. Physical exposures, as on the moor midst drenching, freezing storms, and passions, and perturbations of the mind, burn out the last remnants of his, in the Galenic sense, kingly choler and his vital fluids; he is left cold and dry and weak in body.

137

Lear's mind also shows the effect of this decay. Draper pointed out that Shakespeare created Lear's symptomatology to follow the theories of medical authorities of the ancient and Renaissance times. Act I depicts Lear's "discernings are lethargied" and soon his memory begins to fail. He grows talkative; he overreacts with disproportionate anger and decompensation of inhibitions; he shows a wayward pettiness and he foresees approaching madness. Long before he decompensates into madness, his daughters remark about symptoms of his senile dementia: "How full of changes" he is (I, 1, 288), and "with what poor judgment" he acts (I, 1, 200), and "old fools are babes again" (I, 3, 19). In Act II, he senses the beginning of "hysterica passio." We then find Lear's wits beginning to turn (III, 2, 19):

> Lear: ...Here I stand...
> A poor, infirm, weak and despised old man.
> My wits begin to turn.

The Fool prophetically declares, "This cold night will turn us all to fools and madmen." By the end of Act III, Lear's wits are gone.

In an erudite psychiatric appraisal of *King Lear*, Andreasen summarized Lear's decline as an old man becoming senile, ill-equipped to deal with changes of any kind.[11] In our daily practices, we clinicians see how such minor changes as visits to places outside the home are enough to decompensate our demented patients' equilibrium. But Lear had to deal with betrayal, loss of his kingship, home and dignity, and all familiar friends, except the fool, and he had to deal with the violence of nature in the form of a storm. A severe stress reaction, or a reactive psychosis, was the result. His prominent symptoms were confusion, visual hallucinations and disorganized thinking. Colman, in a paper on Shakespeare and DSM III (*Diagnostic and Statistical Manual of Mental Disorders*), discussed features of Lear's symptomatology.[12] His article is fascinating in that it points out that visual, as opposed to auditory, hallucinations usually imply an organic, in contrast to functional, etiology. Decompensation of organic cerebral lesions is what one would expect in an aged, senescent person, and hence, visual hallucinations would be more likely than auditory hallucinations. Today, MRI brain scans show how common structural abnormalities, such as ischemic areas and cortical atrophy, are. A perceptive and thoughtful contrasting view of Lear is offered by Dr. Joseph M. Foley of Cleveland; he suggests that Lear was delirious, and not demented, because Lear clearly regains his mental functions at the end of the play.[28]

An apt clinical description of wasted, sickly senescence is given by Hamlet as he jeers old Polonius in *Hamlet* (II, 2, 196):

> ...old men have gray beards,...their faces
> are wrinkled, their eyes purging thick amber
> and plum-tree gum and that they have a plentiful
> lack of wit, together with most weak hams...

The following description of severe dementia, typical of senile dementia of Alzheimer's type, could lead the reader to believe that Shakespeare visited a modern long-term care facility in the reader's own community; Polixenes depicts a vegetative old dement in Winter's Tale (IV, 4, 390):

> ...Is not your father grown incapable
> Of reasonable affairs: Is he not stupid
> With age and alt'ring rheums? Can he speak?
> Hear? Know man from man? Dispute his own estate?
> Lies he not bed-rid? And again does nothing
> But what he did being childish?

Convalescent and nursing home chronic care for the aged and frail were apparent social needs in the Tudor England of Shakespeare. *Part I Henry VI* depicts the feeble old Duke of Bedford in a chair outside of the besieged Rouen, watching a battle. Lord Talbot says to him (III, 2, 87):

> Talbot: ...Come my lord,
> We will bestow you in some better place,
> Fitter for sickness and for crazy age.

Encephalopathies

Hepatic encephalopathy is effectively argued by Summerskill as being responsible for the personality of Sir Andrew Aguecheek in *Twelfth Night*.[29] Summerskill believed "so astute were Shakespeare's observations...that his creation of Aguecheek may have anticipated by more than three and one-half centuries a case report of the syndrome of chronic dementia in liver disease due to intolerance of nitrogenous substances." Aguecheek was obtuse, inappropriate, and his name implies a pale, tremulous cheek – because the coward was constantly in fear. Other characters in the play say that Aguecheek is "drunk nightly." Sir Toby Belch comments (III, 2, 54): "...For Andrew, if he were opened and you find so much blood in his liver as will clog the foot of a flea, I'll eat the rest of his anatomy."

The diagnosis of cirrhosis, with the resultant decompensation into encephalopathy following a nitrogen overload, is supported by Aguecheek's own observations. With accurate insight that is so out of character, he confesses (I, 3, 76): "...Methinks sometimes I have no more wit than a Christian or an ordinary man has. But I am a great eater of beef, and I believe that does harm to my wit."

Alcohol And Its Effects

Elizabethan audiences were well acquainted with alcoholism and the changes it creates. The Bard's poetic observations of those "addicted to the sack" are timeless. The initial depressant action of alcohol, which diminishes one's inhibitions, is described by Falstaff in *Part II Henry IV* (IV, 3, 92):

> ...a good sheeris-sack ...It ascends me into the brain, dries me there all the foolish and dull and crudy vapors which environ it, makes it apprehensive, quick, forgetive, full of nimble, fiery, and delectable shapes, which, delivered o'er to the voice, the tongue, which is the birth, becomes excellent wit...If I had a thousand sons, the first humane principle I would teach them should be to forswear thin potations and to addict themselves to sack.

Octavius Caesar declines a drink in fear of its mental effects in *Antony and Cleopatra* (II, 7, 97): "I could well forbear't. It's monstrous labor when I wash my brain and it grows fouler." In *Othello*, loss of self-possession through the drinking of alcohol is bemoaned by Cassio, embarrassed upon being so discovered by Othello (II, 3, 268):

> ...Drank!...O thou invisible spirit of wine...let us call thee devil! ...O God, that men should put an enemy in their mouths to steal away their brains... and...transform ourselves into beasts!

A rare humorous episode in the tragedy of *Macbeth* centers around the tipsy porter who insightfully announces that alcohol induces rhinophyma, acts as a soporific and diuretic, and causes impotency (II, 3, 23):

> ...And drink, sir, is a great provoker of three things...Marry, sir, nose-painting, sleep, and urine. Lechery, sir, it provokes and unprovokes: It provokes the desire but it takes away the performance.

A significant sociological aspect of alcoholism is succinctly pointed out by Berowne in *Love's Labor's Lost* (IV, 3, 45): "One drunkard loves another of the name."

The Neurological Complications Of Syphilis

The "pox," referring to the venereal disease syphilis, is mentioned in many of the works. It became known in Europe around 1500 A. D. Timon of Athens, which was written sometime between 1604 and 1609, contains many references to syphilitic symptoms. Timon shows a marked personality change himself; he initially is a cultured and prominent Athenian leader. As the play proceeds, his intellect pathologically weakens, and at the conclusion, he is angry, violent, and, as his steward Flavius cries out, "a ruinous man...full of decay." Evolution of a syphilitic into a paretic dement, I offer in pointed speculation.

Of special interest, which again emphasizes Shakespeare's powers of observation, are symptoms included in Timon's malignant tirade directed at two prostitutes. He encourages them to "give them (men) diseases" and cause lawyer's voices to "crack." Tertiary syphilis can create an aneurysm of the ascending thoracic aorta, which compresses the left recurrent laryngeal nerve, paralyzing the left vocal cord resulting in a hoarse voice; this clinical entity is known as "prostitute's whisper."[30] Is this what the Bard described, or was it gummas of the larynx, which could cause the same result? (IV, 3, 153):

> Timon: ...Crack the lawyer's voice,
> That he may never more false title plead
> Nor sound his quillets shrilly...

Tabes dorsalis is the neuropathologic form of syphilis which affects the spinal cord. It is responsible for the lightning-like pains in the extremities, and for impotency, which also did not elude the great author.[31] Timon continues to upbraid the prostitutes (IV, 3, 152):

> Timon: ...strike their sharp shins,
> And mar men's spurring...Plague all
> That your activity may defeat and quell
> The source of all erection...

Incontinence, another symptom of tabes dorsalis, is mentioned by Shylock in the *Merchant of Venice* (IV, 1, 49), as is an additional complication of tertiary syphilis, gummas of the hard palate and/or nasal septum. This can lead to nasal speech: as Shylock mentions: "...and others, when the bagpipe sings i' th' nose / Cannot contain their urine..."

Plant Poisons And Neurology

The actions of herbs, plants and their juices upon the nervous system were obviously well-known to Shakespeare; his observations on their appearances, uses and lore, are cited countlessly. Tabor deduces that Banquo, in *Macbeth* (I, 3, 84), may have spoken of henbane, which is the shrub *Hyoscyamus niger*, when he said of the vision of the three witches, "...or have we eaten of the insane root that takes the reason prisoner?"[32] Extracts from this plant yield scopolamine, which in toxic doses can be lethal. Englishmen of the sixteenth century believed that drugs could reach the rest of the body through the ears, including henbane. In *Hamlet*, the ghost of his father tells him (I, 5, 59):

> Sleeping within my orchard,
> My custom always of the afternoon,
> Upon my secure hour thy uncle stole
> With juice of cursed hebenon in a vial
> And in the porches of my ears did pour
> The leperous distillment...

Of interest to the clinician is that hyoscine, as well as other chemicals, can be absorbed into the circulation by contact with the tympanic membrane.[33] Another possible mechanism for the poisoning was suggested by Eden and Opland in the New England Journal of Medicine in 1982.[34] These authors suggested that since Shakespeare and Eustachio were contemporaries, Shakespeare's ever-absorbing intellect could very well have learned about Eustachio's re-discovery of the tube connecting the middle ear and the pharynx, first described by the Greeks in 500 B. C. Why couldn't a liquefied poison pass through a perforation in an eardrum, which must have been commonplace in medieval Europe, and enter the digestive system after draining into the throat?

Conclusion

This presentation of the neurological symptoms, signs, and diseases that appear in the canon of William Shakespeare will hopefully make the reader more aware of the richness of life's experiences from the point of view of that literary genius. The reader also should not be discouraged from further study of Shakespeare, simply because the author admonished, in the voice of Kent in *King Lear* (I, 1, 162): "Kill thy physician, and thy fee bestow upon the foul disease."

How current his ideas are, even though they were written four centuries ago! In our era, as we minister to our poly-intubated and ventilatory-assisted patients in intensive care units, and as we agonize over the appropriateness or inappropriateness of our life-prolonging activities, the Bard of Stratford-upon-Avon admonishes us, as did Kent in *King Lear* (V, 3, 314):

> Vex not his ghost. O, let him pass! He hates him
> That would upon the rack of this tough world
> Stretch him out longer.

And, similarly, our hospital ethics committees should keep in focus Angelo's admonishment, in *Measure For Measure* (II, 4, 165):

> ...he must not only die the death,
> But thy unkindness shall his death draw out
> To ling'ring sufferance...

Jorgensen observes in *The Comedy of Errors* that the two Dromio twin slaves are repeatedly beaten on the head, yet they always rebound. Shakespeare seems to be telling us that man's head is fundamentally ridiculous, not too important in any robust view of life. These blows, to our most pretentious part, serve as a universal leveling virtue! [35]

REFERENCES

All Shakespeare quotations are from *The Complete Pelican Shakespeare,* edited by Alfred Harbage, Penguin Books, N.Y., N.Y. 10022; 1981.

1. Owen, O.W. *The Medicine in Shakespeare.* Transactions of the Detroit Medical and Library Association 1893: 103.

2. Ehrlich, G.E. *Shakespeare's Rheumatology.* Ann. Rheum. Dis.1967; 26: 562-3.

3. Vest, W.E. *Shakespeare's Knowledge of Chest Diseases.* JAMA. 1950; 144: 1232-34.

4. Kaltreider, D.F. *Was the Bard an Obstetrician?* OB GYN. 1964; 24: 491-96.

5. Woods, A.H. *Syphilis in Shakespeare's Tragedy of Timon of Athens.* Am. J. Psychiat. 1934; 91: 95-107.

6. Goldbloom, A. *Shakespeare and Pediatrics*. Am. J. Dis. Child. 1936: 51: 653-65.

7. Simpson, R.R. *Shakespeare on the Ear, Nose and Throat*. J. Laryng. and Otol. 1950; 64: 342-52.

8. Vest, W.E. *William Shakespeare, Gerontologist*. Geriatrics. 1954; 9: 80-2.

9. Thomas, C.E. *Shakespeare and Teeth*. Brit. Dent. J. 1919; 90: 845.

10. Rubin, E.L. *Shakespeare and Radiography*. Radiography 1950; 16: 67-72.

11. Andreasen, N.J.C. *The Artist as Scientist: Psychiatric Diagnosis in Shakespeare's Tragedies*. JAMA. 1976; 235: 1868-72.

12. Colman, E.A.M. *Squibb Academic Lecture: Shakespeare and DSM-III*. Austral. And N. Zeal. J. Psychiat. 1986; 20: 30-36.

13. Edgar, II. *Shakespeare*, Medicine and Psychiatry. New York: Philosophical Library, 1970.

14. Simpson, R.R. *Shakespeare and Medicine*. Edinburgh: E. and S. Livingston Ltd.,1959.

15. *Encyclopedia Britannica Micropedia* vol. 19. Chicago, IL. 1974:363.

16. Richardson, B.W. *Shakespere* {sic} and the Pia Mater. Lancet 1888: 757-58.

17. Laurentius, A. *A Discourse of the Preservation of Sight; of Melanchol- like Diseases; of Rheumes, and of Old Age*. Transl. by Richard Surphlet (1599). Shakespeare Assoc. Facsimile No. 15: 79.

18. Schmidt, A. *Shakespeare Lexicon and Quotation Dictionary*. Third Edition revised and Enlarged by George Sarrazin. New York: Dover Publications, 1971.

19. Seward, D. *Richard III, England's Black Legend*. New York: FranklinWatts, Inc., 1984: 22.

20. Nicoll, A., Nicoll, J. *Holinshed's Chronicle as Used in Shakespeare's Plays*. London: J. M. Dent and Sons, Ltd., 1927:151.

21. Adler, J.J. *Did Falstaff Have the Sleep-Apnea Syndrome?* NEJM 1983; 308: 404.

22. Junghans, R.P. *Falstaff Was Drunker Than He Was Fat*. NEJM 1983; 308:1483.

23. Charcot, J.M. *Clinical Lectures on the Diseases of the Nervous System*. Vol. III. The Classics of Neurology and Neurosurgery Library. Birmingham, AL: Gryphon Editions, LTD., 1985: 292.

24. Schenck, CH., Bundlie, SR. et al. *Chronic Behavioral Disorders of Human-REM Sleep: A New Category of Parasomnia*. Sleep 1986; 9:293-308.

25. Price, G.E. *William Shakespeare as a Neuropsychiatrist*. Ann. Med. Hist. 1928; 10: 159.

26. Cuffe, H. *Differences of the Ages of Man's Life*. London, 1607.

27. Draper, J.W. *Shakespeare's Attitude Towards Old Age*. J. Gerontology, 1946; 6:118-26.

28. Personal Communication.

29. Summerskill, W.H.J. *Aguecheek's Disease*. *Lancet*, 1955; 2: 288.

30. Boyd, W. *A Textbook of Pathology*. Philadelphia: Lea and Febiger, 1961:533.

31. Cecil, R. *Textbook of Medicine*. Philadelphia: W. B. Saunders Co. 1982: 1578.

32. Tabor, E. *Plant Poisons in Shakespeare*. Economic Botany 1970; 24: 81-94.

33. Macht, D.I. *Physiological and Pharmacological Appreciation of Hamlet, Act I, Scene V, Lines 59-73*. Bull. Hist. of Med. 1949; 23: 2.

34. Eden, A.R. And Opland, J. *Bartolommeo Eustachio's De Auditus Organis and the Unique Murder Plot in Shakespeare's Hamlet*. NEJM 1982; 307: 259-61.

35. Jorgensen, PA. *Introduction to the Comedy of Errors*. In: Harbage, A., Ed. The Complete Pelican Shakespeare: The Comedies and the Romances. New York: Penguin Books, 1969: 12.

David C. Frauman, PhD, is a Clinical Associate Professor in psychiatry at the Indiana School of Medicine in Indianapolis where he lectures on the theory and practice of analytic self psychology. He also has a private practice in clinical psychology in Indianapolis.

Dr. Frauman has been studying the psychology of creativity, art, and artists for twenty years and has presented at numerous regional and national conferences on these topics. Some of the artists he has researched in depth include Vincent Van Gogh, Paul Gauguin, Pablo Picasso, Freda Kahlo, Maynard Dixon, and Dorothea Lange.

Believing that if one wants to understand creativity at any depth, one needs to actually be involved in creative work, Dr. Frauman is active in his community as a singer, songwriter, and guitarist. Among his recent projects, he wrote the music and lyrics to a locally-produced play entitled Remember Who Made You, a drama about the challenges of being both gay and Christian. This play has been performed for decidedly appreciative audiences at theaters and churches in several states in the Midwest.

His current research interests include an examination of the possible connections between creativity and narcissism and of the role of artistic pursuits in the maintenance and survival of the self.

*I have always tried to hide my efforts and wished
my works to have the light joyousness of springtime,
which never lets anyone suspect the labors it has cost.*

– Henri Matisse

Van Gogh and Gauguin: The Self Psychology of Creativity

By David C. Frauman, PhD

In the fall of 1888, two artists, Vincent van Gogh and Paul Gauguin, lived and worked together in Arles, a town in the south of France. There have been several books written about this collaboration, and The Art Institute of Chicago and The Van Gogh Museum in Amsterdam mounted a major exhibit to display the works created during the nine weeks the two artists spent together in Arles. Although they came together with differing expectations and needs, both artists envisioned it as a time of mutual benefit, where they could stimulate each other creatively and share models and expenses. They thought that Arles would be an environment conducive to their art. Although it started with much promise, it ended tragically with the well-known incident of Van Gogh cutting off his ear, and the two artists never saw each other again. Van Gogh's mental health continued to deteriorate afterward, and he committed suicide a year and a half later.

Although much has been written about the artists' collaboration, something seemed to be missing in the explanations of what happened in Arles. My in-depth focus will explain what happened through the lens of psychoanalytic psychology. In particular, I will focus on how the interaction between the two artists enhanced orimpeded their creativity. I hope also to describe how the relationship with Gauguin was both a stimulus for great art in Van Gogh and a catalyst for his destruction. In order to better understand the artists, I will briefly examine their early histories.

Van Gogh's Early Life

Vincent van Gogh was an extremely complex person, and over the years, clinicians have diagnosed him with more than one hundred and seventy medical and psychiatric illnesses. Nearly everyone agrees that he was a person with extreme needs that were seldom met. He had the misfortune of being born one year to the day after a still-born brother, also named Vincent. His mother was in a deep depression when he was born, still grieving over the first infant's death. She seemed to have been a cold and distant person even at her best. Given her depression and personality, it was likely that she had little connection with her son when he was an infant and toddler. I also suspect that she compared him to the stillborn Vincent who would have been seen as the perfect child, never having lived long enough to disappoint. The boy may have felt unconsciously that he could never measure up to the other or that he had some basic flaw that interfered with his mother's ability to love him. This phenomenon is often referred to as "the survival child syndrome."

As an adolescent, Vincent turned from his mother to his father for attention. The senior Van Gogh was a stern and rigid minister in a Dutch Protestant Church. Attempting to connect with him, Vincent became interested in religion and began to study for the ministry, initially gaining his father's approval. However, he took religious self-sacrifice, a tenet of the religion, to the extreme and became almost masochistic. He slept without blankets, gave away his clothing, and wanted to live in poverty like the parishioners he served. This fanaticism eventually angered his father who then disowned him. In turn, Vincent became disillusioned with religion and, by association, with his father.

Vincent became closer to Theo, his younger brother, who worked in a relative's art gallery. Through Theo, he was exposed to art and began painting. He poured his emotions onto the canvas, and Theo was encouraging of his work. Vincent began to see himself as an artist and found some self-validation in his painting. During this time, he began to forge his own identity separate from his parents.

He announced that he was no longer a Van Gogh, and began signing his art as simply "Vincent."

Gauguin's Early Life

Paul Gauguin grew up physically and emotionally close to his mother. His father died when Paul was one year old. His mother felt she should have been part of the Spanish-Peruvian aristocracy. She did, in fact, have some Peruvian blood but was only a distant relative to nobility. She traveled to Peru with her son and then returned to Paris in search of her fortune, believing it was due to her. The fortune never materialized, and she felt cheated that she had to live dependently on relatives. Her son also had this sense of importance, of feeling part of the aristocracy as well as the bitterness of being denied the title and money that he felt should be his. He was left with the narcissism of feeling he should be important and wealthy, but this never materialized.

Gauguin was close to his mother as a child, but as an adolescent, he developed hypermasculine and rebellious attitudes and behaviors. I am reminded of Alfred Adler and his idea of "masculine protest." The masculine protest refers to a boy who identifies strongly with his mother as a youngster but then feels threatened and emasculated as an adolescent. The adolescent protests strongly against a feminine identity and swings the other way, taking on an extreme masculine identity to compensate. Gauguin saw himself as very sexual and attractive to women.

As a young adult, Gauguin spent five years traveling the world with the French navy and merchant marine. He married a Dutch woman, Metta Gad, and had five children with her. He actually spent little time with his wife and family, preferring to travel to exotic locations where he would paint.

Gauguin's narcissism left him with a great need for admiration. He saw himself as a teacher and mentor to young artists, and he often had one as a companion on these painting trips. The trips would frequently end disastrously for Gauguin and his acolyte because of

Gauguin's overreaching optimism. Often he and his protégé would return to Paris sick and destitute, but these adventures did not seem to harm the relationships significantly.

Self Psychology Theory

I want to introduce some psychological theory at this point to help structure my remarks. Heinz Kohut's self psychology is a theory that can help to organize the events as they occurred and can make them easier to understand. Self psychology has to do with a person's subjective feelings about himself. These feelings are greatly influenced by the person's experiences with important people in his life, called selfobjects. Selfobjects are those persons who are experienced as helping the self feel vigorous and alive. If a person's experience with selfobjects, especially early in life, is generally positive and adequate, then the person has a reasonably cohesive and resilient self, and can withstand the disappointments and reversals of life. In contrast, if a person's experience with selfobjects is generally inconsistent or negative, then the person remains vulnerable to depression or fragmentation when disappointments arise. An example of this, as I will demonstrate, is Vincent van Gogh. Selfobject needs are only partly conscious and they vary in intensity from slight to intense. An example of slight selfobject neediness would be needing the presence of someone to feel acceptable about one's self. Almost everyone has experiences like this at times. An example of an intense selfobject need would be a feeling of frantic desperation if the needed selfobject were not available. Most stalkers are probably in this group. As we will see, Vincent is of this latter type. Kohut spoke of two general types of selfobject experience: mirroring selfobject experience and idealizing selfobject experience.

Mirroring Selfobject Experience

The mirroring selfobject experience is the feeling that one is the "apple of someone's eye." It is feeling valued by the attention of someone else. When this selfobject experience goes well, the person has stable self-esteem and ambition.

The mirroring selfobject experience can go awry, however. With Vincent, we can suppose that there was insufficient mirroring. Remember that Vincent's mother was depressed and unavailable when he was born, and her depression probably made it difficult for her to attend to Vincent and to value him.

When there is a failure of one type of selfobject experience, the child often intensifies his search for the other type of selfobject experience in an attempt to bolster his fragile self-regard. Vincent most likely gave up trying to be mirrored and instead felt that his self-esteem could be better served through finding selfobjects he could idealize. This leads us to the second type of selfobject experience.

Idealizing Selfobject Experience

The idealizing selfobject experience is feeling enlivened and enhanced because you can look up to someone, admire him or her, be a part of that person's perfection and to feel a part of something good and strong. When there is adequate idealizing selfobject experience, the person becomes an adult with adequate self-esteem as well as inspirational values and ideals.

Unfortunately for Vincent, his lack of mirroring was so pervasive and his need to idealize so all-consuming that he spent a lifetime searching for and attaching himself to idealizable figures and causes. Remember that he tried to idealize his father, religion, self-sacrifice, and finally art. Problems can also occur with this idealization experience. The idealized person can fail. For example, Vincent tried to idealize his father, but when his was rejected, his father was no longer an idealizable selfobject. The idealized person can also become uncomfortable with the demands placed upon him, and later we shall see that this was the case for Gauguin.

Vincent's need to idealize was so pervasive and intense that I would call him an ideal-hungry personality. This personality can only feel good about himself when he can find someone to look up to and believe in. The ideal-hungry personality tends to be drawn to charismatic figures throughout his life. For Vincent, this became Gauguin.

Problems with Mirroring

Sometimes there is not a problem with the amount of mirroring but with the type of mirroring. Think of the mirror as distorted in some way. When mirroring is distorted, it is typically in the service of what the parent wants or needs. Instead of reflecting and approving the child's independent and vigorous self, the parent mirrors behaviors that keep the child dependent or that confirm the parent's values. When mirroring is faulty, the child often feels a heightened need for appropriate mirroring and an intensified need for approval and praise.

This is apparently what happened to Gauguin. Although his mother doted on him, it is probable that her mirroring was faulty in some way, resulting in Gauguin's great and unrealistic need for admiration, approval and praise. A mirror-hungry personality is someone who feels good about himself only when he is being actively admired and praised. This is emblematic of Gauguin's life. Remember that he felt he should be respected as a member of the aristocracy and that he saw himself as attractive and irresistible to women. He often traveled with a young painter who would admire him and praise his work, and he pursued and lived with much younger women, often in their teens. This occurred in Paris, Pont Aven in Brittany, and during his stays in Tahiti. In Tahiti, he built his "maison de jouir," his house of pleasure, and lived there for several years with a number of adoring and sexually willing young girls. They and their families considered it an honor for the girls to live with Gauguin, a sophisticated Frenchman. He later had difficulties with the local authorities that drove him from Tahiti to one of the more remote Marquesas Islands.

Vincent and Gauguin Meet

Vincent and Gauguin began their relationship in Paris in 1887. They probably met in the art gallery where Theo worked, the Paris branch of the family's art business. Vincent was living with Theo who was showing some of Gauguin's work in the gallery. Gauguin, in his narcissism, claimed to be a better artist than the others whose works were being displayed, and his self-confidence probably made

154

him impressive. Vincent was effusive in his praise of Gauguin, saying that he was "a great painter." We already can see the beginnings of Vincent's idealization of him. The two artists decided to trade paintings, and Gauguin mentioned that he liked those of sunflowers he received in the exchange.

The two artists went their separate ways after Paris. Gauguin left for Brittany where he could live cheaply and could paint the Bretons in their native dress. Vincent left for Arles where it was warmer and where he could be away from the competitive Paris art scene. Theo was supporting Vincent financially by this time with a monthly stipend. The two artists continued to exchange letters and paintings, and they agreed to exchange self-portraits.

Vincent's self-portrait depicted him as a Buddhist monk, symbolic of his desire to be a follower and to look up to someone strong and wise. In his self-portrait, Gauguin depicted himself as Jean Val Jean, the misunderstood hero of Victor Hugo's novel, *Les Miserables*. Gauguin saw himself in this painting as unappreciated and misunderstood. This is symbolic of his need for admiration and his frustration when this need was unmet.

The Studio of the South

While he was in Arles, Vincent developed an ambitious idea to establish the "Studio of the South." His plan was to have an artists' cooperative in Arles, a commune for several artists to live and work together. The idea was for the artists to share expenses and to stimulate each other creatively. Part of the plan was to have Theo sell the paintings in Paris. An important element of Vincent's idea was that Gauguin would come to Arles and be the leader of the commune and the artists would be able to learn from him.

Gauguin's response to the invitation was lukewarm, but Vincent's need was so strong that he was undeterred in his attempts to create the Studio of the South. He rented a house near the railway station, which he called the "Yellow House," where the commune was to be located. The house had a studio and a kitchen on the first floor and two bedrooms on a second floor. Convinced that Gauguin would come, Vincent prepared a bedroom for him and tried to make it cheery and attractive. Knowing that Gauguin liked the sunflower paintings, he placed some on the wall.

Vincent also bought thirteen chairs for the Yellow House: twelve plain stiff masculine looking ones, and one curvaceous tufted feminine one. The twelve plain ones were to be for the artists coming to the commune; the fancy chair was to be Gauguin's. The Christian symbolism is evident here: twelve disciples and one Christ figure in Gauguin. Once again, Vincent is creating a highly idealizable selfobject figure in Gauguin as Christ. With Vincent's chair stern and masculine and Gauguin's chair softly padded and feminine, it suggests a tacit homoeroticism in Vincent's mind.

Notice the elaborate fantasy that Vincent created. No one, especially Gauguin, had agreed to come to Arles, yet Vincent already had furnished a house in preparation for everyone's arrival. In self-psychological terms, Vincent had created: 1) an idealizable selfobject in Gauguin, the Christ figure, and 2) an idealizable symbol, the Studio of the South, where he could be part of something admirable and grand. In other words, Vincent had created a fantasy that he could idealize and that he unconsciously hoped would heal him.

Vincent's Creative Period

Vincent began an extremely creative period, from February to October of 1888, as he prepared for Gauguin's arrival. He completed over two hundred paintings and over one hundred drawings in these eight months, sometimes completing one or two paintings a day. (Compare this to Gauguin's usual pattern of spending a week or more on one painting.) Most critics feel that this period is Vincent's best work. He wrote to Theo that he had hit the "high yellow note" and was pleased with the outcome of his work. Yellow was always Vincent's favorite color, and by comparing himself to a singer hitting a difficult high note, he was also implying that this was his best work and that he was hitting his stride as an artist.

Why would Vincent have this masterful creative outburst? His creativity was fueled by the promise that his dreams would come true, that the Studio of the South would happen, and that he would be a part of it. Vincent was enlivened by the idea that Gauguin would also come to Arles to assume his place as leader of the commune. In self-psychological terms, Vincent had hoped that his need to idealize would not be frustrated as it had been in the past. Because of this hope and of a transcendent feeling of finally belonging to something good and grand, Vincent's creativity flourished. This was the happiest time in his life and, not coincidentally, it was the most prodigious. It was a halcyon time when Vincent could bask in the feeling that soon his plans and dreams would come to fruition. This was before Gauguin actually arrived and before disillusionment set in. Gauguin was not going to be all that Vincent imagined.

Gauguin Arrives in Arles

In October 1888, after Theo agreed to pay him a monthly stipend, Gauguin arrived in Arles. The two artists probably could not have had more differing expectations. For Gauguin, arriving in Arles meant that he could have a steady income through Theo's stipend. Gauguin also wanted to do a favor for him because Theo was selling some of his paintings in Paris. Undoubtedly Gauguin wanted a loyal and appreciative companion, and he expected Vincent to be like the young artists who had traveled with him. In short, Gauguin expected Vincent would continue to mirror him.

By contrast, Vincent's expectations were extremely high. He saw this meeting as the beginning of a utopian artists' colony with Gauguin as the leader. Vincent apparently viewed Gauguin's coming to Arles as the turning point for his whole life. He thought of it as the place and the time when his needs to be part of something grand and noble and his need to admire a perfect person (Vincent's selfobject needs) would be met completely and gratifyingly. Vincent wrote to Theo after Gauguin's arrival that the "artistic brotherhood will be more lasting than ourselves, and Gauguin will stay with us always."

It was almost as if Vincent were talking about a marriage; his expectations were so overreaching that he was expecting commitment and connection for the rest of his life.

The Artists Live Together

As further demonstration of Vincent's soaring needs, he immediately demanded Gauguin's time and attention. Gauguin was accustomed to privacy, but Vincent set up the bedrooms so that Gauguin had none. In Vincent's need to idealize, he had arranged the bedrooms to guarantee contact. I mentioned that there were two bedrooms on the upper floor of the Yellow House; Vincent arranged it so that Gauguin had to walk through Vincent's room on the way to his own. He would hear Gauguin come in late at night, wake up, and insist on talking to him about philosophy and other topics. Vincent was well read in religion, art, philosophy and literature. Because he was hungry for intellectual stimulation, he liked to debate these topics with Gauguin. Note that it was a form of idealization to be able to argue with Gauguin because Vincent saw him as all-knowing. Gauguin was accustomed to being attended to and listened to by a rapt listener, but Vincent did not defer to him. Gauguin wrote to Theo that he was reduced to agreeing with Vincent to silence him. For Gauguin, it was irritating not to receive the adulation he needed and expected. I mentioned how the idealized person can feel overwhelmed by the demands of the idealizing person, and I suspect that Gauguin was not only irritated but also shocked by Vincent's demands.

The two artists were of differing temperaments and not terribly compatible. Vincent liked to work quickly and worked all the time, whereas Gauguin worked leisurely and deliberately. Vincent was disorganized and made a mess of their finances and cooking; Gauguin was more organized and reluctantly took over the budget and meals. Gauguin liked to go out to the bars and brothels at night, and Vincent did not care for them. True to his hypermasculine image, Gauguin was a success with the women of Arles. Vincent wrote to Theo that "although Gauguin is married, he doesn't act married."

Even in the midst of these conflicts, Vincent remained desperate to make the Studio of the South work. After the two artists had an argument, Gauguin wrote to Theo: "Vincent and I can absolutely not live together without trouble because of our temperamental incompatibility." Vincent wrote to Theo about the same incident: "Gauguin was a little out of sorts with the good town of Arles, the little Yellow House where we work, and especially with me." You can see how Vincent desperately needed the relationship to work and so he minimized the conflict. Vincent's selfobject needs were so great that he could not allow himself to recognize the conflict and was in denial about it.

Although the selfobject needs of both artists were pressing, they were able to form a working relationship. They shared models and went on painting excursions together. Their styles began to show similarities, indicating they were beginning to influence each other. For example, Gauguin tried to paint from nature using thick coats of paint as Vincent had suggested. Vincent attempted to paint from imagination with thin coats of paint as Gauguin had advised.

Conflict

Unfortunately, in December of 1888, the conflicts and tensions between the artists escalated. It rained the majority of the time, confining the artists in the Yellow House even more. Vincent's manic work schedule made Gauguin uncomfortable, and the two artists started arguing about philosophy and what constituted good art. Gauguin began to realize that he would not receive the mirroring he expected and started hinting that he would go back to Paris. Vincent sensed that his needed idealized selfobject was threatening to leave so he became more intrusive and persistent in trying to convince Gauguin to stay in Arles.

The situation came to a head around Christmas time. On the evening of December 23, after an argument in the Yellow House, Gauguin stormed out into the snow. Vincent followed with a knife in his hand and confronted him on the street. Gauguin acknowledged that he intended to leave Arles. Vincent became agitated and tore off a piece of the newspaper he was carrying. He placed the newspaper fragment in Gauguin's hand. The piece of newspaper read: "The murderer took flight." Gauguin was alarmed by Vincent's agitation, did not return to the Yellow House, and spent the night in a hotel.

The next day, Gauguin returned and found a crowd gathered outside. He inquired and was told that Vincent had cut off part of his ear with a razor and was in his bed in a pool of blood. Gauguin avoided seeing him and returned to his hotel. Vincent was taken to the local hospital.

On December 25, Christmas Day, Theo arrived from Paris to visit his brother in the hospital. Vincent called repeatedly and desperately for Gauguin to visit him. Once again, Gauguin avoided him and left for Paris on the evening train. The two artists never saw each other again.

Vincent's Psychology

In Vincent's mind, he created the precise situation that would meet his needs and allow him to flourish. He did all he humanly could to make this a reality. The Studio of the South was the situation that would fill his needs and allow him to paint. Gauguin's departure and refusal to participate in the experience was probably the worst thing that could have happened to Vincent. I am sure that he saw Gauguin as a murderer because he had killed Vincent's dream. This explains the writing on the newspaper fragment that Vincent had given Gauguin. For Vincent, the situation was probably intolerable. His fragile sense of self depended totally upon the fabrication of an idealized utopian situation; that is, he needed the Studio of the South and a firm sense of belonging to it.

Kohut noted that when idealized selfobject needs are intense and when there is a massive and precipitous de-idealization of the selfobject, the core of the personality—what Kohut calls the nuclear self—can fragment, resulting in a pervasive decompensation and a resultant psychosis. This is apparently what happened to Vincent.

He could no longer maintain the illusion that he would be saved by merging with an ideal. The glue that held his self together, his idealization, had failed. He became psychotic-agitated, incoherent, and self-mutilating. Vincent was coherent enough to call for Gauguin but decompensated to the point of self-mutilation. As to why he focused on his ear as the offending part, I can only speculate: Perhaps he did not want to hear Gauguin's refusal to stay in Arles; Perhaps he turned his rage toward himself and, in an act of displaced self castration, he cut off part of his ear. We do know that he placed the ear fragment in a box and intended to give it to Rachel, one of the town prostitutes. Perhaps he was renouncing his masculinity as well as castrating himself.

Gauguin's Psychology

Gauguin was probably overwhelmed and suffocated by the primitiveness and desperation of Vincent's needs. He undoubtedly felt that he had to leave Arles to save himself and to avoid being engulfed by Vincent's neediness. Gauguin was not as regressed as Vincent was so he did not deteriorate to the point of psychosis. Gauguin was able to leave an untenable situation. He undoubtedly felt victimized when he did not receive the mirroring from Vincent that he felt deserved; Gauguin was angry because Vincent had failed him.

Aftermath

After his release from the hospital, Vincent returned to the Yellow House and began painting again. He painted the themes that he and Gauguin had begun before the incident. Reworking these old themes seemed to stabilize him and perhaps helped him feel close to Gauguin again. This may have negated his fear that Gauguin would be gone forever. The work may have taken Vincent back in time and revived memories of when the fantasy of Gauguin's continued presence was alive. In fact, self-psychological theory would predict that Vincent would try to preserve his needed fantasy and ignore facts that ran counter to it.

Vincent and Gauguin continued to write and Vincent pleaded with him to return. In his letters, Vincent suggested that they resume their old relationship. This probably helped him to deny that his fantasy was over and to preserve his needed idealized relationship. Three months after Gauguin left, Vincent began acting strangely, and the neighbors petitioned to have him committed to an asylum outside of Arles. The Yellow House was closed at that time.

A year later, Vincent moved to a hospital near Paris to be closer to Theo. Around this time, Vincent received word that his brother was going to be a father. A son was born and he was named Vincent. Theo started his own business as an independent art dealer. I wonder if this was yet another abandonment for Vincent. Theo had been functioning quietly and enduringly in the background as a self-object for Vincent. He had been encouraging of Vincent's art, silently mirroring him. Perhaps at this time, Vincent realized that Theo would have less time and attention for him. A year and a half after Gauguin left Arles, Vincent walked into a cornfield outside the hospital and shot himself in the chest. He died two days later with Theo by his side. Gauguin did not come to see him or to attend his funeral. In fact, Gauguin said to a friend that "Vincent was better off out of his misery."

What was the aftermath for Gauguin? Unfortunately for him, Theo died only six months after Vincent, and Gauguin's paintings did not sell without Theo to promote them. When Gauguin heard that a fellow painter was planning an exhibit of Vincent's work, he tried to dissuade him. Gauguin certainly had a history of feeling misunderstood and under-appreciated, and it must have been galling to him that Vincent was beginning to receive posthumous acclaim.

Gauguin perceived himself as a learned teacher. He denied that Vincent influenced him and said that Vincent was "floundering around in Arles until I got there." In addition to the reality that this was not true, I think that Vincent had a significant impact on Gauguin. A ceramic piece that Gauguin completed shortly after his time in Arles was a self-portrait mug, and, interestingly, the face had no ears, and it looked like blood was running down from where ears would be. The mug suggested that Gauguin was the one who was injured in Arles and that Vincent was the victimizer. There were also subtle changes in Gauguin's artwork that indicated Vincent's influence. For one, Gauguin began to use more yellow, Vincent's favorite color, in his paintings. Secondly, he began to paint sunflowers, Vincent's major theme, when he had not painted sunflowers prior to his association with Vincent.

Why would Gauguin make these subtle nods to Vincent? Although Vincent could not ultimately give Gauguin the praise and adulation that he required, I am sure that Gauguin remembered and appreciated the mirroring that he did receive from Vincent when the artists were together in Arles. Gauguin died in the Marquesas Islands in 1903, thirteen years after Vincent's death. His death was probably a suicide, as a vial of arsenic (a tincture he was taking as treatment for his syphilis) was found near his outstretched hand.

Conclusions

Because of his history of faulty and disappointing selfobject experiences, Vincent was left with an extreme need to find sustaining selfobjects, particularly ones he could idealize. His fantasy of the Studio of the South with Gauguin as its leader provided him with the longed-for idealizable selfobject and allowed his creativity to flourish. The fantasy (that the need to idealize will not be frustrated) strengthens the self, allows for hope and purpose to emerge, and facilitates self-expression. Vincent's realization (that once more his longings would be dashed) became a massive and abrupt de-idealization, and led to despair and suicide.

For Gauguin, I believe that he hoped Vincent would be an admiring and appreciative companion, a longed-for mirroring selfobject. Initially, Vincent may have fulfilled that need for Gauguin, but as Vincent's idealizing selfobject needs became more primitive and extreme, they threatened to engulf Gauguin, and Gauguin had to leave to save himself, angry that his needs for mirroring were not fulfilled.

What conclusions about creativity in general can be drawn from the study of these two artists? First, this study suggests that creativity needs nurturing to emerge. By nurturing, I mean that there needs to be a milieu of selfobject responsiveness around the artist for creativity to flourish. Vincent is an example of this. He had much to say artistically, but he only reached the apotheosis of his art when he felt that his selfobject needs would be satisfied.

Secondly, the muse that some artists speak of as a source of inspiration seems to be closely related to the selfobject. The muse is someone who does not necessarily participate in the creation of art but whose presence is necessary for the artist to feel inspired. This is very similar to the function of the selfobject as I have tried to explain it.

The sunflower was one of Vincent's favorite themes and he painted them more than a dozen times. It is an amazing plant in that the seed head moves throughout the day, turning in order to face the sun squarely as the light moves across the sky. This is symbolic of Vincent's struggle: As long as he could look up to an idealizable person or thing, he could flourish. When he could no longer see that idealizable selfobject, he perished.

REFERENCES

Druick, D. W., and Zegers, P. K. (2001). *Van Gogh and Gauguin*: The Studio of the South. New York: Thames and Hudson.

Metzger, R., and Walther, I. F. (1998). *Vincent Van Gogh*. New York: Taschen.

Nagera, H. (1967). *Vincent Van Gogh, a Psychological Study*. New York: International Universities Press.

Silverman, D. (2000). *Van Gogh and Gauguin: The Search for Sacred Art*. New York: Knopf.

Louis A. Gamino, PhD, ABPP, is a Diplomate in Clinical Psychology through the American Board of Professional Psychology. He has been on staff with the Scott & White Clinic/Hospital in Temple, Texas since obtaining his doctorate from the University of Kansas in 1980. In addition to a clinical practice specializing in treatment of bereavement-related problems, Dr. Gamino is an Associate Professor who teaches about death and dying at the Texas A & M Health Science Center College of Medicine. Together with Ann Cooney, he is the author of When Your Baby Dies Through Miscarriage or Stillbirth (Augsburg Fortress, 2002). He is currently writing a textbook dealing with ethical practice of grief counseling. He is former Editor of The Forum, the official (quarterly) publication of the Association for Death Education and Counseling (ADEC) and the 2008 recipient of ADEC's Clinical Practice Award given in recognition of demonstrated excellence in care of the bereaved and the dying. Dr. Gamino has published several articles based on his empirical research on the phenomenology of grieving, from which he is developing a model of adaptive bereavement. He has presented at Creativity and Madness conferences on Mark Rothko and Kathe Kollwitz, and has previously authored a chapter on Kollwitz in Sandra Bertman's Grief and the Healing Arts: Creativity as Therapy (Baywood, 1999)

> *The meaning of a word to me is not*
> *as exact as the meaning of a color.*
>
> *Georgia O'Keeffe*

MARK ROTHKO: A CASE STUDY IN SUICIDE

LOUIS A. GAMINO, PhD

Mark Rothko (1903-1970) was one of the most recognizable American painters of the twentieth century. As a member of the New York School of Abstract Expressionism, Rothko was active from the 1930's until his death. His work evolved from the representational to the symbolic to the abstract as he sought to find purer ways of communicating his message about universal human emotions. Rothko's huge floating rectangles of saturated color constitute a visual signature not easily forgotten by even the casual observer. Yet, over the course of time, the palette of brilliant color evident during the height of his career devolved into a restricted range of somber and severe hues by the time he took his life. Rothko's suicide left many unanswered questions regarding the relationship between his life, his work and his mental health.

Rothko was psychiatrically troubled and suffered from depression and alcoholism. Personally, he was difficult and arrogant. Even one of Rothko's most sympathetic biographers, Dore Ashton, acknowledged that he was a highly complex individual whose "...nature revealed itself reluctantly, even to friends, and they often had totally opposite reactions." He could be charming, engaging, even beguiling in his romantic sentimentality, while at other times he was sullen, irascible and defensive. Rothko brooded in an angry loneliness and languished in a conviction that he was fundamentally misunderstood and unappreciated. Klepser and Weinberg (in Suicide and Life-Threatening Behavior) agreed that Rothko's medical care was undermined by his obstinate non-compliance resulting in his physicians bickering and competing rather than cooperating.

This chapter is a psychological inquiry into the life and death of Mark Rothko as an idiographic case study that exemplifies the nomothetic relationship between creativity and suicide. Several major biographies (by Ashton, Barnes, Breslin, Seldes, Stewart, and Waldman) were consulted to develop this synopsis. My objective is to present the evolution of Rothko's artistic work in the context of his personal history, the sociopolitical era in which he lived and worked, and the nature of his psychiatric problems that contributed to his suicide in 1970.

Developmental History

He was born Marcus Rothkowitz on September 25, 1903, in Dvinsk, Russia (part of modern day Latvia). He was the youngest child of four born to Jewish parents who were ardent Zionists and feared for their lives under the persecution of the Russian Czar. His father Jacob, a pharmacist, immigrated to the United States in 1910 joined his brother, a clothier, in Portland, Oregon. Jacob sent first for his older sons who were nearing conscription age, while Marcus, his sister and his mother came later in 1913.

Shortly after arriving in Oregon at age ten, Marcus' father died, leaving the family in economic hardship. Young Marcus grieved the loss for years afterward. As a poor, fatherless immigrant, he did not always have enough to eat and had to work at jobs, including delivering newspapers, to help support the family. He gravitated to the local Jewish community center where he distinguished himself as a debater defending leftist labor causes such as the Russian revolution. After completing high school in only three years, he won a scholarship to Yale University in New Haven, Connecticut, in 1921.

A combination of Yale's subvert anti-Semitism and Rothko's natural disaffection with conformity and conventional pedagogy led him to drop out after his sophomore year. In 1923, he went to New York City, as he described in a letter to a friend, "...to wander around, bum about, starve a bit." At age twenty-one, he enrolled in the Art Students League and began his lifelong work of painting. By 1929, he had taken a part-time position as art teacher at the Center Academy of the Brooklyn Jewish Center.

In 1932, he married for the first time, impulsively, to Edith Sacher, a sculptor and jewelry designer who came from a business background. She was pragmatic and pushed for Rothko to join her thriving jewelry business. He preferred to remain a melancholy Bohemian who just wanted to be taken seriously as a painter.

1930's: Social Realism

Influenced initially by German Expressionists and by radically leftist political views, Rothko's early works focused on a critical commentary of the isolation and dehumanizing effects of living in densely populated urban centers. Paintings from this early phase of his career included elongated figures in postures of alienation and aloneness, existing in a tension-filled dynamic with the architectural forms, such as cityscapes and subway interiors, that entrap them. "Underground Fantasy" (circa 1940) is a good example of this genre (Figure 1). For Rothko, powerlessness, immobility and incommunicability characterized one's existential position in the modern world following the Industrial Revolution, leaving one utterly alone to confront the prospect of mortality.

In the 1930's, Europe experienced pre-war tensions and the United States grappled with an economic depression. The Works Progress Administration (WPA) instituted a Federal Art Project to produce murals and paintings for public buildings and Rothko was one of the artists employed. Ever the activist, his evenings consisted of drinking and debating philosophy at various popular artists' haunts in Greenwich Village. Within this camaraderie, Rothko emboldened his position as an iconoclast and evolved to the next era in his career.

Early 1940's: Mythic Period

Having obtained his citizenship papers, in 1940 he decided to shorten his name from Marcus Rothkowitz to Mark Rothko and signed his works as such thereafter.

With the world engulfed in war, Rothko searched for universal truths about the human condition and was drawn to themes of frailty, destruction and doom. He became fascinated with archetypal images from Greco-Roman myths, and this led him to a new type of composition using stratified combinations of heads and limbs, both animal and human, resulting in hybrid, allegorical figures. The influence of the Surrealists was also visible in his work such as the piece from 1944 entitled "Hierarchical Birds" (Figure 2).

New York Times art critic Edward Alden Jewell challenged Rothko by declaring himself befuddled by these mythical-allegorical works exhibited in the annual Federation of Modern Painters and Sculptors Show in 1943. Rothko eagerly seized the bait and, together with fellow exhibitor and intimate Adolph Gottlieb, responded with a tart letter outlining five key points of their artistic philosophy. The Times published their letter on June 13 of that year.

1. To us art is an adventure into an unknown world, which can be explored only by those willing to take risks.

2. This world of the imagination is fancy-free and violently opposed to common sense.

3. It is our function as artists to make the spectator see the world our way--not his.

4. We favor the simple expression of the complex thought. We are for the large shape because it has the impact of the unequivocal. We wish to reassert the picture plane. We are for flat forms because they destroy illusion and reveal truth.

5. It is a widely accepted notion among painters that it does not matter what one paints as long as it is well painted. This is the essence of academicism. There is no such thing as good painting about nothing. We assert that the subject is crucial and only that subject matter is valid which is tragic and timeless. That is why we profess spiritual kinship with primitive and archaic art.

These five points, considered an aesthetic manifesto of Abstract Expressionism, were the heady vision and uncompromising philosophy of the members of the New York School who were later dubbed "The Irascibles" from an infamous group photograph by Nina Leen that ran in Life magazine on January 15, 1951.

In 1944, Edith divorced Rothko. Their marriage foundered over the untenable conflict between his temperamental autonomy and her entrepreneurial rejection of the "starving artist" lifestyle. Shortly thereafter, Rothko met and married his second wife, Mary Alice "Mell" Beistle, an illustrator of children's books. "Slow Swirl by the Edge of the Sea", painted in 1944, is a period piece of their courtship, a shimmering, vibrant surreal rendition of male and female energy sources connecting in an archetypal mating ceremony (Figure 3).

Late 1940's: Transition and Multi-forms

Now in his 40's, Rothko evolved toward totally abstract painting, devoid of any figural or representational elements. He stopped titling his paintings and simply assigned them numbers. He described his progression as "...toward clarity: toward the elimination of all obstacles between the painter and the idea, and between the idea and the observer." This elaborated a previous statement (by Rothko and Gottlieb) on why abstract paintings cannot be explained: "[The] explanation must come out of a consummated experience between picture and onlooker. The appreciation of art is a true marriage of minds. And in art, as in marriage, lack of consummation is ground for annulment."

Rothko's personal life hit major turmoil in 1948 with the death of his mother. He became depressed and his output dramatically declined. In 1949, the art school started by Rothko and his compatriots failed. This frustration of generativity strivings left Rothko very despondent and he even described himself on the verge of a nervous breakdown. Examination of his works from the latter half of this decade shows disintegration that paralleled his personal anguish, then regrouping in "multi-forms" from which were born the full flowering of his mature style by 1950.

1950's: Mature Style

In 1950, Rothko's daughter Kate was born, given the American name taken by his mother at immigration. He achieved prominence in the early 1950's with the emergence of his mature style—large canvases filled almost to the edge with juxtaposed rectangles of glowing color. Most of his works of the 1950's reflect a brilliant palette, fully alive. These signatory expanses of color are what most readily identify a painting as "a Rothko." Like symphonic music, his abstract color fields expressed a wide array of atmospheres and feelings. Critics Novak and O'Doherty wrote: "For one to whom music was the supreme art, Rothko viewed color as capable of expressing a comparable profusion of moods in painting...In the delay between the recognition of a mood and its verbal translation, Rothko's most successful work is poised." Rothko's son Christopher (born in 1963 and known as "Topher") agreed when he wrote of his father: "His work communicates on a level that is explicitly preverbal. Indeed, it would be hard to find less narrative painting. Like music, my father's artwork seeks to express the inexpressible—we are far removed from the realm of words." (Figure 4 shows Rothko in his New York studio during this era.)

However, critical adulation and admiring flattery were only momentarily soothing to Rothko's entitled ego. In 1951, he was appointed assistant professor of design in the Art Department at Brooklyn College, but he was denied tenure in 1955 due to his rebelliousness and iconoclasm. By the mid-50's, Rothko was depressed and melancholic; he was drinking heavily and afflicted by gout, hypertension and hypochondria, and his paintings moved toward a darker palette.

Late 1950's, Early 1960's: Mural Commissions

In 1958, Rothko received his first major commission to produce wall murals for the Four Seasons Restaurant in the new Seagram's Building in New York City. Darker hues began to prevail in these works. Instead of splashing brightness, somber tones of plums, maroons and black emerged along with doses of angry and seething reds. Rothko ultimately refused to deliver the murals and returned the commission after deciding that the restaurant setting was too banal and commercial for his work. Instead, he eventually negotiated with the Tate Gallery in London for his works to be displayed in a room of their own where the lighting conditions and their relationship to each other could be carefully controlled according to his aesthetic sensibilities. "Since I have a deep sense of responsibility for the life my pictures will lead out in the world, I will accept with gratitude any form of their exposition where their life and meaning can be maintained and avoid all occasions where I feel that this cannot be done."

With mounting fame and expectations, Rothko became more depressed and felt increasingly isolated and entrapped by the art establishment that he had made a lifelong crusade of loathing. Despite acute depression, he also executed a series of murals for the Holyoke Center at Harvard University, employing a similar spectrum wherein charcoals and grays dominated, punctuated by red and white. Curiously, Rothko once described this series as an expression of Christian themes from Crucifixion to Resurrection.

Mid 1960's: Rothko Chapel

The signal accomplishment of Rothko's career came with a commission in 1964 to create a series of panels for a Catholic Chapel on the campus of St. Thomas University in Houston, Texas (Figure 5). Plans for the octagonal building were eventually changed to become a non-denominational chapel. Rothko had always hoped for a suitable setting for his works in which their metaphysical message could be appropriately absorbed and appreciated by the viewer. The epitome of his life ambition was to create a monument following in the storied tradition of Western religious art, albeit without icons or altarpieces. He sought a sacred space wherein the universal truths of the human condition could be communicated in an atmosphere that connects the viewer with the spiritual core of existence.

Rothko threw himself into this Chapel project with an obsessive and extraordinary attention to detail. In his New York studio, he had a life-size mockup constructed of the chapel walls and spent hours sitting in a chair, facing those walls, contemplating the medium and the message before actually painting the panels. The result was a highly reductive product finished in 1967 that included only plum, maroon and black in a series of fourteen panels.

Of my own visits to the Rothko Chapel, I can say that the enormous panels are overwhelming and evocative. They draw the viewer into an inner world completely free of the trappings and encumbrances of our everyday environment, an authentic quiet place of centered awareness. They also convey, in my opinion, a sense of depression, foreboding and death, but not a terminal death. Rather, the sensation is of a death that transports one to a different plane of experience—a metaphysical or spiritual one. This, I believe, is the effect Rothko wanted.

An opposing view was articulated by Novak and O'Doherty, describing the contemplative fallacy: "At a certain threshold of perception, virtually any blankness (or blackness), given an appropriately solemn context, may return to the viewer self-generated illusions that he or she mistakes for profundities…The Rothko Chapel in Houston [is] liable to this fallacy." I encourage the reader to make a personal visit to the Rothko Chapel in order to reach his/her own conclusion.

That Rothko was moved by completing the chapel commission is evident from a hand-written letter to his benefactors, John and Dominique de Menil: "The magnitude, on every level of experience and meaning, of the task in which you have involved me, exceeds all my preconceptions. And it is teaching me to extend myself beyond what I thought was possible for me. For this I thank you."

Late 60's: Reprise

After the Chapel panels were finished, Rothko experienced increasing health problems including hypertension, arteriosclerosis and an aortic aneurysm that limited his physical abilities and rendered him highly irritable. He was restricted to working on smaller pieces, often acrylics on paper. During this time, Rothko seemed to reprise briefly his earlier delight with brilliant color. Perhaps the enthusiasm of accomplishing his piece de resistance, the Chapel, gave Rothko a surge of creative energy. Whatever the reason, this period proved to be short-lived.

Late 1960's: Descent to Suicide

What had been chronic depression throughout the 1960's now spiraled downward into pervasive melancholia. Rothko's drinking increased. He was also taking prescription tranquilizers, anti-depressants and sedatives. Always a difficult person, Rothko became impossibly truculent and bellicose. He was paranoid of art dealers whom he suspected of trying to bilk him out of his lifetime oeuvre now that he had achieved critical acclaim. He began cataloging his voluminous and mostly unsold works as if preparing for death. He had a new will drawn up bypassing his wife Mell and largely excluding his children so that most of his works would be conveyed to a Mark Rothko Foundation. In 1969, he separated from Mell and began keeping company with Rita Reinhardt, widow of artist Ad Reinhardt. Despite this association, he was essentially alone.

Rothko was famous, but his risk profile for suicide was high. He was older, sick, depressed, separated from his wife, isolated, self-pitying, believed himself to be misunderstood, and alone. He continued to chain-smoke, drink too much and take enormous amounts of prescription medicines. It did not matter that he was made a member of the National Institute of Arts and Letters or that Yale University awarded him an honorary Doctor of Fine Arts degree. Rothko, the misanthrope, was reduced to abject despair. His last series of "Brown on Grey" and "Black on Grey" chronicled his denouement. The world these paintings convey is a stark, ominous, doom-filled void of entropy, as if one is looking at vapid moonscapes. The life has gone out of them.

175

Epilogue

On February 25, 1970, Mark Rothko stood alone at the sink in his studio. He had ingested an overdose of choral hydrate, a medication prescribed for sleep. In hand was a double-edged razor blade with tissue padding one end. It is believed he slashed his arteries at the crooks inside his elbows, at first hesitatingly, then savagely and held his arms under the running water until he passed out. On the floor, arms outstretched, he completely ex-sanguinated and died. He left no note.

In the end, Rothko's suicide was a case of death imitating art. When discovered the next morning, his body lay in a large pool of dark red congealed blood. Ruled a suicide, Rothko's death was enigmatic, unexplained, and full of fury, just like his paintings. His suicide seemed the ultimate enraged rejection of the external world of relationships and things. It constituted a dramatic de-cathexis from people, situations and events. It appeared to be a self-absorbed, autistic withdrawal into a more salubrious inner reality where tranquility, harmony and total control were possible. Seldes (in "The Legacy of Mark Rothko") described the suicide as a selfish, vindictive "action painting", a deliberate act of departure that secured for him the last wrathful word against a world that, in his estimation, never fully appreciated or understood him. Ironically, the Rothko Chapel was dedicated almost a year to the day, February 28, 1971, after Rothko's suicide.

In his own words, which might be a fitting epitaph for his life and work, Rothko was quoted as saying,

> "I'm interested only in expressing basic human emotions—tragedy, ecstasy, doom, and so on—and the fact that lots of people break down and cry when confronted with my pictures shows that I communicate these basic human emotions. The people who weep before my paintings are having the same religious experience I had when I painted them. And if you...are moved only by their color relationships, then you miss the point."

Commentary

Post-mortem studies of suicide in the general population reveal clinically familiar findings. Suicide rates are higher among those older than age sixty-five and continue to increase with age. The vast majority of suicides are completed by divorced or widowed white males who use highly lethal means such as firearms or hanging. Ninety percent of suicides are associated with mental or addictive disorders, especially mood disorders like depression that feature reduced serotonin levels. Family history of completed suicides is also a risk factor. Finally, the social position of the victim is extremely important. Completed suicides most often occur in the context of social isolation or when interpersonal relations are "suicidogenic", meaning negative, conflictual or stressful. Every one of these suicide demographics matches Rothko's death scenario with the exception of family history.

When suicide rates among creative and artistic persons are considered, clear evidence of an increased incidence rate emerges, i.e., the "creativity and madness" linkage. Interestingly, Andreasen compared rates of mental illness in a small sample of creative writers and their first-degree relatives compared with matched controls. She found higher lifetime prevalence rates of mental illness (mostly affective disorders with a tendency toward the bipolar subtype) and higher rates of alcoholism among the writers. There was also a higher prevalence of mental illness among the first-degree relatives of writers, suggesting that these traits run together in families. Stack studied a large, diverse sample of artists (e.g., musicians, composers, actors, directors, painter, sculptors, craft artists, printmakers, and dancers) in an epidemiologic analysis and found—when statistically controlling for factors of gender (male), race (white) and age—that the suicide risk was 125% higher for artists than non-artists. He hypothesized that the field of art may attract those with some emotional instability wherein artistic production becomes an attempt at healing the self and/or that living with the rejection or devaluation of one's creative products is a precursor to suicide. Again, Rothko's circumstances parallel these findings.

177

In a chilling confirmation of how these arguments apply specifically to the fifteen Abstract Expressionist artists of the New York School, Schildkraut, Hirshfeld and Murphy compiled some sobering statistics on a cohort that included, among others, Willem de Kooning, Robert Motherwell, Barnett Newman, Jackson Pollock, Ad Reinhardt, Clyford Still and Mark Rothko. Over half of the group had some form of psychopathology, predominantly mood disorders often compounded by alcohol abuse (including Rothko). At least 40% sought treatment and 20% were hospitalized for psychiatric reasons (including Rothko). Two committed suicide (including Rothko) while two others died in suspicious single-vehicle accidents while driving. Almost half of the cohort died before the age of sixty. In a formulation that certainly seems to recapitulate the anguish and struggle of Mark Rothko, the authors concluded:

> "Depression inevitably leads to a turning inward and to the painful reexamination of the purpose of living and the possibility of dying. Thus, by bringing the artist into direct and lonely confrontation with the ultimate existential question, whether to live or to die, depression may have put these artists in touch with the inexplicable mystery that lies at the heart of the 'tragic and timeless' art that the Abstract Expressionists aspired to produce."

REFERENCES

Andreasen, N.C. (1987). "Creativity and mental illness: Prevalence rates in writers and their first-degree relatives". *American Journal of Psychiatry*, 144, 1288-1292. Ashton, D. (1983). *About Rothko*. New York: Oxford University Press. Barnes, S.J. (1996). *The Rothko Chapel: An act of faith*. Houston, TX: The Rothko Chapel.

Breslin, J.E.B. (1993). *Mark Rothko: A biography*. Chicago: University of Chicago Press.

Jamison, K.R. (1993). *Touched With Fire: Manic-Depressive Illness and the Artistic Temperament*. New York: The Free Press.

Klepser, M.B. (1995). Comment. In J.T. Maltsberger, (Ed.). "Diffusion of responsibility in the care of a difficult patient". *Suicide and Life-Threatening Behavior*.

Lester, D. (1993). *Suicide in Creative Women*. Commack, NY: Nova Science Publishers.

Lester, D. (1995). "The suicide of Mark Rothko". In J.T. Maltsberger, (Ed.). "Diffusion of responsibility in the care of a difficult patient". *Suicide and Life-Threatening Behavior*, 25, 415-417.

Maris, R.W. (1997). "Social and familial risk factors in suicidal behavior". The Psychiatric Clinics of North America, 20, 519-550.

Moscicki, E.K. (1997). "Identification of suicide risk factors using epidemiologic-studies". *The Psychiatric Clinics of North America*, 20, 499-517.

Novak, B., & O'Doherty, B. (1998). "Rothko's dark painting: Tragedy and void". In J. Weiss (Ed.). *Mark Rothko*. Washington, DC: National Gallery of Art.

Rodman, S. (1957). *Conversations with artists*. New York: Devin-Addair.

Rothko, C. (2004). "Introduction". In C. Rothko (Ed.). *Mark Rothko: The Artist's Reality, Philosophy of Art*. New Haven, CT: Yale University Press.

Rothko, M. (1952). [Statement] In 15 Americans, an exhibition catalogue (March 25-June 11, 1952). New York: The Museum of Modern Art. Reprinted (in part) in S.J. Barnes (1996). *The Rothko Chapel: An act of faith*. Houston, TX: The Rothko Chapel. p. 22.

Rothko, M. (1952). Letter to Lloyd Goodrich dated December 20, 1952. Papers of Whitney Museum of Art, Archives of American Art. New York. Reprinted (in part) in L. Seldes (1978). *The legacy of Mark Rothko*. New York: Holt, Rinehart and Winston. pp. 27-28.

Rothko, M., & Gottlieb, A. (1943). Letter to Edward Alden Jewel dated June 7, 1943. *New York Times*. Published June 13, 1943. Reprinted (in part) in J.E.B. Breslin (1993). *Mark Rothko: A biography*. Chicago: University of Chicago Press.

Schildkraut, J.J., Hirshfeld, A.B., & Murphy, J.M. (1994). "Mind and mood in modern art, II: Depressive disorders, spirituality, and early deaths in the abstract expressionist artists of the New York School". *The American Journal of Psychiatry*, 151.

Seldes, L. (1978). *The Legacy of Mark Rothko*. New York: Holt, Rinehart, and Winston.

Stack, S. (1996). "Gender and suicide risk among artists: A multivariate analysis". *Suicide and Life-Threatening Behavior*, 26, 374-379.

Stewart, J. (1998). "Chronology". In J. Weiss (Ed.). *Mark Rothko*. Washington, DC: National Gallery of Art.

Stillion J. & McDowell, E. (1996). *Suicide Across the Life Span*: Premature Exits. Washington, DC: Taylor and Francis.

Time. (1961). Published March 3, p. 75.

Waldman, D. (1994). *Mark Rothko* in New York. New York: Guggenheim Museum Publications.

Weinberg, E. (1995). Comment. In J.T. Maltsberger, (Ed.). "Diffusion of responsibility in the care of a difficult patient". *Suicide and Life-Threatening Behavior, 25.*

FIGURES

Figure 1

Rothko, Mark. *Underground Fantasy*, Gift of the Mark
Rothko Foundation, Inc., Image © 2006 Board of
Trustees, National Gallery of Art, Washington, c. 1940,
oil on canvas.

Figure 2

Rothko, Mark. *Hierarchical
Birds*, Gift of the Mark Rothko
Foundation, Inc., Image © 2006
Board of Trustees, National
Gallery of Art, Washington, c.
1944, oil on canvas.

Figure 3

Rothko, Mark. *Slow Swirl at the Edge of the Sea.*
Bequest of Mrs. Mark Rothko through The Mark
Rothko Foundation, Inc., The Museum of Mod-
ern Art, New York, NY, USA, c. 1944, oil on can-
vas. Digital Image © The Museum of Modern
Art/Licensed by SCALA/Art Resource, NY.

Figure 4

Rothko Contemplating *No. 25*, 1951.
Photograph by Kay Bell Reynal, c. 1952.
Permission by John R. Kennedy.

Figure 5

Rothko Chapel in Houston,
Texas with *Broken Obelisk* by
Barnett Newman (1971) in
reflecting pool in foreground
(Author's photograph).

Dana L. Hadley-Carder, MA, RN, PHN, is a School Nurse. She is part of her School District's Crisis Response Team. She has been an Instructor for National Association of School Nurses for Managing School Emergencies. She has done critical care hospital nursing and corporate nursing. Dana is an artist at heart. She loves family, friends, travel, art and life, not necessarily in that order!

Scott L. Carder, MD, PhD, is in private practice of psychoanalysis and psychiatry in Pasadena, California. He is a Clinical Professor of Psychiatry at the University of Southern California and a Training & Supervising Analyst at the New Center for . Scott was author of Richard Wagner in Creativity & Madness - Vol. I. He loves his wife, Dana, family & friends, travel, running, snowboarding and much more!

MARY CASSATT
AN INDEPENDENT WOMAN WHO WAS DRIVEN TO BE A GREAT ARTIST

BY

SCOTT CARDER, MD, PhD

AND DANA L. HADLEY-CARDER, RN, MA

Often today, people who know only a little about the artwork of Mary Cassatt (1844-1926) may think, "She so captures attachment" or "She really could paint mothers and children." An example is Breakfast in Bed (1897, Figure 1). A much richer perspective opens as one comes to know Mary Cassatt's life and her work in greater depth and complexity. Some recent authors of books about Cassatt agree with G. Pollock who stated that her art became "...increasingly so sentimentalized that the very association with the subject (child/adult relation) at all later threatened to submerge everything else about Cassatt's complex artistic history and intensely intellectual preoccupations with art-making." However, as we will see, the psychological theories of attachment and separation-individuation help us understand how some of Cassatt's childhood problems influenced her adult life and her art and why in her later life, she focused so much of her work on mothers and children.

Figure 1

Breakfast in Bed, 1897,
Huntington Library

Mary Cassatt came from a successful American aristocratic background. She lived her adult life in Paris, France, and became the dominant American woman artist representing the Impressionist period. She lived as a single woman who was closely connected to her family all her life. She followed her passion to work hard to develop the skills and training to become the best avant-garde painter of her time. She lived and learned among a group of now famous artists, many whom she joined to advance the new Impressionist style of art. Some of these contemporaries were Paul Cezanne, Gustave Courbet, Edgar Degas, Edouard Manet, Claude Monet, Berthe Morisot, Camille Pissarro, Auguste Renoir, and Alfred Sisley.

The focus of this article is to highlight some of the components and to see the likely psychological issues that led Mary Cassatt to achieve such success. One aspect of her development was the background and training that provided her with a very privileged beginning. From her early teens, Mary showed an enthusiastic, drive to become a great artist. Her attachment to both her mother and her older sister and the support of her father were important influences on her identity and her work. As a woman, Cassatt was able to reveal with subject, style, and manner some of the essence of femininity during a time of struggle for women's increased acceptance as equals in the world of professional activity. Her creativity was shaped by emotionally significant factors from both her internal and external worlds. She can be seen from the perspective of later nineteenth century art, from the feminist movement of that period, and from being on the cusp of the twentieth century. She painted during a time in which feminism was a political and a social force for change. She was able to integrate her studies of the old masters with the changes of the new independent Impressionists and with both her ambition and her feminine perspective.

A Very Privileged Beginning

Mary Cassatt's family background was one of significant pride from success in American business and politics. Her parents came from hard-working successful American aristocrats who were leaders during American's early history. Mary's paternal family began in America when Jacques Cossart sailed from France in 1662. Mary's father Robert was a successful investment person who retired in his early forties to help raise his children. Katherine Johnson Cassatt, Mary's mother, had known Robert Cassatt all of her life as they both came from prominent families in the Pittsburgh area of Pennsylvania. Katherine was nineteen and Robert twenty-nine when they married. Katherine had been educated by a woman who was raised in France and taught her several languages, giving her a broad European type of education

Louisine Havemeyer wrote in her memoirs: "Anyone who had the privilege of knowing Mary Cassatt's mother would know at once that it could be from her and from her only that she (Mary) and her brother, A.J. Cassatt, inherited their ability. Even in my day, when she was no longer young, she was still powerfully intelligent, executive and masterful and yet with that same sense of duty, that tender sympathy that she had transmitted to her daughter, Mary." The close connection and support of her capable and 'tender' mother helped Mary identify with her and to be comfortable with both her femininity and her capabilities.

The Robert and Katherine Cassatt family moved several times in Mary's early years. Mary was the fourth of six children with an older sister and two older brothers. When Mary was two years old, a baby brother, George, died in infancy. Then when Mary was five years old, the last child, Gardner, was born. Nothing is known about how Mary and her family were affected by George's death or Gardner's birth. It would not be unusual to expect some emotional injury to the relationship of two-year-old Mary with her mother who must have grieved the loss of her infant son. According to the noted psychoanalyst and child development specialist Margaret Mahler, MD, two-year olds are just finishing the rapprochement stage of the separation-individuation process of development. At this stage, children are developing their ability to separate from mother and to be more independent. Katherine must have been less available while pregnant and giving birth to a new fifth child who was quickly followed by grieving the infant's death. Gardner's birth, when Mary was five, may have helped her mother and the family work through their grief but it would also have displaced Mary from being the special 'baby' of the family. Throughout her career, but especially after age forty, she created many paintings and drawings about the intimate bonds between mothers and their young children.

When Mary was five years old, the Cassatt family moved to Europe. Robert and Katherine wanted to enjoy the good life of Europe and to give their children the cultured multi-lingual education that Paris could provide. Mary and her older brother Robbie were close, but about the time they moved, he developed a chronic bone disease and suffered with it for five years. The Cassatt family lived in Paris

190

two years and then moved to Darmstadt in Germany so that Alex, the oldest brother, could study engineering. It was there, when Mary was eleven years old, that Robbie died at age thirteen. The family's grief likely motivated them to move back to America.

On the way home from Germany, the Cassatt family stopped in Paris to see the Exposition Universelle, the 1855 World's Fair. Here Mary and her family saw paintings by important French artists. They saw Eugene Delacroix's huge paintings of famous historical events, and in a different exhibit at the same time, they saw Gustave Courbet's paintings of *Realism*—ordinary scenes from the modern world. Art and its many differing aspects were a very important part of Paris, the Mecca for Western art. While they lived in Paris, Mary had often gone with her mother to the museums where she had seen students copying the old masters. When she returned for the World's Fair, she saw a wonderful, exciting event that had new art at its center.

Grief from the loss of Robbie likely had a deep emotional effect on Mary, and may have led her to be both more independent and to be more cautious in getting close to a man. The loss of the two brothers closest to her in age, baby George and then Robbie, may have motivated Mary to try to make up for these losses and could have given her a sense of her own specialness at being the survivor. In addition to English, Mary learned French and German and later also Italian and Spanish. Her parents supported the children's individual talents and encouraged a broad education that included European art and literature. In childhood, Mary was "high-spirited, athletic and aggressive." Alex, her brother, later wrote that she was "…always a great favorite of mine. I suppose because our taste was a good deal alike. Whenever it was a question of a walk or a ride or a gallop on horseback, it didn't matter when or what weather, Mary was always ready, so when I was at home we were together a great deal. We used to have plenty of fights, for she had a pretty quick temper."

A Strong Independent Drive to be a Great Artist

At fifteen years of age, Mary demonstrated her strong individual opinions and passions by deciding to become an artist. The traits, strong of opinion and passion and a love of art, were some of her most important life-long qualities. Her family supported this decision and took her out of regular schooling, and for three years (1862-65), Mary studied at the Pennsylvania Academy of Fine Arts. At that time, the school was considered the best in the United States.

About 25% of the students at the Fine Arts Academy were female. There were significant prejudices against women as professional artists. However, both Mary Cassatt and her close friend Eliza Haldeman were aware of many successful women artists in America as well as in Europe, and both young women were determined to succeed. They became the top women artists of their class, and over time, Mary's self-assuredness led her to evolve and assume a natural position of superiority among her classmates.

As we look back today, it is somewhat shocking that the Civil War, with all its horror and toll in human life and suffering, went on around them, but the Cassatt family seemed above it all. In fact, this period for Mary was very pleasurable. She addressed letters to her friend Eliza as "Dearest Love" and would talk of pleasures of flirtations with young men as "a quite agreeable employment." She also expressed her self-confidence and ambition as an artist, and she enjoyed days of painting and horseback-riding with her brother Alex. Both Alex and their father Robert achieved great financial benefits from the immediate post war conditions.

Mary enjoyed living in the country, drawing local models, and then going to Philadelphia to continue the practice of copying great art. In 1865, at twenty-one years of age, her passion to be a great artist meant only one thing. She had to return to Europe to study in Paris, the art capital of the world. Her father was opposed to this, and in a fit of anger, he said, "I would almost rather see you dead!" Mary was determined, however, she knew she had much more to learn and that Europe was the place to do it. Within the year, her father agreed and gave her an allowance, and with her mother, she sailed for France.

Katherine Cassatt stayed six to eight months to help her daughter get settled. Mary boarded in the home of a trusted family and met other Americans who had come to Paris to study art. Elizabeth Gardner was one of these Americans who had arrived a year earlier. Since women were not admitted to the principal academy of Art in France—the Ecole des Beaux-Arts—they typically took private lessons from the best available painters of the day. To the amazement of her friends back home, Mary was accepted by the young master Jean-Leon Gerome, a professor at the Ecole. Gerome was a traditional academic painter who focused on realist precision of detail in classical subjects. Along with her friend from Philadelphia, Eliza Haldeman, Mary also attended classes given for women by Charlie Chaplin at his *atelier*, or studio. In Chaplin's class, they worked from live models and Chaplin was known for his decorative portrait style. Cassatt and Haldeman's work and skill helped them become the best in Chaplin's class.

Mary Cassatt was granted permission to copy paintings at the Louvre. From 1865 to 1870, she and many others spent much time copying and often sold their works to visiting tourists. With her friend Eliza Haldeman, Howard Roberts, and Elizabeth Gardner, some of the French copyists at the time were Jenny Sisley, Edgar Degas, Eugene Delacroix, Paul Cezanne, and Berthe and Edma Morisot.

One measure of success in the Paris art world was having a painting accepted in the annual competition for showing in the Paris Salon. More than a thousand paintings won the honor but thousands of others were rejected. In early 1867, Mary Cassatt and Eliza Haldeman moved to Ecouen in the countryside north of Paris to live and paint together. Both Haldeman and Cassatt were impressed with the polite and mannerly behaviors of the French peasants that contrasted with their American backgrounds. They attempted to paint this noble simplicity, and with guidance from Charlie Chaplin, both submitted paintings to the Salon in 1867. Despite the fact that both of their paintings were rejected, they decided to continue this genre and took instruction from Paul Soyer, a famous French painter of local peasants in the countryside.

Mary attended an important art show that was part of the Paris World's Fair in 1867. As she did years before during her childhood, Mary saw Gustave Courbet's realistic style. She also saw Edouard Manet's work and realized that both of these artists hated academic painting. They painted realistic pictures that did not follow the strict rules or the aim of beautiful perfection that they believed deprived paintings of feelings that would engage viewers. Cassatt was passionate about learning to be the best painter, and this newer, less traditional style of Courbet and Manet's work inspired her. Through her friend Eliza, Mary told Eliza's mother, Mrs. Haldeman, that "she wanted to paint better than the old masters..." This sense of potential great ability and talent shows the healthy narcissistic sense of herself. In 1868, Mary and Eliza both again submitted paintings to the Paris Salon and both were accepted. Mary's was displayed on the prestigious eye level. This first painting of hers to be accepted to the Salon is called *La Mandoline* (1868, Private collection).

Mary and Eliza moved from Ecouen to Paris that spring to enjoy being a part of the Salon as exhibitors. A short time later, Mary moved to a boarding house in the town where Thomas Couture, teacher of Edouard Manet, had a studio. Mary began working with him, and with his help, "...Cassatt followed her romantic leanings and returned again and again to themes such as the solitary, almost melancholy woman living her life and displaying her talents, a version of which she had used for her Salon picture, *La Mandoline*." These themes were also an expression of Mary's own feelings and of her life. At this time, she lived on her own, worked with her own talent, and must have been lonely without her family.

Eliza and Mary were aware of the difficult dilemma women faced in regards to marriage and children versus continuing their careers as artists. Cassatt had wealth, intelligence and culture, but other qualities would not endear her to male suitors. She was very independent, brash, outspoken, and so dedicated to her work that charming men was now only a pastime for her. In the summer of 1868, Mary, Eliza, and Eliza's brother Carsten were in Paris together, and upon seeing a beautiful, expensive wedding veil in the window of a shop, Mary impulsively told Carsten that she would marry him if he got it for her. For some weeks after, Carsten joked about their being engaged but the veil was never bought. Carsten had known Mary since she was sixteen, and he was an engineer as was Alex, Mary's favorite brother. Alex had just recently announced his own engagement to Lois Buchanan, the niece of the former president James Buchanan. This is the closest report of Mary Cassatt's possible choice of the traditional woman's roll of marriage to that of her chosen path of competing in the male-dominated professional world of art.

In 1869, Mary stayed near Ecouen where she could consult with Couture, Soyer and Frere. She prepared a painting for the Salon of 1869, planning to exhibit once more and then return to America. She hurried to get it in by the deadline. Unfortunately, it was rejected by the jury as not sufficiently finished. She learned that it was possible to get a negative decision reversed and she asked the Ecole professor Gerome to do it. He was willing but she was one day too late. This showed that she was willing to exploit the system for which she had developed such contempt over time. Cassatt was very discouraged by the rejection, and her mother likely sensed the distress and came to visit. They went to Rome where Mary began studying with another master, Charles Bellay, a Frenchman. While working in Rome, she submitted another painting to the Paris Salon of 1870 and it was accepted. She also had paintings accepted in Italian exhibits and felt recognized by the art worlds of both Rome and Paris.

In 1870, Napoleon III began the Franco-Prussian War and this interrupted Cassatt's studies. She returned with her mother to America that summer. In 1871, Prussia defeated the French and took Napoleon prisoner. Paris was severely damaged and the Paris Salon was not held that year.

When Mary and her mother arrived in America, they rejoined the Cassatt family in the small town of Altoona, Pennsylvania, where Alex, his new bride Lois, and their baby Edward had been the center of attention. Robert, Mary's father, lived in a hotel in the town with

Lydia and Gardner. Suddenly the focus of attention was on Mary and Katherine, not Lois Buchanan Cassatt and her baby. Mary and Lois clashed from the beginning. They were intelligent, educated and determined women but they took very different life paths. Ten years later, Lois wrote, "The truth is I cannot abide Mary and never will— I can't tell why but there is something to me so utterly obnoxious about that girl. I have never yet heard her criticize any human being in any but the most disagreeable way. She is too self important, and I can't put up with it." This harsh critical quality of Mary's personality stands in stark contrast to the tender love and kindness expressed in her paintings. We saw earlier that her brother Alex also commented on her quick temper. The angry critical quality in her personality may have had its origin in the disruption of her attachment to her mother during the early childhood phase of separation-individuation mentioned earlier.

Disruptions in the rapprochement or approach-avoidance phase also can lead to ambivalent feelings about intimate relationships. We see this demonstrated when Mary, although happy to be with her family, almost immediately upon arriving in Altoona, desperately wanted to return to Europe. Her family refused to support this. Mary developed funding on her own, and in 1871, she went to Europe with her friend and fellow painter Emily Sartain. Mary's passion was now to transform herself from a student into a professional who could earn a living from being the kind of artist she wanted to be.

In 1872, Mary received a commission from the bishop of Pittsburgh to copy two of Correggio's paintings in Parma, Italy. While there, she worked on a painting to submit to the Paris Salon of that year. Both the professors and the students of the Parma Art Academy were amazed at her skill. Her colleague and companion Emily Sartain wrote to her father, "All Parma is talking of Miss Cassatt and her picture…The compliments she receives are overwhelming…One of the assistants (in the academy) assured her she was much more 'brava' than any of the professors."

Figure 2

Photo of Mary Cassatt in Parma, Italy, 1872,
Pennsylvania Academy of the Fine Arts Archives

Cassatt then traveled alone to Spain and spent a year, mostly in Seville. Although lonely and often unhappy, she worked arduously painting models in traditional Spanish costumes. In 1873, she again submitted a painting to the Paris Salon and was accepted. Both of the Salon paintings, for those two years of 1872 and 1873, were scenes of flirtatious women.

Figure 3

On the Balcony, 1872,
Philadelphia Museum of Art

It is clear when a comparison is made of the women's facial expressions in Figures 2 and 3 that Mary Cassatt painted about her own feelings. It was only a few years before this that she described her own flirtations as "a quite agreeable employment." This is an example of the frequent observation that many creative people (painters, writers, musicians, actors, etc.) often project their own feelings into the work they do. Cassatt was able to artistically express her femininity. It can also be inferred that the later mother and child themes were, in part, also examples of her own feelings and desires.

The next year, 1874, Cassatt's fourth consecutive and fifth accepted painting exhibited at the Paris Salon received unusual attention from artists and critics. Titled *Ida*, it displays her further movement into a style of her own that opposed the traditional Academic style. At this time, neither Cassatt nor Edgar Degas knew each other, but when Degas saw that painting, he reportedly said, "There is someone who feels as I do."

1874 found Miss Cassatt returning to Paris to work and study. With the acceptance of many paintings into the Paris Salon, she had become known and respected as an American woman who success-fully competed in the male-dominated world of French art. She began accepting commissions to do portraits, often of American tourists. One young nineteen-year-old American woman, Louisine Elder (later Havemeyer), said, "I felt then that Miss Cassatt, (at thirty years old) was the most intelligent woman I had ever met..." On one walk together, Louisine and Mary saw a painting in a shop window, *Ballet Rehearsal* by Edgar Degas. Mary was so impressed by the pastel colors and the artist's freedom and skill of bringing the dancers to life that she inspired Louisine to buy it. This was the first artwork purchased by the now famous collector and contributor to the New York Metropolitan Museum.

Although friendly with both the French and American artists in Paris, Mary's harsh, opinionated outspokenness, and her inde-pendence and drive to be the best had distanced her from many of them. This may be one reason Mary's sister Lydia came to live with her and be her companion that year in Paris. Cassatt's development of her own independent style resulted in the rejection of several submis-sions to the Paris Salon in 1875-77. Her dislike and skepticism of the Salon deepened when a previously rejected painting was accepted the next year after she simply darkened the background.

Many other prominent young painters also felt conflicted over the Paris Salon. On the one hand, the Salon's power of acceptance gave recognition to striving artists. On the other hand, the judges of the Salon were Academics who maintained tradition, discouraged change and independent styles, and were known to be influenced or biased. In the mid-1870's, several noted Parisian artists, including Cezanne, Degas, Manet, Monet, Morisot, Pissarro, Renoir, and Sisley, rebelled against the Salon by refusing to submit works and instead held their "Independent" exhibitions that were free of judges and awards. This group painted their own impressions of the modern world instead of idealized historical or mythological scenes. These "Independents" were criticized by the academics and traditionalists. One critic, Louis Leroy, upon seeing Claude Monet's *Impression, Sunrise* (1876), sarcastically called these artists "Impressionists" and that name has become their identity.

It was with joy that Mary Cassatt accepted Edgar Degas's invitation in 1877 to join the "Independent" exhibition instead of the Salon. "I hated conventional art," said Cassatt. At this time, she was very influenced by such "Independent" contemporaries as Renoir and Degas, and in her series of spectators at the Opera, the influence of both can be seen.

Figure 4

Woman with a Pearl Necklace in a loge,
1879, Philadelphia Museum of Art

And yet, the outspoken Cassatt could be as critical of the Impressionists as she was of the academic traditionalists. For example, she spoke of "...Renoir creating his 'fat, red women,' and Monet painting the reflections in water that [she] dubbed 'glorified wallpaper.'" Cassatt and Degas became life-long friends and had many similarities. They respected each other's talent, came from wealthy backgrounds, were harshly outspoken and critical, and worked hard with great skill at developing their own independent styles.

Although Mary's brothers Alex and Gard were both married with families in America, her attachment to her older unmarried sister Lydia and to her mother led the Cassatt family to move to France in 1877 to support Mary, and all four Cassatts—Katherine, Robert, Lydia, and Mary—lived the rest of their lives there. John Bowlby, a British psychoanalyst, pioneered work with attachment and published a three-volume series on Attachment, Separation, and Loss (1965-1980). Bowlby's last clinical book was "A Secure Base: Parent-Child Attachment and Healthy Human Development" (1988.) The work of Bowlby and those attachment researchers who have followed him help us recognize the importance for Mary to have a secure base of family for her to function optimally in the art world in Paris. These theories concerning a child's need for attachment also further our understanding of why an early abrupt likely loss of connection with her mother could have been very traumatic to the two-year-old Mary.

In 1879, Cassatt showed eleven paintings together in one room at the "Independent" (Impressionists) exhibition. Her works received good reviews. One critic wrote that there was not a painting or a pastel by Cassatt that "is not an exquisite symphony of color." And that "...Mary Cassatt is fond of pure colors and possesses the secret of blending them in a composition that is bold, mysterious, and fresh." The conflict between academic traditionalists and the Impressionists continued over some time and it would be another decade before the new art was recognized by the world as an accepted part of French painting. Those who bought the Impressionist paintings in the 1870's were wealthy Parisians who were sophisticated in contemporary art. Mary Cassatt was now accepted by the Parisian avant-garde as the leading American woman Impressionist. Her self-portraits of this time reveal many of her qualities. They show a confident engaging facial expression on this lone woman dressed in the fashion of her time and class. Her *Self-Portrait* (Figure 5) from 1878 shows her light open impressionistic style that allows the eyes to focus on the person, her face and her fashion.

Figure 5

Self-Portrait, 1878,
Metropolitan Museum of Art

By the age of thirty-five, this amazingly strong independent woman had achieved her goal of becoming a great artist. The 1880's were filled with continuing success for Mary Cassatt. She broadened the expression of her great skills and talent by working with print-making in addition to her continued creations in oil and other individual pictures. The themes varied but they continued to show her impressions of the life of well-to-do women and families, dressed in the fashions of the times and carrying out the daily activities of their lives. She had a series of paintings of women at teatime, of women at the opera, and of her family members. She enjoyed her life, her work as an artist, and her success.

Mary Cassatt turned forty in 1884, and shortly after began to develop what has become her most popular theme of women with children. She had, of course, painted some before, but never with such frequency. In oils, prints, and other media, she would repeatedly capture moments in the lives of mothers and children. For example, in her prints, she did work such as *Baby's Back* (1889) and *Mother's Kiss* (1890). Each of these show a mother holding a child, as does the oil painting *Breakfast in Bed*, 1897, mentioned at the first of this article. Cassatt's art continued to develop this theme through the rest of her career. Since she did not have any children of her own, it is likely that she replaced in her work what she missed in her life. Also, the earlier mentioned attachment theory emphasizes the importance of early childhood on the child's development. A stable and secure mother/child attachment was likely something that Mary experienced as a traumatic loss with her mother's grief over baby George. As a woman in her forties, Mary had to deal with the loss of her own ability to be a mother with a child. It is probable that her repeated focus on this theme in her work as well as her adult need to remain close to her family were her means of coping with these painful mother/child loss experiences.

During the 1880's and after, Mary was severely impacted by family health problems. Her older sister Lydia died in 1882 after a long struggle with kidney trouble. Mary was deeply in pain from this loss and for months could not produce any artwork. She turned to caring for her aging parents. She visited her brothers in America and became close with their wives and children. Even Lois, Alex's wife, became close with Mary at this time. Gradually, Cassatt returned to her art. The challenge and focus helped her recover and move her life forward. She had remained close friends with Louisine Havemeyer, and with her encouragement, Mary supported the struggle for women's increased recognition and treatment as equals in all aspects of life.

In 1891, Mary's father Robert died, creating another painful time for this strong woman. She was already financially successful from her artwork, and within two years, for the first time in her life, she bought a home. It was a forty-five acre eighteenth century country estate that came to be called "Beaufresne" or "Chateau of the Beautiful Ash Trees." For the rest of her life, Mary split her time between an apartment in Paris and this country retreat.

Mary Cassatt, although living permanently in France, was considered by Americans as one of the best American women artists. She was commissioned to create a mural on *Modern Woman* for the Woman's Building of the World's Fair of 1893 in Chicago, Illinois. She created three panels. The first one depicted young girls pursuing an infant who flies away, indicating that young women should be free to live their lives as they wanted. The central section had women dressed in nineteenth-century fashion and plucking apples, the fruits of knowledge, indicating they were free to explore whatever they wanted. The last section was of women dancing and playing the banjo. Cassatt showed the modern woman as strong and free to live her life as she pleased, and to pursue her desires and talents to the fullest. This, of course, was just what Mary Cassatt had done with her own life.

Katherine Johnson Cassatt, Mary's mother, died in 1895, and this loss was also what likely led the artist to continue exploring the mother and child interactions in her work. The death of her sister and then of her mother permanently severed Cassett's attachment to these life-long caregivers. She continued to live in France to the end of her own life in 1926 at the age of eighty-two. She outlived her parents, her siblings, and many of her artistic peers. Vision problems and arthritis caused her to retire from painting in 1915 after more than fifty years of work. The world of art is blessed with the enduring fruits of her labor and talent. Evidently, with some regrets at the age of eighty, Mary Cassatt said, "My mistake was in devoting myself to art, instead of having children." In her straightforward somewhat harsh manner, Cassatt is also known to have said, "We die in inches" and "How we try for happiness, poor things, and how we don't find it. The best cure is hard work if only one has the health for it."

Creativity and its Madness

We make choices in life and this process has its consequences. Even those who appear to just live and not pursue their desires are making that choice with or without awareness. It has been said that luck is "opportunity meeting preparedness." This definition would apply to Mary Cassatt who chose to follow her dream and to strive to be the best artist possible. As we saw earlier, her desire, skill and drive likely came from the crucible of family influence. This included her family's background and all her childhood experiences. The traumas and triumphs of her early years contributed to this woman's 'luck' of achieving international fame in her lifetime in the field of art. Her family heritage was one of success and upper-class achievements. Her mother's inspiring gifted parenting and her father's business success and devotion to his children were very important elements in the successes of both Mary and her older brother Alex, who became one of the wealthiest men in America and the president of a railroad company.

As mentioned earlier, Mary's position in the birth order of her family was that of the surviving girl between two brothers who died in childhood. This may have contributed to her drive to be independent and led her to feel special as one who needed to make up for the family losses. The close childhood relationship with her brother

Alex must have helped her succeed in a male-dominated career world. While admiring Alex, she also played and participated in activities with him as an equal and this must have been a very positive influence. She had help, companionship, and a model of femininity in both her mother and her older sister Lydia. While remaining very upper-class and feminine, Cassatt participated, competed, and succeeded in the Parisian art world dominated by men who came from all different social classes.

Social class is a definite influence on an individual's opportunities. Living in Europe as a child, from the ages of five to nine, in an upper-class status and learning several languages, was a gift few Americans were given. The opportunity to study art in her teenage years at the best American academy with apparently very little detrimental influence from the devastating Civil War was a definite advantage of her upper-class social position.

Mary Cassatt had, as often is the case, many biopsychosocial factors that combined to form the conflicted and complex aspects of this very creative artistic woman. She demonstrated that to really achieve in a creative field such as art, one needs an extraordinary drive, determination, ability, opportunity, and willingness to sacrifice other aspects of life. In some ways, this surely is a form of madness that most people do not show.

In addition to being bright and gifted, Mary, from her early years on, had a drive to be the best and an active aggressive manner that was backed by strong emotions. While driving herself to be the best she could in art, she sacrificed the opportunity to have marriage and children. Also, as discussed earlier, the likely difficulties with attachment and separation issues in her childhood may also have led her to put aside marriage and children of her own. Her early childhood issues and the lack of having her own children, plus the loss of her sister/mother and of her own mother, likely led her to repeatedly create mother/child works in her later life. Evidence of her own sexual interests beyond early flirtations of youth is not available. "As for Degas, whom some view as the great male love of her life, the haughty Cassatt dismissed such a notion in her later years with 'What? That common little man? What a repulsive idea.' (For his part, the finicky Degas told art editor Forbes Watson that 'I would have married her, but I could never have made love to her.')"

In art, Cassatt proudly revealed the essence of femininity at a time when women were struggling for equality. "Cassatt's art expresses her notions of feminism through her portrayal of women as contemplative and spiritual beings as opposed to decorative objects." This was a comment by Erica H. Hirshler, associate curator of American paintings at the Museum of Fine Arts in Boston. The contrast that captures the truth of this comment is comparing Cassatt's feminine portrayal of women as subjects involved in their lives to Edgar Degas' paintings and drawings of girls and women as sensual objects seen from a man's perspective.

Figure 6

The Tea, Mary Cassatt, 1880,
Photograph © Boston Museum of Fine Arts.

Figure 7

School of Ballet, Edgar Degas, 1873,
Corcoran Gallery of Art, Washington, D.C.

From the beginning, Mary Cassatt painted and drew the women of her times with the fashions and activities that accompanied them. She depicted women as capable and pleased with doing womanly activities, from flirting with men to inquisitive interest in the world to their roles as mothers with children.

Mary Cassatt proved herself not an equal, but better than most of her contemporary male colleagues. Although the world around her still discriminated against women and denied them equal opportunities in professional life, this woman pushed ahead to make herself one of the most successful artists of all times. She had, indeed, creatively, and with some madness, achieved her youthful desire to be better than the great artists of the past.

Figures

1. Breakfast in Bed, Mary Stevenson Cassatt, 1897, Huntington Library, Art Collections, and Botanical Gardens, San Marino, California.

2. Photograph of Mary Cassatt taken in Parma, Italy, 1872, The Pennsylvania Academy of the Fine Arts, Philadelphia. Archives. Baroni and Gardelli, photographers. Medium: Carte de visite, albumen print.

3. On the Balcony, 1872, Mary Stevenson Cassatt, Philadelphia Museum of Art: Gift of John G. Johnson for the W.P. Wilstach Collection, 1906.

4. Woman with a Pearl Necklace in a Loge, 1879, Mary Stevenson Cassatt, Philadelphia Museum of Art: Bequest of Charlotte Dorrance Wright, 1978.

5. Self-Portrait, 1878, Metropolitan Museum of Art. This image is in the public domain because its copyright has expired. (see Image: Mary Cassatt-Selfportrait at www.wikipedia.org)

6. The Tea, about 1880, Mary Stevenson Cassatt, American, 1844-1926, Oil on canvas, 25 ½ x 36 ¼ in., Museum of Fine Arts, Boston, M. Theresa B. Hopkins Fund.

7. School of Ballet, Edgar Degas, 1873, Corcoran Gallery of Art, Washington, D.C.

REFERENCES

Barter, J.A. *Mary Cassatt: Modern Woman.* New York: The Art Institute of Chicago & H.N. Abrams, Inc., Publishers, 1998.

Bowlby, J. *Attachment, Separation, and Loss.* A Trilogy published between 1969 and 1980. Also: *A Secure Base: Parent-Child Attachment and Healthy Human Development.* 1988.

Gouveia, G. *The Essential Mary Cassatt.* New York: The Wonderland Press, 2001.

Hale, N. *Mary Cassatt.* Garden City, New York: Doubleday & Company, Inc., 1975.

Hale, N. *Mary Cassatt.* Reading, MA: Addison-Wesley Publishing Company, Inc., 1987.

Havemeyer, L., *Sixteen to Sixty: Memoirs of a Collector*. New York: Ursus Press, 1961, 1993.

Meyers, J. *Impressionist Quartet: The Intimate Genius of Manet and Morisot, Degas and Cassatt*. New York: Harcourt Inc., 2005.

Mahler, M. *The Psychological Birth of the Human Infant*. 1975.

Mathews, N. M. *Mary Cassatt: A Life*. New York: Villard Books, 1994.

Mathews, N.M. *Cassatt: A Retrospective*. New York: H. L. Levin Associates, Inc., 1996.

Moffett, C. *The New Painting: Impressionism 1874-1886*. Fine Arts Museum of San Francisco, 1986.

Pollock, G. *Mary Cassatt: Painter of Modern Women*. London: Thames & Hudson, 1998.

Rosen, M. *Mary Cassatt: Prints and Drawings from the Artist's Studio*. Princeton, NJ: Princeton University Press, 2000.

Segard, A. *Mary Cassatt: Un Peintre des enfants et des meres*. Paris: Librairie Paul Ollendorff, 1913.

Streissguth, T., *Mary Cassatt: Portrait of an American Impressionist*. Minneapolis, MN: Carolrhoda Books, Inc., 1999.

Wealand, S. *Bibliography: Women Impressionists*. Unpublished, 1993.

Janet Helton Hasegawa, PhD, was raised in Indiana and moved to Colorado in the late 1970's to begin her graduate studies. She earned her PhD in psychology from Colorado State University in 1983, completed her clinical internship in Child Psychology at the Denver Children's Hospital and a postdoctoral fellowship in Pediatric Psychology at the University of Colorado Health Sciences Center under the supervision of Gail Gardner, PhD She worked as a pediatric psychologist at National Jewish Hospital and Research Center and served as an Assistant Professor at the University of Colorado Health Science Center where she worked as a pediatric psychologist and trained psychology interns with a joint appointment in the departments of Psychiatry and Pediatrics. She currently lives in Tulsa, Oklahoma with her husband and children, works part-time as a Senior Research Associate for Q2 Consulting, and pursues her interests in art and literature.

WOMEN, NONCONFORMITY, AND MADNESS

JANET HELTON HASEGAWA, PhD

Le Grande Guerre,
painting by Rene Magritte, 1964

Much Madness is divinest Sense
To a discerning Eye
Much Sense—the starkest Madness—
Tis the Majority
In this, as All, Prevail—
Assent—and you are sane—
Demur—you're straightway dangerous
And handled with a chain—

Emily Dickinson, c.1862

213

This poem was written by the famous nineteenth century nonconformist Emily Dickinson who many people of her day thought was mad herself. Dickinson clearly articulates the connection between dissent from society and the perception of insanity. She highlights the very real question of whether or not madness may not truly be sense if it is divergence from a norm that is itself nonsensical. In eight lines, she elucidates the essential conflict between what society deems normalcy and what the individual judges to be truth. Moreover, she succinctly emphasizes society's tendency to label divergence from accepted norms as madness. Dickinson changed the way in which poetry was structured and conceived. Her sparseness and lack of formality were unique in the poems created in the late 1800s. However, she never had a poem published during her lifetime. The first poems by Dickinson that were published were "edited", and the punctuation and form for which she is now so famous were altered so that her poetry would fit in better with the popular poetry of her day. Dickinson's life and her struggle to have her own unique perspective heard by a larger society exemplify many of the themes of female nonconformity and creativity and their relationship to societal perceptions of madness.

Relationship Of Creativity And Nonconformity

Every act of creativity is by definition an act of nonconformity. To create is to bring forth that which has not existed previously. Creativity frequently challenges the established structure and assumptions of society and brings into question the prevailing views of society. Modern art, for example, is defined by the destruction of the societal assumptions about what constitutes the structure of art. The popular stereotype of the artistic genius as an outsider is often an accurate one. What makes ancient artistic masterpieces still relevant is not just that they captured the time period during which they were created, but that they challenged the prevailing views of their culture and in that process, conveyed and still convey significant information to us about what it means to be human. Pablo Picasso,

214

arguably the greatest artist of the modern art movement, understood the role of the artist as a potentially threatening agent of social change and the consequent danger that creative individuals pose to the status quo. In a conversation in 1935, he asserted: "There is nothing more dangerous than justice in the hands of judges, and a paintbrush in the hands of a painter. Just think of the danger to society! But today we haven't the heart to expel the painters and poets from society because we refuse to admit to ourselves that there is any danger in keeping them in our midst." Picasso's statement presages the oppression and censorship of artists during the Nazi Party's regime in Germany during the 1930s and '40s. Furthermore, Picasso viewed the creative process as an active weapon in the fight against oppressive societal forces: "… A painting is an offensive and defensive weapon against the enemy." The painting "Guernica" (1937), Picasso's response to the slaughter of innocent civilians in the Spanish Basque town of Guernica by the German Luftwaffe, is widely considered to be one of history's most effective propaganda statements. Its continued power to speak to the horrors of war was recently accentuated when authorities of the United Nations covered up a tapestry of "Guernica" when United States Secretary of State Colin Powell announced that the United States planned military action in Iraq in February of 2003.

While nonconformity to expectation is necessary for the creative process, there is a razor's edge between what is recognized as creative genius and the divergent view that is ostracized. Societal divergence is also often labeled madness; this connection is what makes the study of the interface between creativity and the designation of madness such a rich area for exploration. "Madness" and indeed its converse, what we think of as mental health, are inextricably linked to issues of social deviance. The intersection between what is considered by many to be great art and others to be madness was emphasized by the public and critical response to the art of the French impressionists in the 1880s. In 1886, the American critic from the *Art Journal* referred to these artists as the "maniacs of impressionism." By the early 1900s, Impressionism had been incorporated into the mainstream of the art genre, but many critics and much of the public at large then viewed the paintings of the early modern art movement as works of "insanity." Reviews from the 1913 International Exhibit of Modern Art (The Armory Show) in New York City labeled the artists as degenerates, psychopaths, and victims of dementia; one critic even accused Picasso and Henri Matisse of feigning insanity in order to make money.

The English writer of the late 1800s, George Eliot (a pseudonym for Mary Ann Evans), satirized the human propensity to see deviance as an indication of madness in her 1871 novel *Middlemarch*: "Sane people did what their neighbors did, so that if any lunatics were at large, one might know and avoid them." The use of labels within a society and the way in which those who are diagnosed are treated cannot be separated from the values of the society at large. This synchronicity between what is judged to be mental disorder and social deviance is a major reason why diagnostic categories are not static but change as society changes. The views of society shift, making some diagnoses obsolete and others seemingly more relevant. One need only consider the increased prominence of eating disorders and the relative disappearance of the diagnostic category of hysteria to see that there is a fluid relationship between perception and frequency of occurrence of mental disorder. Therefore, prevailing diagnostic criteria change over time and we have not just one "Diagnostic and Statistical Manual" for all time but we have many revisions, such as DSM III, IV and V.

The philosopher Michel Focault took the view of madness as social construct to its extreme in his work *Madness and Civilization*. He claimed that all "madness" is not only a social construction but "madness" is a label that enables the powerful to punish those who do not accept their practices. Thus, deviation from prevailing views is not just labeled to be wrong but also to be "mad." Expression of divergent opinions can lead to incarceration, censure, social isolation, and to either voluntary or forced mental treatment for personal or political reasons.

Women have been subjected to a greater degree of social constriction over the course of history than men. Consequently, it was more likely that they would be labeled as mad because of the narrow view of what constituted normal female behavior. Moreover, women have traditionally been denied equal access to positions of power within the social institutions (of religion, law, and medicine) that determine deviance and sanity. Recent statistics from the Humphrey Institute at the University of Minnesota indicate: "Women represent fifty percent of the world's population; they perform nearly two-thirds of all the working hours; receive only one-tenth of the world income; and own less than one percent of world property." These numbers provide overwhelming evidence that women still do not possess even close to half of the world's resources while contributing more than half of its productivity.

In this chapter, the relationship between female nonconformity to societal expectations and society's determination of madness will be examined through the avenue of significant stories handed down from ancient Greek culture. While Greek culture may seem far removed from present-day attitudes, I will argue that our concepts of women and of mental disorder are far more connected and influenced by the assumptions of the Greek culture of 2500 years ago than we realize. Western society's culture, politics, art and science are based on Greek values and these templates are the underpinnings of our own society, an observation made by Romantic poet Percy Bysshe Shelley who stated, "We are all Greeks—our laws, our literature, our religion, our arts all have their roots in Greece."

A hundred years ago, any educated person, regardless of their field of study, had to have a thorough knowledge of the Greek and Roman classics and was expected to even know how to read and write Latin and Greek. Few people today, unless they are classical scholars, study or even know much about classic literature. As knowledge of these works slips away, it becomes more difficult to make a case for the relevance of their lessons to our current lives. However, people and their motivations, emotions, and perceptions are much the same as they ever have been. Thus, as William Faulkner stated: "The past is never dead, it is not even past." Moreover, during significant periods of time, such as the Victorian era in England, references to Greek culture, laws and art have been used effectively to reinforce societal views of women as passive and inferior. Joseph Kestner, in his book *Mythology and Misogeny*, presents convincing evidence for the linking of the active suppression of women's civil rights in the 1800s and the use of myth in classical-subject painting. Even more significant to an examination of the concept of female madness, the context of psychiatric medicine and psychological mental health are based upon Greek models, from the words that we use for diagnosis to how we structure scientific inquiry.

Stories are the way in which culture perpetuates itself. These ancient Greek classical stories are particularly important because they have been a part of the cultural lexicon for thousands of years and they form the basis of many other great works of literature and visual art. In an eloquent exploration of the biological versus social aspects of the concept of gender, Val Plumwood emphasizes how biological sexual designation is itself a story that is imbued with social attributes. Physical aspects of the male or female are given a particular significance that is culturally determined: "Gender thus incorporates a theory, or a story, of how the body is, and how the person is, as well as material treatment." The representation of women who do not conform to society and are judged troubled or mad in Greek myth and art can inform us about some of the earliest stories linking gender, societal perceptions, and madness.

In spite of the overwhelmingly misogynistic laws and values of Greek society in fourth century BCE, only one of the extant Greek tragedies does not contain any female character. Several of the greatest tragedies focus upon women who are nonconforming, strong, and even heroic in their actions. In the remainder of this chapter, I will address the history of sex role expectations and female behavior in ancient Greece and its relevance for today. I will connect these stories to historic and contemporary women's struggles and underscore the relevance of Greek female archetypes to modern day views of women.

218

I will suggest ways in which these ancient artistic masterpieces can help us to see more clearly the challenges that women face today. The ways that these tales are directly linked to our present perceptions of gender are multifaceted:

- First, these stories communicate important information about the archetypes of women in Western culture.

- Second, these artistic masterpieces serve as a template for the understanding of human behavior that has informed human culture for 2500 years.

- Third, the social commentary inherent in these parables raises questions about and challenges to the role of women in ancient and contemporary society.

- Fourth, consideration of the themes of these works allows us to metaphorically examine gender roles that extend into our present-day consciousness and affect current assumptions about mental health.

I will use four female figures in Greek myth and tragedy that portray nonconformist women to further explore this issue: the myth of the nymph Echo, and the characters of Cassandra, Clytemnestra, and Antigone from Greek epic and tragedy.

Zeus and Thetis,
painting by Jean Auguste Ingres, 1811

History Of Sex Roles In Ancient Greece

The Greek belief in the male's absolute sovereignty over women is clearly expressed in Aristotle's great philosophical treatise *The Politics*. Greek women were almost completely dependent upon men for their very existence. In ancient times, women were sacrificed to the gods at the will of their fathers, as depicted in Aeschylus' tragedy *Agamemnon*, and they were routinely enslaved and sometimes sacrificed by their captors in war, as occurred in Homer's *Iliad*. And yet, women's physical beauty, sexuality, and ability to bear children as a benefit to the state were extremely political matters. The Trojan War, arguably the single most pivotal story upon which most Greek tragedy and visual art grew, was, at least symbolically, based upon the possession of Helen of Troy.

Sex roles in ancient Greece were very clearly delineated: men were duty-bound to risk their lives in battle for the protection and advancement of society, and women were expected to risk their lives in childbirth for the replenishment and continuation of the community. The laws of ancient Greek society did not give women the right to refuse to bear children even though childbearing was an exceedingly high-risk proposition and remained so until the mid 1900s. Once children were born, women had no parental rights. This lack of any maternal jurisdiction over what happened to children mirrored Aristotle's philosophical supposition that children belonged to the father because he believed that sperm were the source of life and women were merely vessels for the progeny of the male. The sharp division of societal responsibilities between the sexes was accompanied by a clear separation between the spheres of influence of men and women: Women had no vote; they had no role in political life; and they had no rights to own any kind of property. Women's influence and physical presence was supposed to be limited to the "oikos", the home.

Rape and abduction were common events for women in ancient societies. Defeat in battle meant the slaughter of the children of the defeated men and the capture of the women to generate children for the victorious side. Slavery always followed capture and sexual enslavement was an acknowledged and accepted part of the slavery of women. Moreover, the almost perfunctory and systematic rape of women in war has continued until the present day with many documented instances occurring just during the past century, including: the "Rape of Nanking" over six weeks in 1937-38 when the Japanese captured Nanking, China, raping thousands of women and forcing many of them into sexual slavery; the systematic rape of women during the genocide in Rwanda in the 1980s; the routine and politically motivated raping of women during the Bosnian war of the 1990s; the recent use of the large scale raping of women as a weapon of war in the Darfur region of Sudan; and the documented use of wide-spread and repeated rape of women and girls of all ages by armed combatants as a part of current conflicts in the Republic of Congo.

Sex roles in the ancient world were very rigid and the price for nonconformity was extremely high. And yet, as we see from surviving literature and history written almost exclusively by men, some of these women did not conform to societal expectations and were both revered and reviled for it. In summary, women's beauty, sexuality, and ability to bear children were very real commodities in the ancient world, and the control of women has been a political issue of the utmost importance that continues until the present.

Women's Legal Status And Impact On Madness

While there were significant fluctuations in the rights of women in Western society between the ancient Greek world and English and American culture of the 1850s, 2500 years later, women had almost exactly the same civil rights and legal status that they did in ancient Greece.

Greek and American Law
Women's Civil rights

Ancient Greek Law	American Law
No Property Rights	No Property Rights Married Women's Property Acts (Mississippi 1839) Rights to keep wages (1860s and '70s)
No Rights Pertaining to Children	Consideration of Maternal Custody Rights (1860s and '70s)
No Vote or Political Role	Nineteenth Amendment to US Constitution (1920)
No Physical Sovereignty	Packard Laws to Prevent Spurious Confinement of Women in Mental Institutions (1860s) 1921 Margaret Sanger establishes American Birth Control League

Legal civil rights reflect the most basic level of change within the life and consciousness of a community. Laws change not just as a function of cultural changes but frequently legal change occurs prior to wide spread attitudinal and emotional change within the society at large. American law was formed on the template of English laws. English law regarding women was, in turn, based upon the ancient legal principle of *femme covert* that asserted a wife had no identity before the law separate from her husband. English common law stated that the "…husband and wife are one person, and the husband is that person"; thus, adult single women were recognized as independent entities before the law, but married women had no legal autonomy and were considered extensions of their husbands. The legal extension of the principle of coverture in practice meant that women had no rights to property, no right to vote, and no right to enter into any contracts or legal agreements. In fact, in 1873 the United States Supreme Court referenced the principle of femme covert when it denied Myra Bradwell the ability to practice law in Illinois because she was married. Even though she had met qualifications, the court stated that she could not sign contracts or represent clients because, as a married woman, the law did not consider her an autonomous individual. This legal interpretation made married women wholly dependent upon their husbands and allowed men to have complete jurisdiction over their wives.

Documenting changes in American laws is difficult because many changes occurred on a state-by-state basis before they were passed as federal laws. For instance, Colorado, Utah, and Wyoming allowed women to vote on local and state issues long before the Twenty-first Amendment federally mandated women's suffrage. (I have chosen to list the date when the first state adopted a change in legal status or to list a range of dates when laws were passed in various states.)

Women had no rights to any personal or other property until the first "Married Women's Property Act" was passed in Mississippi in 1839. However, women still had no rights to keep their wages, even if they were divorced, until laws were passed in the 1860s and '70s. Women exerted no control over the fate of their children and were not even considered as a potential custodial parent until the 1860s and '70s. "Packard Laws" in the 1860s attempted to prevent the spurious commitment of women to mental institutions. The laws were named for Mary Packard who was institutionalized for over two years by her minister husband for expressing theological beliefs that differed from his. Until the 1900s, women had no rights to physical sovereignty or even access to information about birth control. It was not until 1921 that Margaret Sanger was legally able to open the first clinic devoted to dissemination of birth control after having been repeatedly arrested. However, it is not until 1972 that the Supreme Court guaranteed nationwide access to birth control regardless of marital status. In spite of the passage of the Nineteenth Amendment in 1920 ensuring women's voting rights, it was not until 1974 that the United States Supreme Court rendered a judgment preventing states from excluding women from jury pools because of their sex. These changes have had a profound effect regarding the role of women in our society and they have all occurred during the past 170 years.

Women And Mental Health

Most people who have even a peripheral connection to the current world of mental health treatment know that women seek out and are the recipients of mental health intervention significantly more often than men. Many epidemiological studies, such as those done by Kessler, et al., demonstrate that just being a woman makes it approximately twice as likely that a person will experience an initial episode of major depression in life. Furthermore, major depression is now considered to be the second most common etiology of "disability" among women in the United States. Various authors and researchers have questioned the use of a male norm as the baseline against which women are compared.

Moreover, separation of mental diagnoses along gender lines reveals an exceedingly complex picture of gender and diagnosis. While women constitute the majority of anxiety, depressive, and eating disorder diagnoses, men clearly display more prevalent difficulties with substance abuse and they heavily outweigh women on diagnoses of psychopathy and rage disorders. It is clear, however, from current epidemiological research, that not only do women seek out mental health advice more often than men but that they also receive more prescriptions for psychotropic medications than men. Unfortunately, the mental health field that women consult has a troubling history in its assumptions about women and their mental functioning. Cultural assumptions about the essential nature of women have influenced historic treatment for women. While a thorough exami-nation of this area is beyond the scope of this chapter, it is worth mentioning some of this background as a way of exploring the traditional views of women and madness in our society.

Insanity itself was initially linked to being female. The Greek concept of hysteria was derived from the word *hystera* meaning womb. The Greeks believed that a wandering uterus caused the excessive and inappropriate emotion associated with a diagnosis of hysteria and this view was widely endorsed even throughout the nineteenth century. By definition, a man could not be hysterical because he had no uterus.

The early field of mental health, like almost all other fields of research, medical, and social endeavor, was profoundly influenced by a society that was organized around the supposed intellectual and emotional inferiority of women. The legal dominion that men had over women lead to many cases of abuse of power when it came to institutionalization, as noted in the history of Mary Packard. In fact, Mary Wollstonecraft, the great English feminist of the late 1700s, set her novel, *Maria, the Wrongs of a Woman*, about the injustices women suffered in society, in a mental hospital. Maria's husband commits her to a mental asylum in order to gain control of her money and obtain his sexual freedom. Unfortunately, Wollstonecraft's story was inspired by a society that allowed men total dominion over their wives, daughters, sisters, and widowed mothers. Once committed to an institution, the patient lost all civil rights and was subjected to treatment without consent. Release from the asylum was only secured at the behest of the warden or the male relative and was almost totally dependent upon cooperation with treatment and submission to the will of male authority.

The relative number of women versus men who were institutionalized in psychiatric facilities varied over time with a peak ratio of 1.38 female to male in the mid-twentieth century. Many authors, such as R.D. Laing and Thomas Szasz, have explored the paternalistic nature of early psychiatric treatment. However, while many men with mental disorders were subjected to enforced incarceration and mistreatment, their abuses were related to their perceived madness and were not directly linked to their gender alone in the way that many women's experiences were. Women were much more affected by abuses of power because of their complete lack of independent legal status as well as the societal notion of the female as the weaker and less rational sex. With the definition of mental disorder focusing upon perceived rationality and ability to reason, women were clearly at a disadvantage within a societal context that assumed women were more emotionally labile and irrational. The sociologist Joan Busfield carefully analyzed the research and writings on gender and mental disorder in her 1996 book *Men, Women and Madness*. She concluded that the concepts of mental disturbance and gender are intricately linked in a way that continues to affect perceptions, diagnosis, and treatment of women. She summarized the reciprocal relationship between gender and mental functioning in the following way:

> Constructs of mental disorder are, therefore, inherently gendered, and are linked with the regulation of gender. And the relationship between gender and mental disorder is reciprocal. For whilst gender is imbedded in constructs of mental disorder, the constructs of disorder which are developed and elaborated by a range of mental health professionals, incorporating ideas about causation and treatment as well as about symptoms, in turn contribute to the way in which gender itself is constructed.

Furthermore, many nineteenth century pseudoscientific theories were presented on the brain structures of women that reflected the prevailing societal bias regarding the desired qualities of a woman. Projection of evolutionary theory into the sphere of social sciences in the mid to late 1800s contained immeasurable societal bias toward women.

An extreme (but not singular example) of this distortion of gender assumptions, behavioral perception, and diagnosis, was Joseph Buchanan's "System of Anthropology." In 1854, Joseph Buchanan superimposed his medical map onto a lithograph of Praxiteles' *Aphrodite of Knidos*. He classified the different areas of the body, linking the psychological and behavioral aspects to the corresponding physical areas. Given society's view holding female mental illness as rooted in feminine physiology and sexuality, it is not surprising that Buchanan labeled female reproductive organs as the "region of insanity" and that he stated: "The selfish or evil propensities are located below the waist...." From the perspective of 150 years, it may seem easy to dismiss these suppositions as being quite ridiculous, however, it is important to note the ubiquity of these attitudes. The significance of this history is to serve as a warning for us in our approach to understanding and treating women in contemporary culture. We are no more immune from the social assumptions of our community than those who came before us. It is next to impossible to maintain an objectivity completely separate from our cultural beliefs, and we can only hope that our own conclusions will not seem quite as ridiculous to those who will discuss them 150 years from now.

Women's Voices

One of the pivotal issues for contemporary historians and feminists is the issue of women's voices. Accounts of history written by women are scarce. Many women, such as the majority of women in ancient Greece, received no formal education and remained illiterate. The writings of women frequently generated little respect as historical records because they were more personal accounts, usually set within the sphere of the home. Writing, however, was one of the few occupations that allowed women to earn an independent living in the 1800s. Even so, popular opinion considered that women writers were likely to become either insane or infertile. For example, in 1873, Dr. Edward Clark, a trustee of Harvard University, attacked the notion of women gaining any college or even high school education because of "medical/scientific" evidence that too much knowledge affects their ovaries and limits their ability to reproduce. Furthermore, some proprietors of insane asylums emphasized that excessive education of women was a precipitant for madness.

227

Only You Can Silence Yourself,
photograph by David LaChapelle

The issue of the female voice is as contemporary as the 2004 election when popular photographer David LaChapelle produced a striking image for the "Declare Yourself" campaign, attempting to educate and inspire young voters to participate in the political process. The Greeks, however, contemplated the issue of the female voice over 3000 years ago in the myth of Echo and Narcissus.

Echo

Narcissus was an uncommonly beautiful man and admirers of both sexes pursued him. He rejected all of these would-be lovers without any seeming pity or remorse. His beauty fueled his pride and a sense of superiority. Capable of inciting great passion and longing in others, he was incapable of experiencing these emotions himself. One day as he was out hunting with friends, Narcissus encountered the nymph Echo. Like many before her, Echo fell madly in love with Narcissus. He never returned her affection or even her interest. Echo became so obsessed by Narcissus, following him, trying to please him, that the gods punished her for a lack of proper self-respect by

228

literally making her into an echo. She was gradually reduced to only a voice as she pined away for Narcissus. Her nonconformity to societal expectation to maintain her individual integrity thus precipitated her fate—the loss of self and the madness of only existing as an echo of another's reality.

Echo Narcissus,
painting by John William Waterhouse, 1880

The story did not end well for Narcissus either. The gods punished him for his self-absorption: They allowed Narcissus to see his reflection in the pristine waters of a glassy pond. He became obsessed with himself and the beauty he saw reflected, trying to embrace and kiss his own image. He drowned, either while trying to merge with his reflection or as he plunged a dagger into his own heart after realizing the futility of having fallen in love with himself. This painting by Waterhouse does a magnificent job of playing upon the mirror images of Narcissus and Echo to show his total absorption with self to the exclusion of others, and her total preoccupation with Narcissus to the exclusion of any sense of self.

The lover of Narcissus becomes a parody of the beloved, only capable of reflecting the narcissist's own thoughts and feelings. Obviously, becoming a narcissistic echo can happen to a male or female, and this fate involves some selection on the part of the individual who idealizes the narcissist. Women, however, are much more likely to fulfill the role of Echo in a society that idealizes men and values them above women. The story is archetypal, not just for Greek society but also for present-day American culture. How often have you heard the story of Echo and Narcissus from female clients or from female friends? This story captures the essential conflict of the female in a society that demands subjugation of one's views, needs, and sense of self to another person. It is an exploration and an archetype of the conclusion of what must ultimately occur if an individual completely immerses his or her sense of self in the identity of another. The symbol of an echoing voice with no identity attached to it is a powerful metaphor for women who are only pleasing to men when they present a reflection of the male viewpoint.

Cassandra

What if you have a voice, express yourself, speak the truth, and not only are you not heard, but everyone thinks you mad even though you are the only one who sees reality? This was the fate of a Trojan princess named Cassandra. Her story, like many of the greatest stories of Greek and Roman history and myth, revolves around the Iliad , Homer's epic of the Trojan War. Scholars disagree over whether the Iliad was written by one author or many, whether the tale was an account of an actual historical battle or whether it was solely a myth. There is disagreement over the actual date of the events in the Iliad , and even the date when it was written. What most scholars do agree upon is that the story was told and retold as oral history before the written version appeared. The Iliad served a central role in educating Greeks, not only about history but also about significant codes of behavior within Greek society.

The *Iliad* was an oral account of one of the greatest events in the Trojan War epic. It documented the events leading up to and including the slaying of Hector, a prince of Troy, by the great mythic Greek hero Achilles. The Greek view of the *Iliad* as a pivotal record of Greek culture is emphasized by the fact that with the development of writing in the early seventh century BCE, the *Iliad* was one of the first Greek stories to be recorded in written form. Although our current society views the stories associated with the Trojan War to be mythical, the ancient Greeks viewed the story as an actual historical account of the events leading to the fall of Troy. The Greeks dated the fall of Troy to 1184 BCE (as it would correspond on the current calendar). The *Iliad* served not only as a form of entertainment, but even more importantly as a historical record that many Greeks viewed as a tale of the accomplishments of their direct ancestors. Perhaps the most important function of the *Iliad* , however, was to teach the younger members of society about Greek identity and Greek values; therefore, the stories contained in the *Iliad* reveal many of the underlying cultural assumptions of the structure of Greek society.

The *Iliad* starts during year nine of the ten-year Trojan War. As with many great conflicts, the Trojan War began with love. Helen of Troy was universally acknowledged as the most beautiful woman in the world. She had many suitors who all agreed to pledge their allegiance to whomever won her in marriage and to come to the assistance of the victor if anyone ever tried to take Helen from him. Helen married King Menelaus of Sparta and lived with him in peace until Paris, Prince of Troy, came to visit.

Paris was the unfortunate mortal chosen by Zeus to judge a beauty contest between goddesses. Against all of the values of Greek culture and to the detriment of his entire society, Paris, the "beautiful", sought more beauty and chose Aphrodite, the Greek goddess of Love. Aphrodite rewarded Paris by compelling Helen to sail with him to Troy. According to some accounts, they took a large portion of the treasure of Menelaus with them. Menelaus, the scorned husband, gathered his troops and set sail for Troy in order to retrieve Helen, inspiring sixteenth century British poet Marlowe to write that Helen bore the "face that launched a thousand ships." After ten years, Troy was eventually defeated and destroyed after the Greeks used a wooden horse to infiltrate the city.

During the sack of Troy, the Greeks went far beyond the bounds of acceptable behavior. It is hard to go beyond the bounds of acceptable behavior when sacking a city but the Greeks did it and thus angered their own gods by their hubris. Cassandra lived through the Trojan War. Her father was the king of Troy and Paris was her brother. The Greek meaning of her name is "she who entangles men", but her story is one of an individual caught in tragic events beyond her control.

Cassandra was widely reputed to be the most beautiful of all of the Trojan women and more than one man reportedly came to defend Troy with the hope of marrying her. The dynamic of male pursuit of feminine beauty and society's emphasis on the importance of beauty for women has not changed over time. In her elegant analysis of the biological, social, and political aspects of beauty, *Survival of the Prettiest*, Nancy Etcoff concluded that our response to beauty is largely inherent, genetic, and universal. In spite of, or perhaps because of, the universality of our response to beauty, the particular significance of physical appearance in a woman's fate continues in the present. Etcoff's exhaustive review of the research shows that beauty has historically been more crucial for women than for men and that beauty remains the single most important attribute of a woman in the modern world. Beauty goes along with other good things. Those who are beautiful are judged to be more intelligent and even kinder than those who are not as good-looking, by women as well as men. Regardless of their own attractiveness, men and women both would prefer to date those whom they judge to be the most beautiful. The best looking women are not only ten times more likely to get married than the least attractive, but the beautiful are more likely to marry men with greater financial status and education than they themselves have. In contrast, there does not appear to be any positive relationship between female intelligence and marriage. One recent study looked at more than 10,000 men and women in Wisconsin and concluded that the women who had never married were significantly more intelligent when compared to the married group.

The significance of female beauty is especially true with regard to a woman's status in society. Results of a series of separate research studies (Blumstein and Schwartz, 1983; Bar-tal and Saxe, 1976) done in the 1970s and '80s concluded that a woman's perceived social status is determined by her own beauty while a man's status is determined by the beauty of the woman he is with. This effect was significant, not just for men but for women who appeared to want to be with the man who was with the most beautiful woman, not to be with the most attractive man. Even in our current-day society, beauty continues to be the most important determinant of a woman's attractiveness. A study by anthropologist John Marshall Townsend indicated that while accomplishment and prestige of employment enhances a man's attractiveness to women, male perception of a woman judged to be physically unattractive was completely unaffected by the status of her job. Ectoff effectively summarizes the continued centrality of beauty as a female commodityin her statement: "Good looks are a woman's most fungible asset, exchangeable for social position, money, even love."

While the possession of great beauty in any period of history including our own is a true challenge, beauty in the ancient world was especially a double-edged sword. Exquisite beauty like that of Helen of Troy could be rewarded with immortality from the gods, but it could also lead, as it did for Helen, to repeated abductions and attempts to control because of the way that possession of beauty reflected upon male status. In addition to this interference from mortal men, great beauty could also lead to persistent attention from the gods, including seduction, that was difficult or dangerous to refuse. The Greek gods frequently behaved much like Lady Caroline Lamb's description of Lord Byron: "He was mad, bad, and dangerous to know."

At a young age, Cassandra attracted the attention of Apollo, one of the greatest of the Greek gods. He was the god of prophecy, the god of art and music. He was handsome and the god of youth. He was both the god of plague and of healing. He was the father of Asclepius, the founder of the field of medicine. *What's not to love?* Apollo fell in love with Cassandra and bestowed the gift of prophecy upon her with the hope of winning her love. Some versions state that Cassandra promised her love and then betrayed that promise, while most indicate that at some point she simply did not return his affections, perhaps she never had. The reason why Cassandra rejected Apollo is never elucidated.

In order to punish her—for one must always be punished for rejecting the advances of a god—Apollo decreed that she would retain the gift of prophecy but that no one would believe her. She prophesied that Paris's trip to Greece would lead to the destruction of Troy. She told the Trojans not to accept the Greek gift of the wooden horse and predicted the doom that would follow. Finally, in Aeschylus' play *Agamemnon*, she predicted Agamemnon's death, as well as her own, while the Greek chorus chanted that she was histrionic, pathetic, and deluded. What could make one feel more mad than seeing the vision of reality and receiving either derision or pity in return?

The symbolism of truth in the story of Cassandra is an extremely powerful one, for what do individuals need to hear the most, and resist at every opportunity, but the truth? The story of Cassandra emphasizes the fragile nature of the truth. It is often easier for people to believe a deception like the Trojan horse because it is what they want to believe is truth. The war-weary and besieged Trojans, who had seen so many of their people die, must have desperately wanted to believe that the Greeks had given up, no matter how improbable that scenario or the gigantic wooden horse would have been. In the ancient world, just like today, the truth often had to be presented as metaphor. Picasso understood the metaphoric nature of art when he stated: "We all know that art is not truth. Art is a lie that makes us realize truth."

The story of Cassandra is iconographic with regard to women's experiences in two very important ways. First, Cassandra rejected a powerful male figure, a stunning act of defiance and nonconformity within the Greek world and throughout history until the present century. Moreover, in spite of the clear legal advantages of being a single woman inherent in female coverture, the structure of Western society has traditionally given social preference to a married woman, regardless of age, over a single one. The social institutionalization of this attitude was expressed with great irony in Jane Austen's *Pride and Prejudice* when the disgraced but newly married youngest Bennett daughter Lydia insisted upon her societal privilege of taking precedent over her sisters simply based upon her married state. Moreover, single women were at greater risk in society. Jane Austen's novels of the early 1800s graphically show the rather bleak existence of women who either chose or were forced to remain single. The economics of a society that insisted women of a certain class could hold hardly any job for pay, making them financial extensions of their male relatives, consigned these women to a genteel poverty of dependence.

The prevailing attitude of dismissal toward single women was forcibly stated in an 1848 Philadelphia newspaper article criticizing the women's suffrage movement: "A woman is a nobody, a wife is everything. A pretty girl is worth ten thousand men, and a mother is next to God, all powerful." This article expressed the prevailing devaluation of women as possessing little value in and of themselves and the exalted status given their role in connection to the male as mother of the male's children, object of male sexual desire, and extension of the male within the marital relationship. Elizabeth Cady Stanton, the American suffragist of the 1800s (herself a married mother of seven children), commented on the severe criticism especially endured by the single suffragists such as her friend Susan B. Anthony. Moreover, Stanton articulated the connection between female independence and the attribution of masculine traits by noting that men labeled the bravest and most independent women as "masculine." Florence Nightingale paid explicit tribute to the iconic role that the story of Cassandra has fulfilled for independent women over the centuries when she entitled her 1854 treatise on the psychological and societal price of enforced female dependence "Cassandra." Nightingale was one of the most prominent women who rebelled against the 1800s determination of a woman's value and role by her marital status.

The second way that the story of Cassandra is iconographic is its emphasis on the price of living without the benefit of male protection. Had Cassandra become Apollo's lover, she would probably have been rescued from her violent fate.

Ajax and Cassandra,
painting by Solomon Joseph Solomon, 1886

In this painting, the city of Troy has fallen, and Ajax the Lesser pursues Cassandra into the temple of Athena, the virgin goddess. He then drags her away from the statue of Athena and rapes her. The extremely proud and virile Ajax is carrying off the almost diaphanous Cassandra. Her veil, a symbol of her virginity, has caught upon Athena's statue and is ripping as he pries her from her refuge. Cassandra's rape is symbolic of the violence that women without male protectors had to endure throughout much of history. The interconnection of violence against women and its consequences upon the entire familial system is further examined in the tragedy *Agamemnon*.

Clytemnestra

The story of *Agamemnon* focuses upon the return from Troy to Mycenae of Menelaus's oldest brother Agamemnon. As the eldest male, he was considered the head of his extended family. Unfortunately for Agamemnon, his family was descended from the House of Atreus, a family characterized by rape, intergenerational incest, parents killing children, children murdering their parents, cannibalism, and violent behavior throughout the family system. Classics professor Elizabeth Vandiver has called the House of Atreus the "original dysfunctional family." Their story demonstrates that Western society's morality is not degrading over time, but in fact, illustrates that the same immoral behaviors we see and horrify us today were happening 3000 years ago. Like today, these behaviors were not the norm or the ideal, but they existed and they wreaked the same intergenerational disasters that they do today. Agamemnon's wife, Clytemnestra, was the half-sister of Helen of Troy. Agamemnon killed her husband in battle, took over his lands, and killed her infant son. And after this whirlwind courtship, he forcibly married her. I think most mental health providers would agree that this situation was not the ideal beginning to any relationship.

By the time that Agamemnon took charge of all the Greek forces and was ready to sail for Troy, he and Clytemnestra had four children, including Electra (of Freudian fame). Greek ships were dependent upon the wind to power their journey and Agamemnon's seer Tyresius proclaimed that the gods demanded from Agamemnon that he must sacrifice his most beautiful daughter, Iphigenia, in order for the winds to blow his ships to Troy. Agamemnon sent a deceptive message to Clytemnestra, telling her to send Iphigenia to him so that she could be married to the Greek hero Achilles. The sacrifice of Iphigenia is described in gruesome and wrenching terms. Iphigenia cried out to her father and the men she had known since childhood while they lifted her to the altar. Her father was, however, the one holding the knife and he indeed sacrificed her life to his ambition.

Clytemnestra received the knowledge of Iphigenia's sacrifice. At the end of the war, she not only learned that Troy had fallen but she also realized that Agamemnon was bringing home Cassandra, considered the grandest prize from the sack of Troy. Clytemnestra had not been whiling away the hours alone either. She had an ongoing affair with Agamemnon's cousin (Aegisthus) who intended to wreak his own revenge upon Agamemnon. When Agamemnon returned to the palace with Cassandra in tow, Clytemnestra came out of the *oikos* to greet them. Now, in Greek tragedies, it is usually a bad sign when women leave the *oikos*. Agamemnon, ever the charmer, told her that he brought Cassandra with him and that she should be kind to her because Cassandra was a stranger in a strange land. Clytemnestra was in no mood for kindness. She feigned delight at his return and rolled out the first red carpet in history. When Agamemnon entered the house to bathe, Cassandra, who could see the future, began keening and wailing that she and Agamemnon would be slaughtered, while, according to the epic, the background voices told her that she was needlessly upset and overwrought. Agamemnon cried out from the bath where Clytemnestra throws a net, which she herself has woven, over him, thus entrapping him, and then she stabs him to death. Thus, she took the Greek ideal of the highest womanly endeavor, weaving, and used it to destroy the patriarch of the family.

Clytemnestra,
painting by John Collier, 1882

Clytemnestra emerged from the *oikos* to tell how she slew Agamemnon. She stated that the murder was in retribution for the sacrifice of her daughter. Then in a truly horrifying turn, Clytemnestra indicated that the acts of killing were sexually exciting to her: "He lies there; and she [Cassandra] ...is laid against his fond heart, and to me has given a delicate excitement to my bed's delight."

At this point in the story, the other voices began chanting that Clytemnestra was evil, treacherous, obscene, deluded—an altogether unnatural and "man-like" woman. In the opening speech of *Agamemnon*, Clytemnestra was described as a woman with the heart of a man. By her actions, Clytemnestra embodied the qualities attributed to men in Greek culture: aggression, action, power, sexuality, and the ability to kill without remorse. She even clearly delineated the connection between violence and sexuality. Her usurpation of the male role led directly to her labeling as mad.

This relationship between sex roles and questions of sanity is long-standing and has been pervasive in the history of our own culture. One of the most clear-cut examples of the equating of sex role

239

definition and sanity in American society was the case of Lucy Lobdell. Lucy's husband deserted her at the age of eighteen and left her with a one-year-old child. She turned to hunting as a way of supporting herself since no other employment and little family support was available to her. She banded together with another abandoned young mother and they lived in the wild with Lucy assuming the role of masculine provider. They were eventually arrested for pauperism and Lucy was declared insane as a direct result of her masculine dress, hunting skills, and an enlarged clitoris. She remained institutionalized for the remaining thirty-two years of her life. In 1891, her physician P.M. Wise wrote an article about her, defending institutionalization as a means to protect her from the ridicule of society. Furthermore, he linked her sexual masculine traits with his determination of her mental illness by stating: "It is reasonable to consider true sexual perversion as always a pathological condition and a peculiar manifestation of insanity."

In recurrent themes in literature and art, the female who assumes the prerogative of male control, aggression, and power is viewed as a threat to society itself. Clytemnestra's murder at the hands of her own son was her punishment for her treachery and the violation of societal prohibitions. Clytemnestra is the prototype for many later figures in Western literature that commit violence upon men and then almost invariably suffer painful deaths themselves. Heroines who have also committed aggression against men consequent to their own suffering include: Sir Walter Scott's *The Bride of Lamermoor*, which was later transformed into the opera *Lucia di Lamermoor*; the great figure of nineteenth century sensation novels, Lady Audley, from *Lady Audley's Secret*; Thomas Hardy's protagonist Tess of the D'Urbervilles whom Hardy used to question Victorian sex roles and the societal victimization of women; and Glenn Close as a modern-day Clytemnestra bent upon the destruction of the offending male in the 1987 movie *Fatal Attraction*.

The tale of Clytemnestra highlights the issues inherent within society of who determines what it means to be a woman. The story questions assumptions about feminine nature and male control of the definition the female role. Our society is still struggling with this issue, from recently proposed legislation to restrict women's role within the military to battles over what constitutes sexual stereotyping. The representation and portrayal of women in culture and the media are frequent targets of feminists who challenge the assumptions of contemporary culture.

La Grande Odalisque,
painting by Jean-Auguste Dominique Ingres, 1814

This is perhaps the most famous image placed on a billboard in New York. It was the work of the "Guerrilla Girls", an anonymous group of women artists and art professionals who have been challenging sexual stereotyping and inequity in the art world and in our society at large for twenty years. This ad was to emphasize the under-representation of women in major museums while highlighting the use of the nude female body as a way of symbolically communicating women's traditional role in society as a passive one. Obviously, the image is a parody of Ingres' *La Grande Odalisque.*

241

Untitled piece,
by Anonymous/The Guerrilla Girls

Some of the most highly publicized and debated remarks of the past few years were those of Larry Summers, the former president of Harvard University. Summers eventually resigned after creating a furor over his comments postulating potential biological differences between men and women evinced in their supposed variant aptitudes and achievements in math and science. A prominent and powerful man was once again weighing in on the definition of female attributes. Many women, especially those with established careers in the math and sciences such as MIT biology Professor Nancy Hopkins, reacted with dismay. The intensity of her emotional reaction (feeling faint and ill) to President Summers' talk was diagnosed by columnist George Will as evidence of hysteria. Will resorted to Victorian logic and rhetorical tactics by criticizing her viewpoints and simultaneously negating her intellect via insinuations of delusion and hysteria.

Even if major biological differences between the sexes are found, the interpretation of what those differences mean will be crucial. Science is always the process of taking raw data, analyzing the results, and then attempting to understand the meaning of that information. The importance of interpretation of physical findings becomes clear if we look at historical treatment of the fact that the average woman's brain weighs approximately five ounces less than a man's brain. This difference in brain size was interpreted to confirm the assumptions of Victorian society that women were intellectually inferior to men. In 1864, Carl Vogt, a scientific contemporary of Darwin's who coincidentally endorsed some of Vogt's theories, used the difference in brain size to conclude that "...woman is a constantly growing child, and in the brain, as in so many other parts of her body, she conforms to childish type." Twenty years later in his 1884 paper "Mental Differences between Men and Women", George Romanes asserted that not only did the finding of a woman's smaller brain size confirm that women's judgment was much poorer than men's but that it explained why women's inferior judgment has been "a matter of universal recognition from the earliest times." Thus, physical findings are always susceptible to the assumptions we use in our interpretation of the meaning of these discrepancies, and our conclusions are always open to societal or individual bias.

We have now presented the archetypes of a woman as a reflection of men, as a victim cognizant of her fate refusing the advances of men, and as a woman who responds to the cruelty and violence of her life by claiming the prerogative of the male role. "But what can one brave girl do against the world?"

Antigone

The question, "What can one brave girl do against the world?" was how the suffragist Elizabeth Cady Stanton would end her popular lecture *"Our Young Girls."* Antigone is a story about what one brave girl with an unshakable sense of purpose and moral rectitude can do. The tale is the embodiment of the struggle between each individual's private morality and the authority of the government to determine what is in the public's best interest. It examines the powerful pressures that can be brought to bear upon the individual for conformity and the individual's sense of right, regardless of the sanction of society. The play *Antigone* was written by in 442 BCE during the apogee of Athenian democracy.

Antigone was a daughter of the ill-fated union between Oedipus and his mother. Oedipus was, of course, the Theban prince who unknowingly murdered his father and married his mother. This travesty caused a great plague upon the city of Thebes and resulted in Oedipus learning the truth of his parentage and blinding himself in shame and guilt. Oedipus then left the city and wandered through the countryside for years with Antigone at his side leading him. After Oedipus left Thebes, his twin sons struggled for power with one son grabbing the authority of the kingship and the other banding together with outside warriors to attack the city. Eventually, the two brothers decided to settle the war by individual physical combat between themselves that resulted in each mortally wounding the other. Their uncle Creon declared himself to be king and decreed that the one brother should be buried with honors while the brother who had attacked the city should have his body left uncovered to serve as carrion for the animals.

To a contemporary reader, this punishment does not have the same meaning as to an ancient Greek. One of the strictest responsibilities and moral obligations of a person in Greek society was to bury dead family members. The disfiguration or desecration of the deceased was a horrific specter to the Greeks and the worst fate one could suffer. It was Antigone's greatest religious duty to ensure the proper burial of her brother. She openly defied Creon's decree that anyone caught covering the body would be buried alive.

Antigone, from Sophocles Antigone,
painting by Marie Spartali Stillman (1844-1927)

This painting depicts Antigone sprinkling dirt on the body as the crows descend to pick at his remains. We see Antigone's younger sister (Ismene) holding onto her. Antigone tries to solicit her sister's help with the burial but Ismene refuses: "You ought to realize we are only women not meant in nature to fight against men." Antigone responds by asserting, "Be as you choose to be; but for myself I will bury him."

Antigone therefore declared her intent to define herself and her own actions as an individual rather than an extension of the government or of the expectations of the society in which she lived, thus earning her the highest rating on Kohlberg's scale of moral development and Creon's eternal enmity. In Sophocles play, part of the intensity of Creon's anger was his feeling of being bested by a woman. Creon's own misogynistic thinking was a major factor preventing him from being able to objectively consider Antigone's viewpoint. Creon's actions did cause the death of Antigone, but her death in turn led to his own destruction.

Clearly, the story of Antigone still has resonance in today's world. Antigone's opposition to Creon is the first recorded treatment of civil disobedience. The selection of a woman as civil disobedient was an interesting one and speaks to both the Greek view of women's sense of filial affection as well as the view of woman as an outsider who can only use civil disobedience to effect societal change. Force and military options were not available to her, so all she had was her own individual beliefs and actions to affect change. She could have a voice as long as she was willing to die for her beliefs. The story of Antigone is a treatise on the limits of not just government but of a monarchy based upon the rule of one individual. Creon is the prototype of the rigid and egocentric ruler who is unresponsive to the will of the people or to the input of individuals including that of his own son.

Summary

If being a nonconformist, especially a female one, increases and sometimes insures the assignation of madness, what can mental health professionals do to counteract that societal propensity?

1. We can have an enhanced awareness of history and the lessons it provides us with respect to assumptions about gender and mental health.
2. We must cultivate an awareness of our own individual propesity to disregard and label new ideas as deviant.
3. We should remain aware of the societal linkage of deviancy with madness.
4. We need to keep these stories in mind and issues in mind when listening to the stories of the women who seek mental health assistance.

The answer to these issues, I believe, lies first, in awareness and secondly, in productivity. I was recently fortunate enough to hear the African-American artist and author Faith Ringgold talk about her art and her long career. She gained success as a visual artist prior to becoming an author. In fact, her writing came about because she strongly felt the need to share the story of her life and wrote an autobiography. No one would publish it. At that point, I think, many of us would have given up on writing and focused upon success in the visual arts. Instead of being discouraged from having a voice through writing, she decided that this rejection meant that she *needed to write more.*

A literary agent saw one of her quilts on display and offered to publish the story behind it, stating that the story would make a wonderful book. Basically, from a psychological perspective, Faith Ringgold performed an incredibly elegant paradoxical intervention upon herself. Instead of giving up and silencing herself, she continued to persist in the face of discouragement and rejection. The only way for women to effectively deal with being discounted or with not being listened to is to talk more, to write more, to paint more, to build more, to find a way to express one's own voice, because the alternative is to become an Echo, lost in impotence and meaninglessness.

BIBLIOGRAPHY

Aristophanes. *Lysistrata and Other Plays.* London: Penguin Books, 2002.

Art Journal. 1880, vol. 6, p. 189.

Astbury, J. *Crazy For You, The Making of Women's Madness.* New York: Oxford Univ. Press, 1996.

Auerbach, N. *Woman and the Demon, The Life of a Victorian Myth.* Cambridge, MA: Harvard Univ. Press, 1982.

Barker-Penfield, G.J. & Clinton, C. *Portraits of American Women From Settlement to the Present.* New York: Oxford University Press, 2nd ed., 1998.

Bonnefoy, Y. (Ed.) *Roman and European Mythologies.* Chicago, IL: The University of Chicago Press, 1992.

Braddon, M. E. *Lady Audley's Secret.* New York: Dover Publications, 1974.

Brown, R. *The Art of Suicide.* London: Reaktion Books Ltd., 2001.

Bullfinch, T. *Bullfinch's Mythology, The Age of Fable,* Garden City, NY: Doubleday & Co., Inc., 191968.

Busfield, J. *Men Women and Madness, Understanding Gender and Mental Disorder.* New York: New York Univ. Press, 1996.

Carr-Gomm, S. *Hidden Symbols in Art.* New York: Rizzoli Pub., 2001.

Chesler, P. *Women and Madness*. San Diego, CA: Harcourt Brace & Co., 1992.

"Cubists and Futurists are Making Insanity Pay", *The New York Times*. March 16, 1913.

Elder, G.H., Jr. "Appearance and Education in Marriage Mobility", *American Sociological Review*, 34, 1969, 519-533.

Etcoff, N. *Survival of the Prettiest, the Science of Beauty*. New York: Doubleday, 1999.

Foucault, M. *Madness and Civilization, A History of Insanity in the Age of Reason*. New York: Random House, Inc., 1965.

Gamwell L., and Tomes, N. *Madness in America, Cultural and Medical Perceptions Of Mental Illness Before 1914*. Binghamton, NY: State Univ. of New York, 1995.

Gantz, T. Early *Greek Myth, (Vol. 1 & Vol. 2)*. Baltimore, MD: Johns Hopkins Univ. Press, 1993.

Geller, J. L. and Harris, M. H. *Women of the Asylum, Voices from Behind the Walls*, 1840-1945. New York: Doubleday, 1994.

Gilbert, S. M. and Gubar, S. *The Madwoman in the Attic, The Woman Writer and the Nineteenth-Century Literary Imagination*. (2nd ed.) New Haven, CT: Yale Univ. Press, 2000.

Grant, M., Hazel, J. *Who's Who in Classical Mythology*. New York: Oxford Univ. Press, 1993.

Graves, R. *The Greek Myths, Complete Edition*. London: Penguin Books 1993.

Greely-Smith, N. "An Alienist Will Charge you $5,000 to tell you if You Are Crazy; Go to the Cubist Show and You'll be Sure of It For a Quarter", *Evening World*. February 22, 1913.

Greene, L. and Sharman-Burke, J. *The Mythic Journey, the Meaning of Myth as a Guide for Life*. NewYork: Simon-Schuster, 2000.

Grene, D. and Lattimore, R. (Eds.) *Greek Tragedies, Volume 1, 2nd Edition*. Chicago, IL: University of Chicago Press, 1991.

Grene, D and Lattimore, R., (Eds.) *Greek Tragedies, Volume 2*. Chicago IL: University of Chicago Press, 1960.

Guerber, H. A. *The Myths of Greece and Rome*. New York: Dover Pub. 1993.

Healy, P. and Rimer, S. "Furor Lingers as Harvard Chief Gives Details of Talk on Women", *New York Times*. February 18, 2005.

Holcombe, L. "Victorian Wives and Property, Reform of the Married Women's Property Law, 1857-1882". In: *A Widening Sphere, Changing Roles of Victorian Women*. M. Vicinus, Ed. London: Indiana University Press, 1977.

Homer. *The Iliad* . Lattimore, R. (translator), Chicago, IL: Univ. of Chicago Press, 1961.

Hubert, S. J. *Questions of Power, The Politics of Women's Madness Narratives*. Newark, NJ: Univ. of Delaware Press, 2002.

Humphrey Institute, University of Minnesota. "Looking to the Future: Equal Partnership Between Women and Men in the 21st Century", quoted in Debbie Taylor, *Women: A World Report*. Oxford: Oxford University Press, 1985, 82.

Johnson, T.J. (Ed.) *The Complete Poems of Emily Dickinson*. Boston: Little, Brown and Co., 1960.

Kessler, R. C. "Epidemiology of women and depression", *Journal of Affective Disorders* (74), pp. 5-13, 2003.

Kessler, R.C., McGonagle, A., Swartz, M.,Blazer, D. G., Nelson, C. B. "Sex and depression in the National Comorbidity Survey I: Lifetime prevalence, chronicity and recurrence", *Journal of Affective Disorders* (29), pp. 85-96, 1993.

Kessler, R. C., Zhao, S., Blazer, D.G., Swartz, M. "Prevalence, correlates, and course of minor depression and major depression in the national comorbidity survey", *Journal of Affective Disorders* (45), pp. 19-30, 1997.

Kestner, J. A. *Mythology and Misogyny, The Social Discourse of 19th Century British Classical Subject Painting*. Madison, WI: Univ. of Wisconsin Press, 1989.

Kiernan, J.G. "Psychological Aspects of the Sexual Appetite", *Alienist and Neurologist*. April 1891, pp. 202-203.

Knowles, E. (Ed.) *Oxford Dictionary of Quotations (5th Edition)*. New York: Oxford University Press Inc, 2001.

Marlowe, C. *Doctor Faustus*. Scene 12, lines 80-86.

Marks, N. F. "Flying Solo at Midlife: Gender, Marital Status, and Psychological Well-Being", *Journal of Marriage and the Family*, 58, 1996, 917-932.

Nightingale, F. *Cassandra and Other Selection from Suggestions for Thought*. Mary Poovey (Ed.) New York: New York Univ. Press, 1992.

Nolen-Hoeksema, S. "Sex Differences in Unipolar Depression: Evidence and Theory", *Psychological Bulletin* (101:2) pp. 259-282, 1987.

Plumwood, V. "Do We Need a Sex/Gender Distinction?" *Radical Philosophy*, 51: 2-11.

Rimer, S. "Professors, in Close Vote, Censure Harvard Leader", *New York Times*, March 16, 2005.

Rodin, J., Silberstein, L., Striegel-Moore, R. "Women and Weight: A Normative Discontent", *Nebraska Symposium on Motivation*. 1984.

Rothblum, E. "I'll Die for the Revolution but Don't Ask Me Not to Diet: Feminism and the Continuing Stigmatization of Obesity" in Fallong D. Katzman, MA, Wooley, S.C., Eds. *Feminist Perspectives on Eating Disorders*. New York: Guilford Press, 1994.

Scott, S. W. *The Bride of Lammermoor.* New York: Oxford Univ. Press, 1991.

Showalter, E. *The Female Malady, Women, Madness, and English Culture, 1830 1980.* New York: Pantheon Books, 1985.

Sigall, H. and Landy, D. "Radiating Beauty: Effects of Having a Physically Attractive Partner on Person Perception", *Journal of Personality and Social Psychology*, 28, 1973, 218-224.

Summers, L. Text of: Remarks at NBER *Conference on Diversifying the Science &Engineering Workforce.* Cambridge, MA. January 14, 2005.

Townsend, J.M. and Levy, G.D. "Effect of Potential Partners' Costume and Physical Attractiveness on Sexuality and Partner Selection", *Journal of Psychology*, 124, 1990, 371-389.

Townsend, J. M. and Levy, G. D. "Effect of Potential Partners' Physical Attractiveness and Socioeconomic Status on Sexuality and Partner Selection", *Archives of Sexual Behavior*, 19, 1990, 149-164.

Townsend, J. M. "Mate Selection Criteria: A Pilot Study", *Ethology and Sociobiology*, 10, 1989, 241-253.

Udry, J. R. and Eckland, B. K. "Benefits of Being Attractive: Differential Payoffs for Men and Women", *Journal of Psychological Reports*, 54, 1984, 47-56.

Ussher, J. Women's Madness: *Misogyny or Mental Illness?* Amherst, MA: The Univ. of Massachusetts Press, 1992.

Warnock, J. "Major Depression in Women: Unique Issues", *University of Virginia School of Medicine Reports on Psychiatric Disorders.* A. Clayton, Ed. 2004, Vol.1, No. 1.

"What Cesare Saw at the Armory Show", *The Nation.* March 6, 1913.

Wiederman, M. W. and Allgeier, E. R. "Gender Differences in Mate Selection Criteria: Sociobiological or Socioeconomic Explanation?" *Ethology and Sociobiology*, 13, 1992, 115-124.

Wise, P.M. "A Case of Sexual Perversion", *Alienist and Neurologist.* Jan. 1893, p. 91.

Wolcott, James. "Caution: Women Seething", *Vanity Fair.* June 2005, pp. 92-98.

Wollstonecraft, M. *A Vindication of the Rights of Women.* Amherst, NY: Prometheus Books, 1989.

Wollstonecraft, M. *Maria, The Wrongs of a Woman.* New York: W.W. Norton & Co., 1994.

Lewis Mehl-Madrona, MD, PhD, grew up in Appalachian Kentucky (Mt. Vernon) with his mother's people who were Scottish Cherokee blends. He attributes much of his contemporary identity to the traditional teachings of his grandparents, Hazel and Archie Price.

He attended Indiana University and received a BA in biophysical chemistry, then graduated from Stanford University School of Medicine, and completed his residencies in family medicine and in psychiatry at the University of Vermont College of Medicine. He received his PhD in clinical psychology from the Psychological Studies Institute in Palo Alto, California, did post-doctoral work at the University of California at Berkeley, and received a Master's degree in narrative practices from Massey University, Palmerston North, New Zealand.

Lewis has taught at a variety of medical schools including Stanford University, the University of Arizona, and, most recently, the University of Saskatchewan. His focus has been aboriginal culture and healing, particularly developing a style of medicine and psychiatry that is indigenous derived and sensitive. He has been addressing the question -- what would medicine and psychiatry be today if they had been created by indigenous people and evolved continually into the present time. In his books (Coyote Medicine, Coyote Healing, Coyote Wisdom, Narrative Medicine and, most recently, Narrative Psychiatry: healing mind and brain in a social world, he writes about a style of healing practice that is both contemporary and indigenous, applicable to both worlds, capable of integrating magic and science, bridging the ancient and the modern worlds through narrative philosophy and practices.

Lewis currently is the Director of the Psychopharmacology Program for Argosy University Hawai'i where he is also Associate Professor of Psychology. He is also adjunct professor of anthropology at Johnson State College in Vermont, where he teaches on-line coupled with long weekends so he can ski and enjoy sub-zero weather from time to time.

Coyote Necessity: Trickster is Required

Lewis Mehl-Madrona, MD, PhD

The trickster is a recurrent image in human cultures around the world (Ricketts, 1966; Hultkrantz, 1979, 1984). Let us consider what trickster does or adds to these cultures. What is his or her role? Is trickster a necessary ingredient of human culture? We can readily see trickster testing the bounds of possibility and order. My suspicion, about which I intend to weave a story in this essay as I focus on one trickster, Canis latrans, or coyote, is that the messages provided by all of coyote's stories (creation, trickster, folk lore, and religious) improve survival. Trickster reminds us about the unpredictability of nature and the Universe. By breaking rules, he reminds us that rules can be broken, which becomes necessary as conditions radically change. By poking fun at our sacred institutions, he reminds us that we, as a culture, choose whatever we do, and that it is not the only choice possible. I suggest these ideas are essential for survival in rapidly changing conditions or catastrophes and that coyote is an ideal candidate for this instruction, since she is a survivor, one of the few animals spreading in distribution in the face of human encroachment.

(Cooper, 1984, 1987) describes how coyote became more negative as people moved from hunting and gathering toward agricultural societies. Trickster's attributes were more appropriate to hunting and warfare than to farming. Bukowick (2004) believes that "negative symbols acquire strength as cultures grow further away from the land they live on and focus on industry and humanity instead of the world around them." She notes also that people tend to bestow unacceptable human characteristics upon animals. For example, coyotes in nature tend to be monogamous, but one aspect of coyote the trickster is that of hypersexual lecher.

Regardless, coyote is a remarkable literary figure who wanders through the oral literature of North America, as well as that of contemporary writers, Native and not (Bright, 1993). Coyote's many roles – trickster, sacred being who helps create the world, folk hero, bringer of omens, stimulus for change, fomenter of chaos that betters mankind, wanderer, lecher, hunter, glutton, outlaw, survivor, and more – contain knowledge about survival that could be conveyed and remembered in no better way than through these trickster tails.

In deviance theory, sociologists argue that a healthy society contains at least 3 to 6% deviants of many forms. This provides a diversity of resources for adaptation to sudden, tumultuous change. Coyote is one of those deviant characters. He lives on the edge, at least two standard deviations from the mean, but ready to adapt. To me, Coyote represents the antidote to what Taleb (2007) calls The Black Swan, or the unpredictable event that brings down the house of logic and rationality. Taleb gives the example of the turkey, happily fed for 1000 days only to find himself on the chopping block on the 1001st day, the day before Thanksgiving. Taleb writes about the defects of inductive logic, for turkeys – that one can safely assume, having been fed for 1000 days, that one will be fed the next day – which he calls Hume's Problem. Coyote would address this problem by sneaking into the turkey pen long before that fateful Thanksgiving eve, exhorting the turkey to wake up and run away. Or Coyote would try to eat the turkey, perhaps alerting the turkey to an awareness of danger, bringing him out of his lulled complacency. Coyote reminds us to expect the unexpected and to prepare for the impossible. In Coyote's world, the improbable is common place, and the impossible occasionally appears.

The broad arena for Coyote's original antics lies in parts of the North American Plains, the Great Basin, California, and the U.S. Southwest. This area may correspond to the original range of coyotes. Carroll (1981) believed that coyote functions socially to portray the simultaneous desire to be uncontrolled coupled with the wish to make the sacrifices that allow orderly social life, yet this would be an unfair reduction of Coyote's richness were we to stop here, for, regardless of how astutely people study animals and nature and their behavior, coyote as trickster is a human construction, and expresses meaning to other humans. Bukowitz (2004) believes that this symbolization operates to make sense out of the uncertainty of the natural world. "To represent an animal through symbols, humans have often taken the most obvious characteristics that animal displays as representative of the animal and have then infused them with meaning congruent with the human culture. This process takes thousands of years, and since the first creation of animal symbolism, each culture has added its own twists before passing it on to the next generation. However, the symbols that are eventually created are often more arbitrary than accurate, frequently layered with negative stereotypes that are not wholly deserved."

For example, Coyote can practice cruelties to mostly unsuc-cessfully gratify his desires (Radin, 1972:165), which would not happen in the wild. He is sometimes obsessed with satisfying his hunger (see Wiley Coyote of cartoon fame who never gets the road-runner) or sexual desire, as in one story in which Coyote gives rabbit his penis to hold so that he can sneak into the women's sweat lodge. When he calls rabbit to slip it under the wall to him, rabbit is nowhere to be found. The next morning he finds that rabbit put this penis to good use all night long (hence, rabbit's current reputation for fecundity). No one suspected that such a small animal could have such a large organ. Coyote forgave rabbit, however, and they remained friends. Most of coyote's excesses are of human design. Coyote may kill an animal in a gruesome manner or break tribally specific sexual taboos. Nature's coyotes are not gruesome or sexually perverse. These are human attributes.

In another genre of stories, coyote serves as a cultural hero to transform the world to be more inhabitable for humans by ridding it of dangerous monsters or by providing the means to live or live well (fire, ways of capturing animals, inspiring the invention of rain, etc.). Between the Okanagan of British Columbia and Washington State, Coyote was given the job of ridding the world of evil monsters who would devour humans. In this context, Levi-Strauss (1963) says that the trickster is associated with the origin of culture.

255

In almost all cultures, Coyote plays an active, sometimes major, role in creation, despite his ambivalent and often bumbling portrayals. For the Dene people of Arizona and New Mexico, Coyote was present from the beginning of creation. He was present when Fire Man made Fire Mountain and watched the invention of fire. He accompanied First Man and First Woman in their journeys from world to world. He remained when the Holy Beings superseded First Man and Woman. Coyote caused the flood that leads the Dine people to emerge into this fifth world. He invented death, interfered with the placing of stars, and generally pokes his nose into everyone's business.

Coyote also has superior knowledge. When there was uncertainty over the desirability of death, for example, when "No one knew what to do, they asked Coyote" (Yazzie, 1971). Coyote wanders off by himself only to turn up and offer advice and instruction when needed. He was enlisted by Changing Woman to steal dreams from people for the Holy people, so that they could give the people forewarning of disaster and disturbance. Having received this, the people could enact a Blessingway ceremony to restore harmony or beauty (hozho) and to exclude evil. Coyote was responsible for ordering proper and necessary life patterns, including crop growing to ensure the people's survival. He provided warnings and signs to travelers. From pieces of his fur and bone come all coyotes (for both the Dene and the Pima of Central Arizona) and different colors for the 4 different directions. In a wonderful, Pima story, Coyote is taken to the Land Above by Buzzard who has discovered a hole in the sky. Coyote wishes to gamble with a new audience who doesn't know his tricks. He gets so caught up in having fun that he forgets that Buzzard must leave at sunset so that his wings will not freeze on the long trip down. Unwilling to wait or perhaps uncertain that buzzard will return for him, coyote makes his own wings out of cedar boughs, launches through the hole, and falls to his death on the earth far below. The animals are at first unmoved and mutter, "good riddance." They soon discover that life without coyote is boring. What's more, there's no one to blame things on. They sing and sing and sing and dance and dance and dance and pray and pray and pray for Creator to bring coyote back. By the next morning, ever bit of fur, flesh, or bone has turned into a baby coyote. Apparently we need this character.

I would interpret this as suggesting that indigenous cultures were well aware of the survival values of Coyote's attributes. To understand that more, we must consider the historical contexts of these cultures. The Dine people are known to have migrated from their main cultural grouping in the sub arctic, (Cooper, 1984). Cooper (1987) has traced the emergence of Coyote from the earlier image of Raven held by the Athabascan Dine of the North. As the Southwestern Dine relocated, raven merged with coyote, who eventually emerged as the dominant figure (as he is in the American southwest). An obsolescent ceremony, the Ravenway remains, which is linked to the Coyoteway. Cooper (1984) describes the Southern Dine's move from shamanism, hunting and warfare to an agricultural/pastoralist economy and to a religious system based on knowledge rather than personal experiences. He wrote:

> The reformulation of Navajo religion--in particular the adoption of Emergence mythology and cosmology, the structuring of the Chantway system, occurred under Pueblo influence following the Pueblo Revolt in the late 17th Century. Warfare adopted many of the techniques associated with hunting, which declined in importance with the adoption of the agriculturalist and pastoralist economy. Both hunting and warfare became associated with witchcraft, particularly following the trauma of incarceration in Fort Summer between 1864-1868, caused by the suppression of widespread Navajo raiding. Emergence cosmology and mythology are dominated by anthropomorphic deities who supersede the animal gods so important in hunting and shamanism. It is not therefore surprising that Coyote, whose power is associated with hunting and warfare, thus became also associated with witchcraft. The transformation abilities of Coyote, both to change his appearance and to throw his skin onto others, are closely identified with the werewolf syndrome, which forms an important part of Navajo witchcraft beliefs (Cooper, 1987).

257

As a predator Coyote is associated with hunting. Hunting is, after all, a form of trickery requiring cunning, and there is no better survivor in nature than coyote. In fact, the paradigm provided by coyote as an animal is ideally suited to the status as Trickster figure. Many have developed an extensive lore regarding coyotes, from observing their behavior in the wild (Dobie, 1961); Hunting strategy is also adaptable to warfare, and the two are linked in Navajo culture. The Navajo word for Coyote, Ma'ii, as well as being a generic term for wolves and foxes and, by extension, all predatory animals, is also an old Apachean word for animal (Cooper, 1987). Illness in Navajo culture came originally from animals, mainly through lack of observance of correct hunting rituals and one of the masked figures appearing at Coyoteway ceremonial is Talking God, guardian of animals.

Coyote's job is to test and experiment. Pacific Northwest stories attribute this function to the Creator.. His role is to test the boundaries and our conceptualizations of the world. For many cultures, knowledge is acquired by disobeying or questioning the established order. Mythical heroes discover their knowledge through disobeying or ignoring rules, becoming ill and receiving ceremonial knowledge from the Holy People. Since Coyote is a god, not a human, he can continually refuse to obey the rules binding everyone else. He not only tests boundaries, but transcends them. He has ensured the people's survival and balanced the world but can also be unreliable, pompous, greedy, disruptive and dangerous. In the assembly of gods, good sits on the south side and the evil on the north. Coyote sits near the door so that he can ally himself with either side as it suits his whim (Reichard, 1963:423). McAllester and Wheelwright (1956), in a study of the Big Star Chant myth note that "The Star People announce that there must always be three kinds of people, Snake Men, Coyote Men and Star Men...The Snake is the awakening, the Coyote is man's animality and the Star is man's spirituality". Thus, not only does Coyote display human characteristics, but humans display Coyote characteristics.

258

Trickster tales stand separate from Creation myths in that they are not as bound to ceremony and ritual. Trickster tales relate to foolish, mischievous and occasionally disastrous activities. They describe encounters with other animals and beings, attempts to trick them, to become like them or to outwit them, attempts which inevitably rebound.

The tales are amusing and entertaining and are frequently told to children. Stories convey both a moral message in an entertaining (and therefore memorable) way, particularly to children, and demonstrate possibilities and limitations in the world (Toelken, 1969). "Coyote, through various actions and responses both extends the area of activities that have been and may be attempted and correspondingly demonstrates the limitations and/or consequences of such actions" (Guy, 1987). Toelken's informant noted that the tales were not taken as making statements about Coyote, but were to do with introducing a method whereby a whole range of topics could be considered; for instance, eye disease and injury and blindness. Coyote is a unique being, one who, in Toelken's words "experiences everything: he is, in brief, the exponent of all possibilities" (Ibid: 231). Coyote challenges and thereby authenticates and legitimizes the order established in the universe.

Let's look at some Dene (Navajo) coyote stories. In "Homes for Coyote and Badger" (Newcomb, 1990: 108-124), Badger is looking for a hill or mesa large enough to burrow into and build himself a house. Coyote has the insight that they will have to build their own mountain to have warm and safe homes. "You will find nothing but hummocks here," he says. Badger had never thought of building a mountain, but Coyote had watched First Man when the four sacred mountains were made, and had been with Fire Man when he started his mountain, so now he thought that he could easily build a mountain for himself. Here is one aspect of Coyote, the mimicry of the spirits, gods, sacred people, and the conveyance to humans and other animals of the sense that we can do anything. Coyote observes and imitates, not always successfully, but almost in a way that stimulates and incites

259

thoughtfulness not previously present. Badger would have never thought of building a mountain in which to place his home without coyote's suggestion.

Most cultures have known that children respond better to animal characters than human. Today, children's books largely attribute human characteristics to animals. Freud (1938) wrote that symbolism was an ancient way of expressing something both in and in waking consciousness. I think it's simpler than that – we just know that animals play well. They make good characters for our moral dramas. Coyote is no exception.

In the story of coyote and badger, coyote knows he needs a rock from the lower world, and finds a way to get Badger to go get it. Coyote is always trying to get others to do his work. I suppose in medicine and especially in psychology, we are always trying to get others to do their work. The problem arises when these others think that our work is to "fix them." Then we must, like Coyote, find a way to "go to sleep" while getting them to go out and do the work – in this case, to go to the four sacred mountains and to get a rock from the underworld from each of these mountains. We need to set our clients upon quests in which they do the work, even if they think they are doing the work for us.

Badger completes his quest, but returns with clay from the Lower World instead of rocks. At first, coyote is angry, but then considers that clay could work after all. Now, however, coyote has a problem. He doesn't actually know how to make a mountain out of clay, or anything for that matter. He knew that First Man had taken some powerful medicine into his mouth to blow onto the tops of the four sacred mountains to cause them to grow tall, and then he had taken something else in his mouth to blow on the two sides so they would stretch along the edges of the land (Newcomb, 1990: 89), but Coyote had no clue what these medicines were and he was too proud to ask First Man. We often find ourselves in Coyote's position. We know what we want to do and we know that others have done it, but we don't have a clue how to proceed. I think Coyote inspires us to go ahead and figure it out as we go. No other character in stories besides Raven, Coyote, and Crow, can start without a plan and improvise as they go. Coyote did just that. He asked Badger to go ask Hosteen Seal for the medicine that would make the mountains grow. Again, Coyote finds logic to persuade Badger why he must go instead of Coyote.

Coyote's constructions are never perfect, nor even good approximations. His mountains turned into three large hills, a small hill, and a huge arroyo where the medicine spilled and trickled down into the ground. Today this place is called Coyote Mountain, because it resembles the pads of a coyote's paw. Nor did Coyote think to build a doorway into his hills, which had turned hard as rock. Then Coyote convinces his digging friends – mole, skunk, gopher, and badger, to build him four doors. When they are done, he throws them out to find their own homes.

At the end of the story, Badger realized he had learned enough to build his own home, and he had retained enough of the sacred dirt and clay from the underworld to have the raw material. He knew where to gather the growing medicine from where coyote had spilled it, and when all this was done, he set about making his home, which is what is now called Badger Mesa. So Badger had learned enough from his trials and tribulations with Coyote to do a remarkable piece of work for himself, and this was Coyote's gift.

In the story of how the First People made piece with Fire Man and his clan so that their world would not be destroyed, Coyote disappears when it's time to work, so that Bat is chosen to negotiate with the Fire Clan (Newcomb, 1990: 95-96).

Coyote steals fire in a number of cultures including the Dine. The theft of fire is motivated by Coyote's personal discomfort (Newcomb, 1990: 139). Coyote causes the world to change. The sun changes his path across the sky, giving rise to the seasons and to uncomfortable temperature variations. Coyote "never did anything for himself if he could find someone else who would do it for him." (p. 139). Coyote steps forward when no one else is available, or all others have given up. Then the task is clear, as is what hasn't worked.

In the Dine story about stealing fire, Coyote cannot convince his friends to get it for him. The burrowing animals have made comfortable homes that are sufficiently warm for their needs without fire. They have insulation. Badger used a flat stone to block the doorway and keep out the cold wind. He built his house small enough that his family's body heat would keep their home warm. Skunk blocked his door with a great mound of leaves and used them inside his home for insulation. Gopher did not even bother with a door, but dug in and out whenever he needed to come and go. Mole did one better, and never came out.

Nor could Coyote convince the Bird People to help. Eagle, Owl, Magpie, and Bluejay all declined, since they already had warm homes. Most of the other Bird People turned away from Coyote because they made their homes of sticks, grasses, and moss, all of which were flammable. Fire seemed like a bad idea. Only Flicker and Hawk were willing to go. In both cases, Coyote convinced them by appealing to their vanity and leaving out key information – namely that Fire Mountain was guarded by Monsters, called Do'tsoh. Flicker failed for that reason. The Do'tsoh through fiery darts at him, driving him away. Hawk failed, but was able to get a good description of the Do'tsoh, enough to give Coyote an idea.

When no one else would go, Coyote does. He created a plan to trick the Do'tsoh into letting him steal fire. He wrapped a bundle of twigs onto his tail so that it could catch on fire. He filled both cheeks with salt crystals, since Hawk discovered that the Do'tsoh have no eyelids. He boldly sauntered up Fire Mountain, offering the Do't-soh the gift of beautiful, multi-colored shells which were "magic," and able to bring moisture to the air and turn rocks to soft sand (Newcomb, 1990: 146-147). Coyote employed deception to gain fire. He got permission to "warm up" by standing with his back to the interior of the mountain from which the fire rose. When the Do'tsoh suspected what he was doing, he threw salt into their lidless eyes while the twigs at the end of his tail caught fire. Then he ran down the mountain, following a zigzag course and catching all of Fire Man's magic arrows on the twigs tied to the tip of his tail. He paid a price. His beautiful white tail was forever singed with black at the tip.

When Coyote brings gifts to the people, trouble is invariably involved. Because Coyote hid behind bushes as he returned with the fire, and, toward the end of his journey, just hopped from bush to bush, he left the mountain on fire. First Women was awarded fire but also the problem of its excess, as Fire Mountain was ablaze, threatening to spread down to where the people camped. Something had to be done.

Is it convenient to have a scapegoat for the problems we see in ourselves but wish not to admit? The Pima story of missing coyote because there was no one else to blame would suggest this possibility. Having someone (coyote) to blame is convenient. Blaming coyote allows humans to continue believing themselves to be inherently good while providing an outlet for their otherwise frustrated unconsciousness that is more "user friendly" than repression or denial. I find that it is much easier in psychotherapy to talk about characters from stories or movies with whom my clients identify than it is to talk about them. Perhaps, as noted earlier, coyote's trickster character provides an opportunity for broaching difficult topics that otherwise would be undiscussed.

In another fire-stealing story from Northern California coastal people (Mehl-Madrona, 2005), coyote deliveries fire to the people but with the same concern that they are ill-prepared to take care of it. In this story, Coyote steals fire from the Up-Country People who have been hoarding it. At first the people are happy, but quickly they discover that the coverings of their lodges are not fireproof like those of the Upcountry People, and that where it had been too dark and cold, now it was too light and hot. In both cases, admiration for Coyote turned to disdain.

In the Dine example, First Woman coached Frog and an assortment of water birds to solve the problem by simulating rain. Then she shows the clouds what they did, and the clouds take over that very useful function. In the California example, Eagle remembered a hole that she found in both sides of the sky. She coached Bear to use his tremendous strength to throw the "big yellow ball" (the source of fire) through one hole so hard that it goes all the way around the earth and comes out the hole at the other end of the sky. One marvels at the traditional knowledge implicit here – that the earth is round and that gravity will keep the "big yellow ball" in orbit.

In the Dine creation story, Coyote and Badger arise in the Fourth World at the same time. The people noticed two columns of whirling dust approaching, one from the north, one from the south, each carrying something that resembled grey tumbleweed at its base. Suddenly the two dust columns came together with a loud noise, then rose up and disappeared in the sky. Where they had met stood two people with dusty, grey coats – Coyote and Badger. First Man observed that the North Wind had brought the people trickery and laziness in the form of Coyote. First Woman observed that the South Wind had brought industry and perseverance in the form of Badger. But Coyote is more than laziness and trickery. When called upon, he responds. No one else could steal fire, so he did. If someone else will work, Coyote is happy to let them, but he does rise to whatever challenge is necessary.

Almost as soon as he appears, Coyote demonstrates his approach. The people need corn. Pueblo People lived in the Fourth World, and cultivate corn. Rather than figure out how to grow their own corn, coyote convinced the people that they could just steal corn from the pueblo people.

Coyote features the lead role in an extensive body of Trickster tales, which Cooper (1987) believes are a separation of his Trickster characteristics from the Creation myths. These tales do not carry the same sacred quality as the Creation Myths (Hultkrantz, 1979), The not as bound to ceremony and ritual. These Trickster tales relate to foolish, mischievous and occasionally disastrous activities of trotting Coyote. They describe encounters with other animals and beings, attempts to trick them, to become like them or to outwit them, attempts which inevitably rebound. Coyote's characteristics are typical of the Trickster figure: greedy, vain, foolish, cunning and, occasionally, displaying a high degree of power. The tales are amusing and entertaining and are, among the Navajo, the most frequently told tales to children, but this does not mean that Coyote has become merely a figure of amusement and ridicule. Toelken (1969) discovered through interviews with a Navajo Coyote storyteller, that the perception of the Navajo was that the stories are not funny per se. He stated: "Many things about the story are funny, but the story is not funny" (p.:221). The purpose of the stories is to convey both a moral message in an entertaining (and therefore memorable) way, particularly to children, and also, as far as adults are concerned, to demonstrate possibilities and limitations in the world. Toelken's informant stated that "If he did not do all those things, then those things would not be possible in the world." Thus Coyote, through various actions and responses both extends the area of activities that have been and may be attempted and correspondingly demonstrates the limitations and/or consequences of such actions.

As Toelken's informant noted, the tales, although often seemingly etiological, were not taken as such by the Dine, indeed were not taken as making statements necessarily about Coyote, but were to do with introducing a method whereby a whole range of topics could be considered; for instance, there is a story concerning Coyote losing his eyes in a gambling game, to be replaced by eyes of pine pitch, which, although allowing him to see, start to melt when he approaches fire. This, superficially, shows why coyotes are afraid of fire and have yellow eyes. But the more important aspect of this tale is that it allows such topics as eye disease and injury and blindness to be considered. These tales are serious, as Toelken's informant emphasized.

The Arizona Dine have taken this notion of Coyote as trickster even further with their concept of "Coyote Sickness" (Luckert, 1979). This sickness manifests as nervous malfunctions; a shaking of the head, hands, or entire body; a twisted mouth; poor vision; loss of memory; fainting; sore throat; stomach trouble; and occasionally; loss of mind (Rutzky, 1998). Coyote sickness is associated with gambling, prostitution, and not unsurprisingly, alcoholism. Those under the influence of Coyote, like alcoholics and addicts, are neither inherently evil nor morally lacking in distinction to mainstream North American beliefs which makes them morally or genetically flawed (Luckert, 1979). When intervening in Coyote sickness, the healer leads the person on a symbolic journey to the center of the world. The journey takes place in progressive steps, beginning with a ceremonial purification and unraveling. Repeated prayers and reparations are made to both gods and humans offended by the patient's behavior. A request is made for deliverance, a search is made for the person's lost mind. In the presence of the divine, the patient is cleansed of shame (Rutzky, 1998).

Coyoteway is a ceremony to restore harmony with an offended Holy person, It has two, five and nine night sequences. It has masked impersonators -- Talking god, a Female Holy Person, and Coyote. The ceremony treats illnesses resulting from attacks by offended Coyote People.

Coyote-induced illness increased dramatically prior to 1948 due to a bounty offered on coyote skins and the subsequent extensive killing of coyotes. Since that time, coyote illness has declined, and today, a Navajo would prefer a white man to kill coyotes.

Luckert also noted that another Coyoteway apprentice believed that an illness could be traced to the great Coyote in the east, who sent illnesses through the Sun and Moon, thence via predatory animals to humans. This is clearly a much more powerful Coyote god, responsible for all illness and utilizing Sun, Moon and all predatory animals to inflict illness on humans. This view corresponds with the etiology of another ceremonial called Excessway, which posits a great Coyote sending illness via Sun and Moon, but thence to humans via game animals who have eaten poisonous or hallucinogenic plants.

Tricksters and Narrative Medicine

Traditional stories reveal a culture's way of life and philosophy. They provide moral guidance (Chanthyda, 2004). They criticize foolish and ignorant characters so that others will not behave like them. They illustrate the proper behavior, qualities, and good deeds needed to transform one's character. Stories embody the various types of conflict between characters (adultery, revenge, various complaints and differences of opinion, issues of power and wealth, etc.) and their resolution. The themes of traditional stories illustrate problems that human beings confront all the time and offer culturally sanctioned ways to solve these problems, including problems that are impossible to resolve. The role of peacemaker is often central to stories involving irresolvable problems. Trickster stories are crucial to cultural evolution and appear in virtually every culture.

Within narrative medicine, we endeavor to listen to the patient's story, to respect his or her version of the problem. Many of our stories do not have an obvious resolution, so dialogue is required, and must, by necessity, acknowledge the absurd, the indecipherable, and the mysterious. Stories can be minimal as Hans Christian Andersen illustrated. He was a mastery of minimalist stories with witty and snappy dialogue, similar to traditional Trickster stories, such as his story of a dialogue between an ancient tree and a day old fly, or "The Top and the Ball," a story of a chance meeting and dialogue between a top and a ball in a drawer (Nagle 2006).

Sometimes self-sacrifice, as in The Little Mermaid, will resolve an irresolvable situation. Sometimes "therapeutic trickery" will avoid the need for sacrifice on anyone's part. When we use our capacity for humor and juxtapose this perspective through multiple stories, we facilitate the patient's or the family's ability to "see something new" which was there all along. We use deception in the sense that we fool another to do something they wouldn't usually do or to see something in a way not typical for them. It is therapeutic because it benefits them in the long run. The ethical dimension emerges in regard to our tricking the person, which generally must be compassionate and non-coercive. In other words, the person must permit and even ask us to trick them for their own good. This "therapeutic trickery" enables the person to have a new awareness from outside their pre-stated values and goals.

We present people with novel experiences so that they can find a new platform from which to evaluate their old views. The court jester was the only character who could safely mock the King, and, yet, he provided the King with necessary and important information about how the King could be viewed and especially about how the common people would see the King and his actions throughout the realm. Couched within humor, the King could consider these possibilities without exacting retribution upon the message bearer. The fool or jester was "immune from prosecution." This trickery is sullied when it becomes manipulative to serve the needs of the trickster. For it to be therapeutic, the others' needs must be primary and must be served. This is consistent with the observation that North American tricksters are also always cultural heroes (Boas, 1898; Lowie, 1909; Radin, 1972:155-169) and not just tricksters.

Epictetus wrote, "It is not the events of our lives that cause us to suffer, but our perspective about these events." Fools, coyotes, ravens, rabbits, and crows, in the popular literature demonstrate for us new ways to see ourselves. They help us change our perspectives on these events.

Trickster may represent an indigenous version of chaos theory. In his role as social transformer, Trickster's activities resemble those described by chaos theory for large group transformation – how large groups interact in patterns, create new forms, or get stuck in old configurations (Pari Center, 2001). Trickster embodies the unfolding process of organizational and societal transformation and offers a holistic picture of "transformation in motion." Trickster stories capture the fluidity of the change process and its non-linear progression. Trickster changes organizations in non-logical, non-rational, non-European ways. Like chaos theory, Trickster shows us the constant process of creation, existing alongside the creativity as renewal and recreation. Trickster is unpredictable like non-linear systems. Trickster disrupts the nice predictability of a linear, business-as-usual world. Trickster is a source of positive feedback which spirals to accelerate change. Like chaos systems, Trickster is autopoetic in constantly recreating him or herself. Trickster is the symbol for the energy that continuously transforms and is transformed by living systems. It disrupts patterns, allowing new patterns to emerge that solve problems that could not be solved before. Tricksters in the various cultures are like "strange attractors" in chaos theory. Strange attractors are associated with patterns for self-similarity, but do not produce exact repetitions. Tricksters are slightly different in each culture studied. Tricksters, like strange attractors, are patterns or tendencies yet with an unpredictable quality. Like Chaos, Trickster represents the extreme high order of complexity, which cannot be described in detail, but can be metaphorically described through story. The apparent absence of order is seen in chaos theory as being simultaneous with extreme order. Trickster's antics gives us a lens from which to see aesthetically the characteristics of extreme order that cannot be described in any other way except through story. Like chaos, Trickster is extremely resilient. Bifurcation points exist, however, beyond which Trickster collapses, as in the Pima Story when Trickster (Coyote) is left behind by Buzzard when they visit the Sky People. Thinking that he has been left forever, Coyote prepares his own wings and tail and jumps to his death. He smashes into many pieces on the ground. At first the animals are glad to be rid of Coyote, but his absence is disquieting. When they can tolerate it no more, they sing and dance all night, praying to bring Coyote back to life. By the morning, each fragment of bone, each fragment of fur, every little piece of Coyote has become a new coyote pup, which explains why there are so many coyotes today.

What we call "narrative medicine" is medicine practiced with the skills to recognize, absorb, interpret, and be moved by stories. These include the stories people tell about themselves and their families, the stories they tell about their suffering, and the stories from within the culture. Trickster stories are part of this package.

To practice narrative medicine -- be it in internal medicine, family medicine, pediatrics, obstetrics, surgery, or psychiatry -- means developing the sophisticated skills to attend to what patients emit, to represent in language what they tell, and to affiliate with them and their families and other healthcare professionals in communities of care. It also means doing so within an environment of respect for the stories of the families and cultures within which we are working. These stories teach us how to approach irresolvable dilemmas (Leach, 1974:57-91), how to manage the inherent contradictions through dialogue (internal and with others), just as Coyote and other Tricksters engage in their internal and external dialogues, moving toward a negotiation of behavior that optimizes the dynamic pulls of the dilemma. On the one hand, for example, Coyote will sell his grandmother to get beautiful spots on his fur, but, on the other hand, we see that no one wins in the end. Everyone loses from excessively selfish behavior.

Narrative medicine had its start in such related efforts as patient-centered care and medical humanities. The clinical cousin of literature-and-medicine, narrative medicine takes those skills that one develops as a close reader or a reflective writer and bends them toward effective clinical practice. The close reader -- whether of fiction, poetry, or memoir -- follows the narrative thread of a story, enters into the teller's narrative world, and sees how that teller makes sense of it. The close reader identifies the images and metaphors, recognizes the temporal flow of events, follows allusions to other stories, and is imaginatively transported to wherever the story might take the one who surrenders to it. The close reader uses traditional stories, like those of the Trickster, to guide therapeutic practices for members of those cultures from which the stories come.

When medicine is practiced with these skills, the clinician or trainee has much to offer the patient. By listening with the close reader's attention, he or she can hear and receive in full complexity what the patient conveys in words, silences, gestures, positions, and physical findings. By representing with accuracy and skill what the patient conveys, the clinician honors what is told in all its detail and contradiction and dimensions and connotation.

This clinician with narrative competence becomes a witness and not a judge, a companion and not an interrogator, an ally and not simply the bearer of bad news or inflictor of discomfort. The clinician or trainee with these skills of attention and representation has the grounds of knowledge and of motive to develop a sturdy and clinically useful affiliation with the one who suffers.

Trickster and Psychotherapy

As I was puzzling over the role of Coyote in life and in psychotherapy, I found myself drawn to Milton Erickson, whose work was inspired from Chippewa healers in Wisconsin, and later, Native people of Arizona. Erickson specialized in helping people find their own hidden solutions in ways that were quite unique to them and drawn out of them through experiences orchestrated by Erickson. I found Erickson to be the essence of "Coyote Psychotherapy."

Erickson's example demonstrated to me that the trickster in psychotherapy is not devious, arrogant, or manipulative. Erickson was none of these. I found myself objecting to Richard Bandler and John Grinder's formulation of Erickson as Neuro-Linguistic Programming, since they removed much of the humor and compassion from Erickson to create something that seemed manipulative and even deceptive to me. I found Milton Erickson to be caring and compassionate, not at all like the image of the therapist scheming behind the scenes that I felt NLP portrayed. Erickson's "trickery" felt loving and in service to the person who came to him. He was not a puppet master, manipulating his characters by their invisible strings. He was engaged as a collaborator, teasing out solutions from people's stories about their problems and situations. NLP's "trickery" sometimes seemed to better serve the therapist's ego and feelings of being smart. That was when I realized that the world's trickster stories can teach us needed moral values to guide the trickery that is also known as psychotherapy.

Comparing Erickson to NLP helped me capture "coyote psychotherapy," which is certainly clever, clearly tricky, always

271

humorous, but never humiliating, patronizing, or malevolent. Those who couldn't get what Erickson was trying to show them left confused, perhaps, but never deprecated. The imposed structure of NLP seemed to describe what Erickson was doing, even convincing others of its truth. However, Erickson's own writings were more consistent with my coyote friends and not the NLP story, which seemed rehearsed, pre-planned, and artificially clever. Erickson appeared spontaneous, intuitive, and inspired. I suspected that he was engaged in multiple levels of connection with the person or persons suffering, that some of these other levels of connection provided him with information that he used to help the person. He never seemed to trick more than he was given permission to do. To my surprise, Erickson was more like the aboriginal world than the world of his imitators, copiers, and students. Erickson was himself a Coyote!

This discussion of "therapeutic trickery" a la Erickson leads us to consider trickery itself, to deconstruct it as a concept. What do we do when people are stuck? What do we do when cultures are stuck? What does it mean to be stuck? Does "trickery" arise spontaneously within cultures to resolve the situation of being "stuck?" Who does the tricking; what is a therapist? Apparently, people and cultures do become unable to see any perspective but their own and must be shocked or surprised or even tricked to see outside the box into which they have painted themselves. Trickster does this.

Philosophers show us that one counter-example refutes a rule, that it is impossible to accumulate enough evidence to prove something, and that, as no one could say better than Coyote, we must expect the highly improbable. Considering Coyote's role for the Dine people of Northern Arizona and New Mexico, Cooper (1987) said, "Coyote is a key figure in Navajo mythology, representing both good and evil, humans and gods, and of course animals. He is unpredictable and ambivalent, a characteristic of these beings. At the same time, however, by testing and pushing the limits…, he demonstrates and reinforces concepts of harmony and order…" I would guess that cultures who remember Coyote and her teachings are less likely to be lulled into complacent expectation of certainty. They are less likely to fall prey to "Hume's Problem" - *that we cannot gather from past experience any data that will give us certainty about the future.* Regardless of their best laid plans, coyote can come along and stir up everything with a simple kick of her hind paw.

But how does Coyote the Trickster "help" people who are sick or suffering. They come to therapists because they can't see an exit from their situation of suffering. They come as individuals, couples, families, and even large groups. Cultures can suffer, as aboriginal culture does today from the after effects of colonization, Christianization, and suppression of the sense of worth as a people that used to shine forth in the traditional stories, practices, ceremonies, dances, and ways of relating. Black Americans have written exquisite sagas of the suffering of slaves in the Southern United States, including perhaps the Uncle Remus tales, whom some think presented Br'er Rabbit as standing for the black slave with the other characters he outwitted representing white plantation owners (Wikipedia, 2006). Help can be seen as a process of dialogue that results in a new perspective on suffering, one in which the suffering can be overthrown or dismissed. People can apparently become so attached to their situation (perhaps habitually so), that, again, a shock, surprise, or trick may be needed. Shamans of old used magic tricks to get the client's attention (Lyon, 2007). Post-modern concepts of participatory action research also move us toward revised concepts of help, one in which the facilitator helps people to see their own local knowledge (Selamna, 1999), yet these techniques can also involve a "slight of hand" when the facilitator empowers local people to see what was always there in front of their nose (or snout).

The world's traditional stories, including coyote stories, provide education, life lessons and entertainment and reflect historical and cultural mores and customs (Yamada 1999: 599). Coe (2004) emphasizes their role in teaching values compatible with social survival – individual sacrifice in service to group survival; respect for children, women, and elders; service to the greater good over

273

individual gain, to name a few. Uncannily, trickster usually serves the higher good, though not always intentionally or even recognizably at first glance.

My involvement with Coyote. As a child, I dreamed of having an affiliation with an animal spirit. I wanted to be visited in visions by bears, eagles, and wolves. I spent time with wolves at various wolf hybrid and re-entry projects. I cultivated the image of the bear and tried to learn its name in at least 10 different native languages. I aspired to fly like an eagle. Fortunately or not, coyotes appeared wherever I went. Thus, as I wrote in Coyote Medicine, I was destined to align with coyote, to challenge the status quo, the champion the unexpected, improbable, and highly unlikely, and to poke holes in concepts that claim premature truth, when, in actuality, there is very little that we do know, except that the things we don't know are far more important than those that we do know.

REFERENCES

Baltimore City Community College: Humanities 207 Text: A Guide to Understanding Myths of Creation and Scientific Theory: Chapter III: Creation by an Emergent Being: North American Indians. http://www.users.erols.com/bcccsbs/c3emerge.htm#zuni. Last accessed 19 September 2006.

Boas F. (1898). Introduction. In Traditions of the Thompson River Indians of British Columbia. Teit J. (ed.). New York: Houghton-Mifflin, pp. 1 – 18.

Bright W. (1993). A Coyote Reader. Berkeley, CA:: University of California Press.

Buckowick KE (2004). Truth and Symbolism: Mythological Perspectives of the Wolf and Crow. Boston: Boston College Honor's Thesis.

Carroll M. (1981). Levi-Strauss, Freud, and the Trickster: A new perspective upon an old problem. American Ethnologist 8(2): 301-313.

Chamberlain AF. (1891). Nanabozho among the Otchipwe, Mississaugas, and other Algonkian Tribes. Journal of American Folklore 4: 193-213.

Chanthyda C. (2004). An analysis of the trickster archetype as represented by the Rabbit character in Khmer folktales. Royal University of Phnom Penh. Master's Thesis.

Chappell J. Living with the Trickster: Crows, Ravens, and Human Culture. PLoS Biol 2006:4(1):e14.

Clark E. (1960). Indian Legends of Canada. Toronto: McClelland and Stewart.

Cooper, Guy H. 1984 Development and Stress in Navajo Religion. Stockholm: Almquist and Wiksell.

Cooper GH. (1987). Coyote in Navajo religion and cosmology. Canadian Journal of Native Studies VII (2): 181-193.

Dobie, Frank 1961 *The Voice of the Coyote*. Lincoln: University of Nebraska Press.

Dorsey JO. (1892). Nanibozho in Souian Mythology. Journal of American Folklore 5: 293-304.

Emery NJ, Clayton NS (2001) Effects of experience and social context on prospective caching strategies by scrub jays. Nature 414: 443-446. Find this article online.

Freud, Sigmund. "Totem and Taboo." *The Basic Writings of Sigmund Freud*. Transl. and ed. Dr. A. A. Brill. (New York: Random House, Inc, 1938)

Hamilton J. (1903). The Algonquian Manabozho and Hiawatha. Journal of American Folklore 16: 229-233.

Harris M. (1979). Cultural Materialism. New York: Random House.

Hill K. (1963). Glooskap and his Magic: Legends of the Wabanaki Indians. New York: Dodd Mead and Company.

Hill K. (1970). More Glooskap Stories: Legends of the Wabanaki Indians. Toronto: McClelland and Stewart.

Hultkrantz A. (1979). Myths in Native North American Religion, in E.H. Waugh and K.D. Prithipaul (Editors): *Native Religious Traditions* pp. 77-97. Waterloo: Wilfred Laurier University Press.

Hultkrantz A. (1984) The Myths of the Trickster and Culture Hero, in M. Bhuriya and S.N. Michael (Editors): *Anthropology as a Historical Science*, pp. 114-126. Indore: Sot Prakashan.

Jacob JM. (1993) *The Cambodian Linguistics Literature and History: Collected Articles*. David A Smyth (ed.), London: School of Oriental and African Studies.

Johnson WJ. (1890). Mythology of the Menomini Indians. American Anthropologist 3z; 243 – 258.

Leach E. (1974). Claude Levi-Strauss. New York: Viking Books.

Leland C. (1884). Algonquin Legends of New England. Cambridge, MA: Riverside Press.

Levi-Strauss C. (1963). Structural Anthropology. Translators: Jacobson C, Schoepf BC. New York: Basic Books.

Lowie R. (1909). The Hero-Trickster Discussion. Journal of American Folklore 22: 431-433.

Luckert KW. (1979). *The Coyoteway: A Navajo Holyway Healing Ceremony.* Johnny C. Cooke, Interpreter. University of Arizona Press: Tuscon and the Musuem of Northern Arizona Press: Flagstaff.

Lundquist SE. (1991). *The Trickster: A Transformation Archetype*, San Francisco: Mellen Research University Press.

Lyon W. (2007). Shamanic Power. Berkeley: University of California Press.

Marzluff JM, Angell T (2005).. In the company of crows and ravens. Yale University Press.

McAIlester, David and Mary Wheelwright 1956 *The Myth and Prayers of the Great Star Chant and the Myth of the Coyote Chant.* Santa Fe: Museum of Navajo Ceremonial Art.

Mehl-Madrona L. (2005). Coyote Wisdom: The Healing Power of Story. Rochester, VT: Bear and Company/Inner Tradition.

Midan, Paul (trans.) (1933) 'Histoire de juge lièvre. Recueil de contes cambodgiens produits et annotés', *Bulletin de la societé des études indochinoises* (Saigon), 8 (4): 1-116.

Midan P. (1986). *Le roman cambodgien du lièvre*, Introduction de Jacques Népote et preface de Nouth Narang, Paris: Centre de documentation et de recherche sur la civilization khmère.

Nagle R. Book Notes: Stories of Hans Christian Andersen. http://www.imaginary-planet.net/essays/literary/hcastories.php. Last accessed 19 September 2006.

Newcomb FJ. (1990).Navajo Folk Tales. Albuquerque: University of New Mexico Press.

Pari Center for New Learning. (2001). Conference Report: Chaos Theory and the Arts in the Context of Social, Economic, and Organisational Development, 18 – 21 March, 2001. http://paricenter.com/conferences/chaos/chaosreport.php. Last accessed 19 September 2006.i9

Radin P. (1972). The Trickster. New York: Schocken Books.

Reid D. (1964). Tales of Nanabozho. London: Oxford University Press.

Ricketts ML.(1966). The North American Indian Trickster. *History of Religions* 5(2):327-350.

Rutzky J. (1998). The Trickster Archetype in Psychotherapy with Alcoholics and Addicts In *Coyote Speaks: Psychotherapy with Alcoholics and Addicts* New York: Jason Aronson, Inc.

Saskatchewan Indian Cultural Center. (2006). Article: Oral Tradition: The Beginning of the Cree World.

http://www.sicc.sk.ca/heritage/ethnography/cree/origin/oral.html. Last accessed 21 September 2006.

Selamna N-E. (1999). Relativism in agricultural research and development: Is Participation a post-modern concept? Working Paper No. 119. London: Overseas Development Institute. http://www.odi.org.uk/publications/wp119.pdf. Last accessed 20 September 2006.

Skinner A, Satterlee JV. (1915). Folklore of the Menomini Indians. Anthropological Papers of the American Museum of Natural History, Vol. 13., No. 3. Published by Order of the Trustees. New York.

Swanton JR. (1913). Animals Stories from the Indians of the Muskhogean Stock. Journal of American Folklore. 26:193-218.

Swanton JR. (1929). Myths and Tales of the Southeastern Indians. Bureau of American Ethnology Bulletin 88. Washington, DC: U.S. Government Superintendent of Documents.

Taleb NN. (2007). The Black Swan: The Impact of the highly improbable. New York: Random House.

Thierry S. (1988) *De la rizière à la forêt: contes khmères*, Paris: Éditions L'Harmattan.

Thompson S. (1966). Tales of the North American Indians. Bloomington, IN: Indiana University Press.

Toelken JB (1969). The "Pretty Language" of Yellowman: Genre, Mode, and Texture in Navajo Coyote Narratives. Genre 2(3):211-235.

Vucetich VA, Peterson RO, Waite TA (2004) Raven scavenging favours group foraging in wolves. Anim Behav 67: 1117-1126.

Wikipedia Encyclopedia. (2006). Br'er Rabbit. http://en.wikipedia.org/wiki/Br'er_Rabbit. Last accessed 21 September 2006.

Wyman, L.C. 1970 *Blessingway*. Tucson: University of Arizona Press.

Yamada T. (1999). Problematics of Contemporary Khmer Literature in English with Transnationals *Khmer Studies: Knowledge of the Past and Its Contributions to the Rehabilitation and Reconstruction of Cambodia*, Sorn Samnang, ed., Proceeding of International Conference on Khmer Studies, vol.II (Phnom Penh, Royal University of Phnom Penh, pp. 595-605.

Yazzie E.(1971) *Navajo History*, Volume I. Chinle: Navajo Community College Press.

Shirley Linden Morrison is Professor Emerita at Notre Dame de Namur University in Belmont, California, where she taught mythology, literature, including children's literature, for forty years. In 2004 she was the recipient of the University's prestigious Living Torch Award; in 2005 the School of Arts and Humanities and the NDNU alumni sponsored an endowed scholarship in her name. With Delmont, her husband of fifty years, she has co-authored Memories of Loss and Dreams of Perfection (Baywood, 2005) and numerous publications on creativity. Her work on Isak Dinesen led to an essay in The Encyclopedia of Creativity; she is also the author of "The Pearl and the Princes": a Tale of Twins, a fantasy romance.

Delmont Morrison, PhD, served as a Clinical Professor in the Department of Psychiatry, University of California, San Francisco, and was Director of the Clinical Psychology Training Program and Director of the Early Childhood Development Clinic. His long-standing interest in imagination and creativity, shared with Shirley, resulted in numerous publications, including "Organizing Early Experience." He also served on the editorial board of Imagination, Cognition, and Personality. Dr. Morrison passed away earlier this year. His contributions, warmth and wisdom will be missed.

C. S. Lewis :
Unsuccessful Childhood Grief Mourning, and Creativity

by Shirley Linden Morrison

and

Delmont C. Morrison

"With my mother's death all settled happiness, all that was tranquil and reliable, disappeared from my life ... It was sea and islands now; the great continent had sunk like Atlantis."

Introduction

Clive Staples Lewis (1898 - 1963)

C. S. Lewis , a prolific writer, may best be remembered for his seven volumes of the Chronicles of Narnia, a fantasy world that has touched generations of readers. It is not insignificant that as a child Lewis lived in an imaginative world that was more important to him than anything in reality. Initially, this world served to mitigate his feelings of isolation and solitude in Ireland. He shared this world with his brother Warnie, and after his mother died (Lewis was 9; Warnie was 12) it became even more significant. Her death alienated the boys from their father who withdrew into a major depression, but it brought the two boys closer together. As is seen in unsuccessful grieving and mourning, both were never shared by the family, and later, as an adult, Lewis was reluctant to trust his emotions.

In his 50's, simultaneously, he experienced a career crisis and the loss of Minto, a maternal figure who was extremely important to him: they had lived together for 30 years. Under this stress, Lewis returned to an imaginary world, different from the one in childhood which had compensatory value for him. Yet this world, too, was a contrast to the reality which surrounded him. In this world, evil could threaten but never triumph because of a powerful, mythical figure of good: the Lion Aslan. Protective and loving, Aslan's sacrificial death incurs loss and grieving, but the Great Lion is resurrected.

It is only after meeting, marrying and losing his wife Joy Davidman to cancer that Lewis explores grief and mourning in a profound way. His reflections on these experiences are recorded in his book *A Grief Observed*, generally acknowledged as a text on the subject. Lewis is the writer who can formulate this grief into words, shape his sorrow into art. It is the creative artist's attempt to understand, to explain, and to accept loss.

C. S. Lewis, or Jack as he renamed himself as a child, was nine years old when he suffered a tragic and irreparable loss: the early death of his mother at age 46 from breast cancer. His brother, Warnie, was twelve.

The real bereavement had happened before our mother died. We lost her gradually as she was gradually withdrawn from our life into the hands of nurses and delirium and morphia, and as our whole existence changed into something alien and menacing, as the house became full of strange smells and midnight noises and sinister whispered conversations. This had two further results, one very evil and one very good. We drew closer together … two frightened urchins huddled for warmth in a bleak world. It divided us from our father as well as our mother. They say that a shared sorrow draws people closer together; I can hardly believe that it often has that effect when those who share it are of widely different ages. If I may trust my own experience, the sight of adult misery and adult terror has an effect on children which is merely paralyzing and alienating. (1955, pp. 18-19)

Much understanding of grief and mourning is based on observations of adults who have lost an emotionally significant person (Neimeyer, 2003). The contemporary view of adult grieving is that it is a meaningful reconstruction of deeply personal and interpersonal dimensions. Because of developmental factors, grief and mourning in children are significantly different psychological processes from the experiences of adults (Webb, 2002). Like adults, children have grief reactions, such as denial, anger, guilt, sadness, and longing for the deceased. However, mourning as a process of understanding the meaning of loss is more complicated because this meaning will evolve over time as the child's developing awareness of self and others occurs. The child's mourning process will take longer and is characterized by strong emotional ties to the deceased and enduring compensatory fantasies. For example, the child may anticipate that the deceased will return, as Lewis believed, or that their spirit is present. The fantasy component of the mourning process is normal in a child and represents the child's continual emotional attachment to the deceased (Klass, Silverman, and Nickman, 1996).

The child's family relationships contribute significantly to the mourning process. Having a family member who can share the meaning of the loss with the child and help construct a positive future in the context of the family enhances both the grieving and the mourning process.

Lewis differentiates the child's viewpoint of grieving from adult grieving. Lewis' father reacted wildly to his wife's death: his emotions, his temper were uncontrolled; his actions were unjust. Thus he alienated his sons and forced them to trust and to rely on one another.

Everything that had made the house a home failed us; everything except one another. (1955, p. 19) Flora Lewis' death divided the boys from their grieving father, who went into a major reactive depression. As Lewis states, they lost a mother and a father.

There had been an operation in the home and an apparent convalescence, then a return of the disease and the increasing pain before death. Taken into his mother's room to see her at her death, Lewis experienced grief overwhelmed by terror. He reacts with horror to the coffin, flowers, hearse, and funeral.

> With my mother's death all settled happiness, all that was tran-
> quil and reliable disappeared from my life. There was to be
> much fun, many pleasures, many stabs at Joy; but no more of
> the old security. It was sea and islands now; the great continent
> had sunk like Atlantis. (1955, p. 21)

This grieving process is also noted in the first book of the
Narnia Chronicles, The Lion, the Witch, and the Wardrobe, where
Lewis speaks in first person, stepping out of his role as the omniscient
narrator. Lewis speaks to the pain that Lucy and Susan feel at the
death of the lion, Aslan.

> I hope no one who reads this book has been quite as miserable
> as Susan and Lucy were that night; but if you have been -- if
> you've been up all night and cried till you have no more tears
> left in you--you know that there comes in the end a sort of quiet-
> ness. You feel as if nothing was ever going to happen
> again.(1950, p. 155)

In successful grieving, the child reaches a point where the
parent is released and doesn't need to be replaced in the child's life.
C. S. Lewis had not achieved successful grieving or mourning in his
childhood.

The boys were also isolated from other children in the Irish
countryside. When Warnie left for boarding school, Lewis states that
his "real life" … was increasingly one of solitude." Lewis refers to the
significance of living in his imagination from the age of six. From the
perspective as an adult, the imaginative experience seems more
important to him than any thing else. Thus his creative paracosm of
"Animal Land" compensated for his isolation and the gradual loss of
his mother before her death.

A paracosm is a child's fantasy world, extended over a period
of time, that can serve as a compensatory function of imagination; it
is rewarding for the child. Developed at ages seven to twelve, it is
usually given up during adolescence. Children are emotionally
invested in this private world, but they can distinguish it from reality.
Paracosms are an integration of preoperational and operational
thought that helps the child adapt to relationships and social context.

282

Paracosmic fantasy (Cohen and MacKeith, 1991) develops during the time children demonstrate a growing capacity to use language, think in more socialized ways, and have a more articulate capacity for reflective thought. It is important to the child that this created world be internally consistent. Favorite toys and dolls often play roles in the stories. However, the range of fantasy is broad, and imaginary islands and countries with people who only live in the child's imagination also occur. Private language and means of communication known only to the child are used in these special places and guarantee the child's ownership. However, although the world is idyllic and private, the paracosm always contains important elements that correspond to real experience.

Lewis staked out a claim on one of the attics of his house as his study and began to write and illustrate his first stories; these began at age five and continued until his early teens. They were an attempt to combine "dressed animals" and "knights in armor." Chivalrous mice and rabbits rode out in complete mail to kill cats.

Warnie, three years older, claimed " Rajah Land" as his domain and filled it with ships, trains, and battles. When Warnie was home from school for holidays, "Animal Land" became modern rather than medieval so that the boys could share their paracosms. This led Lewis to attempt to write a full history of "Animal Land." Soon there was a map of "Animal Land," then several maps, always consistent, and geographically related to Warnie's "Rajah Land." Their paracosms were peopled with consistent characters, and they shared them with each other. These characters wouldn't surface again until Lewis was 48 years old.

Later, when Lewis was 19, he became a cadet in the British army, sharing a room with Paddy Moore, whom he rather disliked and found to be somewhat childish. However, Paddy's mother, Mrs. Janie Moore (separated from her husband for many years) became an important figure in Lewis' life. He spent weekends in her company, and his month's leave, to his father's dismay, was spent primarily with her; the last few days were with his father in Belfast.

There may have been a few young women whom Lewis noticed, but before any romantic relationship could even begin, there was Janie Moore.

When they met, Mrs. Moore, or Minto (so named because of her favorite peppermint candy), was 45, divorced, lively, attractive. Lewis was 19 and clearly looking for a mother; his own mother had died at age 46. She was poorly educated, but she made Lewis feel wanted, needed, comfortable. Before Lewis left for the front lines in France, he telegraphed his father to meet him in England to say good-bye. Some misunderstanding occurred and his father never came. Lewis turned to Minto for affection. When Lewis was wounded in 1918, Minto came to London to be near his hospital. He convalesced in Bristol, where she lived. And when he returned to his regiment , Minto spent the rest of the war following Lewis from camp to camp, to camp, setting up homes as near to him as possible. Finally when the war ended and Lewis went back to Oxford, she packed up her Bristol belongings and came too. They shared the rent on a furnished house in Oxford. In 1921 Lewis, Minto, and her daughter, Maureen, set up housekeeping together.

Much about Lewis and Minto has been eliminated from numerous biographies, including Lewis' autobiography, Surprised by Joy. In his words:

> I returned to Oxford;- "demobbed" - in January 1919. [He is 21 years old]
> But before I say anything of my life there I must warn the reader that one huge and complex episode will be omitted. I have no choice about this reticence.(1955, p. 198)

Lewis never mentioned Minto in his published writings, and this "reticence" that he states may have been to protect Minto's family from any scandal. His relationship with Minto was not conventional.

There is always the sexual titilation regarding their relationship. The significant part of that relationship is the emotional intimacy: Lewis' need for affection, support, stability -- all the things he lost at his mother's death at age 46.

When Paddy Moore died in the war, Minto wrote to Lewis father, saying that Paddy had asked Lewis "to look after me if he did not come back." This is the explanation found in most accounts of Lewis' life. The fact that the relationship between Lewis and Minto flourished well before Paddy's death is probably more relevant to the reality of the situation. Maureen married in 1940, but Minto and Lewis remained together till her death in 1951. Warnie called them "30 years of tyranny" and documents details of their relationship in his diaries and in his book, *Brothers and Friends*.

WEDNESDAY 17TH JANUARY, 1951

Minto died of influenza at Restholme about 5 o'clock on the evening of Friday 12th, and was buried in the churchyard at 2.30 on Monday … And so ends the mysterious self imposed slavery in which J [C. S. Lewis named himself Jack] has lived for at least thirty years … It would be Macaulayesque to say that he took a First in the intervals of washing her dishes, hunting for her spectacles, taking the dog for a run, and performing the unending futile drudgery of a house which was an excruciating mixture of those of Mrs. Price and Mrs. Jellaby, but it is true to say that he did all these things in the intervals of working for a First. Did them too with unfailing good temper (towards her) at any rate … Most infuriating to the onlooker herself as J's benefactor: presumably on the grounds that she had rescued him from the twin evils of bachelordom and matrimony at one fell swoop …

In the last fifteen years of her reign, I don't think I ever saw J work more than half an hour without the cry of "Baw-boys' … 'COMING, Dear!', down would go the pen, and he would be away perhaps five minutes, perhaps half an hour: possibly to do nothing more important than stand by the kitchen range as scullery maid. Then another spell of work, then the same thing all over again: and these were the conditions under which Screwtape, and indeed all his books, were produced. (pp. 236-237).

While Warnie describes Mrs. Moore's character in deprecating terms, it is clear that she meant something very different to Lewis. He and Mrs Moore had set up housekeeping without Warnie and even felt an intrusion into their privacy when he moved in with them. Lewis, Warnie, and Minto lived in the Kilns since 1930. The house was named after the brick kilns that stood nearby. The garden was the size of a small park -- eight acres of land with a lake. Being the dutiful son to a demanding mother became rewarding for Lewis, and when Mrs. Moore declined, physically and mentally, and was finally moved to a convalescent center before her death, he visited her every day. His loyalty was unquestionable; sharing daily life with someone for 30 years constitutes a marriage of sorts. Yet when she died, her mind and body had both deteriorated previously, and she was no longer his Minto. Lewis never wrote about her death, and although Minto was a mother figure for him, her death was psychologically not the same for him as the loss of his mother. Minto's death was expected: age and disease had claimed her. Lewis was relieved to be released and told a colleague it was one of his best years (Carpenter, p. 233).

Clearly, Minto was a powerful maternal figure for Lewis: the mother he lost, and, subsequently, the Boyhood that evaded him. Minto was difficult and demanding. Yet Lewis treated her with a far more adult patience than most blood sons could ever muster under the circumstances. For thirty years he played the "dutiful son"- an extended adolescence.

This boyishness pervaded portions of his life. His autobiography, *Surprised by Joy*, written when he was 57 years old, is deeply concerned with the crises of childhood, the demise and loss of his mother, the wild behavior of his father, and his unhappy boyhood school memories. As an adult his special fondness for re-reading childhood favorites like *The Wind in the Willows*, Beatrix Potter's books, and fairy tales also illustrates this "boyishness."

It was in his boyhood that he first experienced "Joy." It is an experience which is an instantaneous sense of seeing into the heart of things, as if an insight into the universe opened itself widely, then disappeared. In his words:

> an experience of a yearning, whose object was unknown ... the intimation of a dimension of reality that common sense and reason could not explain" (1955, pp. 17-18)

Lewis' first experience of "Joy" was in his early boyhood: an awareness of Nature in Warnie's toy garden, a simple concoction of moss and greens planted in a biscuit tin. Beatrix Potter's Squirrel Nutkin provided the second experience of "Joy." It gave him "the idea of Autumn" and a spontaneous revelation that the memory of the toy garden gave him: an insight into another world, a dimension of reality that is inexplicable. Again, it is tied into the world of Nature. The third experience evolved from reading Longfellow's *Saga of King Olaf*. The words Lewis quotes "Balder the Beautiful is dead, Is dead" lifted him into regions of the Northern Sky. These boyhood experiences of yearning for an unknown object that defied rationality finally, among other factors, led to his conversion to Christianity.

While Lewis demonstrated a "boyishness," he was also a respected scholar at Oxford. His Allegory of Love is still used by medieval scholars. He is also a Christian Apologist.

Before his mother's death, Lewis prayed every night for her recovery. When she died, he became an atheist. This lasted until his 30's, when he embraced Christianity, and, later, the Anglican Church. Then, in the 1940's, he wrote several volumes of Christian Apologetics: Miracles put him on the cover of *Time* magazine in 1947. He gave radio talks related to his books. In short, he became very popular.

This popularity did not sit well with his colleagues. By 1946 Lewis had been a Fellow of Magdalen College for 21 years and was a strong candidate for a professorship. He was competing with his good friend, J.R.R. Tolkien, who received the professorship at Merton College that same year. When another professorship opened up the next year, Lewis again was passed over. In 1951 another professorship became available; another colleague was chosen:

the vote was 173-194. Lewis was experiencing major stress. Besides the academic rejections of his colleagues, he was without Minto who died that year and the domestic security and stability she brought to his life.

It was at this point that Lewis returned to the compensatory world of fantasy and began writing the Chronicles of Narnia. His imagination had always served him well; writing was a creative venture that greatly rewarded him. He stated that a series of nightmares about lions led to his creation of Aslan in *The Lion, the Witch, and the Wardrobe.* (Incidentally, that particular wardrobe was carved by his grandfather and resided at his childhood home in Belfast. It now resides at Wheaton College in Wheaton, Illinois.) The work is not allegorical, per se, but a Christian analogy. Lewis stated that he raised a basic question regarding Christ and Christianity in a strange world.

Lewis wrote rapidly. He wrote all seven books in less than four years. After the first book, he wrote the next three books in one year, though they were published annually from 1950 - 1956. Lewis refutes the idea that his childhood paracosm had influenced his creation of Narnia. He claims there is no sense of wonder or romance in his original Animal Land. This may be because he needed to share this paracosm with Warnie, and Warnie demanded trains, steamships, and the country of India.

The year after finishing the Narnia Chronicles, 1954, Lewis was offered a Chair at Cambridge University: he was 56 years old. Reluctantly, he left Oxford but returned to the Kilns on weekends. After Minto's death, he and Warnie were alone together - until Joy Davidman Gresham and her two sons entered their lives.

The story of Lewis and Joy has been documented in books and in films: their correspondence; Lewis' initial reluctance to see her; her eventual divorce; their civil marriage in 1955 to maintain her sons in English schools; the awakening of love between them and a Christian marriage. And her fight with breast cancer. Finally, her death at age 45 from the same disease that destroyed his mother.

Once again Lewis shared the process of watching a loved one suffer, endure pain, and fight to live. It had to evoke childhood memories of his mother, of his unresolved grieving and mourning as a boy, of feeling abandoned and insecure.

Unsuccessful grieving in children results in a failure to master the personal meaning of the child's loss. This results in the preoccupation of and vulnerability to loss in adulthood. The association between early loss and later adult creativity has been documented (Simenton, 2000; Goertzel, Goertzel, Goertzel and Hansen, 2004). In the creative adult, like Lewis, this preoccupation with early loss can be expressed by telling or writing stories (Morrison and Morrison, 2006). These stories are compensatory: they may be an idealization of the experience of death, and the relationships in the stories are frequently attempts to control and master death and loss and come to a psychological state of successful grieving and mourning.

Successful mourning in childhood results in the child's capacity to think about death and loss that will allow the child as an adult to master the personal meaning of this loss. Clearly, Lewis was not prepared for his loss of Joy, who was brave; he admired her courage, her sharp wit, her humor. Married for four years, Lewis had finally found the relationship he had craved, in his words:

> Do you know I am experiencing what I thought would never be mine. I never thought I would have in my sixties the happiness that passed me by in my twenties. (Carpenter, p. 241)

And now he had lost it.

Initially, Joy had been in remission from the cancer; she and Lewis thought she was cured: but in 1959 an x-ray revealed that cancer had returned to many of her bones. Later, secondary cancer developed, and she had to have her right breast removed. Shortly after this, she died; Lewis was devastated:

No one ever told me that grief felt like fear. The same fluttering
in the stomach, the same restlessness, the yawning. I keep on
swallowing … then comes a sudden jab of red-hot memory and
all this" common sense" vanishes like an ant in the mouth of a
furnace. (1976, pp. 1-2)

Writing had always been a way for Lewis to cope with life.
While the compensatory venue of the paracosm had previously
worked for him when he was under stress: his mother's death, the
professorship rejections, and Minto's death, now his deteriorating
health, his lack of energy, and his depressed spirit could not conjure
another meaningful fantasy world for himself. However, he began to
write again. In *A Grief Observed* he records his thoughts and his feelings in the days and weeks after Joy's death. It is his personal mourning process.

Part of every misery is, so to speak, the misery's shadow or
reflection: the fact that you don't merely suffer but have to
keep on thinking about the fact that you suffer.

I not only live each endless day in grief, but live each day
thinking about living each day in grief. (1976, p. 9)

In the film *Shadowlands* (Attenborough & Eastman, 1993)
depicting Lewis' life with Joy, there is one son. In reality, Joy had two
boys. The film demonstrates Lewis and the one son commiserating
over their loss together. As children both had lost a mother, and they
share their grief. Indeed, they weep together. That never happened.
Lewis was unable to speak to the boys about Joy's death. In his words:

I cannot talk to the children about her. The moment I try, there
appears on their faces neither grief, nor love, nor fear, nor pity,
but the most fatal of all non-conductors, embarrassment. They
look as if I were committing an indecency. They are longing for
me to stop. I felt just the same after my own mother's death
when my father mentioned her. I can't blame them. It's the way
boys are. (1976, pp. 8-9)

Again, Lewis goes back to his mother's death ; it is a dual grief that he is experiencing:

> Cancer and cancer, and cancer. My mother, my father, my wife.
> I wonder who is next in the queue (1976, p. 12).

According to Thomas Attig, the functions of adult grieving in bereavement are twofold: a need to come to terms with the pain and anguish of the loss and a struggle to put one's life back together. He calls it "relearning the world" (Neimeyer, p.33). Lewis was trying to do precisely that.. In the text Joy is thinly disguised as "H."

> At first I was very afraid of going to places where H. and I had been happy-our favorite pub, our favorite wood. But I decided to do it at once-like sending a pilot up again as soon as possible after he's had a crash. Unexpectedly, it makes no difference. It's not local at all … Her absence is like the sky, spread over everything. (1976, p. 11)

Lewis struggles to relearn his life; he must also relearn himself: emotionally, psychologically, he is forced to deal with feelings that as a child he never coped with at his mother's death or had to cope with at Minto's death because of her age and deterioration.

> I thought I could describe a state; make a map of sorrow. Sorrow, however, turns out to be not a state but a process. It needs not a map but a history, and if I don't stop writing that history at some quite arbitrary point, there's no reason why I should ever stop. … Grief is like a long valley, a winding valley where any bend may reveal a totally new landscape.
> (1976, pp. 68- 69)

Another "relearning" transpires in a physical, sexual way. Lewis was almost 60 when he was married. His sexual union with Joy brought him tremendous pleasure. Now there is an enormous feeling of loss, of being divorced from his own body.

> There is one place where her absence comes locally home to me,
> and it is a place I can't avoid, I mean my own body. It had such
> a different importance while it was the body of H's lover. Now
> it's like an empty house. (1976, p. 12)

The one compensation which Lewis possesses is his memory of Joy. While initially these images invoke pain, he eventually realizes that they will bring him closer to the woman he still loves.

> I will turn to her as often as possible in gladness. I will even
> salute her with a laugh. The less I mourn her the nearer I seem
> to her. (1976, P. 66)

Obviously reliving childhood emotions and feelings evolving from his mother's death, there is a danger for Lewis to return to his anger at a cruel God who would take Joy from him, just as his mother had been taken from him. In his words:

> Not that I am (I think) in much danger of ceasing to believe in
> God. The real danger is of coming to believe such dreadful
> things about Him. The conclusion I dread is not "So there's no
> God after all, but "So this is what God's really like. Deceive
> yourself no longer." (1976, p. 5)

In less than 100 pages Lewis pours out his grief, his rage, his anger at God and the world. He published this book under a pseudonym: N.W. Clerk (a pun on the Old English for "I know not what scholar"), for in the midst of his agonized bereavement, he records new insights that clash with the Christian certainties in his previous writings. Later, posthumously, it was published under his own name.

Lewis' relationship with God pays a vital role in his development. His response to God's absence from saving his mother's life is recorded from his adult perspective. While some critics maintain, this was Lewis' first religious experience, he refutes this point. As a child, he had been taught that "prayers offered in faith would be granted" (1955, P.20), so he willfully prayed for his mother's recovery. When she died, he shifted gears and believed a miracle would bring her back to him. Nothing happened. Lewis' adult perspective of this event states that as a child he approached God "without love, without awe, even without fear" (1955, p. 21). God, the "Magician", didn't succeed and so Lewis thought God would simply disappear. Yet Lewis' boyhood experiences of yearning for an unknown object that defied rationality are defined in his search for "Joy." While Nature, not God, is the venue for Lewis' search, he describes it as "an unsatisfied desire which is itself more desirable than any other satisfaction. I call it Joy. (1955, p.18). Later, at Oxford, he redefines Joy as "aesthetic experience": something valuable that seldom appeared and "when it came it didn't amount to much" (1955, p. 205).

At Oxford, some of his Christian colleagues, Nevill Coghill, J.R.R. Tolkien, among them, influenced Lewis' gradual conversion to Christianity. Joy becomes transformed as a symbol. The images of Joy (the toy garden Squirrel Nutkin, Baldar) were "merely the mental track left by the passage of Joy - not the wave but the wave's imprint on the sand" (1955, p. 219). This led to his acceptance of Theism, followed by a conversion to Christianity.

Now, years later, Lewis' faith is again tested at the death of his wife Joy. The unsuccessful mourning he experienced as a child at his mother's death is intensified as he grapples with his loss, his grief, his faith.

> Meanwhile, where is God? . . . go to Him when your need is desperate, when all other help is vain and what do you find? A door slammed in your face ... bolting, and double bolting ... after that, silence. (1976, p. 4)

Lewis rages against his personal God who, he feels, has abandoned him, who has taken from him the person dearest to him:

> Oh, God, God, why did you take such trouble to force this creature out of its shell if it is now doomed to crawl back - to be sucked back - into it? (1976, p. 20)

Significantly, Lewis didn't express this grief, this rage with another person; his personal relationship with God was at stake, and he saw God as a person, albeit omniscient and powerful as a Deity, yet his personal monologues address God in a human way. And his venue to understand and to express this grief is writing. Though his previous crises involved his creation of compensatory fantasy worlds, this time Lewis can't escape his reality, and he addresses the process of mourning that he had never previously experienced. His target is God:

> Time after time, when He seemed most gracious, He was really preparing the next torture.
>
> I wrote that last night. It was a yell rather than a thought ... Is it rational to believe in a bad God? ... the Cosmic Sadist, the spiteful imbecile? (1976,p. 35)

Yet Lewis recognizes what he has written and states, "I think, it is, if nothing else, too anthropomorphic" (1976, p.) It is a step toward his spiritual reconciliation with his personal God:

> I have gradually been coming to feel that the door is no longer shut and bolted. Was it my own frantic need that slammed it in my face? (1976, p. 53)

His resolution and recognition of his rage continues:

> God has not been trying an experiment on my faith or love in order to find out their quality. He knew it already. It was I who didn't. (1976, p.61)

Lewis sorts out the sequence:

> The notes have been about myself, and about H. [Joy] and about God. In that order. The order and the proportions exactly what they ought not to have been. (1976, p. 72)

Lewis ruminates about his placing H., Joy, before God and what a conflict it could have presented. He feels the order is now restored, as is his faith.

> His [God] love and His knowledge are not distinct from one another, nor from Him. We could almost say He sees because He loves, and therefore loves although he sees. (1976, p.84)

It is a dramatic conclusion to the beginning of his book on grieving. He demonstrates his resolution to the mourning process. He has come to terms with Joy's death, with his personal God and with himself.

Lewis wrote one more work: *Letters to Malcolm, Chiefly on Prayer*. Begun in 1952, he completed it in May, 1963. His own prayers seemed less desperate, but his health was deteriorating. During Joy's first recovery from cancer, Lewis contracted a non-malignant bone disease and was losing calcium. He needed an operation on his prostate, but his heart and kidneys were not in good condition. Restricted with a surgical belt and a catheter, he was forced to give up his teaching, and indeed his social life as well. A heart attack in 1963 left him weak, and he died at age 64 on November 22, 1963, the same day that President John F. Kennedy was assassinated. His death occurred within three years of Joy's death. Though he never lost his faith, he never quite recovered from his loss of Joy.

Lewis' initial unsuccessful grieving at Joy's death reopened his childhood grief at his mother's death. The insecurity, instability, and fears resurfaced. This time, however, his grieving extended to a personal God with whom he thought he had made peace and established a personal connection. The devastation, the betrayal were doubled.

Significantly, in Lewis' personal catharsis of his grief, he reached a state of mourning: an acceptance of his loss, of himself, and of his faith. He could remember his beloved wife with joy; he could reconstruct his life.

C. S. Lewis had always lived in the richness of his imagination, including his paracosms, and had always used his writing to cope with life. His creativity emerged despite of or because of these circumstances. His works will remain his gift to humanity: his creativity born from his own pain shall speak for him in generations to come.

Barry M. Panter, MD, PhD, is the director of the Creativity & Madness—Psychological Studies of Art and Artists Conferences. He, along with his late wife Mary Lou Panter RN co-founded The American Institute of Medical Education and the Conferences in 1981. Prior to his retirement from clinical practice he was Clinical Professor of Psychiatry, USC School of Medicine, Training and Supervising Analyst for the Southern California Psychoanalytic Institute and Member of The American Psychoanalytic Association and The International Psychoanalytic Association. He is the co-editor and co-author of Creativity & Madness—Psychological Studies of Art and Artists Volume 1 and the author of Thirty-Three Poems for Mary Lou.

Wolfgang, Leopold and Sigmund Meet at the Opera

Mozart's Psychodynamics as Revealed in his Opera Don Giovanni

Barry M. Panter, MD, PhD

> *"All art is autobiography"*
>
> *Pablo Picasso*

There has never been and there never will be a composer greater than Mozart. He excelled in nearly every genre of music. We have no way of comprehending how this short, pockmarked, relatively unattractive man was the holder of such genius. We can enjoy his works. We can marvel at his genius. We can try to understand what motivated him to choose to create some of the works he did. But we will never comprehend how his genius and creativity came to be. The following is as good an explanation as possible: At 8pm on January 27, 1756 a hand reached down from above the city of Salzburg, Austria and touched a newborn infant. A voice said, "You shall become one of the most magnificent gifts that I will ever bestow on mankind." Perhaps his father Leopold knew or wished for this even before Mozart was born, for he named him Joannes Chrysostomus Wolfgangus Theophilus Mozart. Theophilus translates to loved by God. In Latin Theophilus would be Amadeus. He was known as Wolfgang Amadeus, but changed it to the French, Wolfgang Amadé Mozart. So throughout the vicissitudes of his short life, he was always beloved by God. We have two of the three named in the title of this paper. How does Freud come into play? I will attempt to use psychoanalytic theory to explain the relationship between Mozart and his father and how this relationship influenced and was expressed in his work, especially his opera Don Giovanni.

299

In act II of Mozart's opera, Don Giovanni says, "I have a talent that is unequalled." Mozart could have been speaking about himself, for he knew that his talent, his genius was unequalled by any of his contemporaries. Mozart's works include nearly every genre of music. They include 41 symphonies, 27 piano concertos, 5 violin concertos, 20 operas, piano sonatas, string quartets, flute, piano, clarinet concertos and even horn concertos. Most of these works, composed more than 300 years ago, are performed regularly around the world. Music speaks the language of the heart and the listener can enjoy the work because the strings of the heart resonate with the work. In opera the composer and librettist add words- words that reveal much more of the composers mind and emotion and issues than his other compositions.

In this chapter I will try to create a psychological portrait of Mozart based on his biography and what is expressed in his opera Don Giovanni *The Punishment of the Rake*, which he created in collaboration with Lorenzo Da Ponte (who also is a fascinating character). He also collaborated with Da Ponte on *The Marriage of Figaro* and *Cosi fan Tutti*. These operas also express Mozart's psychodynamics, but I will leave that for another time.

The soaring lasting success of these 3 operas is due in part to the psychological needs and issues of both men. Artists of the highest caliber who create their greatest works are motivated by deep, usually unconscious psychological needs and issues. Da Ponte and Mozart both were trying to work through their individual needs and issues in their work together. Each was inspired, motivated and driven to achieve the highest level of creativity. This level is reached when there is a combination of genius, inspiration, and an intense emotional need. These combine to create a drivenness to work through psychological conflicts by creating the work of art. Gustav Mahler's wife Alma complained bitterly about his working on *Kindertotenleider*- a work with words that focuses on the loss of children. His reply to her was, "I don't choose to work on the deaths of children, the works choose me."

300

Mozart and Da Ponte shared the same emotional needs. Their psychological conflicts were similar. Both men were driven to create by these forces. Two hearts and minds devoted to the same emotional task. Their three collaborations are among the greatest operas ever created. They are among the most performed, enjoyed and appreciated operas of all time.

Let's try to understand these issues by looking at Mozart's life – especially his relationship with his father. Mozart's father Leopold was a musician – a very accomplished violinist, composer and teacher. Some of his compositions are performed today. He wrote a widely used book of instruction and examples for playing the violin. He taught his son, and his daughter Nannerl how to play the piano. He recognized Mozart's prodigious talent very early. The following vignette that took place when Mozart was 6 years old beautifully illustrates this.

Leopold was a member of a string quartet that met and played in his home every Thursday night in Salzburg. One evening because of a snowstorm the second violinist was unable to attend. The three members were deciding what they would do without their fourth member. Wolfgang or Wolfie as he was known said, "Papa, I'll play the second violin." Leopold was surprised since his son had not studied the violin, only the piano, so he said, "No Wolfie, you don't know how to play the violin." Mozart said, "Please papa, let me try, anyone can play the second violin." Because of Mozart's pleading Leopold agreed and the four began to play. The three members were astonished that Mozart did in fact play the second violin part very well. When they finished playing the composition tears streamed from Leopold's eyes. At that moment he realized that he didn't have a talented son, he had a son who was a genius— A genius that the world sees once in hundreds of years. How was it possible for Mozart to play the violin without ever studying it? To know where to place his fingers? To know how to read the music for the notes and the rhythm? We will never know the answers to questions like these. But I offer you my opinion. Mozart was wired differently than we are. Somehow his brain could think or function or deal in music as easily as in words. Stimuli were processed in musical terms rather than verbally.

In his recent book *Musicophilia: Tales of Music and the Brain* Oliver Sacks MD describes a man of little musical interest or talent, who was struck by lightening. Following this he developed an intense interest, which led to his becoming familiar with the classical repertoire. He learned to play the piano well. Some of the neural pathways in his brain must have been altered. I suspect they were altered toward the patterns that were innate in Mozart. In Mozart these pathways were such that he could read music, play the violin, hear and put feelings into musical compositions effortlessly because that is the way he thought – in musical terms. One of his compositions is known as the *Kegelstatt* Trio, which translates to "the bowling trio" He, and some friends were bowling. While he was sitting waiting his turn, musical ideas came to him; he put them on paper and by the time the game was over he had composed a trio for piano, violin and clarinet!

To appreciate this genius even more, let's consider this: If you were to make a list of the great composers of western music you probably would have 40-50 names on your list. Western music began in approximately 1600. So in more than 400 years there have been only a small number of composers of genius. A musical genius is born once a decade. If you listed the 3 greatest composers, Mozart probably would be on your list.

Leopold devoted himself increasingly to developing and nurturing his son's gift. He became an impresario, taking Mozart and Nannerl on tour throughout Europe. Mozart during these childhood years performed seemingly magical feats on the piano. He played blindfolded. Given a two or three note theme he could improvise and develop the theme in more and more complex music. He could play with his back to the keyboard. He astonished European aristocracy. He climbed onto Maria Theresa's lap and she kissed him. He was adored, admired, celebrated wherever he went.

At the same time, Leopold as his mentor, guide, ruler, enforcer and constrainer, controlled every aspect of Mozart's life—not an unusual situation for a child of 6-10 especially one who is traveling all over Europe and performing. However this pattern of being constrained and controlled led to a major psychological and emotional issue for Mozart. He was unruly, undisciplined, likely to go beyond the limits without the stern discipline of his father. Inevitably, when Mozart reached adolescence and early adulthood he rebelled and attempted to overthrow his father's authority.

In 1776 Mozart was 20 years old. In America the rule of the controlling British was overthrown. In France the revolution was brewing and soon, King Louis XVI and Marie Antoinette, daughter of Maria Theresa, would be beheaded. At 20 Mozart was a man of the world. He had traveled extensively, his name was known throughout Europe. In his 20th year in a period of 6 months, he composed 5 violin concertos, which are performed regularly and are considered to be among the best pieces ever composed for the instrument. The forces of revolution and rebellion were brewing all over the world. Mozart undoubtedly was aware of these events. This tide, flowing along with the river of his own emergence into manhood and his desire to be his own man, free of his father's rules were among the forces driving him at that time.

This rebellion was exacerbated by the adulation that he had received for many years of his childhood, developing in Mozart the conviction that, "I am the greatest. There is no talent equal to mine." Mozart's narcissism also had been fed by the unwavering and unquestioning love that he received from a devoted mother. But are these words, "there is no talent equal to mine" the words of a braggart if the person speaking them is in fact the greatest at what he does? Mozart was simply stating a fact.

When Mozart was 29 years old a performance of several of his string quartets was given in Vienna. Joseph Haydn was in the audience. Haydn who was recognized and celebrated as one of the greatest living composers, was 34 years older that Mozart. After the performance, Haydn said to Leopold, "Sir, as a man of honor and before God, I tell you that your son is the greatest composer I have ever heard. He has taste, and, what is more, the most profound knowledge of composition." Mozart was so moved and probably so starved for words of praise from a father figure, that he dedicated the 6 quartets to Haydn. This was not just a gesture, for in dedicating them to Haydn, he also was turning over any future royalties from the works. Royalties that Haydn didn't need because he was supported very well throughout most of his career and lived in the castle of the Esterhazy family. Here is Mozart's letter to Haydn after he was so complimentary about the string quartets. "You, yourself, dearest friend, told me of your satisfaction with them during your last visit to this Capital. It is this indulgence above all, which urges me to commend them to you and encourages me to hope that they will not seem to you altogether unworthy of your favor. May it therefore please you to receive them kindly and to be their Father, Guide and Friend! From this moment I resign to you all my rights in them, begging you however to look indulgently upon the defects which the partiality of a Father's eye may have concealed from me, and in spite of them to continue in your generous Friendship for him who so greatly values it, in expectation of which I am, with all of my Heart, my dearest Friend, your most Sincere Friend."

Although Mozart made a great amount of money in his lifetime, he spent even more. So he often was impoverished. At the end of his life he was a very poor man and was buried in an unmarked grave with others who didn't have the means for an individual grave with a marked site.

How does this flow into the world of Don Giovanni?

The opera begins as Don Giovanni kills the father of his most recent conquest in a duel. So the opera starts with the victory of the son over the father. He is proud and unrepentant. In the catalog aria his servant Leparello recounts the list of his conquests – country by country: "In Italy, six hundred and forty. In Germany, two hundred and thirty-one; A hundred in France; in Turkey, ninety-one; But in Spain already one thousand and three." He has seduced a total of 2065!

Mozart, like Don Giovanni was proud of his ability. He would not bow to others of inferior gifts. He was proud of his "talent" and unrepentant. He took pleasure and was driven to utilize his ability, his gift, and his genius and sought more and more opportunities to demonstrate it.

In the final scene, the statue of the Commendatore, the father, comes alive. The father, seemingly dead lives on. Doesn't the father always live on – in our minds, in our memories, influencing our values, our behavior, our sense of right and wrong, the course of our lives? In the opera the son invites the father to sit and have dinner with him. The commendatore/father tells Don Giovanni that he has sinned and must repent. If he does not he will perish. Don Giovanni refuses to repent. In some productions the floor opens and Don Giovanni sinks into it….descending into hell. In others he exits through the side of the stage enveloped by flames. The subtitle of the opera – *The Punishment of the Rake* clearly implies that Don Giovanni is going to hell. But when he exits into flames it could be that he is ascending….climbing into the highest reaches of human aspiration and achievement. Did Mozart see him this way? And if so, why? Throughout the play Don Giovanni is exuberant, confident, exciting. He is the motivating force for nearly everyone else in the play. He is the source of excitement and life. Why? Because he has energy. He has desires. His desires cause the action and the achievements. Isn't this divine? The opera could be saying that Don Giovanni is the supreme example of human aspiration and achievement. He is the best in the entire world at what he does. No wonder he is exultant and exuberant. Why should he repent? He gives life to everyone. So too, Mozart, the best at what he did, and he knew it, was exuberant throughout his life. He did not defer to the royalty. He did not bow to authorities in his life that had power over him but had only the meagerest of musical knowledge and ability according to Mozart's standards and abilities. Why should he repent? And at the end, why should he go to hell? Shouldn't he be given the highest respect and admiration for what he has created and given to the world? I think

Mozart resonated with these ideas. He and Don Giovanni were kindred spirits.

In the opera, the father figure, the commendatore, whom Don Giovanni has killed, returns to curse him "You will be punished for your sins against me." The father has the final victory as the son dies.

But, what if Mozart had had a good psychoanalysis? Let's look at this from the classical Freudian perspective and from the self-psychology perspective of Heinz Kohut.

If Mozart had been in analysis with a classical Freudian analyst, his transference would have led to his seeing the analyst as the father. He would have become argumentative, rebellious, confrontive. The analyst would not have reacted the way Leopold did. Mozart would have realized more and more that "this man is not pressuring me, he is not trying to control me, and he is not criticizing me." Mozart then would have had the opportunity to observe himself, and to see that his behavior and his attitude were not appropriate for the situation – that it was coming from within himself and not being imposed on him from outside. If he could have incorporated these insights into his personality, he would have had less and less need to be argumentative and rebellious and confrontive. If we look at only one of the important relationships in his life, that with Colorado, The Archbishop of Salzburg, we can see how the course of his life might have been changed. The Archbishop was essentially the ruler of Salzburg. He determined who would work, who would receive help, who would be honored, who would be rewarded, who would be punished. He was like a king of Salzburg. No one could have been successful in Salzburg if he had alienated the Archbishop. Mozart alienated the Archbishop, as he did many men in the course of his life. The archbishop was not very interested in music. He did employ musicians in various capacities – performers, composers, and the supporting players. These were in the service of Church functions. If the Archbishop had wanted to, he could have employed Mozart full time as a composer and/or performer. Mozart could have had a very comfortable life with time for composing, as did Haydn.

The Archbishop did offer Mozart work. Mozart felt demeaned and unappreciated by the offer and the salary. He delivered a letter of resignation to the Archbishop. No one ever refused the Archbishop. Upon receiving his letter, the archbishop, literally kicked Mozart out of the castle. Instead of an easy life, Mozart was unemployed and impoverished. He went to Vienna where he supported himself by teaching, performing and composing. Mozart was one of the first composers to earn money by selling tickets to a concert. Prior to this, musicians were invited by the nobility to perform, or invited to compose a work for a specific occasion. Payment was at the largesse of the King, or the Prince or the Count. There was no negotiation. There was only service, compensated or not at the discretion of the nobleman. A very humiliating and usually intolerable situation for Mozart who knew that musically he was far superior to those who employed him or criticized him.

Initially Mozart did well in Vienna. His 26th year was one of the best in his life. He married Constanza Weber, his opera *The Abduction from the Seraglio* was premiered and was a great success – the first great success of any of his operas. He was in demand as a performer, teacher and composer. He earned a great deal of money. He and Constanza lived very well – too well. He spent beyond his means on clothes, parties, moving to better and better quarters. He often had to entreat or beg friends or members of the nobility to loan him or give him money. If Mozart could have gotten along with the Archbishop his life would have been very different from his teen years onward.

Mozart won an early Oedipal victory over his father. What are the consequences of such a victory? He was confident in his abilities. He composed many of his works without any editing. What he first put on paper often was the finished work. This contributed to his tremendous output. In his 36 years he composed 636 works. Many of these are long works, e.g. his symphonies, concertos and operas. So we are grateful that he brought so much undying beauty into the world.

Because his genius was recognized early it was nurtured and developed while he was still a child.

Picasso also experienced such a victory. When he was 12 years old his father who was a curator and painter and teacher assigned him the task of painting a picture of a dove. When Picasso handed his father the work, the father said, "You have so far surpassed me that I shall never paint again." And he never did. The early victor might intimate others, which can lead to envy, and attacks of various kinds. Solieri who was the court musician envied Mozart. He could have helped Mozart but he didn't. The play and movie *Amadeus* depict Solieri as Mozart's murderer. He supposedly poisoned Mozart. There is little evidence for this. Many researchers have concluded that Mozart died from the complications of glomerulonephritis. This illness is a late consequence of childhood strep infections. If you are reading this book and have not seen the movie *Amadeus* I recommend it very highly. It is a beautiful absorbing work that presents a great deal of Mozart's music and fascinating biographical information.

His victory contributed to his arrogance and narcissism, which created interpersonal problems for him. Mozart didn't abide by the customary rules. He was so confident that he thought that he should live at the highest level. Even though he earned a great deal of money he lived far beyond his means. During the year of his tour of Europe as a child he earned 50 times what his father earned in his best year. He was frequently short of money and had to entreat friends and other supporters to assist him. He didn't enjoy the comfort of a secure financial position. His defiance of the rules was held partially in check while his father was alive. Mozart was 31 years old when his father died. He became even less responsible and created greater and greater problems for himself. He spent wildly, went to many parties, and probably began having affairs with a number of women. All of this dissipated his energy and compromised his health.

Picasso too felt that the rules didn't apply to him. He was notoriously cruel to the women in his life. Two of them committed suicide. Two had psychotic episodes. He put a lit cigarette to the cheek of Francoise Gilot. She had the good sense to leave him. The others captured by his genius and the force of his personality stayed with him and suffered for it.

Mozart won a very early Oedipal victory over his father. He surpassed his father as a violinist, as a pianist, as a composer, as an earner at a very early age. He knew it, as did his father.

What are some of the consequences of such a victory? We see them in Mozart: irritating narcissism, conflict with authority, and work flowed easily. He felt no need to make corrections because the thought the first draft was perfect. (It often was). Unconscious organizing principals by which he lived and governed his behavior were: Rules do not apply to me because I am special; I do not need to worry about money or the future because my talent will provide everything I need.

If Mozart had been in analysis with a follower of Heinz Kohut's Self Psychology, the analysis might have gone like this: Mozart's narcissism would have come into focus early in the analysis. If the analyst attempted to interpret the origins or degree of the narcissism, he probably would have lost Mozart as a patient. The better course would be to allow Mozart to recount his adventures, dreams, hopes, and resentments. The analyst would have become the mirroring mother. As the infant/child perceives that she adores him, he begins to internalize some of her thinking. "If she thinks I am so wonderful, then I am wonderful." This gives confidence and brings wholeness to the personality. Mozart probably didn't need too much of this as he already had self-confidence. What he lacked from this perspective was the acceptance and approval of the father. Kohut posits that a person will be emotionally healthy if he has one of two benefits from his parents. If he has adequate mirroring from his mother or if he is allowed to idealize and then merge with his father. Mozart had the former but didn't have the latter. If he had, it would have gone like this. "My father is powerful and wonderful." If the father allows the child to share in his power and wonderfulness, the child begins to think, "I am like him, therefore, I too and powerful and wonderful." Mozart's father was not able to do this for his son. A number of reasons probably were responsible: Mozart needed to be controlled as a child and prodigy; Leopold's nature would not allow him to give his son the permission to become an adult; and there probably were good financial reasons to keep Mozart childlike. His earning power was much greater as a child prodigy than as an aspiring adult musician and composer. If during the analysis, Mozart began to see the analyst as the powerful and wonderful authority, and the analyst, not criticizing, but actually enjoying Mozart's abilities, claims, and achievements, Mozart might have been able to merge with the authority and power of the analyst and feel more and more his own man. This would have made him less contentious and rebellious.

Psychoanalysis wouldn't have protected Mozart from kidney disease or strep throat or any organic disease that might have killed him. However, psychologically, he would have been a healthier man he might have been able to work on a steadier basis. He might have had better nutrition and a better immune system. He might have had the ability to fight off whatever illness killed him. If all this had happened, and since I don't like unhappy endings, let me tell you what should have happened.

After lying in a coma for 2 weeks, Mozart's fever broke. He regained consciousness and miraculously made a full recovery. He was so inspired, excited and exhilarated by his phenomenal recovery that he immediately set to work on his 42nd symphony, which we know as the *Miracle Symphony*. - One of the most beloved of his works because of its exuberance and rushing rhythms. His next work was his *Resurrection Symphony* the themes of which deal not only with his physical recovery, but also with his emergence from under the shadow of his father. He was reborn as his own man, no longer needing to defy or rebel against the father, but able to live his life with the natural born energy and genius with which he was endowed.

These works were performed first in Prague then in Vienna then even Salzburg and throughout all of Europe. They were so successful that they brought about a resurgence of interest in his music that saw performances of his orchestral music and his operas all over Europe. This brought financial success and at last he no longer had to worry about money.

He went on to write 7 more symphonies, which went from the splendors of the 39th 40th and 41st and culminated in the majestic affirmation of his final work the 49th known as *The Sublime Symphony*. These works showed an expansion of his emotional expression - deepening the experience for the listener and leading directly to the emotionalism that evolved into the symphonies of Beethoven - who credited the later Mozart with the opening of the great river of feeling that inspired his works. Indeed it sometimes is difficult to distinguish the later Mozart from the early Beethoven.

His ebullience mellowed from an intrusive provoking characteristic into a quickness of wit and a humor that entertained rather than annoyed. He was sought after not only as a conductor and composer but also as a guest in the homes of music lovers everywhere. He wrote toward the end that he felt that he had recaptured the success of his early years of touring Europe during which he was so celebrated.

Finally at the age of 76 at his second home in Vienna - on vacation from his residence in Prague, he enjoyed an evening with Clemenza and their children during which they had a festive dinner, and then played one of his string quartets for assembled guests.

The Archbishop of Salzburg who was in attendance toasted Mozart not only as the greatest musical genius of all time, a judgment that has been shared by many for centuries, but also as a man beloved by his children and all of Europe for the magnificent gifts that he gave to the world. After the concert of his works amid family and friends, He retired to bed. Later that night he died peacefully in his sleep.

Mozart's compositions are among the most magnificent gifts ever given to the world. They inspire, they sooth, they fascinate, they uplift. No one has ever given more. Imagine the gifts he would have given us if he had lived another 40 years.

Kohut, Heinz., (1972) *The Analysis of the Self*. International Universities Press. New York.

Solomon, Maynard. (2005) *Mozart: A Life*. HarperCollins Publishers. New York

Da Ponte, Lorenzo, and Rosen, Charles. (2003) *Memoirs of Lorenzo Da Ponte*. New York Review of Books. New York.

Richard A. Paskowitz, MD, was born and raised in Birmingham, Alabama. He attended Vanderbilt University in Nashville and the Medical School at University of Tennessee in Memphis. He served in the United States Navy from 1967-1970 He was Staff physician U.S. Naval Hospital Charleston (Department OB-GYN) He returned to Memphis for Obstetrics and Gynecology Residency at The University of Tennessee and Baptist Memorial Hospital. His medical practice includes: Private practice of Obstetrics and Gynecology in Memphis And Clinician Permanente Medical Group Sacramento/Roseville California.

His published articles include:

1. Townsend D, Richart RM, Paskowitz RA, et al: "Rollerball" co-agulation of the endometrium. Obstet-Gynecol 1990; 76: 310-313

2. Richard A. Paskowitz, MD "Rollerball" Ablation of the Endometrium. J Reprod Med 1995; 40:333-336

He is a Fellow American College of Obstetrics and Gynecology (FACOG)

Volunteer Faculty University of California, Davis 1979-2008

Clinical Professor Obstetrics and Gynecology University of California, Davis

Author of three books about George Horatio Derby (John Phoenix, Squibob) Soldier Joker, Soldier Joker the Cartoons and Soldier Joker The 1849 Surveys

He currently is involved with the Wheatland Historical Society:

He is married to Jane Stineman Paskowitz (40th Anniversary this year 2008)

They have two children and five grand girls.

Dr. Paskowitz lives in Wheatland, California but travels frequently to Memphis

> *"I have done an in depth study of drug abuse*
> *and communist brainwashing techniques*
> *and I am right in the middle of the*
> *whole thing where I can and will do the most good.*
> *I am glad to help just so long as it is kept very private."*

> *Elvis Presley*
> *Letter to President Richard Nixon*
> *December 21, 1970*

LESSONS LEARNED FROM THE DEATH OF ELVIS PRESLEY

RICHARD A. PASKOWITZ, MD

Very few people can say they had a personal relationship with Elvis Presley, and yet he touched millions with his music and personality. His early appearance on The Ed Sullivan Show was electrifying. Later, after his stardom was firmly entrenched, there were newspapers and television broadcasts showing a conscientious young man going into and returning from the army. His generosity was famous, and long before Oprah, he gave cars away to strangers. He did not drink alcohol. He did not smoke cigarettes. He did not use illicit drugs. Nevertheless, the death of this charismatic super-star had a tragic lesson to teach his contemporaries and future generations.

Mentors, Minds, And Minions

There were several key players in the medical life and death of Elvis Presley:

THE MENTORS: Dr. Harold Sexton and Dr. Claude Ledes

Dr. Sexton was in charge of the toxicology following the autopsy of Elvis Presley. He was a Pathologist at Baptist Memorial Hospital in Memphis Tennessee on that hot August day in 1977. Dr. Sexton also had specific expertise in cardiac pathology.

Dr. Claude Ledes was a practicing internist in Memphis in 1977 and covered the practice of Dr. George Nichopoulos when he was on tour with Elvis Presley.

THE MINDS: Dr. Eric Muirhead and Dr. Rodger Haggitt

Dr. Eric Muirhead was the Chief of Pathology at Baptist Memorial Hospital in Memphis Tennessee in 1977. Known as "The Chief", he was highly respected by all with whom he came in contact, be they residents, medical staff, or the ten or so pathologists he supervised. He was responsible for Clinical and Surgical Pathology for the sixteen hundred-bed Baptist Memorial Hospital. He had an interest in and was an authority on renovascular hypertension.

Dr. Rodger Haggitt had been a brilliant medical student and was one of the pathologists at Baptist Hospital at the time of the autopsy. He became Chief of Gastroenterology Pathology at the University of Washington after leaving Memphis. Sadly, he was shot and killed by a deranged resident in Seattle.

THE MINIONS: Dr. George C. Nichopoulos and Dr. Jerry Francisco

Dr. Nichopoulos was the personal physician to Elvis Presley in Memphis. He traveled on his tours and was known to Elvis's entourage as "Dr. Nick." He eventually lost his license for the practice of medicine due to over-prescribing. He is currently living in Memphis, Tennessee.

Dr. Jerry Francisco was the Medical Examiner for Shelby County in Tennessee at the time of the death. He was on the faculty of the University of Tennessee in the Department of Pathology and was at Baptist Memorial Hospital during the autopsy as observer. He issued the "Cause of Death" and was interviewed on the topic.

The Patient: Elvis Presley

On August 16, 1977, the patient, the person, the celebrity was found face down two feet from his commode in his home, Graceland. At that time, he was forty-two years old.

In his twenties, Elvis was thin, agile, virile, vigorous and full of life. In photographs early in his career, his complexion appears ruddy and healthy. An early photo showed the six-foot Elvis with the shorter Nichopoulos.

Later in his career, Elvis was over-weight, and radio personalities kidded about him and his "jelly-filled donuts." His weight gain was blamed on these and the legendary "fried peanut butter and banana sandwiches" that he consumed. Food and weight were blamed for his bloated appearance, captured in photographs in 1977. In that year, the performer had a paunch, was pasty-faced, peaked, and pale. His double chins were obvious and at least one fan observed that Elvis moved sluggishly.

The comparison between 1955 when Elvis was twenty and 1977 when Elvis was forty-two is striking. Something had happened to him and it was not good. As his song said, "I'm caught in a trap...I can't walk out." But before he was caught in a trap, what did he do? Who was this person, this Elvis Presley?

Elvis Aron Presley: Celebrity Wonder

He was born Elvis Aron Presley on January 8, 1935, in Tupelo, Mississippi. He made thirty-three movies. Fifty-five of his records sold more than one million copies each. To date, one billion records have been sold.

He arrived at Sun Studios in Memphis, Tennessee, in July of 1955 and recorded his first hit record. The recording, "That's All Right Mama", put him on the charts and started his amazing career. Sam Phillips, the owner of Sun Records, recalled that Elvis Presley enabled "white kids" to listen to "black music" and "black kids" to be on an equal footing with "white kids", joined by the rock-and-roll music of the times. That legacy lives on.

Of the thirty-three movies Elvis Presley made, thirty-two were less than memorable. One movie, "Flaming Star", made in 1960, captured the artistic worth of a serious actor, but he was relegated to showy and insubstantial roles for the rest of his career.

317

Some of the songs he sang include: "Blue Suede Shoes,",", "Jail-house Rock", "Heartbreak Hotel", "Hound Dog", "Love Me Tender", "Your Cheatin' Heart", "In the Ghetto", "How Great Thou Art", and "Tutti Frutti."

Some of his movies include: "Love Me Tender", "Jailhouse Rock", "King Creole", "Blue Hawaii", "Girls, Girls, Girls", "Viva Las Vegas", "Harem Scarum", and "Frankie and Johnnie."

Where will Elvis Presley be in history? This leads us to The Mystique. There are now thirty-five thousand Elvis impersonators around the world. Not a day goes by when someone does not mention the name "Elvis". The search for him is world-wide and Elvis sightings have gone from Rangoon to Roswell. The First Presleyterian Church of Elvis The Divine in Australia is dedicated to the gospel of "The King", and regular sermons are given to extol the primacy and cabalistic meaning of his music.

The Reality

What really happened to the King of Rock-and-Roll? When did it happen? How did it happen? How did he die? The end came at Baptist Memorial Hospital in Memphis, Tennessee, on August 16, 1977. Prominent physical findings noted at autopsy were: "Forty-two-year-old white male weighing 250 pounds with an enlarged heart and a megacolon." The report of the county medical examiner signed by Dr. Jerry Francisco included autopsy at Baptist Memorial Hospital Hypertensive Cardiovascular Disease associated with Atherosclerotic Heart Disease.

The Baptist Memorial Hospital autopsy report stated that the colon of the patient was three-and-a-half to five inches in diameter (with two inches as normal). "[The] mega colon was packed from the base of the descending colon to and halfway across the transverse colon...The content was a white chalk-like fecal material and the impaction had the consistency of clay which seemed to defy efforts with the scissors to cut it out."

The Drugs

As part of the autopsy at Baptist Memorial Hospital, toxicological studies were done on blood samples. The person in charge of the toxicology was Dr. Harold Sexton, one of the staff pathologists at Baptist. Dr. Sexton sent the samples to Bio-Science Laboratory in Van Nuys, California. The label on the specimen was "Ethel Moore" to mitigate the celebrity status of the patient. Ten drugs, identified by Bio-Science Laboratory, were in the body of Elvis Presley at the time of his death. They were: Codeine, morphine, methaqualone, diazepam, diazepam metabolite, ethinamate, ethchlorvynal, pentobarbital, butabarbital, Phenobarbital.

The Codeine was ten times greater than the therapeutic range. Methaqulone (Quaalude) was at toxic levels. Diazepam (Valium) was in the low therapeutic range. Ethinamate (Valmid) was in the high therapeutic range. Ethchlorvynol (Placidyl) was on the toxic borderline. Pentobarbitol was in the high therapeutic range. Butabarbital was within the therapeutic range and Phenobarbital was in the low therapeutic range. These were the drugs that were tested.

Pathogenesis

Elvis had been a robust youth with incredible talent. This raw talent and energy was detected and harnessed. The talent was discovered and expressed. As energy waned, leading to fatigue, external energy motivators were sought and a complicit resource was found.

The Impact Of Power And Prestige

An autopsy serves as a vehicle to discover the truth. How did a patient die? What lessons can be learned from an unfortunate demise and untimely death? Benefits can accrue and preventive measures can be taken based on the findings so that history does not repeat itself. Autopsies are done for the advancement of knowledge.

Such was not the case in the autopsy of Elvis Presley. There was indeed the impact of power and prestige to the effect that truth

319

was not initially served and facts were misrepresented. Dr. Jerry Francisco, the Medical Examiner of Shelby County, Tennessee, signed out the Death Certificate. Because he wanted "to protect the family", he stated and signed "Cause of Death: Cardiac Arrhythmia." To this day, he maintains that was the cause of death of Elvis Presley.

The Progression : How It Happened

According to friend Marty Lacker:

> "He started in the 1960's while making movies. He took appetite suppressants, because he always had a weight problem. He was a hyper person anyway...he just needed something to unwind, to put him to sleep. So, you know, he was prescribed some sleeping pills. He began to take more than the prescribed amount in about 1975."

He was admitted to Baptist Hospital in 1973 after receiving a massive dose of cortisone from a doctor in Las Vegas. At that time, he had a distended colon and no bladder control but improved with treatment. As an entertainer, he complained of a need for increased excitement with his shows and then the need to relax afterwards. He had been performing two shows a night in Las Vegas and did not follow advice to limit himself to one show per night.

> The "protocols" for his shows were as follows:
>
> Stage 1: 3:00 pm prior to the show was the first "voice shot" that included three appetite suppressants and testosterone.
>
> Stage 2: One hour prior to his performance was the second "voice shot", comprised of a decongestant laden with codeine, amphetamine, and dilaudid.
>
> Stage 3: Just prior to the show, he took a dose of caffeine, Dexedrine, and Dilaudid.
>
> Stage 4: This was immediately after the show and included an antihypertensive, an antihistamine, a tranquilizer, and dilute Demerol.
>
> Stage 5: At bedtime, his protocol included Quaalude, Placidyl , amphetamine, a laxative, an antihypertensive, and three other sedatives.
>
> Stage 6: In the middle of the night if he was restless, he was given more Demerol.

Dr. George Nichopoulos, Elvis's personal physician, eventually lost his license for improperly dispensing potentially addictive drugs to a variety of his patients.

This Has Got To Stop

From the time before 1977 until 1988, the subterfuge and the lies persisted. The official word was that Elvis died of a "cardiac arrhythmia." This was perpetuated by the Shelby County Medical Examiner. The autopsy and toxicology results were kept private and under closed wraps. The Death Certificate was private. The public was unaware. The Elvis entourage was closed-mouth. "Hero" status and the need to keep the Elvis image intact got in the way of the truth. The image, the profits, and the support of the hangers-on were the only important matters to those who knew the truth.

Harold Sexton cared for the truth. For eleven years, he had known about the toxicology report that he had supervised. For eleven years, he had a copy of the Baptist Hospital autopsy report that concluded that prescription drug abuse was responsible for the death of Elvis Presley. Dr. Sexton was an authority on heart disease and heart pathology, both professionally and personally. Dr. Sexton knew for eleven years that in the case of Elvis Presley, "cardiac arrhythmia" was a gross exaggeration of the truth, perpetrated and perpetuated by the authorities.

Dr. Sexton died in 1988 and had made arrangements for the Baptist Memorial Hospital autopsy and toxicology reports to be made public after his death. Because of Dr. Harold Sexton, *The Death of Elvis: What Really Happened*" was written by Charles C. Thompson II and James P. Cole, and the book was published in January of 1991. (The information contained in this monograph is based on this well written and researched book.)

Implications: The Lessons Learned From The death Of Elvis

Elvis Aron Presley appeared to "have it all". His talent and fortune could have taken him anywhere he wanted to go. Instead, his life was cut tragically short at age forty-two by his addiction to prescription drugs. The lessons learned from this include:

1. Prescription drugs are easy to abuse.
2. Prescription drugs are the fastest growing group in the illicit drug market.
3. Thirty percent of all drug-related deaths involve prescription drugs.
4. PRESCRIPTION DRUG ABUSE WIL DESTROY YOU.

BIBLIOGRAPHY

1. The Death of Elvis: What Really Happened, by Charles C. Thompson II and James P. Cole, January 1991
2. Memphis Commercial Appeal
3. Substance Abuse and Mental Health Services Administration (SAMHSA)
4. California Board of Pharmacy statistics
5. University of Tennessee, Memphis, Medical School Yearbook, 1967

Carol Salus, PhD, is Associate Professor of Art History, Kent State University. She teaches late nineteenth and twentieth century American and European art history courses. Dr. Salus is co-editor of Out of Context: American Artists Abroad (Greenwood Press, 2004). Carol has spoken at national and international conferences as well as at the Cleveland Psychoanalytic Society and Creativity and Madness conferences. Carol had certification as a school counselor.

Dr. Salus has published articles in Art Bulletin, Art Journal, Sculpture, International Journal of the Arts, Ceramics: Art and Perception, Landscape Architecture Journal, Analecta Husserliana, Celestinesca, Schatzkammer der Deutschen Sprache, Dichtung, und Geschichte, Shofar: An Interdisciplinary Journal of Jewish Studies, Jewish Art, Journal of Contemporary Literature and Aesthetics, Printmaking Today. Carol has written exhibition reviews and encyclopedia entries. Her current work is focusing on the impact memorials dedicated to genocide have when developed in an abstract rather than representational mode.

The Pigeon in Picasso's Art and Life: An Abbreviated Look

Carol Salus, PhD

This paper studies the meaning over time of Picasso's attachment to the pigeon. Whether pigeon or dove (the former connotes a larger bird, the latter a smaller one; they are one and the same for purposes discussed here), this bird is a life-long symbol of importance, one that undoubtedly resonated with Picasso. The dove images by Picasso are known all over the world as strong political statements associated with peace, yet the early roots of this bird reveal fascinating insights into his thought and interests for the artist who acknowledged the diary-like nature of his oeuvre.

As the tender, maternal parent, Don José Ruiz Blasco (1840-1913), Pablo's artist-father, was a painter of pigeons. The fact that pigeons/doves were bred and painted by his father as his favorite subject helps explain why it figured in both Picasso's art and even related to his fears of growing old and dying. Among his earliest known drawings are those of pigeons created when he was nine years old. The repetitious appearance of the bird in his art and his life is a selection of psychological significance.

Early Signs of Attachment to Father and His Symbols

Picasso started school in Malaga at about age six and became phobic of going to school. He found all sorts of excuses to avoid attendance, among them, feigning illness. He refused to go unless taken and brought back by Don José. Father took over the mothering role since mother, to whom he appears to have developed a detached relationship, was emotionally unavailable. On the way to school, Pablo clung to his father until Don José agreed to leave some possession, an object that the child deemed important, as a guarantee that

325

he would return. The boy preferred his father's paintbrushes as collateral or, failing these, one of the pigeons that Don José used as models. When Picasso entered the classroom late, clutching a pigeon or perhaps his father's walking stick, everyone burst into laughter. Both the pigeon and the walking stick perhaps can be said to function as symbols of great importance or as labeled by the late psychiatrist Dr. Rachel Baker, matured transitional objects. Pablo told Jaime Sabartés, his personal secretary and life-long friend, that he was so worried about whether his father would return that he scarcely noticed his schoolmates' reaction.

Furthermore, when he was six years old, the year of his entrance into school appears to have coincided with the birth of his sister Concepción, nicknamed Conchita. This event repeated the loss of mother's attention as had happened three years earlier with the birth of his first sister Lola. The trauma of the birth of yet another sibling and his resentment over his parents' attention to her undoubtedly added to his separation-anxiety.

Transitional Object and Its Maturation

As stated above, Dr. Rachel Baker felt the pigeon/dove represented the maturation of the transitional object in terms of Picasso's great attachment to doves/pigeons. D. W. Winnicott, the British child analyst, described in 1951 this special first possession designated by the infant (that is not part of the infant's body) as a symbol most likely of the breast. Its importance supersedes symbolization. It implies a process as well as an object, what the English psychoanalyst called a "journey of progress toward experiencing." The object can be anything from a stuffed animal to a pacifier, a soft or hard toy, to the ragged corner of a blanket; it appears at some time between four and twelve months old. In Picasso's case, as will be described, like the original transitional object, Winnicott's definition involves issues of separation from, and re-attachment to, not the original object, which is the mother, but rather the father.

The transitional object, displayed by babies in the recognition and use of the first "not-me" possession, comforts the infant in times between sleeping and waking when fantasies develop. The object enables the child to stand frustrations, deprivations, and the presentation of new situations. Dr. Baker explained its fulfilling function: "A need for a specific object that started at a very early date may reappear at a later age when deprivation threatens. This may be a time of loneliness or when a depressed mood is near."

The source of Picasso's attachment to his father is rooted in early traumata. An earthquake, followed by the immediate birth of a sister, and the tragic death of another sister at a young age—each contributed to chronic preoccupations with fears of aging, loss, and death, and manifested themselves early in extreme separation-anxiety from his protective father, Don José.

The Earthquake

Various events in Picasso's childhood are important to discuss in understanding the significance that pigeons/doves held for him. Dr. Richard Lightbody, a psychiatrist, felt it was preferable to designate the pigeon/dove as a symbol of life-long importance rather than regarding it as the maturation of a transitional object. As Pablo remembered it, at Christmas time when he was three years old, his sister Lola was born shortly after the family fled to a neighbor's house during an earthquake that rocked his native Malaga from December 25 to 27, 1884. Dr. Mary Matthews Gedo, the art historian and psychoanalyst, stated: " Being displaced by a little sister can be earth-shaking and enraging to a little boy who was adored by his mother till then. It seems likely that little Pablo, unable to distinguish between internal rage and external devastation, came to believe that he had caused the Malaga earthquake." Don José apparently made a special effort to provide Pablo with companionship because he noted the child's deep distress at this time. Gedo observed that the ambivalent attitude following the births of Picasso's own children reflected his own unresolved feelings towards the arrival of his sisters.

Death of Conchita

Pablo's younger sister Conchita died of diphtheria when he was fourteen. There are numerous paintings and drawings he created commemorating this tragedy. They range from images showing his mother praying for her child's life in front of a cross on the wall as she kneeled by Conchita's bedside to deathbed scenes to a portrait of a grieving family. All of his life, Picasso avoided those closest to him when they lay ill or dying, as though he might escape his own human mortal fate. For example, at the death of Henri Matisse, with whom he had established close affectionate and artistic ties during Matisse's last years, his behavior was frankly avoidant. Matisse's daughter called about her father's funeral. Picasso would not acknowledge her call or attend the service. There are many examples of his tendency to react to illness and death with phobic avoidance. One could say that he painted to the end of his life as if to push death away.

Picasso's Father

Picasso's father, Don José, was a mediocre painter who had an unstable career. As a student, his father never earned a single honor grade, nor won a prize fellowship to study abroad. His appointment as professor at Malaga's Academia de San Telmo had nothing to do with his artistic gifts. It was argued that San Telmo should fill vacant places with "more modest artists, who are natives of Malaga and sons of this school (as the father was)...in order to establish these modest places as a prize for young artists." In Malaga, his income from teaching at this local school of arts and crafts was barely enough to support his family. Through family connections, he was also appointed as a restorer at Malaga's Museo Municipal and had a studio there, but in 1890, the collapse of the local economy forced the museum to close. He was never elected to the local academy of artists, failed to win a medal at a national exhibition, and lost the senior position at San Telmo to a more qualified painter.

He and his family were forced to relocate in 1891 to La Coruña. There he took a new position at another art school, the

Instituto da Guarda, obtained through connections, and formally became his ten-year-old son's teacher. Don José dreaded leaving sunny Malaga, where two generations of his family had lived, for the isolated life in La Coruña, a remote Atlantic port city on the northwestern coast of Spain. Don José suffered bouts of depression and began to neglect his painting. It is difficult to ascertain when Picasso made this observation as related by his longtime friend and personal secretary, Jaime Sabartés: "In Coru a, my father did not leave the house, except to get to work. Upon returning home, he amused himself painting, but not so much any more. The rest of the time he spent watching the rain through the windowpanes."

Don José was a disappointed artist of limited range; his primary interest, as stated above, was depictions of pigeons. He also created still life paintings of flowers and occasional genre scenes. Primarily, he spent time breeding pigeons in Malaga and La Coruña. In Picasso's mind, pigeons would become symbols of his warm feelings for his father. The apartment where Picasso grew up in Malaga faced a plaza lined by pigeons. Under his father's guidance before he was ten, Pablo was encouraged to draw and to sketch the pigeons that he could watch in the branches of the plaza's plane trees. Pigeons were always a part of his parents' household. Sometimes they were kept in the dovecot, and at other times they flew freely about the rooms, leaving their droppings everywhere, as often as not upon the canvases of his father, whether at Malaga or at La Coruña.

The interest in art that Pablo and Don José shared helped the relationship flourish. He hoped that his son would win the prestige he himself had failed to achieve as an academic artist, and, for this reason, he set up a rigorous program for Pablo's preparation.

Picasso always insisted that his father, who was his first art teacher, functioned as the only effective art instructor he ever had. Don José provided young Pablo with instruction in drawing from an early age. He gave him drawing lessons at home and taught Pablo how to paint with oils.

With tireless dedication, Don José taught his child the academic skills and artistic techniques he knew. In La Coruña, they lived across the street from the Institute where Picasso's father held a professorship in art. Dr. Gedo described how the son spent much of his time there under his father's tutelage. When he was eleven, Pablo officially enrolled in the Instituto de Guarda, studying drawing (generally from plaster casts) with his father. His sketches from 1892-94, the years when he was eleven to thirteen years old, show precocious powers of observation and drawing.

Natasha Staller, in her study of his early years, wrote that Picasso also studied with Isidoro Brocos, whom he remembered as "an exceptional teacher." Brocos was one of the leading artists in Galicia and he embraced the classical tradition in a way Picasso's father never did. Brocos trained at the local academy (which preceded the Instituto da Guarda), won chances to study in Paris and travel to Rome, and won third prize at the National Exhibition in Madrid.

The Legend about His Father Giving Up Painting

With his prodigious artistic gifts, during his early teen years in La Coruña, from 1891-95, Picasso had become so skilled at painting that his father permitted him to execute details of his canvases, particularly the feet of the dead pigeons in his still life paintings. Picasso described to Sabartés: "My father would cut off the legs of a dead pigeon and pin them down on a board, in a convenient position, and I would copy them minutely, until they met with his approval." According to Picasso, when his father noticed his son's great skill painting claws, "...he gave me his paints and his brushes, and never went back to painting." Picasso, who relied for comfort and protection on his father, was possibly frightened by his exposure to Don José's cruel impulses. He fantasized that Don José had relinquished his brushes and palette to him.

The myth of Don José passing his brushes to his son is perpetuated by various Picasso biographers without careful examination. Françoise Gilot, one of his mistresses, and Jacqueline Roque, his second wife, have clarified Picasso's exaggerated tale. He omitted the fact that his father's gesture was motivated primarily by his failing eyesight. While Pablo's skills grew, not only had Don José's sight begun to deteriorate in La Coruña, but this was coupled by a loss of steadiness in his hand. He confided to Jacqueline: "After my father's eyes couldn't draw the pigeons' feet any more, I made them for him."

Gedo explained this tale as follows: The story may be yet another chapter of that personal mythology created by Picasso, showing a retrospective condensation of separate events—recognition by Don José of Pablo's progress occurring along with an aggravation of the father's depression and difficulties about working, unrelated to his son.

In a study of Picasso and his father, Dr. Jan Ehrenwald erroneously compared Don José's alleged abandonment of his painting, upon recognition of the mature talent of his son, to that of Mozart's father. The psychoanalyst wrote: "It is interesting to recall that Leopold Mozart's career likewise came to an end with the first few minuets and other early works which he wrote down when little Wolfgang composed them." Don José did not give up painting entirely. Well into the twentieth century, he continued to paint the annual portrait of the pigeon-of-the-year for Barcelona's Colombofila Society (pigeon fanciers), of which he was the president. Furthermore, as will be explained, the family moved to Barcelona in 1895 so that Don José could teach at the art school known as La Llotja. Picasso was the sole source for the story of his father passing the brushes to him and vowing never again to paint. Sources vary at what age this mythic story took place, but Picasso was probably about fourteen years old.

The tale of Don José's renunciation of his brush is enlightening. Manuel Pallarés, who met Picasso at age fourteen in 1895, remained a life-long friend to both him and his father, and always maintained that the father never renounced painting in favor of the son. This tale of self-denial on the part of the father has been passed on significantly

331

by Picasso himself. It reveals Picasso's fantasy in which he clearly saw himself as triumphing over his father, thus expressing his own cruel wishes. Picasso chose to think that his career—his skill, vision, and power—was launched at the expense of his father's career.

Father's Dedication to Promotion of Son's Career

Picasso said later in life that he preferred the paintings he did under his father's supervision in La Coruña (1891-95) to the work he would subsequently do at art school in Barcelona. The artist kept several of his La Coruña canvases in his personal collection until his death. When Don José took a new teaching position at the Barcelona Academy of Fine Arts, he did various forms of promotion for his son as a promising painter. He arranged for Pablo to work on a canvas in the studio of the established Andalusian artist José Ramon Garnelo (Don José's colleague at La Llotja from 1895 to 1899).

His father used his Andalusian connections to win his fifteen-year-old son a commission to copy two altarpieces by Murillo for a convent in Barcelona. In 1897, his father, as he had previously, dictated subjects to his son that were typical of the School of Malaga—first communions and altar boys. For an allegorical painting, Science and Charity, in which a doctor and a nun stand on either side of the bed of a dying patient, he prepared the canvas and served as a model for the doctor in this sentimental sickroom scene. The painting was exhibited and won an honorable mention at the Exposición de Bellas Artes in Madrid. He wanted his son to have a solid background in order to teach art in Spain.

Move to Barcelona

Don José switched teaching positions with a colleague in Barcelona and the family moved again in 1895 following Conchita's death. He taught at the Barcelona Academy of Fine Arts, a national art school of high ranking known as La Llotja, (the art school is called this because it is located in the old stock exchange, Casa Llotja). According to Sabartés, Picasso's father became increasingly morose in Barcelona, and he avoided the company of his friends and colleagues, and except for brief walks to his school, he refused to leave his house. The rest of the time he spent watching the rain through the windowpanes. Pablo took classes there while Don José increasingly withdrew.

Don José convinced his wealthy physician brother Salvador to invest financially in Pablo's future so that they could send the boy to study in the Royal Academy of San Fernando in Madrid, which the father regarded as the greatest art school in Spain. There he was taught, as Staller wrote, "...not by exalted artists" but by two former colleagues of his father including the professor who received the senior position in Malaga for which Don José was turned down. Gedo wrote that Picasso seldom if ever attended classes there, claiming that he "forgot" to go.

During these years in Malaga, Coru a, and Barcelona, Don José guided his son's artistic progress. Picasso surpassed his father when he demonstrated in his adolescence that he could draw with enormous mastery according to academic formulas. Don José seems to have instilled a high level of ambition in his son with expectations of the future success of his prodigy. Significantly, during Picasso's teenage years, his dejected academic painter-father was young Pablo's favorite subject, and he recorded the subtlest changes in his mood in sensitive paintings and drawings. In these studies, Don José never smiled and often appears depressed. His depression deepened after the death of his younger daughter in 1895. In contrast to these intimate examinations of his father's psychic state, Picasso rarely did detailed pictures of his mother. In fact, only two real portraits of her exist.

At age fifteen or sixteen, Picasso did a pen-and-ink sketch of Don José that indicated his own feelings. Picasso depicted his bearded father, seated on a plain chair, with a bevy of pigeons beneath him. It was sketched with greater animation than his father could ever achieve. Surrounding Don José, a few words apparently written in his own hand refer to the system of honor grades in which he so fervently believed. Above and to each side are the judgments

333

"suspenso, suspenso, suspenso" (in Spanish, "failure, failure, failure"). Farther out, as though beyond his grasp, are the words "sobresaliente, sobresaliente" (the highest examination grade), which Don José never earned but which he and others had awarded his son from the very beginning.

Don José came to represent everything in art Picasso fought against—a sterile academic tradition. At age sixteen, he stated: "In art it is necessary to kill one's father." The profound revolutions Picasso developed in his career stem not only from his great talent and ambition, but were propelled by his rebellion against his father and the limits of the artistic vision he embodied. John Richardson, Picasso's long-time friend and most objective biographer, wrote that "...this oedipal maxim lies at the heart of Picasso's creative process."

In 1900 at age nineteen, in defiance of his father's wishes, Pablo left Barcelona for Paris. After four years and four major trips to Spain, between October 1900 and April 1904 for periods of varying lengths of time, he made Paris his new home. John Richardson described Don José's condition at the time of Picasso's initial departure as follows: "...Failing eyesight, melancholia, and a lack of rapport with his incomprehensible son had exacerbated Don José's bitterness." He was a frustrated and disappointed man at the time of his death in 1913. One can guess that had Pablo not left in 1904 for the opportunities, experimentation, and support he found in Paris, his enormous talent could have never flourished.

The Visual Evidence of Father, Son and Pigeon

The association of father and pigeons/doves clearly held deep meaning for the artist since these birds are even depicted in his mature *oeuvre*, a body of work, as mentioned above, that is known to be autobiographical. Picasso told Françoise Gilot: "I paint the way some people write their autobiography." In the last of his trips between Barcelona and Paris, he was able to sever the family ties binding him to Barcelona, to stay in Paris, and become a permanent French resident, though never a naturalized citizen. During these four years, his art changed and matured rapidly, stimulated by the new influences to which he was exposed in his stays in Paris, as well as by his own great talent.

Figure 1

Child with a Dove (1901)

When the adult Picasso found himself alone and depressed in Paris at the onset of his Blue Period, he painted this sensitive picture of a child tenderly cuddling a dove. In Figure 1, *Child with a Dove* (1901), a little boy with a gentle and innocent expression hugs a dove to his chest. It seems, as Dr. Mary Gedo states, the way the child clings to the pigeon brings to mind the thought of Picasso clutching one of his father's birds to comfort himself when he had to separate from his father and enter the classroom in Malaga. The child seems to want to be cuddled. The dove/pigeon came to represent aspects of his father—security and protection. The bird continued to stand as a strong symbol, source of comfort, remembrance of good times past between father and son, in his life.

Olga Picasso's Illness

Olga Koklova, whom Picasso met while artistic designer for The Ballets Russes in 1917, married Picasso in 1918 and became pregnant the following year. There were changes in her mental health as she began showing delusional tendencies. Picasso worried about how to keep Olga functioning until their child was born. Gedo suggested that he may have been terrified that he might go under with her. The more advanced Olga's pregnancy, the more out of contact she became. Descriptions by people who knew her later reveal that, by the late 1940s, Madame Picasso behaved in a manner so aberrant that it does not seem speculative to label her a chronic schizophrenic personality. The hollow, repetitive, inappropriate quality of her behavior closely resembled that of chronic schizophrenics who have made certain adjustments to their psychosis, Dr. Gedo wrote in her dissertation. Olga's unbearable behavior made it impossible for Pablo to function normally.

New Love

In 1927, Picasso met Marie-Thérèse Walter, a seventeen-year-old blonde athletic-looking beauty, with whom he would have a child and a steady relationship until the 1940s. She was a dream of classical perfection, and because of this, he picked her out as she was leaving for the Metro from the department store Galeries LaFayette. She was perhaps his greatest muse in terms of artistic inspiration and appears in countless works including both a photograph and a 1930 blue charcoal in which she holds a dove.

In 1934, Picasso's artistic productivity declined alarmingly. His rage and guilt, created by his predicament between his disturbed wife and his now pregnant mistress, prevented him from focusing on painting or sculpting. Curiously, he portrayed himself in a series of etchings as a blind Minotaur groping along a shore. The blind creature probably represented both Picasso's fear of disloyalty toward his sick wife and his mistress, as well as his apprehension about his future career. He was torn between a sick wife whom he could not totally leave and a mistress who loved him and he grew tired of. Marie-Thérèse was innocent, beautiful, and in the end functioned solely as a muse; she was far from an equal partner. A close friend and biographer of Picasso, Roland Penrose, referred to her as "the only non-intelligent woman, the only really vulgar woman to have been part of Picasso's life."

In a mixed-media print comprised of color aquatint, engraving, and drypoint, Marie-Thérèse appears in *Blind Minotaur Led through the Night by Girl with Fluttering Dove* (1934) as the beautiful little girl who guides the monster (as he undoubtedly saw himself at times) by the hand. She clutches a fluttering dove. Gedo felt the image recalled Picasso's nostalgia for his tender childhood relationship with his father, represented by the dove.

Figure 2

Blind Minotaur Led through the Night by Girl with Fluttering Dove (1934)

In his later relationships with women, Picasso often behaved with his beloved as his father behaved with him. He played the nurturing, mothering role with Marie-Thérèse, while she enacted that of the little girl. Gedo noted that, as is always the case with role reversals, Picasso soon tired of his assumed role, for his underlying wish to be the beloved child himself was just beneath the surface.

The Years of World War II

In 1943, during the German Occupation, Picasso painted the ironic *Child with Doves* (in the Musée Picasso; see www.angel-art-house.com) in which an adult appears seated on the ground. Adjacent to him is an empty wooden chair on which one dove stands on the seat and another remains at the top of the chair's back. The setting is a rather dark room with a constricted space, the same kind of oppressive environment seen in some other examples of Picasso's wartime *oeuvre*.

The two doves indicate Picasso's cynicism at the time. While he was never in active combat in any of the wars during which he lived, news frequently arrived that Jewish friends had been deported to concentration camps or that others had been tortured or put to death because of their clandestine activities in the resistance movement. With all the evil uncertainty that went with the Occupation, Child with Doves can only be interpreted as a mocking look at a childhood scene.

The Post-War Years and Associations with the Dove

In 1947, Picasso settled in the Communist-ruled town of Vallauris with Françoise Gilot, who was forty years younger than the sixty-two-year-old artist was when she met him. During this year, he became intensely involved in ceramics and revived the industry in this ancient Roman pottery town. His dove appeared on the pottery and even was depicted nesting on a ceramic platter.

Like many French intellectuals, Picasso joined the French Communist Party. His famous poster of the dove for the Communist World Peace Congress held in Paris and sponsored by the French Communist Party in April 1949 was actually a lithograph he had made with no specific purpose in mind. Louis Aragon, the Surrealist poet and a fellow Party member, looked through a folder of his prints and selected his lithograph of a white dove to symbolize the 1949 meeting. (See this famous image printed by Mourlot in 1949 at www.On-lineWall.com.)

This lithograph of a white Milanese pigeon, with its small tuft of feathers behind the head and distinctive feathery feet, appeared on a black ground, titled *Dove of Peace*. It was a depiction of one of Matisse's pigeons that Picasso had been given by the elder painter. It is interesting that from the place of honor in his loge during the mass meeting of the 1949 Peace Congress, he described what he watched: " …five hundred thousand participants parading on the grounds with billboards figuring naïve and clumsy imitations of doves, cut-out doves, small doves and large doves."

His initial lithograph, *Dove of Peace*, which was printed in multiple copies to advertise the congress, appeared on the billboards and walls of many European cities and was adopted by the peace crusade as its international symbol. His dove image ultimately reached worldwide fame as it appeared on stamps, on various posters hung on factory and workshop walls, students' dormitory rooms, museums, and exhibitions.

His second daughter, the future jewelry designer, was born during the Peace Congress, and he named her Paloma ("dove" in Spanish.) (His first daughter Maya was the child of Marie-Thérèse Walter; Paloma was his second child with Françoise Gilot.) During the late forties and early fifties, Picasso was actively involved in the Communist-backed International Peace Movement, which included attendance at world peace conferences in Poland, Italy, and England, as well as the creation of numerous peace posters with more singular images of doves as illustrated and discussed by Gertje Utley.

Figure 3

November 1950 Peace Congress in London

This poster was created specifically for the November 1950 Peace Congress in London in which a dove spreads its wings over the globe. Picasso told the gathering, how, as a child, he had learned from his father to draw pigeons: "How it would please him if he were alive today and could see my modest doves have circled the world. I stand for life against death: for peace against war." He was awarded the Lenin Peace Prize in 1950 for the dove posters, but after that year, Picasso declined to take part in Peace Congresses, deeming them as too time-consuming.

Dove in Late Life

As an adult in emulation of his father's habit, Picasso allowed pigeons to fly freely through his homes, despite the mess their droppings created on the surfaces of his paintings. There is a photograph of him that is owned by the Musée Picasso in which he is holding one of the birds. When he moved to the south of France, he often kept dovecotes on the roof of his chateaux.

At age 76 in 1957, Picasso returned to the doves as subject matter for his work. He first started a painted dialogue with Velázquez' *Las Meninas (The Maids of Honor)* (1656), a study of the court painter who stands in front of a canvas as he portrays the Spanish royal family with their dwarfs. This series of paintings, which resulted in a four-month painterly dialogue, was a form of recognition that he belonged to the lineage of great Spanish artists.

He painted this series after Velázquez, as reinterpretations of the Baroque masterpiece, in his pigeon loft studio. After Picasso finished his first seventeen variations on *Las Meninas*, on the same day he interrupted the series to paint a group of canvases of his doves in their dovecotes, eight views of his pigeons and their nests. He recorded the view framed by his window of a pigeon roost and cage that stood on the balcony overlooking the Mediterranean in the bright summer light; over six days he painted nine canvases of the scene. *The Pigeons* (1957) shows this view he saw outside his studio window lined by his doves.

Figure 4

The Pigeons (1957)

The interest in *Las Meninas* appears to have ties to his early years with his father and thus holds significance for this study. In 1895, Don José took his fourteen-year-old son to the Prado to expose him to great art. Before the family moved to Barcelona, they took a summer vacation in Malaga. They traveled by train and stopped for the better part of a day in Madrid so that Don José could take Pablo on his first visit to the Prado and they undoubtedly saw *Las Meninas*. It was his first exposure to great art in the original. Already in 1897, Pablo's first direct reference to the painting, a sketch of two figures from *Las Meninas*, was drawn during a period of study in Madrid when he was sixteen years old.

The return to this late-life series of paintings after Velázquez' masterpiece seems to have been associated in Pablo's mind with early, tender times spent with his father who in 1895, as stated, initially introduced Pablo to the master's works. There appear to be intimate connections between his memories of Don José and seeing this Baroque painting with him in Madrid years before and the birds.

Picasso saw the pigeon paintings as integral to the *Meninas* series as a whole. He created forty-five paintings based directly on Velázquez' masterpiece and an additional thirteen related works. Importantly, when he donated his reinterpretations of *Las Meninas* to the Museo Picasso in Barcelona in 1971, he included this suite of pigeon paintings with them, and they remain on display together. These birds created a comforting bridge between Picasso and his father over whom he had triumphed.

Significant Late Life Associations of Picasso

Picasso's attachment to his father is apparent in many instances. Brassa , the famous Hungarian-born photographer who met Picasso in 1932 and remained friends for forty years into late life, discussed Picasso in the 1960s. He related that for a long time, little canvases by Don José were hung on the walls where Picasso received visitors . Picasso also said to Brassa : "Everytime I draw a man, automatically I think of my father... I see all the men... with his features."

The life-long importance of the bird symbol and its connection with Don José is particularly significant in this story from his final years as his well known fear of aging and death are mentioned. Typically, as noted above, he responded by avoidance behavior. His difficulty is seen in this incident from his last decade with his wife Jacqueline Roque, who was forty-five years younger than Pablo when they married in 1961.

John Richardson, recounted in a video, *The Bull in Winter: The Final Years of Pablo Picasso*, that Picasso kept some birds in a cage. Richardson used a French name for the small white birds;

nevertheless, they function as substitutes for the first bird, the dove or pigeon. He related how Jacqueline in her protective manner, had new birds bought for him and placed in the cage before he could realize that one of them had died. The artist commented curiously, "My birds never die." This must have been a comforting self-deception, possibly representing a fantasy of the undying tie to father, thus keeping a part of him and himself immortal. As he worked daily and obsessively to try to ward off death, he died of a lung edema while still recovering from an influenza attack. The pigeon, a life-long symbol of importance, represented father's care. It helped him cope with separation-anxiety and the ultimate separation of death.

Special thanks to Dr. Richard Lightbody for his reading and thoughtful suggestions in the preparation of this article.

BIBLIOGRAPHY

Burglin, Timothy Anglin. "Picasso and Appropriation," *Art Bulletin*, September 1991, LXXVIII, 3, 479-94.

Ehrenwald, Jan. "Picasso: Father and Son: Patterns of Contagion and Rebellion in Genius," *Neurosis in the Family and Patternsof Psychosocial Defense: A Study of Psychiatric Epidemiology*. New York: Harper & Row, Hueber Medical Divisions, 1963, 109-124.

Gedo, Mary. Picasso: *Art as Autobiography*, Chicago: The University of Chicago Press, 1980.

Gedo, Mary. Picasso's *Self-Image: A Psycho-Iconographic Study of the Artist's Life and Works*, PhD dissertation, 1972.

Richardson, John. *A Life of Picasso*, Vol. I: 1881-1906, Random House, New York, 1991.

Sabartés, J. Picasso: *An Intimate Portrait* , trans. A. Flores, New York, Prentice-Hall, 1948

Staller, Natasha. "Gods of Art: Picasso's Academic Education and Its Legacy," *Picasso: The Early Years*, 1892-1906, National Gallery of Art, Washington, D.C., 1997, 67-81.

Fabian Ulitsky, MEd, is an Associate Professor of Psychology, at the University of The Arts in Philadelphia, Pa., where he has been teaching for 42 years. He also founded and directed for 25 years a Master's Degree program in Group Psychotherapy and Organizational Dynamics at Hahnemann University, in Philadelphia. He has participated frequently at the Creativity and Madness Conferences, giving presentations on Ben Shahn, George Nakashima, Robert Rivera, Georgia O'Keeffe and Antonio Berni. His special interest in art and creativity was deeply influenced by his exposure to Japanese culture, while serving in the United States Air Force, and his many years of doing play therapy with emotionally disturbed children.

"Nobody sees a flower really; it is so small.
We haven't time, and to see takes time -
like to have a friend takes time."

Georgia O'Keeffe

GEORGIA O'KEEFFE
VISIONS INTO FLOWERS, BONES AND SKY

FABIAN ULITSKY, MEd

This remarkable contemporary American artist achieved legendary status in her lifetime and still remains as the only female artist to have ever had a museum named in her honor. Located in Santa Fe, it attracts thousands of visitors each year and the places in New Mexico where she lived, and worked are still referred to as O'Keeffe country. She was a prolific painter and produced an enormous body of work throughout her career, consisting mostly of flowers, animal bones and landscapes. Much of the credit for the initial years of her fame and success must be given to her husband, photographer and gallery owner Alfred Stieglitz, who organized her first show. He also managed her career and created a special image of Georgia, which fostered the public's interest and fascination with her, which she sustained throughout her long life. However, after eleven years of living together in New York, and strains in their marriage, she began spending her summers in New Mexico, apart from her husband. She fell in love with the way of life and the land there, which provided her with renewed artistic inspiration and an increased amount of independence. Three years after his death, she moved to New Mexico and permanently resided there for the last 37 years of her life. She particularly cherished her solitude, hiking, gardening, music and painting, with which she continued for many years until her vision finally failed her. When she died in 1986, at the age of 98, her estate was worth millions of dollars.

347

Georgia's Childhood

Georgia was born on November 15, 1887 on a dairy farm, near Sun Prairie, Wisconsin, the second of seven children and the first girl. Her father was a hard working, fun loving Irishman who married one of the daughters from the family who lived on the next farm. Georgia's mother came from a higher social order and wished to become a doctor but her family convinced her to marry and raise a family instead. She was an intelligent woman who emphasized education and a love for learning in her children. Georgia was an athletic, highly competitive youngster who liked climbing trees, swimming, hiking and roaming around in the hundreds of acres of farmland, owned by her family. Her sex education, like that of most farm children, came from her observation of the natural practices of the farm animals.

Her mother arranged for her children to receive private art lessons, at home, when Georgia was about 12 years old. The following year they began receiving painting lessons from a local artist. It quickly became apparent that Georgia was very talented in this area and her family thought that she might become an art instructor one day. While playing with a friend and talking about future plans she suddenly stated that she was going to be an artist when she grew up. An insight into her personality can be discovered from an analysis of the feelings she expressed then, "I decided that the only thing I could do that was nobody else's business was to paint. I could do as I chose because no one would care."

In 1901 her parents sent her to an exclusive Catholic Boarding School where she performed well academically and earned a medal of improvement in art. The following year she and her brother were sent to live with relatives in Madison and to attend high school there. It was here, in her art class, that Georgia became fascinated with the variety of colors and flowers that were carefully studied. The following year she and her family moved to Williamsburg, Virginia as her parents wished for a warmer climate. They hoped this might help them all to avoid developing tuberculosis, which had killed several of

348

their sons. In the fall Georgia attended Chatham Episcopal Institute, a girls boarding school, a few hundred miles away. Her artistic ability and plain style of dress were the two things that most distinguished her from the other students. Mrs. Willis, an art teacher and the school principal, was so impressed with Georgia's talent and work that she gave her a special diploma in art, at her graduation in 1905.

Art Education and Employment

In the fall, at the urging of Mrs. Willis and with the encouragement of her mother, she went to live with relatives in Illinois, so she could study at the Art Institute of Chicago. Although the school was highly competitive, after just one month, because of her talent and industriousness, she was transferred out of the beginning group of students and placed in a more advanced group, where by the end of February she ranked first. Over the summer, while visiting at home, she came down with typhoid fever and went through a lengthy bedridden recovery period. In 1907, instead of returning to Chicago, she moved to New York to study at the Art Students League, the alma mater of Mrs. Willis, her former teacher. New York was a wonderful change of pace for Georgia, as she enjoyed the excitement and energy level of the city and the friendlier and less competitive atmosphere in her classes. At the end of her first year she won the League's still-life prize for an oil painting, which was a scholarship to the League's outdoor summer school at Lake George, New York. At the end of the summer when she returned home to Virginia she discovered her father's business had failed and her mother was ill with tuberculosis. Realizing that there wasn't sufficient funds for her to return to New York she went to live with relatives in Chicago, where she was hired as a freelance illustrator, drawing lace advertisements for a newspaper. Although she was successful as a commercial artist, the work proved boring and she was lonely and found Chicago to be cold and dreary. After working at this job for two years, she developed measles, which affected her eyes and so she returned home to Virginia. She attended art classes with her sister Anita, at the University of Virginia, taught by Alon Bement. He introduced his students to the methods of Arthur Dow, who stressed their experimenting with abstract shapes instead of traditional representational art. This appealed to Georgia who was ready for a new painting approach that encouraged more freedom and creativity with design and color. From 1912 to 1914, she taught art and penmanship in the public school system of Amarillo, Texas, and in the summers she worked as Bement's teaching assistant. Her attempts at introducing new and innovative ways of teaching art there proved popular with her students but provoked controversy and were strongly opposed by the Amarillo school board. She quit her position after two years so she could return to New York and take classes with Dow, at Columbia Teachers College.

While studying in New York she and her fellow art students began attending some of the opening shows at 291, the art gallery where Stieglitz was introducing the American public to the art of Picasso, Cezanne, Matisse and the sculpture of Brancusi. She enjoyed listening to the spirited and informative art discussions that Stieglitz would frequently engage in with students, artists and visitors who came to his gallery. Unfortunately, after one year, because of limited finances, she had to leave New York and in the fall of 1915 she accepted a college teaching position in South Carolina. One day, after a few months of working there, she began carefully examining and evaluating her own body of work and decided she needed to start anew with a fresh and original approach. This was the beginning of her successfully integrating the lessons she learned from Bement and Dow concerning the oriental principle of in-yo, shadow and light. She also freed herself to follow the theories of Kandinsky, who emphasized the internal world of the artist. She would no longer adhere to the traditional conventions of accurately copying nature, but would begin expressing her deeply, personal feelings and interpretation in her colors, shapes and designs. In the evenings, after she had finished teaching her classes, she began a series of abstract charcoal drawings and mailed a few of them to Anita Pollitzer, a former school friend. Anita was so impressed with Georgia's new work that on January 1st,

1916 she hurried over to 291 and showed them to Stieglitz who was so excited with them that it led to the beginning of a correspondence between Stieglitz and Georgia that would continue for thirty years. At the beginning of May, she was very saddened by the death of her mother, who had been living in poverty. Georgia's career really began a few weeks later when Stieglitz included several of her sketches in an informal group show without her knowledge or permission. When she finally learned of the show, she stormed into his gallery intent on demanding their instant removal. However when she saw the prominence he had given to her work, her rage subsided and Stieglitz took her to lunch and persuaded her to let them remain on display.

In the fall of 1916 she began college teaching in Canyon, Texas, where she painted a number of watercolors of the surrounding territory, mailing some of them to Stieglitz. The year 1917 contained two special events in her life; in April, she had her first solo show at 291, and in the summer, while traveling with her younger sister Claudia, she visited New Mexico for the first time. She was so captured by the clear light, intense colors, simplicity, and beauty of the Southwest that she promised to return one day. That winter she came down with influenza and took a leave of absence from the college, and moved to a warmer part of the state. Steiglitz, concerned for her health, wrote and proposed that she return to New York, where he would make arrangements for her to live and to continue painting. She resisted this offer until the summer when Stieglitz sent his photographer friend, Paul Strand, to Texas to make sure she was well and to see if she would come back to New York. A mutual romantic attraction developed between the two of them while together in Texas but Strand reluctantly realized the financial impossibility of their situation. However, he was successful in his assigned task and she returned to New York with him. When they arrived on June 10th at the train station, Stieglitz was waiting there to claim her; Georgia was 30 years old and single and Stieglitz was 54, married and had a teen-aged daughter.

He moved her into a studio apartment that his niece wasn't using and shortly thereafter began a 20 year period of photographing her and every aspect of her body. Several weeks after her arrival, he invited her to his apartment and proceeded to take nude photographs of her, while his wife Emmeline was out shopping. However his wife returned early, became enraged at what she observed and threw the embarrassed Georgia out and demanded that Alfred move out. This may have been what he was hoping for as he then moved in with Georgia and they soon became lovers. Several weeks later they were invited to the Stieglitz summer home at Lake George to meet his family. Never overly fond of Emmeline, when his mother saw how alive and happy her son was with Georgia , she welcomed her and gave them her blessing. The rest of the summer spent there was like a wonderful honeymoon for the two lovers who also enjoyed the natural beauty of the area.

Life with Stieglitz

In the fall, upon their return to the city, Alfred borrowed a thousand dollars from a friend so Georgia could remain and dedicate herself to painting for one year. He had closed 291 the previous summer and now his time and energy were invested in photography, and in Camera Works, the magazine that he started and still edited. He was now required to become more economically realistic as his wife ceased supplying the considerable financial support that he routinely relied upon. While Georgia was much more accustomed to financial hardship, she had always managed to find employment and to support herself. In sharp contrast, Alfred had always been indulged with financial assistance from his wealthy family, even during his marriage, and had never been forced to depend upon his own efforts.

In spite of major personality differences that existed between them they were able to enjoy a successful relationship for a number of years because of the core interests and artistic values they both shared. A major factor was the high level of trust and respect they had for each other's professional talent and artistic integrity.

Alfred was a brilliant, gregarious, dynamic, opinionated, erudite and eloquent spellbinder, who needed a crowd. He enjoyed being the center of attention and displaying his vast fund of information and knowledge on a wide variety of topics. Already established as one of the greatest living photographers in the world, he derived satisfaction from introducing Modern art to the United States and assisting in the development and success of his creative associates. On the negative side, he was also selfish, controlling, manipulative, deceitful, hostile, destructive and a womanizer, who betrayed his wife, daughter and finally Georgia.

Georgia was an intelligent, opinionated, forthright person who was very goal oriented and tenacious when she set her mind on something. She was competitive, industrious, disciplined and initially reserved in most social situations. Spirituality was a major component of her personality as was her need for solitude. She required tranquility to work and found this mostly in nature and music. She loved Oriental art and was deeply influenced by the "Book of Tea", about the Japanese tea ceremony. In New Mexico, her way of living and painting were very Zen like, a striving for simplicity and harmony. Even her style of dress reflected this, as she owned over 100 wraparound dresses, virtually all the same except half were white and half were black. She was very health conscious, careful of her diet, enjoyed walking for hours in the surrounding hills and canyons, skinny dipping in nearby streams and caring for her vegetable garden. As she aged she achieved an oneness with life and never tired of appreciating and enjoying the eternal beauty of the land she so deeply loved and ultimately became a part of.

Alfred and Georgia lived in a number of different apartments in Manhattan from 1918 to 1925. Every year, they would spend several months, from spring to fall, vacationing and working, at his family's country estate at Lake George. As she hiked around the lake she discovered inspiration for painting a number of landscapes and a series of flowers, but was bothered by the many family members and guests who interfered with her privacy and disrupted her work.

353

In February 1921 the Anderson Galleries in New York held a Stieglitz retrospective exhibit that included several nude photographs of Georgia. It quickly became the buzz of New York as it created a sensation with both the critics and the public, who became as interested in the artist as in her art. In the beginning of 1923 Alfred opened an O'Keeffe exhibition, containing over 100 of her works. The show was extremely successful, and earned her recognition as a remarkably talented artist. Alfred continued to arrange annual exhibitions of her work for the next 23 years until his death.

His divorce from his wife was finalized in September 1924 and Georgia reluctantly married him in December, but insisted on keeping her own name. He was now 61 years old and she was 37. That same year, influenced by Strand's use of magnification in his photography, Georgia painted a series of flowers huge in size and explained that in the busy city people are in such a hurry that they don't really notice a flower, but now they will see it whether they want to or not. These gigantic flower paintings exhibited in 1925 generated an increasing number of sexual interpretations. Freudian theory was very popular then and some critics saw in these paintings a female artist, struggling with sexual tension caused by the frustration of not having a child. Other paintings in this series were like a Rorschach blot in which critics saw phallic objects and female genitalia. Amused at first, Georgia over the years became increasingly irritated and tired of these repeated interpretations. Alfred was ambivalent, although he was jealous of her popularity and growing celebrity status he realized that the publicity produced by the sexual controversy would increase the financial value of Georgia's paintings. In November 1925 they moved to the Shelton Hotel, one of the tallest buildings in the city, with a panoramic view from their balcony that led to a series of skyscraper paintings over the next five years. The following year he was able to open The Intimate Gallery where he arranged an exhibit that included the first of her New York architectural paintings. Several of her flower paintings were sold during this time for such astronomical sums of money that her fame increased and the public's interest in Georgia reached new heights.

In 1927 Dorothy Norman, a 22 year old attractive, married and wealthy aspiring poet began making frequent visits to Alfred's new gallery. She was in awe of the breadth of his artistic and cultural knowledge and was easily seduced. This love affair continued for many years and history repeated itself as Alfred began a nude photographic series of Dorothy, a few of which he publicly exhibited. Georgia was humiliated and enraged by this and the openness of the affair. She stopped going to the gallery after Alfred hired Dorothy as its manager. As Georgia could not tolerate being second best to anyone the strain and tension in their marriage deepened and she was particularly disturbed by the time and energy Alfred invested in helping Dorothy with her writing career. Depressed by all of this and in need of new artistic inspiration in 1929 she accepted an invitation and traveled to Taos, New Mexico accompanied by Strand's wife, Beck. She was immediately enchanted with the desert and mountains, the wide-open spaces and the many beautiful vistas. Thousands of miles apart from her husband she experienced a renewed sense of spirit, freedom and independence. From now on she would regularly return and spend a part of each year in New Mexico. In her daily hikes she began picking up some of the animal bones she found and sent a barrel of them back east. She began a series of New Mexico paintings and in 1931 Alfred arranged the first exhibit of her bone and skull paintings at his new and final gallery, An American Place. Many believed these paintings reflected a fear or preoccupation with death, but for Georgia, who saw beauty in all aspects of nature, picking up animal bones in the desert was no different than picking up shells while strolling along a beach.

In 1932 Georgia asserted her independence from her husband by accepting a commission from Radio City Music Hall to paint a mural. Alfred became furious, unsuccessfully tried changing her mind and even attempted breaking the contract she had signed. Their marital relationship continued to deteriorate which made Georgia increasingly anxious and depressed. When she went to inspect the area that had been specially prepared for her to begin painting, a portion began to peel off from the wall and she became hysterical, left and never returned. Over the next few months she became increasingly withdrawn, developed severe neurotic symptoms, had a nervous breakdown and was hospitalized for one month. Weakened by the entire experience she recuperated with friends in Bermuda for a few months, then came back to Alfred but was unable to paint for the next year and a half. In 1934, she returned to New Mexico, discovered the area around Abiquiu, including, where she stayed nearly every summer, from then on, sometimes for as long as six months. She purchased a car, learned to drive and spent endless days exploring the area, seeking locations to paint. She felt so integrated there, alive and at peace with herself that she bought residence near Ghost Ranch and during the war years she purchased a second home in the town of Abiquiu. Similar to desert cactus, Georgia blossomed in this region and was able to follow her bliss, no longer feeling produced or controlled by Alfred. Over the next decade she continued with her New Mexico paintings, achieved world recognition and earned many honors and awards.

Alfred died in 1946 and Georgia spent the next three years in New York settling his estate. Afterwards she moved and permanently resided in New Mexico. In 1951 she took her first real trip outside of the country, visiting Mexico. For the next ten years she also took trips to Asia, India, the Middle East, South America and Europe. In 1971 she lost most of her central vision, due to macular degeneration. Two years later, when almost blind, a young potter named Juan Hamilton entered her life. His presence restored her life spirit and he assisted her with her final artwork, exhibits and the publication of her biography. She died in 1986 at the age of 98. As she had instructed, she was cremated without a funeral or memorial service and her ashes were scattered over the land at Ghost Ranch.

Analysis and Conclusion

Although she was certainly the favorite child of her father, she unfortunately was her cold mother's least favorite, which in later years contributed to the speculation of Georgia's bisexual orientation. Several informed researchers explained her frequent outbursts of uncontrolled rage as indicative of repressed homosexual desires and childhood sexual molestation. Georgia occupied a separate private upstairs bedroom in the family home where incest possibly occurred with both her father and her brother. Throughout her entire life she vigorously defended her father's financial failures and after his probable suicide, falling off a roof at night, no one was allowed to remind her of his passing, as it caused her so much emotional distress. Her love of the outdoors can be partly explained as a defense against being confined and trapped in a room; one of her favorite activities in New Mexico consisted of sleeping outdoors on the flat roof of her home, under the stars. Her attraction to and marriage with Alfred, when she was 37 and he was 61, serves to reinforce the belief concerning the occurrence of childhood sexual abuse.

She obtained her father's love for music and her mother's love for reading, both of which continued to provide her with meaning and joy throughout her long life. From her early childhood days of growing up on a dairy farm she learned that long hours, hard work and responsible behavior are required for successful survival. The sense of freedom and exhilaration she enjoyed as a youngster roaming the open acres of farmland were re-experienced as an adult in the hills, canyons and desert of New Mexico. She often felt stifled and claustrophobic living in Manhattan and it wasn't until she and Alfred moved to the top floors of the Shelton Hotel, with its panoramic view that she felt comfortable enough to start painting city scenes. When she was a schoolgirl her physical skills and ability allowed her to successfully compete with boys, and generated confidence and high self-esteem. This positive self-regard continued into adulthood where it was now her talent and discipline that allowed her to successfully compete in the masculine art world, and she derived considerable gratification from being the primary female artist in Alfred's inner circle of talented professionals. She kept her own name when she married and nobody ever referred to her as

Mrs. Stieglitz more than once, after receiving her angry response. She snubbed many of the feminists eager to praise her accomplishments and also refused to participate in a famous Guggenheim show honoring female artists, as she insisted on being recognized as an artist, not as a female artist.

An examination of Abraham Maslow's theory of Self Actualization is helpful in providing additional knowledge and understanding of Georgia's personality. Maslow, a founder of Humanistic Psychology, describes Self-Actualizers as individuals who are achieving their potential, fulfilling themselves and doing the best that they are capable of doing. Based upon his hierarchy of needs satisfaction, it is the highest level of personality development to be achieved and is only accomplished by less than one percent of our entire population. While Self-Actualizers function generally in a most healthy manner, they are not perfect beings and often struggle with the common failings of the average person. Some of the personal characteristics of Self-Actualizers that directly apply to Georgia are:

A more accurate and efficient perception of reality and an ability to tolerate uncertainty.

Throughout her long life Georgia usually demonstrated realistic attitudes and healthy behavior in both love and work. She was a hard working, responsible and pragmatic individual who established realistic goals, for her self, and invested the necessary time and energy required to achieve them. She accepted the financial limitations of her family to finance her professional art education and took jobs to support herself for several years at a time. When she accepted Alfred's invitation to leave Texas and come and live and paint in New York for one year, financed by him, she had a very accurate picture of what was involved. She was also willing to tolerate the uncertainty of what her life would be like when she allowed him to move in with her and became his mistress.

Increased acceptance of self and simplicity.

Even as a youngster Georgia recognized that she was different, in a number of significant areas, from most of her peers. Over the years she learned to be proud of these differences and developed a healthy acceptance of her own nature. In adulthood and middle age she would often take delight in the confusion and discomfort of others when she would make a point of demonstrating the differences that existed between them. The term simplicity captures the essence of her life style, from her manner of dress, her diet, the way she furnished her home, her garden, etc. There was a monastic quality to the manner in which she lived the last half of her life.

Increased detachment and desire for privacy.

Like most creative individuals Georgia was a private person and valued solitude, which she required to work at her best. Nothing provided her with more enjoyment than listening to her music albums and the many hours she would spend on her daily and solitary hikes in the mountains and desert of New Mexico. She much preferred establishing deep, satisfying interpersonal relationships with a few, rather than many people. She was very selective as to who she allowed into her life and even relatives and friends were not welcome to just stop by for a visit, unless they were invited. Unlike many people today who equate being alone with loneliness, Georgia preferred her own company and was very comfortable being alone.

Increased autonomy, and resistance to enculturation.

She possessed core beliefs that she expressed in a variety of situations that she knew were unpopular and she was willing to endure the consequences. In her early years as a teacher many of her pacifist viewpoints were angrily received during the war years. She was able to rely on her own judgment and forge her own autonomous values, resisting identification with cultural stereotypes. She also rejected the cultural mores of the day by living openly with a much older and married man, and even years later when Alfred was finally divorced

Georgia was in no rush to be married, nor was she willing to surrender her own name. After years of dependency on Alfred, in the management of her art career, she asserted her will to become independent and finally was able to accomplish this, when she began spending months living in New Mexico, separate from him.

Increased freshness of appreciation and creativeness.

She had a child like sense of awe concerning nature, which was successfully communicated in her creative works. She never tired of experiencing the beauty of nature, the stunning rock formations, the brilliant blue sky and the fragrant and lovely cactus in bloom. She could spend hours observing the same mountain and desert areas noticing the constant changes in color and shadow caused by the moving overhead clouds and the special quality of light in this region. During her daily hikes, she was frequently in the habit of finding something that appealed to her which she would pick up and take home with her. Over the years she amassed a large collection of river rounded rocks that she displayed in her Abiquiu home, along with a select number of animal bones and reptile skeletons. Her creativeness extended way beyond her artistic works and was reflected in many of the daily tasks of living, such as her home decoration, gardening and cooking. Some of these special qualities are fully captured and revealed in a beautiful photographic book, "O'Keeffe At Abiquiu," by Wood and Patten.

Higher frequency of peak experiences.

Peak experiences are profound moments of love, understanding, happiness, or rapture, when a person feels more whole, alive, self-sufficient and yet a part of the world. Georgia would often describe those special moments of rapture when she would experience the silence of the desert during the day or the star filled sky at night. It was those special fleeting moments of feeling completely at peace with her self and the universe that made life in New Mexico so special for her.

Imperfections

Georgia was known for having a short fuse and for often losing her temper. She could also be very abrupt, cold and impolite with strangers, as well as with people she had known for many years. On numerous occasions she demonstrated ruthless and inconsiderate behavior with others, in both her business and social affairs. However, there were also a few times when her kindness toward others allowed an individual to take undue advantage of her.

*   *   *

Her rafting trip along the Colorado River at the age of 76, and the several camping trips in the mountains, taken with Ansel Adams are good examples of her risk taking and adventurous spirit. She did not practice an organized religion but was very spiritual and enjoyed visiting The Monastery of Christ in The Desert, located near Ghost Ranch. She appreciated the chapel, built by George Nakashima, and the simple, austere furnishings, similar to those in her home. She valued the theories and philosophy of art expressed by Albert Calder and Frank Lloyd Wright and the natural and clean lines contained in their work. An analysis of her work reveals her constant efforts to reduce the object she was painting down to its very essence, similar in fashion to a therapist assisting patients in gradually stripping away their defenses to reach their inner core.

The application of Rorschach theory to her landscapes and flower paintings is suggestive of a tendency to withdraw from intellectual competition and to isolate oneself from competitors and critics. This rings very true in her case and also explains her admiration for Alfred's intellect, breadth of knowledge and his willingness and ability to engage anyone in meaningful debate. The interpretation by art critics of unresolved sexual tension contained in many of her flower paintings seems valid to me. Rorschach believed that responses containing bones and skeletons are chiefly found in neurotics who complain of inner emptiness, of loneliness, of emotional coldness, and are suggestive of hypochondriasis. While the majority of art experts interpreted the animal bone paintings as her concern with her own mortality, I believe that they primarily reflected her preoccupation with the death of her marriage. When Georgia suffered her nervous breakdown in 1932, her symptoms included excessive crying, severe headaches, breathing and sleeping difficulties, inability to walk, and phobias. She struggled with these neurotic symptoms for approximately seven weeks, was quite regressed and terrified of going outside, unless accompanied by her sister, Anita. During most of her hospitalization Alfred was only allowed to visit her for ten minutes, once a week, as his affair with Norman was one of the major causes for her breakdown. Georgia did not continue with therapy when discharged from the hospital but stayed with Anita briefly and then went to Bermuda with friends where she recuperated for several months before finally returning to be with Alfred again. It took her approximately 18 months to regain her emotional strength and confidence before she could resume working once more. In addition to Alfred's blatant affair, the fiasco she experienced with the Radio City Music Hall mural had taken its toll, as she felt inferior, rejected, humiliated and a failure.

She initially relied heavily upon Alfred's artistic judgments and opinions, appreciated the persona he created for her, and was thankful for his tending to all of the business details in the arrangement and sale of her art. However, after several years, she tired of the tight control he maintained over her and tried to assert her independence. She found it almost impossible to win arguments with him, as he was so persuasive, never gave in and argued tirelessly until she surrendered. After recovering from her nervous breakdown, she realized that living for part of each year in New Mexico was an ideal solution for her in both love and work. She often referred to this as her divided self, wanting to be with her husband but feeling the call of the outdoors that she described as being in her blood. When she would leave Alfred each year to come to New Mexico she wanted him to be happy in New York, but not because of his emotional and sexual involvement with the young and attractive Norman. Alfred never came west, which allowed Georgia complete freedom in every way, and their fondness for each other was gradually renewed by the months spent separated from each other. In New York she often felt in Alfred's shadow, and because of his need for an audience, people frequently dropped in and disrupted her work. In addition, the silence of the desert and its harsh, rugged beauty appealed to her and were a constant source of inspiration. Her daily walks, for hours in the hills and canyons, kept her physically fit, and the combination of the desert in bloom and the scattered animal skeletons encountered provided a reminder of the eternal struggle for existence.

Georgia is certainly one of the greatest 20th century artists. She was an original who followed her bliss and chose to paint what she felt and in her own style rather than continuing to copy or imitate others. Her use of vivid colors reflected her passion and range of inner emotions and her New Mexico paintings clearly convey her love and reverence for the land. She achieved the status of a living legend by age 60, and throughout her long life and career she demonstrated personal and artistic integrity.

Lisa M. Wayman, MSN, RN-BC, AHN-BC, a registered nurse with a master's degree in holistic nursing and a clinical background in intensive care, acute care, end-of-life care and nursing education, works for Banner Boswell Medical Center in Phoenix, AZ. She is currently a clinical nurse educator who specializes in developing programs to improve nurse recruitment and retention. Lisa has given talks for AIMED and for other national healthcare organizations on a variety of topics including: spirit in practice, the paradox of suffering and joy, end-of-life ethics, and support of nursing practice. She has published articles in nursing journals and has been a contributing author to several books. Her special interest lies in improving nursing practice through the integration of holistic principles in acute care settings. Lisa is also a visual artist who creates primarily in acrylic and collage.

Lisa has been married to Charlie for 25 years. They enjoy living in sunny Arizona. Charlie is a computer guru with a passion for photography. Their daughter Katie lives in Las Vegas.

"For what then matters is to bear witness to the
uniquely human potential at its best, which is to
transform a personal tragedy into a triumph, to turn
one's predicament into a human achievement."

(Frankl, 1984, p. 116)

WALKING WITH PERSEPHONE: A JOURNEY TOWARD HEALING

LISA M. WAYMAN *MSN, RN-BC, AHN-BC*

It may seem strange to discuss aspects of healing in the twenty-first century from the framework of a myth thousands of years old. I find, though, that myth—stories that hold archetypal meaning—can still inform and enlighten the human journey. I was thirty-two years old when Persephone captured me. I had not thought very much about myth before that time, and what I had learned about Persephone I didn't like. She was too passive, too dark, too mysterious for me. Then life turned unexpectedly and I was her disciple, walking her path and learning the lessons illuminated by her story millennia ago.

Demeter is the great grain goddess of agriculture. When you see a wheat field wave and respond to the smallest breeze: that is Demeter. When food is eaten, from the simplest meal to the greatest feast, she is there, goddess of full bellies and contented children. Demeter had a daughter, Kore, who was the most beautiful of maidens, young and alive as small shoots of grass and little flowers blooming in shade. Kore danced in her mother's green light, content to be fully aligned with light and life, unaware of the shadows that exist beneath all light.

I was once Kore, young and focused on light and life. I will admit some longing for darkness, some secret yen for depth, but caught in the business of life, I did not heed that call. At that time in my life, I was a young wife and mother. In myth, maiden or virgin can

365

mean physically virgin, but it can also mean a oneness of self. I was independent and though in relationship with others, those relationships did not touch the very core of my being. I was not thoroughly Kore. "Kore" means maiden, and she is the most undefined of all the virgin goddesses. I was a person, a strong full woman with many facets.

As Kore, it was easy to step over any stones of suffering. My husband Charlie and I became adept at sidestepping suffering. If we were sick, we were young and would recover. If we were poor, and we were, we would work hard. Whatever suffering there was, we put it behind us, ignored it and went on. Life was good.

How I knew myself is best illustrated by a meditation I had at that time. In this meditation, I was walking along a canyon with steep, black rock sides. At the very bottom was just the glimmer of a little stream. Now, in my life, I am very afraid of heights, but in this meditation, I fearlessly jumped off the cliff. It was wonderful. I was free with the air rushing through my hair and across my body. As I got closer and closer to the bottom, I realized that the water at the bottom was not a little stream, but a large river that had just been far away.

I dived into the water, not with a hit or a splash, just a changing of medium. I love to swim, and I started to swim toward the bottom. I didn't have to breathe, and the water flowed around me. The water was green, shot through with yellow light. As I swam, the light got stronger and stronger. Soon I could see the bottom of the river—bedrock—that had been cut away, like diving into a quarry. The rock was glowing yellow, the source of all the light. I put out my hand and touched it, and when I did, I knew that I had touched the very bedrock of my soul, and that it was joy.

Dancing with God

I painted this painting as an exploration of self and an expression of my spirit. It is a response to that meditation. I posed for this painting and it was a way of learning how to love myself. I have always had a sturdy peasant body, one that caused me some distress at not fitting the modern ideas of beauty. When I stood in front of the mirror and sketched, I began to notice the lovely curve of my chin, the graceful bones of my ankle, and on and on. Drawing is a way of paying attention. I began to feel that I was beautiful and feminine in my own unique way. I felt my spirit connections to the unnamable spirit as I painted the light around me and through me.

Questions

What am I?
Surely more than this sturdy flesh;
Work worn hands,
Large feet, muscled limbs,
My peasant heritage.

What else?
Surely more than these swirling thoughts;
Sadness, loss, joy,
Mosaic of ideas
With no discernable pattern.

What is that light?
It shines through my sturdy practical life
To make it more;
Sacred, beautiful,
Holy with borrowed light.

Goddesses are not without their shadows, and I had all the shadows of a virgin Goddess. I knew that I was right, and I was so independent that I had the tendency to be removed from others. I could be judgmental and self-righteous. During that time, I went to nursing school. I was so sure that I would learn the right way to be a nurse, and that I would be able to do nursing without changing who I was or how I interacted with people. I would not be in relationship with patients, but would be in charge, in control, a separate entity.

H. Lea Gaydos (holistic nurse of the year 1999) was one of my instructors. She was fond of saying very bizarre things in class like: "Caring is the essence of nursing." I had listened to this for most of the semester, and had enough. I wanted to learn real nursing, not some fuzzy concept of caring. I raised my hand and said, "Could we get to the point? If my patient's blood pressure is dropping, they want to know if I know how to titrate Dopamine, not if I care." She told me that I did need to know how to titrate drugs, but that I also needed to care. I was sure that nursing was only a science, not an art, and I did not believe her. I continued to work only from the science of nursing in my subsequent career as an ICU nurse. I was in charge; I knew what needed to be done, and I felt no need to enter into a relationship with my patients for their health or for mine. I thought I would be able to live this way forever, but for me, and for Kore, the time of the virgin goddess could not last forever.

One day Kore was in a field of flowers dancing with the other young virgins. She had been in that field many times, but today she saw a flower that she had never seen before, the beautiful Narcissus. She went closer to the flower and bent down to smell the sweet white blossoms. The scent overwhelmed her and she had to pluck it and hold it to her breast. As she did, the ground beneath her opened. Out rode Hades, Ruler of the dead, on a great black horse. Before her mind could even grasp his terrible presence, he had her. He rode with her to the very kingdom of hell, totally unhampered by her struggle, unmoved by her screams. Kore was his prisoner, his victim, raped and pulled from the life she loved. Demeter heard Kore cry out and ran to her, only to find the ground closed, no sign of her beautiful daughter but for wilted flowers on the ground. No witness remained with the courage to tell her what had happened.

The abduction of Kore can be any experience of suffering. Patients are abducted to hell when they get the heart-stopping diagnosis—cancer, stroke, multiple sclerosis— or when a trauma suddenly interrupts their lives. For me, it was an experience with my son. A few weeks after Joe's eleventh birthday on September 7, 1996, he was diagnosed with a brain stem glioma. He died on February 21, 1998.

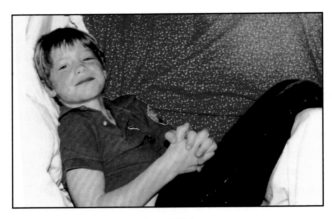

Joe, 1996

Joe's diagnosis filled me with terror. I did not want to go to the depths of hell. I had seen others go down, and not everybody came back. I thought of the psych hospitals and the hospital beds filled with patients beaten down by life. I knew I was going to dangerous territory, and the prospect filled me with dread. For the first time in my life, I felt a gut-wrenching connection to Demeter, and a longing to hold my son to me.

> I want to tuck him into my darkness
> Open muscle separate rib
> Fold him, knees to chin
> Into a space beside my heart
> Safe once again in my
> Personal red ocean
> Comfort him with the wave-beat
> Of my pulse.

I was Kore, ripped from my familiar safe life and taken through the door to hell. I painted that door years after Joe's death. The event was too sudden, too painful to paint a piece at that time with as much depth and reflection as *Persephone's Door.*

Persephone's Door

The door to hell deserves examination. This painting taught me as I created it. I found that I had an idea of what would be in the painting, but as I completed parts of the painting, they spoke to me and informed me in ways I had not expected. I will explain this process with a few insights from this painting.

I knew I needed to define the doorway. I had some nice Japanese paper, and I thought, "I will cut this paper into triangles to symbolize change, and that will be the doorway." I put the paper on the canvas, and suddenly I could see how sharp the doorway to hell is. It cuts to go through. To stand in the doorway, as in denial, hurts with a hurt that will only be relieved by going through into the dark. When I created the doorway, I was flooded with the memory of being in denial.

371

The day Joe was diagnosed, I had a curious split of person. My nurse self was very upset. I understood almost instantly what a long painful illness a brainstem glioma would be. I knew it was an almost certain death sentence. My mother self could not let that truth in. It was not that I did not believe that the MRI showed a tumor, or that I didn't believe that my son had cancer. It was just too much information to let in, so I remember saying to myself, "They do so much with kids' cancer now—It will be fine." I repeated my mantra even as I stood in the nurses' station discussing his films with the doctor. It took about four hours for me to allow those selves to come together, until all of me could accept the catastrophic news that my son had a terminal illness. I used that time to gather my strength, to retouch the depths of my joy, and to prepare. For a long time, I was ashamed that I—I who knew better, who was a professional—had struggled with denial.

Creating *Persephone's Door* let me see how painful it was to enter the door. The symbol helps me understand denial in a visceral way. I struggle here to explain in words the depth of understanding I had with the creation of this painting. It allowed me to forgive, not only myself, but also my patients who need time in denial. Now when I care for a patient in denial, I think of this painting, and how painful a place that is, to not be able to go back on the path, back to life as you knew, but to also be unable to move forward into and through the dark. Living denial helped me understand. Painting the denial brought a depth of understanding that fosters compassion.

The path to the door is clear. It is rough and hard to walk on, but clear. I painted the path by dipping rocks into paint and applying the paint on the canvas with rock. I wanted the paint to stand up. I wanted the path to hurt the feet that walk on it. Painting it that way made it clear of overgrowth. I realized that everyone goes this way at some time in life. It is an unavoidable path. I walked that path, but I am not alone. My suffering was easy to see. It is difficult to ignore a bald child in a wheelchair. The path reminds me that all people suffer. Their suffering may be less obvious than mine, but the path to hell is clear from all the feet that have walked it.

Kore has abandoned the stalks of wheat that symbolize her mother and her above ground life. In this painting, the wheat is actual stalks sewn on to the canvas. They are obvious poignant reminders of the life left behind. My patients abandon the life they once knew when they are taken down the rough path to hell. I abandoned things that I thought would be so easy to attain. When I had Joe, I never questioned if I would see him graduate from high school or have girlfriends. Dreams of daughters-in-law and grandchildren were lost. I also lost the joy of seeing what kind of man he would become, dreams abandoned on the side of the path to hell. Leaving the stalks of my prior life and its expectations was the most difficult part of the whole experience of Joe's illness and death. His diagnosis demanded a change of paradigm. With his diagnosis, I was no longer separate from my patients. When I abandoned my beloved virgin life, I joined the society of the suffering. I walked into the valley of death.

When the ground closed over her and the dust settled, Kore found herself in the dark with the fearsome Hades. She was terribly frightened, but she did not close her eyes. Kore looked around the kingdom of the dead, peered into the dark shadows, and knew where she was. She missed Demeter and the light of the upper world with a fearsome longing, and could not help but weep. Hades offered her great feasts and the treasures of his kingdom. Kore refused. She did not belong in the dark and would not make her home in the kingdom of the dead. She waited to be rescued, knowing her mother would come to her aid.

Above ground, Demeter was frantic in her search for Kore. She searched the world for her, and appealed to the other gods for help. Kore's father Zeus had given Hades permission to take Kore as his bride. He thought the ruler of the underworld was a fine match, and ignored Demeter's plea for information and help. Finally, Hecate, the crone, the wise woman, old enough to fear neither death nor gods, came to Demeter's aid. It was not in her power to bring Kore back, but she told Demeter where Kore had gone. Deep crone knowledge was able to speak the unspeakable, and bring the dark to light.

Demeter wailed, and through many adventures and mishaps, finally disguised herself and found work as a nursemaid for a royal family.

The day Joe was diagnosed was a terribly busy day, still a blur in my mind. I had had him at the doctor's office all summer for changes in behavior, temper tantrums, and something vague going wrong. I had been dismissed as a troublesome mother. Then at the end of August, he started to have a facial droop and complain of double vision. His doctor still would not take his symptoms seriously, so I found another doctor. The first time he was seen by a new doctor, an MRI was ordered. That was Friday night and the MRI was done first thing Saturday morning. It showed a five-centimeter tumor in his brain stem. The family practice doctor admitted him to the hospital. All day we talked to doctors and called specialists. Then came the night.

At night, hospitals are quiet, and the fears held at bay by the business of the day loom even larger, magnified as all shadows are at night. Joe was no longer the brave eleven-year-old of the day, but now simply a scared child. I ignored any rules I had once learned about hospital beds and climbed in with him, held him in my arms as he cried. I will never forget his tears, my tears, and Charlie's tears. Charlie, my poor Charlie, sitting on the other side of the bed holding Joe's hand and crying like he hadn't done since he had been a small child himself. Charlie is not prone to tears, yet in the dark, we were broken and aware of our entrance to hell. Like Kore, I opened my eyes and knew where I was. Joe was very ill and not likely to get better. I cried in paint. My tears turned into the paint that flowed onto the canvas.

Blue Prayer

Soon after Joe was diagnosed, I painted this painting, *Blue Prayer*. Unlike *Persephone's Door*, this painting is not a reflection on my journey into hell. This painting is a cry, a prayer in the moment. I went down to my studio and painted it in one sitting. I poured my feeling out onto the canvas. I cried, "Please let my son get better, please let my son get better." *Blue Prayer* expresses feelings for which I still do not have the words. Art became a container for feeling and enabled me to continue living my daily life. I could not withstand the intensity of emotion without art. Dissanayake (1992) postulates that all human societies make art because it has survival value. I did not paint this painting because I hoped it would be good enough to hang on a museum wall. I painted this painting because it helped me survive the intense grief I was experiencing.

375

Prayer
Blue paint, green, purple,
Curve together,
Bend, then reach for heaven.
My prayer, sadness, hope,
Too heavy for words,
In paint on canvas.

We were in the dark, and it hurt. Joe quickly gained weight from his high-dose steroids. During his illness, he gained a hundred pounds, going from eighty-five to one hundred and eighty-five pounds. He lost his hair from his chemo; his face was crooked from the tumor; he became wheelchair-bound from the weight gain, the loss of balance, and the steroid-induced microfractures in his bones. We could not go around this suffering. We could only recognize that he had cancer and deal with it as best we could.

We still could hold hope. Kore sat in the dark, fed by the hope that her mother would come for her. We did not hold much hope that Joe would recover, but we had boundless hope that he could live the rest of his life fully alive. Joe's primary way of dealing with the dark was humor. By the beginning of October, 1996, his hair had started to fall out in big clumps. It drove him crazy falling into his food, filling his bed, so he asked me to shave it off. I did, and he cried. I said to him, "Well, if you are going to be bald, you should be something cool for Halloween." He pondered it for a few days and then came to me with his idea. "If I'm going to be bald, I should be Daddy."

Chemo

Two bald heads
Bent over pumpkins;
Matching shirts, discs in pockets,
Pens protruding, ID badges swing.

My man and my son,
Clones of each other
Well mom, if I'm going to be bald
I'm going to be dad for Halloween.

376

We started to live every day as sacred. Joe went to school and Scouts. He did crafts and made new friends. He had always been my troublesome kid. If there was mischief to get into, he would find it. When he was diagnosed, it was as if he woke up and said, "Oh, I have one life—I need to do my best at it." He still got into trouble on occasion, but his whole attitude on life was different. As was mine.

It was important for me to go into the dark with Kore, a journey of my unconscious self. It was also important for me to struggle above ground with Demeter, a journey of my conscious self. My Demeter self was very busy doing. Joe's care was demanding, especially as he became more and more ill. I was very busy with doctor appointments, chemo sessions that lasted all day, radiation five days a week for six weeks. Then there was the daily physical care. Many nights, I did laundry at 3:00am when he had been incontinent or had vomited, and as he became more and more ill, he needed higher levels of care. I was the one to do it.

I also needed to remain available to my daughter Katie, then age ten. It is so difficult to be the well child. As the focus of everyone around us turned to Joe, Katie often felt left out. We made huge efforts to attend every school event, to take her to the music lessons that she loved, and to spend time with her. I know that she still felt abandoned as Joe became increasingly ill, but I hope she knew that she was still loved.

It was important to be both Kore and Demeter. I needed unconscious and conscious effort to deal with the challenge of suffering. Neither is more important than the other but need to exist in a balance. I needed both to wait in the dark with my eyes open and to do the tasks of daily life. The challenges of the unconscious and conscious suffering stripped me to the bare bones of my being. Anything unnecessary was abandoned, and I wondered who I was becoming.

Waiting for Spring

They stand naked now,
Throughout the city, stripped
For the cold, every
Beautiful detail etched in
Snow.

I watch their skeletons
Scrape against the full
Winter sky. Patient, quiet
They stand, simply waiting for
Spring.

If you should strip me
To my skeleton, would people
Wonder at the beauty of
My bare bones against the darkening
Sky?

Kore waited in the dark, stripped to the bone by the experience of being in hell. She waited for a very long time. Months passed as she cried in the dark, fed only by her hope. Finally, finally, she was hungry, tired of waiting. Kore accepted a few pomegranate seeds. With the eating of those seeds, she took some of the dark into herself, not all the dark, but part of it. By accepting part of her own shadow, she was no longer the maiden victim. With the acceptance of shadow, she became Persephone Queen of the Dead, full ruler with Hades.

She now saw Hades in a new light. He was still fearsome, and would always be, but she also saw him as necessary. All people die, and all people spend some time walking in the shadow. To not do so is to lack depth and insight. Hades, fearsome as he was, was the keeper of great treasure, available only to those who had traveled in his realm. Persephone could balance Hades' dark with compassion. As Queen, the former victim could give guidance and care.

Out of the Cocoon

As the months passed, it became apparent that Joe would die. My beloved son would leave his body and become something else, transformed. When I knew that in my very heart, I painted *Out of the Cocoon*. It is a painting of acceptance and of stepping into the mystery. I did not go to bed praying with Blue Prayer, "Please let my son get better, please let my son get better", to wake up in the morning with an acceptance of his death and a surrender to the mystery. I made that change in fits and jerks and with great difficulty. The following story illustrates the turn, the shift of perception.

In May of 1997, Joe was very ill. He was now totally wheelchair-bound, a loss which he would mourn the rest of his life. He had decubitus ulcers in his inguinal folds from the weight gain and the sitting. He had micro fractures from the steroids. Then he started to vomit. He threw up all the time. We couldn't figure out why. He was long done with chemo, radiation was over, but still he vomited. We tried every drug we could think of to relieve this horrible nausea. No luck.

379

Perhaps it was just the way his tumor was growing. I don't know. For Joe, this was terrible. All of the other things, he had worked around and adjusted to. This, however, interrupted his whole life. He could no longer go to school or Boy Scouts or out with his friends, couldn't even do crafts at home. All he could do was be sick.

By the weekend, he had worsened. He couldn't hold down his meds, including his long-acting morphine, so his pain wasn't being addressed. He couldn't hold down his steroids so he had a horrible headache. We decided to give him some IV fluid, and also give his meds intravenously. He had a central line, so this was no problem. The medical supply people came out with a pump and tubing. The pharmacy sent fluid, steroids, and a morphine drip. The home health nurse called and asked me if I needed her to come out and start the IV. I told her that I didn't. It was Sunday night, and I had hung plenty of drips, was familiar with the pump. I could do it.

That is how I found myself standing in his room with 50 milligrams of morphine in my hand. I looked at him lying in his bed, so ill, and I thought, "If I ran this bag wide open, shut the door, and didn't come back until morning, he would be done suffering, and we wouldn't have to watch him suffer." I stood there for a very long time thinking that. This was my baby, and it hurt incredibly to watch him so. I was afraid that it would get even worse for him. What would I do then? How could I handle that? I was so afraid that he would suffer more, so afraid that I couldn't do it any longer. I wanted to be done, for me and for him. Then I thought, "I have never, ever done this to a patient. I don't know what is best. I don't know when he should die." I hung the morphine at two milligrams an hour which relieved his pain, kissed him goodnight, and left the room.

Was that decision a gift of grace or a decision made from a habit of choosing life? I don't know. I do know that it was my pomegranate seeds. I faced and accepted part of my shadow in those long minutes in his room. I had always needed to be in control, in my own life, and in my work with my patients, and here was something I had no control over. I also had a fear of the future. What would happen, what could happen? Both those flaws, both those aspects of my shadow robbed me of the now. I could not be present in my life without confronting my fear of the future and the way it manifested in my need for control.

If I had given him all the morphine at once, I would have sat down to a dark feast, not just accepted part of my shadow, but aligned myself with the shadow. I would never have come out of the dark. As it was, I took part of my shadow into myself and was able to let go of enough of my fear and enough control to start coming out of the dark. Now I realize that *Out of the Cocoon* is not just a symbol of Joe's release from who he was, but a symbol of my own transcending. I did not get over my fears and my problems. I was able to see them differently and become someone else. The butterfly was not a metaphor I consciously chose. It just rose from inside of me and asked to be painted. At the time, I thought it was only about Joe. Now I know that it was also about me. I needed to be in the dark cocoon. I needed to lose my form, lose who I was, surrender to what was happening in order to change and grow wings. I think that I should have changed my name—Just as Kore experienced, I am not who I was.

To Joe

I remember, little caterpillar,
When you came to me, hungry for the world.
I joyfully opened my life to you,
And stuffed your ravenous heart full.
I fed you
  Love,
  Laughter,
  Discipline,
  Tears,
  Jokes,
  Starshine.
I watched you grow.

Soon, oh too soon for me,
You pulled the silken strands
Of your chrysalis close
And wrapped yourself in

Love,
Friendship,
Suffering,
Humor,
Loss,
Courage.
I watched you change.

Your beautiful, strong body
Bloated and weak, unrecognizable,
But for the mischief in your eyes,
And the logic in your hands.
You grew
  Stronger,
  Lighter,
  Deeper,
  Closer.
I caressed you with strong hands.

Then you were something different;
A mystery glimpsed through the web,
Too lovely for the chains of earth.
As you left you showered me
With sweet gifts
  A flash of color,
  Light of knowing,
  Blinding love,
  Enduring joy.
I cried.

I cried with selfishness.
I yearned to hold you forever,
To not release you to the
Unfathomable lover.
I'll remember you with
  Joy,
  Music,
  Sadness,
  Laughter,
  Love,
'Til we meet in the singing JOY.

Joe stopped throwing up all the time. We never did figure out why he was vomiting, and I cannot say why he stopped. In the rest of the time he had, I was able to love him more deeply and fully than I had before. I started living more connected to the people I love, even knowing that it would increase my pain. I did not want to miss any part of his life, willing to take joy and sorrow both. I continued to be his mother, giving him both love and structure. I remember a time when Joe was sitting at the table near Katie. She was trying to do her homework, and he was harassing her. He was telling her what she was doing wrong, what she should be doing, generally being the bossy older brother. I finally had to wheel him to another room and scold him. He may have been ill, but he did need me to be his mother.

Joe wanted to live to the fullest in the time that he had. In June of 1997, he went to a camp for kids with cancer. He still could not eat camp food and generally avoided the dining hall, existing on dry cereal. One day some of the counselors were sitting around and asked themselves, "If we were twelve and knew we were going to die, what would we want to do?" Being guys, they came up with wanting to drive. Definitely not a camp-sanctioned activity, but they decided to take the risk. Jamie had an old beat-up truck, but it was a standard transmission so Joe could not drive it. Austin had a new truck that was an automatic. He foolishly offered it for Joe's adventure. They put Joe behind the wheel during a mealtime and let him drive around cones in a field. He was doing much better than they expected so they decided they needed more excitement. They told him to try going up the hill, so Joe putt-putted up the hill. He had gone a little way when they guys said, "This isn't going to work. You'll have to back up, put it in fourth, and floor it." So Joe backed up, put it in four wheel drive and put the pedal to the metal. When they were almost to the top, one of the guys said, "Isn't there a big log up here?" After they came to a sudden stop with the big log unexpectedly lodged behind the front tire, Joe looked around... When they stopped, Joe looked around like, "Boy, am I in trouble!" and then he started to laugh and laugh. To him, it was OK to live with an illness as long as you got to live. His zest for living, even at the end of life, taught me that you can't control the circumstances of your life, but you can control your response. He chose to respond with joy.

Eventually even his joy in life and all the varied interventions we did were not enough. His body grew weaker and he prepared to die. He wrote scrapbooks to reflect on the importance of his life. In one, he wrote, "My body is worse but my spirit is better." Isn't that the point of being alive? We will all die eventually—Everybody's body ages and dies, but to go with your spirit better, that is living well.

He did not want to speak to anyone else about dying, but asked me what would happen. I felt woefully inadequate to the task of answering that question. I knew I could not placate him with stories. He was not going to buy the 'St. Peter and angels with wings' explanation. I had to tell him the truth. I told him that I don't know what happens when we die. Do any of us really? But I have faith. I had faith that he would be OK. I clearly remember sitting in his wheelchair beside his bed, holding his hand and telling him, "Faith is jumping off into the dark and knowing you will be caught." That satisfied him. It was not a lie and he trusted my faith. He died on the twenty-first of February, 1998, in his own bed, under the quilt his grandmother had made him, in his own time, in his own way.

Goodbye Joe

We said goodbye to Joe through art. We did not want a cold stone to remember him by, but needed color and warmth and some of the things that he had loved. We wanted to memorialize his life, celebrate the fact that he had lived. The photographs are by Katie Tartikoff of Children's Legacy. Charlie did the purist part around his picture, and our Katie, who was eleven at the time, did the frameworks. I did the swirls of color. We also put parts of Joe's life on the canvas: Legos, puzzle pieces, medals, music. This piece always makes me smile and remember what a joy it was to have him in our lives.

Goodbye Joe was also the first project we worked on as a family of three. It is very strange to go from a family of two children to a family with one child. All the ways that we interacted and the patterns of our family life changed. This painting was not just a way to remember Joe, though it is that. It was also a way for the three of us to start being a family in a new way. I have always loved the way that all of our styles and color choices revealed who we are, but also worked together to make one whole piece.

After many months without her daughter, Demeter reached the end of her endurance. She simply was not complete without her daughter. She needed to come into her goddess self and bring Persephone back. Without the help of other deities, she was forced to take drastic measures. She withdrew her gifts. Enough of talking, pleading and hoping for help. Nobody would eat until she got her daughter back. The crops turned to chaff in the field, fruit withered on the vine, and the people went hungry. The mother bared her teeth, angry now and unmoved by cries, her patience gone.

At first, the gods were not concerned, Demeter would relent soon and human misery did not move them. After a while, the gods did not get their offerings. Demeter was being more of a problem than they had anticipated. Now they got worried and sent messengers to her, "Be reasonable; he is a fine son-in-law." She would have none of it. Her gifts were hers to give or not, and without her daughter, she could not go on. Finally, they relented; Demeter's daughter could come home.

At first, Persephone had to close her eyes against the brightness of the sun. Even with her eyes closed, she could see the brightness of the day. The breeze—how long had it been since she had felt the play of a breeze on her cheek? As she walked, lilies of the valley and daisies bloomed in her path. The sweet smell of lavender rose from her skin. The land greened before her, first in little hesitant shoots, then in the full riot of spring. And then Demeter was there, green again in her full goddess power. Kore, uncaring that she was no longer the maiden, greeted Persephone in a warm embrace. She welcomed her back without reservation. Hecate the crone was also there to be Persephone's constant companion. Into this spring greenness, Persephone brought gifts and deep treasures from the underworld.

I am not a goddess. No amount of tempering or withdrawing of my gifts could bring my son back. I could only bring myself back. I had wandered in the dark, wrestled with my shadow for long enough. It was time to come back to myself. My unconscious self was brought back from the netherworld by my need to be whole. I had entered the dark strong enough to withstand it, not unchanged, but still intact, and now it was time to come back. I started by being selfish. I needed to take some time off, and then changed jobs to work at a hospital where the nurses cared for each other. My wants and needs were important. My conscious self needed my unconscious. I had to come back, and I came back bearing gifts.

> I walk with you
> Among the aspen
> Aquiver with green gold,
> Newly minted leaves.
> I hold your hand, and know
> That it is spring.

My gifts have changed my life. Some of the ways I have changed are external and recognizable by those who love me. Most of the ways I have changed are internal, changes in attitude and in ways of being rather than in ways of doing. I am reminded of the Buddhist saying that before one is enlightened, you chop wood and carry water. After enlightenment, you chop wood and carry water, but what a difference. I am not enlightened. I am transcending myself, but even doing the tasks I did before is different, different in the being.

My life lesson that keeps repeating is the lesson to let go. Let go; surrender to the unknown; trust what is happening. The control and perfectionism that I had before Joe died did not allow me to let go. I am still struggling to learn. Now when I clutch what I want and have a momentary fear that it will go, I remember Joe. I remember that I let go, I surrendered to what was happening, and in doing so, I was able to enter my life more fully. So I let go. After all, not much can be worse than what I have already been through. I find that I am more open to joy and gifts that life has to offer when I am not so attached to it, when I can step into the flow.

Pacific Ocean Lessons

I walk where
The land is not land
And the sea not sea.
One moment land
One moment sea.

A place of negotiation
Change, ease of
Letting go.
Continuously made new
Virgin land before and behind me.

The ocean rumbles deep,
Moaning, remembering depth
Even at the shore.
Cresting, breaking
Powerful even here.

But when the salt fingers
Reach my feet
They froth with news
Little whispery chatting

Murmurs to the sand.

Up to my knees
Buzzing, bubbling,
Caressing, pulling.
Sand slides, perception
Bends, and I am unsure.

I no longer know
Why I hold on.
I want to throw
My spirit into the deep
Be remade with every breath.

Slide with the sand
Glint with the shells,
Know my impermanence
But not care,
Fly headlong into life.

I had always been a terribly busy person. I rushed from *doing* one task to the next, afraid that I would not get it all done, too busy doing to be. Now I find a deep stillness in myself, a profound being-ness. Now when I am busy working, even when things are at their worst and I am in the midst of a storm of activity, there is a calm still point at my center. From this point, I can be present to my patients and my nursing students, to the art of nursing, even when I am busy with the external, to the science of nursing. I have not left the science behind, but have deepened it with the art. There is a difference in doing a task just to do a job and in doing a task because you really care. I am now able to also be more fully with my family. I am not rushing to finish a conversation with Katie or a meal with Charlie to get on to the next thing. I am, not always, but more often, truly present in what I am doing right now.

I still struggle with the wish to be perfect. That struggle doesn't have the intensity that it had when I needed to be in charge and in control. I am not in control. I am not the master of the circumstances of my life, only of my response, so I choose to respond to the best of my ability, but with an awareness that things may not turn out as I had planned. I used to expend precious energy beating myself up when a patient got worse or a family was upset. Now I put my best effort in what I do, try to weigh the possible outcomes, but know that I am not ultimately in charge. This new attitude has shown itself in a willingness to not take myself so seriously. When I am not in charge, I can afford to be silly, to play.

I also know that I am impermanent. I was fond of living as if my life would never end. There would always be time tomorrow to do what was important. I was busy with what was necessary. Now I know undeniably that I am mortal. Like the reeds that stand in sunlight, I am only here for a short time. They stand in the shadow and the sunlight, beautiful, necessary even though they are not permanent. I too can live that way. Beautiful in my light and shadow, the now important because it is all we have and it is fleeting.

Reeds in Sunlight

Before, I was able to see the soul light in myself, seeping up from the bedrock of my soul. Now, I can see that light shining forth in my life. The light in me is connected to the light in others. I do not exist as a separate entity, my light alone. I am part of the web of life, all of us shining in our own way, connected and interdependent. Now I could see my patients not as separate entities, but as part of the web. There is no way that I can be a nurse without relationship. What Lea Gaydos said to me about caring, way back when I was an undergraduate, now came back to me. My patients are dependent, as am I, on my ability to connect. Before Joe, I knew this with my head. Now I know it with my heart. I have joined with my patients by becoming part of the community of suffering. I do not tell them about my loss with my words, but they know it in my hands and in my presence. I am a nurse who cares, who knows I am not truly separate. I could try to separate, exclude, control, but that would mean severing part of myself.

> I have walked with the angel of death,
> Her hand warm and full on my shoulder,
> Her blue cloak protecting me from hospital sterility.
>
> In her face full memory of every
> Suffering, aged, tortured body I have ever
> Caressed and cajoled to live, breathe.
>
> Their lives a constant reminder of all
> The dark forgotten wastelands of my soul,
> An unforgiving mirror of my own mortality.
>
> This darkly beautiful Goddess has taken
> My eyelids, I cannot look away.
> I have paid her tithe with weary heart and salty tears.
>
> Still she leads me, gently, gently, in love.
> Her shadows deepening the cartoon drawing of my life.
> Her presence in every life a reminder.
>
> A touch of a brow becomes benediction,
> Small sweets; a laugh, a look, end of day
> Homecomings, now great feasts.
>
> I have walked with the angel of death
> Until my feet kiss the ground with every step,
> And all life sparkles in diamond leafiness.

I still have patients I do not like. I work with people who are unpleasant or drunk or simply stressed beyond their endurance. They, more than anyone, need my love. Yes, *love*. Not the emotion love, but love with sweat on, as in Heyward's description: "Love, like truth and beauty, is concrete. Love is not fundamentally a sweet feeling, not, at heart, a matter of sentiment, attachment, or being 'drawn toward'. Love is active, effective, a matter of making reciprocal and mutually beneficial relation with one's friends and enemies. Love creates righteousness, or justice here on earth" (Heyward, 1991). I do not work from this attitude because I think it is the right thing to do. I work from this attitude because I cannot work any other way.

Family Portrait

Family Portrait is a painting that expands on *Dancing with God*. Here I see not only my spirit gold and glowing, but all spirits gold, glowing and connected. I named it *Family Portrait*, but as the

391

net expands and expands, I realize that the family is everyone. In a very real way, I am connected not just to Charlie, Joe and Katie, but to even my most difficult patient. I have worked intensive care, hospice, palliative care, and as an educator. Holding this painting in my mind allows me to be more capable of approaching others with a deep respect.

I don't need to control or understand every mystery. I find that I have a tolerance for the shadow that I never had before. I am still not perfect. I have been to the dark and struggled with my shadow, but I have not completed my tasks. I go back, as does Persephone.

Every year in her season, Persephone begins to draw into herself. She turns quiet and inward and finds herself longing for the respite of the dark. She kisses Demeter, leaves her with the promise to come back, and returns to Hades. Some say that she goes back because she has eaten in hell and can never be free. Others know that once the sweetness of the depth is tasted, there is no wish to be totally free. She goes back to hell with a love for Hades. Her fearsome husband still fierce and wild but loved, for even the shadows need love. It is also now her duty, her reason for being to be the Queen of the Dead. She cannot abandon others on their path through the shadows. She knows the way and will always be there to guide.

Demeter is sad, drawing back her gifts. Not abandoning her divinity or inflicting famine, simply resting. Even that rest is beautiful. Fall comes upon the land, and all are invited to rest and deepen and trust that in its own time, spring will come again.

Aspen

I too go back to the shadows, not as deeply as before, but in need. I have other parts of my shadow to meet and struggle with and take into myself. I often find my feet reluctant to go, forgetting the beauty of the turning of the season. But go I do, with less fear, knowing that I will survive and be changed. I also find myself spiraling back to my grief in the winter, rediscovering its lessons, knowing it again. I will not ever get 'over' my loss. I am transcending it and knowing it in a different way. I am grateful for the lessons, but that does not mean the suffering has gone.

Winter

His ashes lie
Under the Ouray snow.
My heart goes there.

Through my willingness to deeply experience my joys and my sorrows, I am stepping into life. I am coming out of the emptiness of certainty, control and separateness. I am climbing the stairs out of hell and taking the treasures of the dark with me. I am living a richer and fuller life than I could have ever imagined. I step into the light and shadows of my life loving them both.

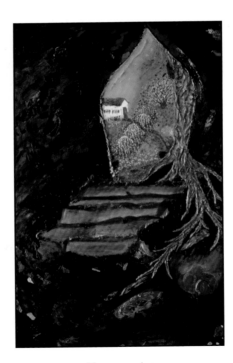

Homecoming

Painting *Homecoming* was at first a recognition and honoring of where I had been. I started the background of this painting with my pallet knife. I was just starting to put texture on the canvas, but I found myself attacking the work with the pallet knife. I sliced at the canvas, threw the paint on in chunks, and scratched at it in a frenzy. This is a very large piece and it took my whole body stretching and dancing in an anger of where I had been forced to go. I may be happy about the gifts of the dark, but it will never be easy or fair. So I sliced until I was exhausted and near tears.

Then I started to paint. I made the dark very dark, hard and fearsome. I started to find little places to hide treasure; a piece of stained glass here, copper paint there, silver gilt over there. Pomegranates, the way to internalize part of the shadow and take it with you, are also there. These were ideas that, just like in the painting *Persephone's Door*, flowed from me to the painting, then from the painting with illumination that can only come from the nonverbal back to me.

I made the stairs glow. I also gave them the foundation of prayer. I wrote prayers under every one of them: "Thy will be done," "Let go," "I surrender." These prayers are now hidden by paint, unconscious to the painting as my lessons often are in my life. The tree that grows into the above ground is the support for the stairs out of hell. I was thinking of the above ground, the consciousness providing the way out of hell. When I was done creating the tree, I realized how it depended on deep roots in order to stand in the light. The balance, the necessity of both, came to me clearly in the symbol of the tree.

Finally, there is the green, the home. All my life, I have searched for my heart's home; where I belong, where I am welcomed. It is so green, the color that most eases my heart. The flowers are blooming because I am ready now to start blooming. When I painted the flowers, I was surprised at how much life and energy has come out of the darkness. I was also surprised by the house. I had a gypsy child-hood, and yet, in my heart, there is a little house with a path that draws me in.

I am not sure that I am completely familiar with the above-ground life. I have been in the dark for so long that the abundance of my life now makes me shade my eyes. This painting tells me that I am ready to come out of the darkness and live life above the ground for a while. It draws me out, not into a place outside of me, but into a place that developed inside me from my trials and journey through hell. I am still working on being able to step into the abundance of my life. My painting gives me a map, Persephone gives me direction.

REFERENCES

Dissanayake, E. *Homoaestheticus: Where art comes from and why.* New York: The Free Press. 1992.

Frankl, V. E. *Man's search for meaning: An introduction to logotherapy* (3rd Ed.). New York: Touchstone Books, 1984.

Heyward, C. "Our passion for justice" (excerpt). In M. Sewell (Ed.) *Cries of the spirit: A celebration of women's spirituality.* Boston: Beacon Press. 1991.

Johan Wouterloot, MD,, was born in Leiden, Netherlands in 1952 of a Dutch father and an Irish Canadian mother. When he was 6, the family moved to Vancouver, British Columbia and it was (close?) this city that he grew up. After high school, he entered university intending to study marine biology, but after (the) first year, medicine became his passion and has remained so.

(Johan) He graduated from the University of British Columbia first with a bachelors of science in physiology, where the major interest was brain physiology and then with his doctorate in medicine. After interning in New Zealand, he returned to family practice in the Vancouver area. After 18 years in practice he ventured into addiction medicine on the pleading of a patient and discovered a rewarding and fascinating area of practice. He (Johan) was subsequently certified by the American Society of Addiction Medicine and during the course of preparing for this, was able to appreciate the importance of brain physiology in addiction and also the importance of fundamental brain research to improve the success of treatment.

Johan and Marietta have been married for 31 years and have had 3 children. The raising of Elise, Kristianna and Karl and their various pets has been the main focus of Johan and Marietta's lives. The freshness and liveliness of the Impressionist and post impressionist periods and the interest in addiction medicine compelled Johan to develop this article on Absinthe.

"A glass of absinthe is as poetical as anything in the world."
"After the first glass, you see things as you wish they were. After the second, you see things as they are not. Finally, you see things as they really are, and that is the most horrible thing in the world."

Oscar Wilde

ABSINTHE, LA FEÉ VERTE (THE GREEN FAIRY)

JOHAN WOUTERLOOT, MD

The Green Fairy, as absinthe was known in France, is best known for the sway that it held over late nineteenth century French society. It is an example of two psychoactive substances being used together to give an additive, complex mood altering effect. I will use the term 'dual acting substance' when a particular drug produces both sedation and stimulation. This dual effect has been sought repeatedly, certainly in recent history and likely during ancient times as well. The effect can be produced both by alcoholic beverages and by other drugs. A widely known historical example of this effect was the use of absinthe during the Impressionist and Post-Impressionist periods in Europe and America. More recent but less extensive and less destructive examples are present today. Alcoholic combinations consist of hard liquor and the new energy drinks. Non-alcoholic combinations include the use of heroin and cocaine (speedballs).

In order to understand the mood altering effects of alcohol and other psychoactive substances, some background discussion of what is in absinthe and how it affects the brain will need to be developed.

Neural Pathways

The main pathway in the brain by which alcohol and all addictive substances exert their effects is housed in the medial fore-brain bundle, situated in the brain stem. This pathway originates in

399

the ventral tegmental area, which is in the front part of the pons. When the substance stimulates this part of the brain, a signal is sent that ends in the pleasure center of the brain producing a euphoric rush. Heroin and cocaine directly stimulate the first part of this pathway. But alcohol produces the effect indirectly by blocking the natural inhibition of this initial area of the path. Freed from its inhibition, the signal passes more readily to the pleasure center of the brain. After the pleasure center is stimulated, it then signals the cerebral cortex. This is where the pleasure is consciously perceived. The signal continues to the midbrain where emotions are put into action.

This is a simplified version of the pathways involved. Other drugs stimulate the pleasure center directly and there are a number of pathways that either enhance or dampen the signals at the beginning of the paths. All nerves interconnect and they do so by releasing small molecules, known as neurotransmitters, at the nerve terminals when the electrical impulses reach the terminals. The neurotransmitters transmit the signals by diffusing across the minute space between the nerve endings. The neurotransmitters then attach onto receptors situated on the next nerve terminal and this attachment activates the nerve terminals, which in turn continues the electrical signal transmission along the next nerve.

Nerve terminals can have more than one type of receptor and the varying degrees of activation of each receptor type can modulate the degree of firing of that nerve. There are neurotransmitters that are excitatory and those that are inhibitory. When excitatory transmitters attach onto their respective excitatory receptors, the usual negative resting potential of the nerve cell is brought closer to neutral, making that nerve cell more likely to fire. Conversely, an inhibitory receptor increases the negative charge inside the cell making it less likely to fire when stimulated by an adjacent nerve. Excitatory neurotransmitters include dopamine, norepinephrine and glutamine. Inhibitory neurotransmitters include GABA (gamma amino butyric acid) and glycine.

Medications and illicit drugs vary in their ability to stimulate various inhibitory and excitatory receptors. For example, heroin and methadone (used to treat heroin addiction) stimulate just one kind of opioid receptor, where other narcotics such as hydromorphone (Dilaudid) and oxycontin stimulate several opioid receptors. Cocaine and methamphetamine stimulate several excitatory receptors, including dopamine, norepinephrine and to a lesser extent serotonin receptors.

No substance, however, can compare with alcohol and its ability to affect a wide range of both excitatory and inhibitory receptors. Excitatory receptors activated by alcohol include dopamine, norepinephrine and serotonin, and inhibitory receptors include the GABA, opioid and glycine receptors. Alcohol, unlike other substances, produces its stimulatory effect indirectly by removing the inhibitory controls rather than by direct stimulation. Alcohol is a truly seductive mix of stimulation, resulting in excitement and euphoria, and inhibition, resulting in relaxation and sedation, which has captivated humanity throughout our existence.

Absinthe and Its Actions

It is important to mention at this stage that the action of alcohol at low levels of consumption is mainly stimulatory, resulting in euphoria. Unfortunately, as one chases the euphoria with further drinking, the result is sedation with depression of brain function. As the amount of alcohol consumed increases, there are increasing levels of inhibition of brain function. At blood levels of 400 mg % and higher, coma and death from acute toxicity can occur. Adding a stimulant to the alcohol may allow the drinker to experience the effects of higher levels of alcohol without falling asleep. Periodically this combination has been tried throughout time and the use of absinthe during the nineteenth century is the most famous example.

Before we get to its history, let's look at the makeup of absinthe and how it produced the effects on people that it did. The unique ingredient in absinthe comes from the shrub Artemisia absinthium and its cousin Artemisia ponticum. These 3-foot high shrubs are members of the daisy family and are found throughout

401

central Europe. All parts of the plant are toxic. It was commonly called wormwood after its ancient use as a treatment for intestinal round worms. The use of wormwood has been around a long time and has received mention in the Bible and the Egyptian Ebers papyrus. It was used historically to flavor wines, as a stimulant and tonic, an antiseptic, and as a remedy for fevers and menstrual cramps.

Building on wormwood's reputation as an ancient remedy, a physician in the town of Couvet, Switzerland, Dr Pierre Ordinaire, combined the herb with alcohol and other ingredients to develop absinthe in 1792. It was originally developed as a remedy for epilepsy, gout, kidney stones, colic, headache, and of course, worms. Using absinthe for epilepsy is especially ironic as absinthe itself produces seizures.

Absinthe, as Dr Ordinaire developed it, was manufactured by assembling a mixture of dried herbs including aniseed, fennel, hyssop, lemonbalm, angelica, star anise, juniper, nutmeg, veronica and Artemisia absinthium. These herbs were soaked in water, boiled and steam-distilled. The oily distillate was then collected and mixed with distilled alcohol made from grape wine. The alcohol was added to the mixture until a dilution of 74% alcohol by volume was reached resulting in a 110-144 proof drink. Following this, further distilled herbs, including Artemisia ponticum, were added. The typical green color of absinthe was due to chlorophyll, possibly from the oil of wormwood, anise, elecampane or marjoram. It certainly was enhanced by the addition of grass, parsley or nettles. In cheaper versions of the drink, the unscrupulous imitators achieved the green color by adding copper sulphate, turmeric, cupric acetate, or antimony trichloride. Also in the cheaper versions of absinthe, grain alcohol distillates were used, resulting in the addition of fusel oil products such as methanol and higher chain alcohols. Deceit in alcohol and drug manufacturing is a recurring norm throughout history. These old practices are similar to modern day clandestine drug manufacturing labs where the methamphetamine produced is laced with toxins or where other drugs sold on the street are regularly cut with talcum and other powders to increase their volume.

The chief unique ingredient found in absinthe is alpha-thujone. This causes excitation by reversibly blocking the GABAa receptor, which, as previously mentioned, is an inhibitory or calming receptor. Thujone gets its name from the eastern white cedar, Thuja occidentalis, the source from which it was originally derived. There are two mirror image forms (enantiomers), with the alpha form being two to three times more potent than the beta form, although the beta form is twice as abundant in the shrub Artemisia. In experimental animals, this compound is broken down in the liver to other less neuroactive compounds, but the metabolism in humans is unknown.

Thujone's excitatory action on the brain is achieved by reducing the inhibition produced by the GABAa receptor. It does so by blocking the GABAa receptor and specifically by stopping inflow of Chloride that this receptor regulates. The blockage is termed reversible, which means thujone can bind and unbind to and from the receptor over and over. Chloride is a negative ion and more chloride in the cell increases the negative charge in the cell, making it less likely to fire when stimulated. The GABAa receptors involved in this effect are located in the medulla (the brainstem) and in the cerebral cortex. There is also a site of action in the dorsal root ganglion where the sensory nerves enter the spinal cord in their ascent to the brain.

Thujone produces excitation and seizures, often preceded by delirium. It has been used experimentally since the 1920's in lab animals to study seizures. Before the use of electroconvulsive therapy in psychiatry, both thujone and a related compound, camphor, were used as chemical inducers of convulsions. High doses of GABA receptor stimulators, such as alcohol, benzodiazepines (such as diazepam), and barbiturates could prevent the seizures induced by thujone.

Thujone is a member of the terpene family of chemical compounds and I would like to briefly discuss how terpenes fit into a chemical classification. The Essential Oils are the mainstay of the flavor and fragrance industry. While there are three groups of compounds comprising the essential oils, by far the largest group is

403

the terpenes. Terpenes are derived from five carbon isoprene units and are named by the multiples of these units in their structure. For example, monoterpenes are ten carbons compounds, diterpenes twenty carbon compounds, triterpenes thirty carbon and tetraterpenes forty carbon compounds. Examples of diterterpenes are chlorophyll and vitamin A. Triterpenes are represented by absinthin (which gives absinthe its bitter taste) and tetraterpenes are represented by lycopene (thought to be a cancer preventative found in red vegetables) and beta carotene.

The monoterpenes are of special interest as they include many common aromatic compounds such as limonene and citronellal, giving citrus fruits their characteristic smell. Other notable monoterpenes include camphor, which can potentate seizure activity like thujone, and which, like thujone, was an addictive substance in the nineteenth century. Menthol is yet another monoterpene and has its primary effect on mucosal and skin receptors, blocking calcium outflow from the nerve cells and thus lowering the firing threshold for cold receptors, giving a feeling of freshness (even though no airway widening occurs). It also has an initial cerebral stimulating effect followed by depression of brain function. These, then, are the constituents of absinthe and how they affect brain function. I turn now to absinthe's effects on society at large.

Substance Use Epidemics

The arrival of a new drug of abuse in society is usually accompanied by a flurry of use by a great many people over a period of time. The intensity of use, the number of people using, and the period of time that a drug is popular varies from substance to substance. One certainty is that each wave of drug use is accompanied by great fear in society as a whole. The press and broadcast media are frequently full of apocalyptic headlines. These spikes of drug use can be seen as epidemics and indeed the term "substance use epidemic" is a valid term. It suggests that each new wave of drug use will likely be temporary. That said, it is not my intention to minimize the damage that can occur with each new drug, only that each epidemic will likely not go on forever at a feverish rate. A substance use epidemic continues until society establishes the mechanisms at all levels of organization, from individual to family to community to national and international, that will control the use of that particular substance.

A classic historical example of a substance use epidemic is found in the London Gin epidemic of 1751. This occurred when the technology for distilling grain alcohol was developed, resulting in the production of much higher levels of alcohol in beverages such as gin than in the beer and wine that people were previously accustomed to. The epidemic had a devastating effect on the population of London.

Approximately one hundred years later, morphine was first produced from opium. Opium was already used in Europe for some time, having been introduced by naval and merchant seamen returning from Hong Kong and Indochina. Following its development, there was an explosion of morphine use lasting fifty years. The Franco-Prussian War saw extensive use of morphine as an analgesic with subsequent addictions, but surprisingly only in a small proportion of those who were originally treated with morphine. Following the War in France, morphine use was taken up in fashionable circles, with custom syringes being made by jewelers. The problem was so great and widespread that medical research produced heroin as a "heroic treatment for morphinism." Other substances used in France during the latter nineteenth century included ether (with strawberries soaked in ether offered as a refined dessert), cocaine (termed a miracle drug against depression by Freud), and camphor, which was smoked. The artist Marcel Proust was addicted to camphor cigarettes.

In the same way, absinthe, with its extra psychoactive effects over plain alcohol, was a novel substance and its pattern of use from 1850 to 1914 was like an epidemic. The great popularity of absinthe was explained, in part, by its alluring clear green color that turned milky when water was added to it. That, however, would not have been enough to explain why large segments of the population were held in sway by absinthe. The double psychotropic effect of the

405

alcohol-induced euphoria and sedation coupled with thujone-induced excitation, including visual and auditory hallucinations, was likely the main reason that absinthe was so popular. And popular it was! From 1875 to 1913 there was a fifteen-fold rise in consumption to a total of 36 million liters, although in perspective, this only represented 3% of the total alcohol consumption of France. By 1906, Paris had 33,330 establishments selling absinthe, but only 17,000 bakers. London and Chicago, by contrast, only had about 5800 liquor establishments each.

Absinthe, the Drink

Absinthe had a bitter taste due to the chemical Absinthin, a triterpene, most of which is alcohol insoluble, but of which small residual amounts remain. Therefore, in order to drink absinthe, the beverage had to be first diluted with water and sweetened with sugar. Hence was developed the practice of placing a perforated spoon with a sugar cube on top of a parfait glass of 30 ml of absinthe and then pouring 150 ml of cold water over the sugar into the glass. The water dissolved the sugar into the absinthe and turned the clear green absinthe opaque or louched it. The louch occurred because water caused the essential oils, derived from the herbal mixture used in the manufacture of absinthe, to precipitate out of the alcohol solution, forming a colloidal opaque suspension. Some essential oils were released or aromatized during this process, thus liberating a floral bouquet.

Asinthism was the term used one hundred years ago to describe the intoxication induced by absinthe. At low doses, it caused a cheerful mood, a sense of wellbeing and a sharpened sense of perception. At higher doses, there were visual and auditory hallucinations. No wonder it was used by artists of the time, believing that it enhanced the brain's activity to develop new ideas and to expand the imagination. Continuing to chase the euphoria and excitement with continued consumption, however, resulted in increasing the toxic effects. These included rapid giddiness, restlessness, hallucinations, vomiting, vertigo, muscular disorders and seizures. There could also be unwanted dysphoria, paranoia, agitation and impulsive violence. Severe toxicity included coma, respiratory arrest and death. Absinthism was distinguished from alcohol toxicity by the sudden onset of delirium, characterized by restless activity and impulsiveness, seizure, vertigo, hallucinations, thickness and embarrassment of speech, and unequal pupils. This delirium would last longer than that produced by alcohol alone.

There was early onset of dependence, or addiction, with continued absinthe use. The chronic use associated with dependence led to gastritis, or chronic inflammation of the stomach, and impaired brain function, including memory loss, restlessness, enormous visions (likely illusions), terrible nightmares, forgetfulness and yet painful reminiscences. Chronic use also could result in tremors, seizure disorders, pica behaviors (compulsive cravings to ingest substances containing terpenes and essential oils) and full-blown psychoses. Altered visual perceptions, with whites appearing violet and later yellow, have been linked to absinthe use, but this linkage has been disputed. Finally, withdrawal from absinthe was more severe than other alcoholic drinks and was associated with increased delirium.

Absinthe and Its Times

Subsequent to the development of absinthe by Dr Pierre Ordinaire, the recipe was eventually passed on to Pernod who established a factory in Pontparlier in the Doubs region of France near the Swiss border. For the first half-century, the drink remained relatively obscure, but the breakthrough in popularity came with the Algerian War of 1844-1847 when the French legionnaires used absinthe as a fever preventative, and after the war, introduced absinthe throughout France.

Initially, absinthe was relatively expensive and used primarily by the middle classes. As previously mentioned, grain-derived alcoholic beverages contain potentially dangerous higher chain alcohols. Moreover, various potentially harmful ways were developed to achieve the characteristic green color. But efficiencies of scale with increased production volume along with the emergence of cheap copies using grain and beet-derived alcohol, allowed the poor to indulge in absinthe as well, but also with increased risk from the cheap copies.

Lower price was not the only factor contributing to absinthe's rapid rise in popularity in the latter nineteenth century. The wine industry in France was devastated by two plagues: oidium, a fungus, and phyloxera, a beetle. The result of these plagues was the destruction of most of the vineyards in France and the subsequent need to replant them. The temporary scarcity of grapes drove the price of wine up. Examples of prices in 1873 are in centimes (1 franc = 100 centimes) and are as follows: a glass of absinthe = 15 centimes; a loaf of bread = 50 centimes; and a glass of Bordeaux (wine) = 1 franc. While the spike in wine prices was temporary, it caused many people, who otherwise would not have, to turn to absinthe and increase the percentage of absinthe drinkers in the general drinking population.

Paris, La Belle Époque

Following the Napoleonic era, France, like England and America, underwent a period of rapid industrialization. This transformed medieval Paris into its modern configuration and resulted in the migration of thousands of workers into the city. The predominant culture of this time was one of confidence in life's constant improvement through the application of science and technology. Original art was shunned by the new bourgeoisie in favor of an expression of an idealized society and portrayals of nymphs, mythical deity and morality themes. The reaction to this blandness, developed in the underworld culture, centered in the Montmartre district of Paris. Stark reality was embraced by this culture and life's darker side was explored in detail. A common theme among the artists was one of martyrdom in nihilistic self destruction. The focal point was to spend long hours in the cafes of the district philosophizing and developing themes, and the social lubricant was found in absinthe.

Absinthe's great popularity was attested to by its inclusion in the language and expressions of the day. For example, "l'heur verte" (green hour) was the Parisian equivalent of happy hour when the cafes and bistros were crowded with people enjoying absinthe. It became an icon of "la vie de bohème" and had many notables of the era under the spell of its charm. For instance, the French poet Baudelaire used wine and hashish, and later turned to laudanum (a morphine preparation) and absinthe. His later life was a downward spiral, and he eventual died of syphilis. Other artists included the Impressionists Eduard Manet, Edgar Degas, the Post-Impressionists Henri Toulouse-Lautrec, Vincent van Gogh and Paul Gauguin, and playwright Oscar Wilde. Later absinthe drinkers included Picasso, Jack London and Ernest Hemingway.

So, what effects did absinthe have on Impressionist and Post-Impressionist artists and why would such a drink be embraced by a broad range of artists? Was it to be outrageous (like Toulouse-Lautrec) or as part of a hedonistic self-destructive vein among some artists (suffering for one's art, like Baudelaire)? Or was it possible to gain insight and to stimulate creativity? Absinthe was also used as an aphrodisiac and probably most importantly, to gain a cheerful mood. Of course, it also had direct effects on the mental and physical health of these artists and the effects could be broken down into the toxic effects of the alcohol and the toxic effects of the thujone. Some of the best examples of this are van Gogh and Toulouse-Lautrec.

As a subject of art, absinthe also had an effect. It was used as shock value, as seen in paintings by Manet, Degas and Jean Francois Raffaëlli. It was also simply included as part of the milieu in paintings by van Gogh and Toulouse-Lautrec.

The Absinthe Drinker
Eduard Manet, 1859

The painting illustrated above is "The Absinthe Drinker" and was painted in 1859 by Eduard Manet It shows an anonymous street person, the lowest order of society, simply as he was with his glass of absinthe beside him. There was none of the heroic air of Bacchanalian pleasure as depicted by Reubens or the moralizing seen in Pieter Breugel's works regarding alcohol centuries before this. As such, the painting was seen to encourage decadence. A similar theme of decadence associated with absinthe for shock value is seen in the 1876 painting titled "L'Absinthe" by Edgar Degas shown below.

L' Absinthe
Edgar Degas, 1876

This painting depicts "l'heur verte" in any Montmartre café and has a look of careless wanton about it. When the painting was exhibited in London in 1893, it caused a scandal and the woman was called a slut. The irony is that the subject, actress Ellen Andree, hardly drank absinthe and lived a long and healthy life. She reportedly regretted sitting for the painting following the reviews.

Vincent van Gogh

A great deal is known of the Impressionist painter Vincent van Gogh. This is mainly due to the voluminous letters that he wrote to his brother Theo who was meticulous about saving them. The same cannot be said about Theo's letters to Vincent as he saved few of them.

411

As a subject for his paintings, absinthe was simply part of the landscape rather than deliberate shock value. Absinthe is important because of the effects it may have had on his health. Van Gogh was born in 1853 in Zundert, a village in the south of the Netherlands. His family of origin was rigid, hard working and God-fearing. Vincent managed to disappoint them repeatedly by failing to attain any vocational goals with his impetuous decisions and argumentative behavior. Prior to becoming a painter, he worked as a lay preacher in the mining district of Borinage, south of Brussels, and lived in deliberate great poverty. His contract was not renewed in 1879, and following a period of indecision and instability, Vincent turned his efforts to painting. Following a brief and incomplete period of formal art education in Antwerp in November 1885, Vincent joined his brother Theo in Paris in March 1885. There he became acquainted with the Impressionist painters of the time, including Gauguin and Henri de Toulouse-Lautrec. He began drinking heavily, both regular alcohol and absinthe, although he was never known to be intoxicated and did not drink more than his contemporaries. He began to experience episodes of sudden terror and lapses of consciousness with initial tonic hand spasms and stares followed by a confused-amnesic state. These episodes were often accompanied by epigastric symptoms. He felt he would have a stroke had he stayed in Paris, so in February of 1888, he moved to Arles in the south of France. His irascible manner and unpredictable behavior had made him unpopular in Paris. Interestingly, the Arles region had one of the highest consumption rates of absinthe in all of France, roughly four times that of Paris.

When he arrived in Arles, Vincent initially limited his consumption of tobacco and alcohol and this afforded him some clarity of thought and improved his health. Unfortunately, this moderation was only short-lived and he resumed drinking heavily, alternating cognac with absinthe. As he explained in a letter to Theo, "If the storm within me gets too loud, I take a glass too much to stun myself." In his letters, Vincent described his symptoms in detail: fits of anxiety, listlessness, emptiness, fatigue, along with attacks of melancholy and of atrocious remorse, and yet at other times, enthusiasm, madness or prophesy, with readiness of speech.

The misguided self-treatment of one's symptoms is common among substance users and can be a common reason for starting drug use in the first place. Vincent used alcohol in small part to calm himself. Today, it is still common to self medicate using alcohol as well as benzodiazepines for prolonged periods to control anxiety and to blunt the manic phase of bipolar disorder. Initial inadequate pain control of an injury is another very common reason why heroin users become addicted. Few of them realize the danger they face in the rapid onset of physical dependency from their home-based pain treatment. It is a principle in mental health and addiction treatment that if there is a concurrent psychiatric or addictive disorder, that treatment of both disorders is mandatory. In Vincent's case, sustained abstinence would not have been possible unless his psychiatric disorder was addressed and treated. Unfortunately, this only occurred for a brief period.

In addition to using alcohol, van Gogh was suspected of using other psychoactive substances. He was once stopped from drinking turpentine, which contains and pinenes and camphene. These substances are known to create a pleasant warmth to the stomach as well as exhilaration and distortions of perception. He also stuffed his pillow and mattress with camphor as a treatment for his insomnia. He also smoked cigarettes, which lower the seizure threshold for thujone induced seizures.

Vincent's brother Theo persuaded Paul Gauguin to join Vincent in Arles in the fall of 1888. Theo was worried about his brother's moods and increasingly erratic behavior and felt that Gauguin could help keep him safe. Ostensibly, they were going to establish an artists' studio of the south. The union only lasted two months, became increasingly quarrelsome and dissolved on Christmas Eve when Gauguin announced that he was leaving and Vincent threw a glass of absinthe in his face. Paul then brought Vincent home and put him to bed. When Paul left the house, Vincent arose, followed him and attacked him with a straight razor. Paul managed to fight Vincent off. Vincent then returned home and cut off part of his left earlobe and presented it to his favorite prostitute.

This famous incident resulted in Vincent being committed to the local hospital. He was diagnosed with epilepsy and lapsed into a psychotic state with no memory of the previous events. His physician, Felix Rey, treated him with Potassium bromide. Vincent recovered after two weeks, was discharged from the hospital, and resumed drinking. At that time, alcoholism was not considered a chronic disease and there was no idea of long-term continuous management rather than just acute interventions in times of crisis. He received rather good care for the time. Bromide had anti-seizure properties and he was spared the usual treatment for the insane that consisted of hydrotherapy or soaking in a bath for five-hour intervals with cold water dousing every half hour.

At the same time, Theo, his brother and main support, became engaged in late 1888, was married four months later, and in early 1890, became a father. It is possible that this perceived threat to his supportive lifeline could have triggered further episodes of drinking. In any event, Vincent suffered two further psychotic episodes requiring hospitalizations and public pressure forced him to be voluntarily admitted to the asylum in the nearby town of St Rémy. His medical care could charitably be described as minimal. He was not treated with bromide, suffered more psychotic episodes, several of which were precipitated by drinking absinthe during outings to Arles. He did, however, produce a great body of artistic work there, including *Starry Night* in June 1889. There is speculation that the halos around the stars were auras from temporal lobe epilepsy. This brings up the issue of whether his illness improved his work. Most authors agree that his creativity existed before his illness became severe and that he was most productive during the periods of wellness between his crises and his illness, which detracted from his creativity rather than enhancing it.

414

After Vincent's discharge from St Rémy, Theo arranged for him to move to Auvers-sur-Oise, northwest of Paris, and for most of his two-month stay there, Vincent remained abstinent, seizure-free and lucid. Unfortunately, this was also where he died from a self-inflicted gunshot to the chest, clinging to life for two days. Over his grave in Auvers-sur-Oise, Theo had a Thuja tree (a well known source of thujone) planted, and when the coffin was disinterred fifteen years later to be buried next to his brother's, the roots were found to be entwined around the coffin in a tight embrace.

An immense volume of literature exists regarding Vincent's psychiatric diagnosis. Compelling arguments have been made to advance many of the possibilities. Several conditions are listed below, and aggravation of some of these by Vincent's alcohol and absinthe use was likely. The longest standing diagnostic possibility is temporal lobe epilepsy. The episodes were first described when Vincent lived in Paris. They were worsened by ethanol, absinthe (containing seizurogenic thujones), tobacco use and malnutrition. Depression between episodes has been described as an interictal dysphoric disorder, and Vincent's psychotic episodes were felt to be associated with the seizures as there is an established link between the two diseases. Temporal lobe epilepsy is linked to a personality trait known as viscosity, which is manifest as clinging to loved ones, persevorating or repeating one's self, endless debating and excessive writing. Van Gogh displayed all of these.

While he did have episodes of depression and mood swings, there is lesser consensus for bipolar disorder. Bipolar disorder has a high concurrence with alcohol and other substance use, especially cocaine and methamphetamines.

A diagnosis of acute intermittent porphyria has been proposed by Wilfert Arnold and his book makes a compelling case for this. For example, Vincent's crises lasted for days, longer than the temporal lobe seizures would have, and were brought on by fasting, unlike seizures. Alcohol, camphor, thujone and carbohydrate restriction stimulate the main enzyme in porphyrin production, which precipitates

415

the porpyria, resulting in neurological disturbances. Also acute intermittent porphyria is usually manifest by abdominal pain and urinary retention, which Vincent displayed. Vincent's condition was improved by bromides, which are known to help porphyria, alcoholic and generalized seizures, but not temporal lobe epilepsy. These facts speak against the diagnosis of temporal lobe epilepsy.

It has been proposed that van Gogh had a pica, or compulsive craving, for terpenes such as thujone, pinene, camphor and eucalyptol. As well, Saturnism, or lead poisoning has been put forward as a diagnosis. Lead poisoning is associated with colic, fatigue, joint pains, headache irritability, altered personality and memory loss with poor learning, but less commonly with seizures and confusion. Lead poisoning is relentlessly progressive rather than intermittent and episodic.

Alcohol could have affected Vincent by acting as a depressant, in lowering the seizure threshold, and in causing malnutrition. Malnutrition can result from a direct loss of appetite from gastritis or stomach inflammation and in substituting alcohol-derived calories for those from a well balanced diet. As previously mentioned, this malnutrition can trigger acute intermittent porphyria.

The thujones in absinthe could be responsible for yellowness of vision, and although this is not a usual absinthe effect, added sun exposure could have brought it on. The effect is more commonly associated with digitalis toxicity, but there is little evidence that van Gogh used digitalis. Another possibility for the yellow chromatopsia was the use of santonin, a sesquiterpene lactone compound found in the plant A maritime. Santanin causes bright objects to appear yellow and dark objects to appear violet. It was recommended as a cure-all in the popular home remedy book of Dr Raspail, which Vincent read.

As well as the alcohol, the thujones in absinthe cause seizures in their own right. It has been proposed that seizures could have influenced van Gogh's work, most notably that the halos around the stars in the painting "Starry Night" represented auras. Hallucinations

416

could have occurred due to the thujones, but it is felt that only a minority of his paintings could have reflected absinthe-associated hallucinations. Most likely those paintings that reflected any hallucinogenic effect were created out of artistic preference, as Vincent was aware that being sober allowed for a better thought process.

The last influence that thujones could have had on the work of the artist was that of directly precipitating porphyria, although his porphyria would have been more likely precipitated by the carbohydrate restriction brought on by the substitution of normal calories by that of alcohol based calories. A drink of hard liquor contains about 80 calories and some sweet red wines contain up to 120 calories.

Let me conclude my incomplete list of possible diagnoses by adding that Vincent seemed compelled to prove himself as worthy and tried to accomplish this by tremendous artistic output.

I would like to limit comments of Vincent's family and his disease to that of his brother Theo and how Theo influenced Vincent's drinking. Theo acted as a codependent or enabler in that he felt responsible for Vincent's welfare and supplied him with regular stipends regardless of destructive behavior and alcoholism. Theo also arranged for Paul Gauguin to join Vincent in Arles as a way of ensuring Vincent's safety after Vincent painted "Wheatfield with a Reaper", which was interpreted as suicidal ideation. As previously mentioned, the plan backfired and precipitated Vincent's hospitalization. Later, Theo allowed Vincent to dictate his own discharge from the St. Rémy asylum with no good indication of a cure. In not maintaining good personal boundaries, Theo allowed Vincent to avoid the full consequences of his dysfunctional behavior. Allowing consequences to occur is one of the few tools that families and professionals have to force individuals with substance abuse and other behavioral disorders to accept treatment. Finally, in the Wegschneider model of the alcoholic family, Theo was the hero and Vincent was the lost and denigrated soul.

Henri de Toulouse-Lautrec

The other artist whose name is directly linked to absinthe is Henri de Toulouse Lautrec. He was born in the village of Albi in northern France, son of an eccentric Count. He derived his living by producing posters, along with more traditional art, and like van Gogh, he lived in Paris. The opening of the Moulin Rouge and its need for posters led to his breakthrough as a poster artist. He had a congenital bone disease that prevented fractures from healing, and after successive femoral fractures, he was left with permanent short stature and chronic pain. He treated this pain with absinthe and wine, and he used the euphoria of intoxication in order to paint. He had some rather unusual practices with respect to absinthe, namely that he would store it in a hollow cane and would drink it diluted with cognac rather than water. This concoction was called a "hurricane" or "earthquake" and was much higher in alcohol content than the usual mixture. It also remained a clear deep green color rather than the traditional opaque yellow-green due to the absence of any essential oil precipitation. This is illustrated in his painting "Monsieur Boileau at the Café."

Toulouse-Lautrec was a friend of van Gogh's and introduced Vincent to hurricanes. Excessive absinthe and other alcohol consumption resulted in anxiety, depression, persecutory delusions and deteriorating work, and led to his treatment for alcohol dependence in March 1899. He had a short period of further brilliance but again relapsed and died September 1901 at the age of 37.

Other artistic personalities have been associated with absinthe use, such as Picasso and Ernest Hemmingway, but overall use declined after the Post-Impressionist period for reasons that will soon become clear.

Opposition Builds

With the rise of substance abuse comes a gradual realization of the dangers, and then the gradual imposition of measures at all levels of human organization to control it. With absinthe, there was first the gradual accumulation of data that showed it posed dangers above those associated with other alcoholic beverages. As early as 1708, the physician Johan Lindestrolphe noted that wormwood essence would lead to great injury to the nervous system. In 1859, Dr. Motet described the syndrome of absinthism and wrote that the toxic effects of absinthe were distinct from those of other drinks. In 1860, Henri Balesta wrote how one man caused his six-year-old daughter to become an absinthe addict. Henri went on to comment that the effect of absinthe on the rich was different than that on the poor. He wrote that absinthe use by the rich and idle resulted in only their deaths but that absinthe use by the poor killed the entire family. These class effects of drug use continue in some form today, both in the different consequences of drug use and also in the different issues regarding treatment. The poor have much more stark consequences from drug use, precipitating in an earlier incapacitation and a tendency to seek treatment earlier. However, even today they have fewer options for treatment.

In 1864, Louis Moncé produced convulsions and involuntary evacuations of the bowels in experimental animals with absinthe. His student Valentin Magnan showed that this special action of absinthe was due to the essential oils and gained the experimental data that was influential in leading to its eventual ban. Following this, the French public health system began collecting data on the consumption of absinthe. Associations were noted between consumption and neurological disorders, stillbirths and psychosis.

In Switzerland, absinthe was linked to two spectacular murders. In 1905, after a series of petitions, a commission report and a referendum, absinthe was banned. Other countries also banned its use: Belgium in 1905, The Netherlands in 1910, and the United States in 1915. It had become the focus of the temperance movement and was linked to Bohemian radicals. Other countries such as Spain and England did not ban it because absinthe use had never reached such dangerous levels. In France, absinthe was not banned until six months into the Great War, when France had suffered a series of disastrous losses and public opinion felt that absinthe use had contributed to a loss of national vigor. The Pernod factories were converted into military hospitals and the bottle crates were used as makeshift beds to support mattresses.

Today

While absinthe was banned in the US in 1915, thujone itself was not included in the Federal Food Drug and Cosmetic Act of 1972 list of banned substances. Other thujone-containing herbs, such as sage and rosemary, have been deemed safe. There are also herbal preparations containing wormwood and cedarleaf oils that contain thujone and are permitted by law. Of interest is that thujone can be given off into the atmosphere and -thujone emissions have been detected near California sagebrush.

Today, absinthe is still available in a number of countries including Canada, Spain, Portugal, England and the Czech Republic. There is also an internet trade in absinthe. The absinthe of today is a shadow of its former self. Today it contains only 45% alcohol versus 74% in absinthe's heyday (still a very high concentration of alcohol). Similarly, the -thujone content is limited by European Commission law to 8-10 parts per million rather than the previous 260 parts per million.

A new twist to the combination of the depressant alcohol with stimulants has occurred in recent years with the use of alcohol and energy drinks such as Red Bull, Rock Star, Monster and others in the club culture. These drinks typically contain about 100 mg of caffeine, the same as a cup of coffee. The danger lies in that the energy drinks can be consumed rapidly, whereas coffee's high temperature forces the drinker to consume it over several minutes. These energy drinks also contain compounds such as the amino acids taurine, the carbo-hydrate glucuronolactone and guarana seed extract. The manufac-turers claim these compounds improve mental alertness, although independent consensus is still lacking and most of the alertness is likely due to the effects of the caffeine. The belief in consuming the energy drink along with alcohol is that the energy drink can keep the alcohol drinker alert enough that he can continue to function, a belief that has recently been refuted experimentally by Maria Sousa-Formigioni. The linkage of alcohol and energy drink consumption with several deaths in Sweden in 1991 has led to public health concerns. Red Bull has been banned in Denmark, Malaysia and France. Similarities in substance use and attempts to control it seem to repeat themselves throughout human history.

REFERENCES

Arnold, WN Vincent; van Gogh: chemicals etc. Boston: Birkhäuser

Blumer, D: The illness of Vincent van Gogh. Am J Psychiatry 159:519-526

Conrad, B III; Absinthe: History in a bottle: Chronical Books, SF (1988)

Höld, K et al: -thujone. PNAS 97(8):3826-3831

Pato ka J, Plucar, B: Pharmacology and toxicology of absinthe:

Sousa-Formigioni, M: Alcoholism Clinical and Experimental Research, April 2006

Woolf AD: Clinical Toxicollogy Review. 18(4):1-4

Absinthe An alcoholic drink made from wormwood, a European bitter herb. Absinthe has been banned in most countries because it can produce irreversible brain damage.

Abstract Expressionism An art movement that developed in New York in the 1940's. Initial members of the movement, Gorky, Pollock, DeKooning, Rothko, and Kline sought spontaneous, unedited freedom of expression, not limited to painting conventional forms.

Action Painting A technique made famous by Jackson Pollock in which paint was dripped, smeared, dropped, or poured onto canvas, and the act of painting was as important as the product.

Ambivalence The condition of holding two seemingly incompatible feelings, ideas, or attitudes toward a person or thing at the same time, e.g. loving and hating.

Antabuse Drug used in the treatment of alcoholism to deter drinking. A person taking Antabuse who imbibes alcohol will become nauseated, sweaty, and shocky.

Art Therapy The use of art as a projective technique for bringing unconscious conflicts, unformulated ideas, and unexpressed feelings into consciousness.

Attention deficit dissorder A condition, usually in childhood, in which the individual has difficulty focusing on a task, is hyperactive, impulsive and sometimes irritable.

Autistic Phase In Margaret Mahler's separation-individuation theory of development, autistic phase refers to the first stage of infantile psychological development, in which the infant has no awareness of anyone or anything outside of the self. He or she is totally dominated and reactive to inner feelings and states, such as hunger, thirst, fullness, etc. Lasts from birth to 1 month.

Capriccios Italian term for caprice. In art, applied to any fantasized or imagined type of paintings. The most famous use of the term is for a series of works done by Goya, which mock society of his time.

Castration anxiety A fear of having the penis cut off. In more recent psychiatric and psychoanalytic usage, the term refers to the fear of offending and therefore experiencing some kind of retaliation from an authority figure. More generally, a loss of power.

Cohesive functions Activities or mental mechanisms that an individual employs in an attempt to maintain feelings of positive self esteem, intactness of body, awareness of self.

Consolation phase In Mahler's separation-individuation theory, this refers to a subphase of psychological development, in which the individual becomes aware that he or she is separate from the other person, but can still keep the other person in mind when away from that person, and at the same time, can experience the selfs intact and not threatened by being alone.

Cubism A movement in painting started by Picasso and Braque in 1907-1908. They sought to portray an object or person from many angles at the some time, rather than from a single perspective. Later Cubists include Juan Gris and in sculpture the work of Henry Moore is sometimes considered to have cubist elements.

Dependency State in which the individual cannot function independently. He or she needs and seeks advice, guidance, support, etc. and cannot make decisions. The presence of the other provides comforting and soothing. If this is not provided, the dependent person may turn to drugs and/or alcohol or other destructive behavior to calm the unpleasant unfulfilled feelings of neediness.

Depression Clinically, a state of sadness and lethargy, accompanied by feelings of helplessness, hopelessness and worthlessness, often one pole of a manic depressive state.

Desynthesizing The act of taking apart into component pieces. Carl refer to a physical act, or to the psychological phenomenon of a coming-apart of the various functioning arts of the mind.

Differentiation Phase The first subphase of the separation-individuation process, usually from 5-9 months, when total bodily dependence on the mother begins to decrease and the infant makes his or her first tentative movements away from the mother.

Digitalis A drug initially prepared from the flower, foxglove, used in the late 1800's as a treatment for epilepsy. It is used today for the treatment of heart failure

Displace of sexual energy According to the classical theory of psychoanalysis, the individual is motivated by one of two drives-sexuality or aggression. The sexual energy or drive can be displaced from one person or object and directed toward another person or object. The energy can also be converted to another activity other than sexuality, e.g. intellectual pursuit, painting, etc.

Disintegration, psychic The disorganization of normal psychological functions, e.g. awareness of self, ability to experience and contain emotions, the ability to think and act appropriately.

Dissociation The separation of any group of mental processes from the rest of the mind. In its most severe form, it is thought to be a factor in multiple personality disorders.

Drives Biological motivations for behavior: e.g., hunger, thirst In classical psychoanalytic theory, the basic motivating forces that determine a11 behavior are sex and aggression, sometimes modified to be Eros and Thanatos, life and death, or love and hate.

Dyslexia Impaired ability to read or understand what is read. Usually associated or attributed to minimal brain damage or dysfunction.

Electroshock A form of therapy, usually for severe depression, in which a small electric current is passed through the brain.

Engulfment The act, or psychologically the fear, of losing one's identity, one's sense of being a separate intact person, due to being overwhelmed by and taken in by another person. Usually accompanied by panic or terror.

Expression A term in art to denote the use of distortion and exaggeration for emotional effect. The paintings of El Greco, Munch, and Kandinsky are examples of expressionism.

Fragmentation Disturbance in thinking, feeling, or psychological functioning in which normal functions become vague and confused, resulting in decompensation of judgment, behavior, and the mind, generally.

Grandiose self In self psychology, this refers to a theoretical agency of the mind in which reside feelings and beliefs of omnipotence and omniscience.

Hemesphericity The theory that the right hemisphere of the brain is the seat of imagery, creativity, and spontaneity; while the left side is the seat of logic, language, and reason.

Individuation The emotional development of the individual or infant, from perceiving the self as enmeshed in and a dependent part of another, to perceiving the self as separate and able to survive and achieve alone.

Internalization of conflict The ability to uke areas of convict from the external world and to struggle with them intrapsychically, e.g. the conflict between father and son, or the conflict with an authority figure, need not be acted out between the two people, but can become an intrapsychic phenomenon or tension within the individual.

Kohut, Heinz Austrian-born psychoanalyst who lived and worked most of his life in Chicago, whose theories of the functioning of the mind and the interpersonal needs and wishes of the individual are referred to as *Self Psychology*.

Laudanum A preparation containing opium and/or morphine.

Mahler, Margaret American psychoanalyst who lived and worked in Philadelphia. Her theory, known as the separation-individuation theory, of the psychological birth and development of the human infant was set forth in her book, *The Psychological Birth of the Human Infant*, 1975.

Manic condition A state characterized by an elated or euphoric, although unstable, mood, increased physical activity, restlessness, agitation, and increased number of ideas racing through the head, and often by bizarre and inappropriate behavior.

Manic depression An emotional illness in which the subjective states of euphoria or manias and depression alternate. Cycles may occur as rapidly as every few reeks or over periods of years.

Mannerism Term in art used initially to describe the style that developed after the High Renaissance had reached its peak. The term initially was derogatory. Later usage referred to the elements used by the Mannerists, e.g. elongation of form, as by El Greco. Thus the term has lost some of its negative connotation.

Mènierè's Disease Disease of the inner ear that causes loss of balance, ringing in the ears, fainting, sweating, and, occasionally, unconsciousness and total incapacity.

Narcissism Self love or positive self regard. The term was originally used in a pejorative sense in psychoanalysis. More recent theories appreciate that it is necessary for healthy functioning in individuals, and need not be at the expense of other people

Naturalism A term in art that refers to the artist's attempt to render subjects as they really are rather than in any stylized or emotional manner.

Neoplatonic philosophy A philosophical school originating in Alexandria about 200 AD, which modified the teachings of Plato. According to Neo-platonism there is one ideal form, which is God. The closer any object, art, or person comes to this form, the closer it is to perfection.

Object hunger The psychological need for another person to provide or fulfill a function for the personality, e.g. a feeling of positive self-regard, or a feeling of emotional comfort.

Object loss The loss of a person who has great emotional significance for the individual.

Oedipal Complex An organized set of feelings in the individual in which the parent of the same sex is seen as a hated rival to be destroyed, in order to obtain the parent of the opposite sex who is desired sexually. This all occurs unconsciously and is at its peak at age 4-5. According to Freud, this is the bedrock of all neuroses.

Organic brain syndrome A group of symptoms consisting of disorientation, loss of memory, impaired intellectual functioning, defective judgment and emotional lability, caused by a physical illness of the brain, such as syphilis, intoxication, hemorrhage.

Organic thrust to Individuation The inborn biological drive to develop one's abilities and skills—just as a flower has an innate program and need to bloom.

Parturition Childbirth.

Pathological grief A morbid reaction to a loss, where feelings of sadness, lack of interest, loss of appetite, insomnia, etc, last well beyond the normal period of time required to mourn a significant loss.

Pathologic identification Psychological process in which an individual assimilates an undesirable aspect, property, or attribute of another person and models himself or herself after that person.

Practicing phase In Mahler's theory, the second subphase of separation and individuation lasting from 9-14 months, when the infant is aware of his or her developing motor skills and is able to actively move away and return to the mother.

Primary process A type of thinking characteristic of the unconscious that includes no awareness of time, the absence of any negatives or limitations, the wish and need for immediate gratification—in essence, thinking that is dominated by the wish for pleasure.

Psychoanalysis A method developed by Freud of investigating mental processes and of treating neuroses. It is based on the assumption that such disorders are the result of the rejection by the conscious mind of factors that then persist in the unconscious as repressed wishes, needs and fantasies. These then cause convicts which may be resolved or diminished by discovering and analyzing the repressions, bringing them into consciousness through the use of such techniques as free association and dream analysis.

Rapprochement In Mahler's theory, the third subphase of separation and individuation lasting from 15-24 months, when the infant, now experiencing himself or herself as a separate individual, can leave and then return to the mother, without anxiety.

Regression Psychologically returning to an earlier level of development or functioning.

Repression A mental mechanism, in which the individual unconsciously repels from awareness, unacceptable thoughts, feelings, images, or memories. For example, repressed hostility is the rejection from conscious awareness of feelings of hatred toward a person or thing.

Right brain dominant people Loosely applied as a term for people who, demonstrating aright brain functions' of imagery, fantasy, rhythmicity, and manipulo-spatial skills, are likely to be creative.

Right-left brain See Hemisphericity.

Rorschach Projective test devised by Hermann Rorschach, popularly known as "the ink blot test'' in which the individual's underlying emotional issues and concerns are seen by the individual in the ink blots.

Self psychology A theory about how the mind works, and how people relate to each other, originated by Heinz Kohut and his followers in Chicago in the 1960's to 80's. The theory emphasizes empathy as a means of understanding, self-esteem regulation as a motive for and factor in relationships, and a degree of narcissism as necessary for emotional health and well-being.

Separation anxiety A feeling of dread that accompanies the awareness that one is alone, and has the perception that he or she cannot function adequately, possibly cannot survive, alone.

Separation-individuation phase According to Mahler, the phase of normal development from 4-5 months to $2^{1}/_{2}$ years that leads from a self that is intertwined with the mother, to the emergence of a separate independent person. There are four subphases: see differentiation, practicing, rapprochement, and consolidation.

Shock treatment See electroshock.

Social realism A movement in art in the United States in the 1930's and 40's that sought to portray the hard working, often dreary lives, of the underprivileged members of society, as accurately as possible.

Splitting A mechanism of the mind, in which the individual, unable to tolerate conflicting emotions toward one person, e.g. love and hate, directs all the love toward one person and all the hatred toward another.

Superego as control system In classical psychoanalytic theory, the superego is an agency of the mind that fulfills certain functions for the individual. It is the repository of the goals, ideals, and rules that govern the individual's actions, feelings, and relationships.

Superego as regular of self esteem According to the above, the individual's self esteem is governed to a large extent by how well he or she is meeting the goals, rules, and ideals of the superego.

Surrealism Movement in art and literature originating in France in the 1920's and 30's. Andre Breton, principal spokesman, said its purpose "is to resolve the previously contradictory conditions of dream and reality into an absolute reality—a super reality.'' Other surrealists include de Chirico, Dali, Magritte, and Ernst.

Symbiosis Condition or state in which the individual experiences the self only as a part of another, i.e. the mother-infant symbiosis.

Symbiotic phase Second phase of Mahler's separation-individuation process, lasting from 1-5 months, in which the individual experiences the self, not as separate and unique, but only as a part of the mother.

Transference The phenomenon of experiencing and directing feelings and attitudes toward people who are currently important in one's life, which were initially experienced in infancy and childhood, usually toward the parents.

Transitional object Something used as a substitute for an unavailable person, e.g. a teddy bear or a blanket, which the child holds fast when the mother is not able to hold him or her.

428